S0-BEH-730

Wissenschaftliche Untersuchungen zum Neuen Testament

Herausgegeben von
Martin Hengel und Otfried Hofius

76

Anton Fridrichsen

Exegetical Writings

A Selection

Translated and Edited by
Chrys C. Caragounis and Tord Fornberg

J. C. B. Mohr (Paul Siebeck) Tübingen

Die Deutsche Bibliothek – CIP-Einheitsaufnahme

Fridrichsen, Anton:
Exegetical writings: a selection/Anton Fridrichsen. Transl. and ed. by
Chrys C. Caragounis and Tord Fornberg. – Tübingen: Mohr, 1994
(Wissenschaftliche Untersuchungen zum Neuen Testament; 76)
ISBN 3-16-146268-8
NE: Caragounis, Chrys C. [Hrsg.]; Fridrichsen, Anton: [Sammlung]; GT

The book was typeset by Gulde-Druck in Tübingen using Times typeface, printed by Gulde-Druck in Tübingen on acid-free paper from Papierfabrik Buhl in Ettlingen and bound by Heinr. Koch in Tübingen.

ISSN 0512-1604

This Book
is Dedicated to

the Theological Faculty
of the University of Uppsala
Scene of A. Fridrichsen's
Exegetical Labours
and Alma Mater
of the Editors

Table of Contents

Part Two
The Fourth Gospel

Part Three
Paul

Part Four
Varia

Preface

The origins of this book go back to the last week of May 1992. In the relaxed atmosphere of the living-room of his Tübingen home Prof. Martin Hengel approached Chrys C. Caragounis with his long-cherished idea of seeing the widely-scattered and thus little known exegetical writings of Anton Fridrichsen made available in book form. To this intent he made available the series of *WUNT*, which he and Prof. Otfried Hofius edit together, and provided Caragounis with a list of Fridrichsen's writings.

On his return to Sweden Caragounis contacted Docent Dr. Tord Fornberg (Uppsala) inviting him to become co-editor of the volume. Together we worked through Fridrichsen's writings in the difficult task of choosing a mere ten per cent of what was available to be included in the present volume.

As we look back, we are happy and grateful that Professor Hengel took this fine initiative, gave his encouragement and made it possible through the *WUNT* series to publish some of the exegetical writings of Anton Fridrichsen – undoubtedly the greatest Scandinavian New Testament scholar of this century. We are also happy that at a somewhat later stage also Herr Georg Siebeck embraced the project with good-will and enthusiasm and did all that was necessary by way of practical arrangements to see the book through the press.

The writings of Anton Fridrichsen have been published in many languages (in his native Norwegian as well as in Swedish, German, English, French, and Latin) and in many journals, some of which are little known to New Testament scholars. At first we decided on a trilingual book: we would use material published by Fridrichsen in German, English and French, and would, moreover, translate a number of Swedish and Norwegian studies into English. We were then planning a larger book. Owing to the economical recession of the times Herr Siebeck requested of us to reduce the size of the proposed volume to no more than 350 pages, and this compelled us reluctantly to excise the French material.

Our choice of material has been guided by several principles and concerns. First, we have included an evaluation of Fridrichsen's person and work, setting him in the theological context of Uppsala at the time of his appointment, and of his significance for Swedish scholarship, written by his pupil, the late Erik

Beijer, in 1988.[1] In this way Fridrichsen's contribution is placed in its proper context. Second, to present Fridrichsen's particular approach to biblical interpretation we have included his programmatic essay, "Realistic Interpretation of the Bible", which sets forth his method, hermeneutical principles, and his particular angle of approach. Third, we have included a number of articles that he had published in English and German as well as a number of his studies, originally published in Norwegian and Swedish. Our selection has been motivated by our desire to give an adequate picture of the man, his theological achievement, and the way in which his own work fitted in the context of the international debate.

Our objective to make available particularly material that was inaccessible or not easily accessible for scholars has led us to include on the one hand a number of studies in German, published in internationally rather unknown journals like the *Symbolae Osloenses,* and on the other hand to translate into English several of Fridrichsen's most important studies that were published in Norwegian and Swedish. Accordingly our translated material from Norwegian and Swedish comprises more than fifty per cent of the book.

Although we have looked into each other's work and inspected together the entire manuscript in its final stage, our respective responsibilities have been as follows: Fornberg has translated the Norwegian material and Caragounis the Swedish material into English. To avoid different styles and format by reproducing photomechanically the existing German and English material, Caragounis scanned this material carrying it over to his computer. One German article, written in old German characters, was typed by Fornberg into his computer. The scanning proved to be more problematic than anticipated and Caragounis had to restore the German and English material by comparison with the originals. He also typed in the Greek for the entire manuscript. Fornberg and Caragounis each read the proofs of the German and English material. The page lay-out has been preserved in as far as this was possible, but a number of editorial changes – as e.g. the use of the same quotation marks in all articles, the consecutive numbering of footnotes throughout each article, as well as the same type for all article titles – had to be made, changes which do not affect the wording or the punctuation of the original. The material published originally in German and English has been left as it was even where syntactical errors were discovered, with the exception of the minimal correction of a few quite obvious inadvertently committed typographical errors.

[1] For a fuller account of A. Fridrichsen's significance as an exegete and theologian of the Church, see A. Smith, *Anton Fridrichsens kristendomsförståelse,* Oslo 1976. For a brief introduction to the life and work of A. Fridrichsen in English as well as a complete bibliography, see the recent booklet by Erik Heen, *Anton Fridrichsen (1888–1953). A Bibliography*, University of Oslo. Faculty of Theology. Bibliography Series 5, Oslo 1993.

Our thanks are due to Mr. Douglas Jackson, M.Th., for his valuable suggestions to improve the English of our translations. Docent Curt Dahlgren, Lund, kindly made available the Theological Faculty's scanner and his expertise to Caragounis for scanning the German and English material. Caragounis' former student, Mr. Per Holmberg, B.D., now a research student at the University of Göteborg, prepared the indices. Last but not least we owe a debt of gratitude to Professor Jan Bergman of Uppsala. He knows why.

As this book leaves our hands, it is our wish that, besides giving all its readers the pleasure of being acquainted with the perspicacious and sober thinking of one of the great New Testament scholars of this century, it may also challenge and inspire particularly the younger scholars with the true nature of their task: to make the meaning and life of the New Testament transparent and relevant for modern man. It was Fridrichsen's deepest concern to put theology and exegesis in the service of the Church.

Lund 20 February 1994 Chrys C. Caragounis and Tord Fornberg

Introductory

Anton Fridrichsen as Academic Teacher in the Service of the Church

by

ERIK BEIJER

Few academic teachers in recent years have had such a significance within their province of research as *Anton Fridrichsen*. During a period of more than twenty years from his appointment in 1928 to his retirement in 1953, he left his mark on the teaching of New Testament exegesis at the University of Uppsala. When he commenced his professorship at Uppsala he was already well-known and respected in academic circles on the continent. At Fridrichsen's invitation a whole array of scholars, chiefly from German universities visited and lectured at Uppsala. This gave the students the opportunity to come in personal contact with international scholarship – it is difficult for us today to understand how isolated the academic milieu at this northern Swedish university was, at least with regards to theological studies. For students and younger scholars to travel abroad before the Second World War was quite simply an exception. Later the War put a stop to all travel. But international winds blew around Anton Fridrichsen, and he generously shared his wide outlook. At his research seminar a number of young scholars were bred, many of whom later came to hold chairs in various foreign universities, both in Europe and the U. S. A. But even for the usual students who, following their graduation, went out as priests or teachers, he had a decisive significance. Even to the church life of Sweden in general he gave stimulating and decisive impulses through his teaching ministry. I believe, therefore that this year – 100 years after his birth on the 4th January 1888 – it would be appropriate to give a few indications in the *Svensk Exegetisk Årsbok* of the significance, which Anton Fridrichsen has had for Swedish church life through his teaching.

Anton Fridrichsen entered his office as academic teacher at a time, when students came as a rule to the study of New Testament Exegesis, with a solid preparatory education. Most of them had taken the classical course of study in high school, which meant that they had had Greek for two academic years. If at the time of the commencement of their theological studies, they had not already taken a Bachelor of Philosophy degree in Classical Languages, they had, at any rate, taken the theological-philosophical examination, "teolfilen", which was an obligatory entrance requirement, in which *inter alia* the study of Koine-Greek formed a part. This was the starting point, at which the study of the New Testament was embarked upon. Anton Fridrichsen was a demanding teacher. From the *Study Manual of the Theological Faculty,* the 1931 edition, it emerges that for the mark of *Pass* "an intimate knowledge of the writings of the New Testament and their contents was demanded, and an ability to translate the entire New Testament in such a way that the text was comprehensible both linguistically and materially". Fridrichsen gives a few reflections on this basic demand: "The requisite familiarity with the Greek NT cannot be acquired in any other way than through an assiduous and protracted study of the text". "A Lexicon and Grammar must be constantly consulted. One should not shun the labor of writing lists of words and learning them by heart. An emphatic warning is hereby given against taking refuge in a translation and learning it by rote". Those were unequivocal words. Consequently, the New Testament was regarded by Fridrichsen's students as a difficult subject. At the Priests' conference in the Archdiocese in 1941 Fridrichsen delivered his oration on "Nya Testamentets enhet".[1] In it he speaks of the narrow road that leads to life: "Only by engaging one's whole being seriously in the search can one discover the path that leads to life. This is the way in which the New Testament, too, in all its parts discloses its inner unity of life only to those who apply themselves to the study of Scriptures with all seriousness and energy ... The task is already large and heavy when one reads the wretched elements that are demanded for getting the first courses in the B.D. degree ... No one can be spared the hours of discouragement in the scientific study of the Bible".[2] Fridrichsen demanded much of his students, but he also gave them much.

In order that we might understand today what significance Fridrichsen's teaching at Uppsala came to have, we need to place ourselves in the situation which prevailed at this northern Swedish university at the time Fridrichsen entered upon his office in the 1920's. One might say an exegetical vacuum prevailed. During the years of 1909–1920 the exegetical chair had been occupied by Adolf Kolmodin. With all his erudition he represented an exegetical conservatism similar to that of Theodor Zahn. Kolmodin had acquired the professorial chair by defeating S. A. Fries, who represented the growing scholarship that was coloured by liberalism. This type of scholarship, therefore, never made itself felt in the exegetical teaching at Uppsala. The break became still greater when Kolmodin was succeeded by Gillis Persson Wetter in 1923.[3]

---

[1] Anton Fridrichsen, "Nya Testamentets enhet", *SEÅ* 6 (1941), pp. 43ff. [This essay is included in the present volume under the title "The Unity of the New Testament" (Tr.)].

[2] Ibid. p. 52f. [in original edition (Tr.)].

[3] Anton Friedrichsen, Olof Linton, Gösta Lindeskog, *Gillis Wetter in Memoriam, Arbeiten und Mitteilungen aus dem neutestamentlichen Seminar zu Uppsala* V, printed in Helsinki 1937.

Wetter was an out-and-out representative of the religio-historical school. For him the great names were *Reitzenstein* and *Bousset*. Early Christianity belonged together with the Hellenistic mystery religions. A great chasm separated the early Christian churches growing on Hellenistic soil from the early Church within the Palestinian context. Wetter came to the professorial chair of the New Testament at Uppsala from the Stockholm *Högskola* [4], where he was professor in the History of Religions. He was a frequent contributor to the daily press, and presented also his views to the educated public through a number of popular-scientific works.[5] In circles close to the Stockholm Högskola Wetter was a respected name. In Uppsala, where he was to educate priests, it would appear that he became quite isolated. Since his teaching-labours came to an abrupt end by a humanly speaking early death in 1926, his work as an academic teacher turned out to be a mere parenthesis. There never was enough time to create a continuity. The chasm between Kolmodin and Wetter was too wide and too deep. Kolmodin was a conservative. Wetter was a radical. This caused a great uncertainty within such a central subject for theological studies as New Testament exegesis.

Such was the situation, when Anton Fridrichsen appeared on the scene at Uppsala. He was made professor on the 27th of April 1928 and delivered his inaugural lecture on the 15th of September the same year. Thereby a new chapter in the history of Uppsala exegesis had begun. The man who was thus installed was a mature man with his eye open to what the hour demanded. He was familiar with all aspects of his subject and had an open mind for new views and ideas. Some professors are strangely finished when they are installed on their chairs. Anton Fridrichsen definitely did not belong to this category.[6]

Among the factors which contributed to the feeling of disorientation among the students, and their difficulty in understanding any inner connection within exegesis, was their difficulty in finding an organic connection between the two Testaments. The study of Old Testament exegesis had been dominated for decades by Erik Stave. During the long period between 1899 and 1922 he occupied the chair of biblical exegesis with the center of gravity in the Old Testament. At Uppsala Stave had performed a pioneer's work by his introduction of the new exegesis, whose foremost representative was Julius Wellhausen. The acceptance of this new kind of exegesis had not taken place without a bitter struggle. Together with Nathan Söderblom and Einar Billing, Stave had tried to show that the scientific study of the Bible was no threat to the Christian faith.[7]

---

[4] [I.e. a university-level institution (Tr.)].

[5] Gillis Persson Wetter, *Det urkristna gudstjänstlivet och Nya testamentet,* 1923; Idem, *Kristendomen och hellenismen,* 1923; Idem, *Johannes' Uppenbarelse,* 1924; Idem, *Innanför Herakles' stoder. En resa i Nya Testamentets värld,* 1926.

[6] Harald Riesenfeld, "Anton Fridrichsen 4/1 1888–16/11 1953," *SEÅ* 18–19 (1953–1954), pp. 7 ff. Axel Smith, *Anton Fridrichsens kristendomsforståelse,* Oslo 1976.

[7] Sven Linder, *Domprosten Erik Stave. En minnesteckning, SEÅ* 5 (1940), pp. 224 ff.

The new radical scholarship which Stave represented, was also in some way easier to apply to the Old Testament than to the New. The center of gravity in Old Testament piety had come to rest with the prophets. These could be seen as representatives for a religious development, which placed ethics before cult, and could therefore be seen as heralds of a portrait of Jesus characterized by ethical ideals – the portrait of Jesus represented by liberal theology. Once Stave sat securely in the saddle, he was untiring in writing manuals and popular writings on Old Testament themes. He was still in his best years when "the young men of the Church"[8] studied. They were ambitious, and in the Swedish countryside many lectures have been given about Israel's prophets. With regards to the New Testament, Stave was pretty conservative. One has the feeling that once he had attained the position of professor he no longer developed appreciably. It is characteristic of the exegetical scholarly situation, that following Stave's departure from the professorship in 1922 that there was no competent successor – it was not until 1927 that the Old Testament chair was occupied.

The new occupant of the chair was Sven Linder. Linder was a competent orientalist, he spoke Arabic fluently and had a deep interest in archeology – he lectured gladly on the archeological investigation of Palestine. On the other hand, biblical theology was not his line. This made it difficult for students to get any grasp of the unity of the Bible, what it was that connected the Old Testament with the New – and yet both Testaments were part of the Christian Church's Bible! To be sure, the prophets could be understood as preachers of an ethically-coloured religion of personalities, but the Messianic prophecies seemed to be an illusion which ended in disappointment and emptiness. That the cult played an important role in Old Testament piety the student learned purely religio-historically – in the course on the Old Testament there was no biblical-theological work. Rudolf Kittel's *Israel's Religious History* was read. When Sven Linder lectured on the Psalms, he referred most dutifully to Sigmund Mowinckel's *Psalmstudien,* but what the cult – when at the New Year's festival the cultic cry *Yahweh is King!* was sounded – meant as a bridge to the New Testament, no one had the slightest idea of. The whole thing was a "bold theory" – "bold" was one of Linder's favorite expressions, though he himself as a scholar was anything but bold. For the students entirely new perspectives were opened up when Anton Fridrichsen lectured during his early Uppsala years on "Jesus' preaching according to the Synoptics". I remember myself what an aha-experience it was, when Fridrichsen drew the line from the Old Israelite New Year's Festival, the enthronement, with its cultic cry *Yahweh*

[8] [The "young men of the Church" were members of a revival movement within the Church of Sweden in the early 1900's to mobilize young people to influence society towards a Christian life-style (Tr.)].

is king!, to Jesus' message: "The time has come, the kingdom of God is near", so near that it is present in Jesus and with its power it works in and through him. Suddenly, one began to picture the prophetic Messianic line with its roots in the message brought at the time of the kings of the struggle and victory of the King, and how from this the trajectory of thought passed over to the New Testament. Fridrichsen has treated this issue in an exposition of the text for the Annunciation of the Virgin Mary (which, to be sure, is from 1946, however the thoughts had already begun to take form early in the 1930's). He writes: What we find in Lk 1:26–38 is *"the renewal and actualization* of the promise. The message of the angel is conveyed in that style. 'The throne of David', 'the king over the house of David everlastingly', 'The Son of the Most High', – all of this connects back to the old prophetic word, which resounded once, when David's scions ruled over Zion ... What the king meant to the old, classical Israel and Judah nationally, religiously, morally, all this in indissoluble unity, we have begun to understand more and more. The King was the Saviour and the Reconciler. It is this aspect of the kingship, which now appears in its eschatological realization ... We see here the organic connection between prophecy and fulfilment, between pre-formation and realization. The person and work of Jesus are incomprehensible without this background".[9]

This understanding of the relation between promise and fulfilment is for Fridrichsen important for understanding the New Testament presentation of Jesus. Time and time again he comes back to this subject. In an exposition of Lk 18:31–43 (1946): he writes "The teaching about that fatal Easter concentrated in a few pregnant sayings, which the Apostles – and through them the Church – receives here is placed under the perspective of fulfilment. All that the prophets have written about the Son of Man must be fulfilled. This concerns both his humiliation and his exaltation. The words about humiliation and death obviously connect back to Isa 53 and related texts. The word about resurrection has its roots in Hos 6:2. These old prophecies become reality through the Son of Man's death and resurrection from the dead. The cultic realities which peer out from behind the prophecies of Hosea and Isaiah, found their fulfilment in the historical Jesus and the risen Lord of the Church, who is one and the same person. For the Church, as for Jesus as well, the perspective of Scripture is of the greatest significance (1 Cor 15:3–4). Prophecy is the cornerstone in the foundation of the Christian faith, and it is shown that the more unreservedly one allows the New Testament witness of Christ to come to its right place, the deeper one is drawn into the Old Testament. The theological and homiletical indispensability of the Old Testament as well as its fundamentality for faith and preaching becomes clearer and clearer, and the time must come again, when

[9] Anton Fridrichsen, *Fyrahanda sädesåker,* 1958, p. 523.

the Church once again dares and is able to connect its witness of Jesus to the prophetic word".[10]

This does not mean – and I believe it is important to point this out – simply an uncritical reproduction of the Old Testament prophets' words. Fridrichsen was too knowledgeable a scholar and well oriented in history to allow himself to come to such a simple conclusion. When he is able to speak of the New Testament word as a fulfilment, in this word there lies just as much of a new creativity in a radically new situation. Characteristic for Fridrichsen's way of seeing the problem are a few words in an examination of Mt 17:9–13 about the disciples on their way down from the Mount of Transfiguration, in which they raise the question of Elijah's place in the context of eschatology. Fridrichsen expounds on how Jesus interprets the situation from the perspective of John the Baptist's appearance, and continues thus: "With superb certainty Jesus expounded the prophecy, unfettered by the letter, in inner harmony with the prophetic intuition. Thereby the position of the Church on prophecy is also given, whether it is concerned with Old Testament or New Testament prophecy. All interpretation, that goes above the purely religio-historical interest, must start with the historical fact of Jesus Christ. But note well: from the *transfigured* Jesus Christ. It was on the way down from the Mount of Transfiguration that Jesus expounded the prophecy to his disciples ... The transfiguration on the Mount received its fulfilment and perfection in the eternal radiance of the resurrection. For us the light that falls on prophecy comes from this light-source. We know that what the old Spirit-filled men of God said ultimately refered to the Son of Man's suffering, death and entrance into glory (Lk 24:25, 27). There prevails there a hidden connection that is revealed in the resurrection of Christ. The 'historical element' of prophecy should not be overcome through false allegorization or through unhistorical literal application. History is a creative act of God, which does not occur in accordance with a detailed program, communicated beforehand. History is full of surprises. But it has an inner connection, which the prophetic spirits are aware of and behold in their own way. That is why the prophetic word of the Old Testament becomes a confirmation for the Church, which has experienced the fulfilment".[11]

The atmosphere in the Theological Faculty at Uppsala at the time of Fridrichsen's assumption of his professorial duties, did not only exhibit the vacuum which prevailed within New Testament scholarship and the difficulty which Old Testament exegesis experienced in finding usable bridges between the Old and the New Testament, but also the difficulty that liberal theology in refined form was represented in the faculty. This theology had a convinced and energetic advocate in the professor of Church History, Emanuel Linderholm, who was

[10] Ibid., pp. 198f.
[11] Ibid., p. 403.

active in the years 1919–1937.[12] His piety towards Jesus, inherited from childhood had found a foothold in the picture of Jesus of liberal theology. Linderholm had received decisive impressions from Adolf von Harnack and his "Das Wesen des Christentums".[13] The formula according to which Linderholm, in immitation of Harnack, solved the problem of early Christianity, was the double gospel, *Jesus' gospel about the kingdom of God* on the one hand and *early Christianity's gospel about Jesus Christ* on the other. This differentiation was decisively important for Linderholm personally, and in his preaching of this Linderholm felt himself called to be a reformer of the Church. We encounter his thought in his programmatic writing "From dogma to the Gospel".[14] He founded "Sveriges Religiösa Reformförbund"[15] with its journal "Religion och Kultur" and prepared proposals for new Church rituals.[16] Linderholm communicated his ideas to his pupils, one obligatory work in the first year courses being his work *"Evangeliets värld"*.[17] This was a kind of a compendium, which was not based on personal research, but which presented uncritically the religio-historical school's view of Christianity. It was the first part of a work which had the same fortune as many other works in Swedish scholarship – the second part was never published. In his preface and his epilogue, however, Linderholm sketched an outline of the whole work: "As soon as time and strength allow, the two above-mentioned parts about *Jesu evangelium om Gud och Guds rike* and *Urkristendomens evangelium om Jesus Kristus* as well as the Church life of the early Christian times will be published."[18] The concluding words are typical of Linderholm's views. In his work he has painted the world of Hellenism and the Jewish background of Primitive Christianity. He writes: "However, the time was now at last fulfilled. He who would bring the new revelation with its inimitable loftiness and simplicity, with its perfect wisdom and gentle power, divine love and wonderful peace, already stood at the door".[19]

I have tried to sketch in some considerable detail the atmosphere at the Theological Faculty of Uppsala at the close of the 1920's in order that we might

---

[12] Anders Jarlert, *Emanuel Linderholm som kyrkohistoriker,* Bibliotheca historico-ecclesiastica lundensis XV, 1987.

[13] To be sure Linderholm tried to distance himself from Harnack underlining his dependence upon Rud Eucken, *Der Wahrheitsgehalt der Religion,* 1901. See Em. Linderholm, *Från dogma till evangeliet,* 3rd ed., 1926, p. 5.

[14] Originally a lecture given at a Sigtuna conference in November 1918, which was first published in the collection *Det andliga nutidsläget och kyrkan.* The lecture was published separately with a foreword typical of Linderholm in a third edition in 1926.

[15] [I.e. "The Religious Reform Covenant of Sweden" [Tr.)].

[16] Emanuel Linderholm, *Svensk Högmässa,* Stockholm 1926. Idem, *Högmässa, dop och nattvard. Några reformtankar,* Stockholm 1927.

[17] Idem, *Evangeliets värld,* Stockholm 1918.

[18] Ib. p. VII.

[19] Ib. p. 299.

be able to understand the real significance of Anton Fridrichsen's appearance on the scene. At the time of his inauguration as professor he was a mature scholar with a long development behind him and always open to new questions and perspectives. He was at home in the university cities of Europe. He had studied with *Ernst von Dobschütz* at Breslau and with *Paul Wendland* at Göttingen. He was a good friend of Rudolf Bultmann's and had defended his doctoral thesis *Le problème du Miracle dans le Christianisme primitif* at Strasbourg.[20] As I have implied, he was not a scholar who had stopped maturing, during his whole life he was open to new ideas. On one point, however, he had come to a result which was to determine his view of early Christianity and its literature in a decisive way. He had learned the approach of the form-critical school and he handled its methods superbly. The Gospels were no biographies of Jesus, but documents of faith, where we meet the early Church's faith in Christ, sprung up from its spiritual reality and characterized by its view of life. Fridrichsen was by this time through with the portrait of Jesus painted by liberal theology. It was an illusion which did not measure up to the demands of a radical research. The Jesus of liberal theology was inspired by the cultural presuppositions of the Germany of Wilhelm, but such a Jesus had never existed. The understanding of Jesus at which Fridrichsen arrived, is met with in a booklet, which was published in 1931. It was one of Fridrichsen's peculiarities that he did not publish big, voluminous books. From his pen flowed small booklets and essays, but behind the flowing presentation the discerning reader could not fail but notice a depth of erudition and reading. The booklet bore the title *Vem ville Jesus vara?* [21] It had an important sub-title, which indicated its concerns: *The Historical Foundation of Faith in Christ according to Present Biblical Research.* For Fridrichsen the matter was clear. The faith of early Christianity in Jesus as Lord had its roots in Jesus' own Messianic self-consciousness. One did not need to look away from dogma to the Gospel. The road to Early Christian dogma led directly from Jesus. "Christian dogma thus has its roots in Jesus' own consciousness and the disciples' personal experience in following him".[22] Jesus made his appearance with clearly Messianic claims and was understood in that way – he was executed by the Romans on account of his Messianic claims. But he avoided using the title of Messiah. It was first during the decisive hearing before the high priest that he admited clearly and verbally his Messiahship. Earlier this idea had made its appearance more in symbolic actions, as with Jesus' entrance to Jerusalem. The reason for that was that the

[20] The dissertation was published in Paris in 1925. ET: *The Problem of Miracle in Primitive Christianity,* 1972.

[21] A.Fridrichsen, *Vem ville Jesus vara?* Studentföreningen Verdandis småskrifter, Nr 346, Stockholm 1931. [This booklet in included in the present volume under the title *Who did Jesus Claim to Be?* (Tr.)].

[22] Id. p.58 [See section under "The Lord" (Tr.)].

title of Messiah was charged with a national-political content. "An old theocratic cliché like the title of Messiah did not fit his idea of the kingdom of God, or his task and personal relationship to it. He needed a new self-designation, and he found it in 'The Son of Man'".[23]

One can come thus far on the road of scholarship, a scholarship which Fridrichsen carried out with all the radicalism to which his many years of research had led him. In other words, this had nothing to do with some type of uncritical reproduction of old conservative ideas. The title of the booklet, which I do not hesitate to characterize as one of the most important works published during the thirties, was surely, *Who did Jesus Claim to Be?* Scholarship can try to evaluate this claim with all the methods which it has at its disposal. A critical scrutiny of the sources by the methods of the form-critical school can establish the faith of early Christianity in Jesus as Lord and then find its way back to Jesus himself. Does such a faith have any connection with him? It is this question which Fridrichsen wants to answer affirmatively. As a scientist he cannot say more. "The secret of this person is great and unfathomable. We can only establish the fact and elucidate the historical presuppositions. The deepest foundations of Jesus' conviction of his high calling lay hidden from our sight; they rest in the inaccessible sanctuary of personal fellowship with God".[24]

The views which Fridrichsen put forward in this booklet, and which characterized his teaching, came to have a liberating effect on the generation of students, who gathered around his Teaching desk in the 1930's. In other words, it was possible to draw a scientifically tenable connecting line from gospel to dogma with a clear distinction between faith and science, when approaching the NT writings as historical sources for the faith of the early Church.

But Fridrichsen's firm conviction that "the historical Jesus" made his appearance with a Messianic self-consciousness, which he clothed in the title "Son of Man", had an important consequence, which Fridrichsen himself also drew as a conclusion. If Jesus regarded himself as the Messiah in any form, this demanded as its correlate a holy people, the people of the Messiah. Thus Fridrichsen was able to take the concept of the Church back to Jesus himself with his Messianic consciousness. When Jesus chose twelve disciples, the figure twelve corresponded to the twelve tribes of Israel, they represented the people of God gathered around its King. Thus, the Church existed before the early Christian mission. Through it new persons were incorporated into the Church, which already existed, where the Lord, who was exalted to heaven, was sacramentally present in the Last Supper and where his word was still sounded in the kerygma. In this Church the common meal stood side by side with the Word. There in a direct connection goes a straight line from Jesus' Messianic

---

[23] Id. p. 45 [See section under "The Son of Man" (Tr.)].
[24] Ib. p. 48 [See section under "The Son of Man" (Tr.)].

table-fellowship with his disciples to table-fellowship with other groups of people, as for example, the meal with the crowds out in the desert, which is narrated by all four evangelists. Thus, the Church and the sacraments have their roots in Jesus. I think that people today, half a century later, find it difficult to understand how liberating these thoughts were in the thirties. The student generation of the twenties had learned from Wetter and Linderholm that the Last Supper was a Hellenistic cultic meal with its roots in the mystery religions. The uncertainty about the Last Supper which this created, had had disastrous consequences for the celebration of the Lord's Supper in the Church of Sweden, in which the twenties proved to be its low-water mark.

With respect to the concept of the Church the situation was somewhat different. Within the Church of Sweden there was a lively concept of the Church. At the turn of the century the growing free-Church movement had spoken with great pathos of "the New Testament Church principle". In that light a church type like the Church of Sweden was a sheer incongruity, with no support in the Bible. Here Einar Billing had cleared a new road and opened up fruitful perspectives with his national church concept motivated by centrally religious concerns. The Church is "the remission of sins to the Swedish People". But though Billing was a biblical theologian – "the last Swedish systematician who had some exegetical training" (Harald Eklund)[25] – his concept of the Church had not originated in his study of the Bible, but was a result of his systematic thought. In an essay Oscar Krook has depicted with great congeniality Einar Billing's view of the Church in its *status nascendi.*[26] Billing's point of departure for his view of the Church was quite literally the parish church. The Word has been carried over the world and has come to it. There the message of prevenient grace is proclaimed. "As it now stands, it proclaims not only the Gospel of God's forgiveness in word, but it is, or it represents itself in reality God's offer of forgiveness to the whole Swedish People".[27] We note here that as far as the history of ideas goes, both Einar Billing and J. A. Eklund ("Stenkyrkan", "Fädernas kyrka"), belong together with the national romanticism of the turn of the century. We get a glimpse of Harald Hjärnes' contribution here. With this religiously motivated national church concept in their theological baggage the men of the Young People's Church Movement[28] went off to the countryside. But in the thirties new winds had begun to blow. The ecumenical movement had begun to take form. New inter-church contacts were made and thereby wholly new ecclesiastical perspectives were opened up, where to speak

[25] Harald Eklund, "Nytestamentlig och modern verklighetssyn", *SEÅ* 13, (1948), p. 1. On Einar Billing's biblical theology see Erik Beijer, "Einar Billings bibelteologi" *SEÅ* 4 (1939), p. 119 ff.

[26] Oscar Krook, "Kyrkobegreppets förnyelse i svensk teologi", *En bok om Kyrkan,* Lund 1942, pp. 248 ff.

[27] Ib. p. 254. Krook is here quoting Billing's *Herdabrev,* p. 68.

[28] [On this movement, see note 8, above (Tr.)].

of "the Church of the Fathers" might sound a little provincial. The Universal Church was beginning to be felt. We experienced a growing high ecclesiasticism, which received its inspiration from the Church of England (Gunnar Rosendal, Albert Lysander). Within church life a new interest in liturgy took shape, inspired by such men as Arthur Adell and Knut Peters. In this area Fridrichsen's ideas acted as a thaw. We received a Church concept that was based on Jesus and early Christianity, which could be transformed into a church outlook functioning in practical church life.[29]

On these matters, too, Anton Fridrichsen was at first more or less alone at the theological faculty. In the early thirties the professor of Dogmatics was Torsten Bohlin. He had strong cultural interests and participated whole-heartedly in the public debate, *inter alia* with Torsten Fogelqvist about Christian morals. But he lacked a deeper interest for the exegetical and biblico-theological problems. Arvid Runestam, who had succeeded Billing as professor of Ethics, had been brought up in the free-church tradition and had a strongly individualistic ideal of piety, which was deepened, when in the second half of the thirties he came under the influence of the Oxford Movement. Runestam was drawn early into the work of the ecumenical movement. In Germany, Nazism put theology before a whole series of questions of socio-ethical nature. Much of the Swedish preliminary work for the great Life and Work–conference held at Oxford in 1937 was done at Runestam's seminar.[30] But faced with a Church concept based on the New Testament, where the Church existed before the individual, Runestam was in doubt, a doubt also that followed him during his years as bishop of Karlstad. Torsten Bohlin became bishop in Härnosand in 1936 and was succeeded by Hjalmar Lindroth. This scholar had shown deep sympathy with Fridrichsen's view of the Church, see his work *Tankar om Kyrkan och sakramenten.*[31] I have a feeling, however, that Fridrichsen and Lindroth were so different as persons, that there never was any deeper contact between them. Linderholm had been succeeded by Gunnar Westin, who with his orientation to free-churchmanship in the Swedish Free-Churches saw a dynamic power at work in the history of churches. He showed no understanding for Fridrichsen's biblically oriented Church concept.

The Swedish systematician, to whom Fridrichsen came to stand closest, both ideologically and personally, was *Gustaf Aulén.* One of Fridrichsen's first works to be published in Sweden was his essay in the *Svensk Teologisk Kvartalskrift* in 1929; "Jesu kamp mot de urene ånder", where Fridrichsen paints Jesus' works of power, especially his driving out of demons, as an element in the

[29] Anton Fridrichsen, "Messias och Kyrkan", *En bok om Kyrkan*, pp. 26ff.; "Nytestamentlig församling" *En bok om Kyrkan*, pp. 45ff.; "Försoningen och Kyrkan i Nya Testamentet" in *Den nya kyrkosynen*, Lund 1945, pp. 41ff.

[30] Nils Karlström (ed.), *Oxford och Edinburgh,* Stockholm 1938.

[31] Hjalmar Lindroth, *Tankar om Kyrkan och Sakramenten,* Stockholm 1948.

restoration of creation which takes place where Jesus passes by and where the powers of the kingdom of God work in and through him.[32] In 1930 Gustaf Aulén held his famous Olaus Petri lectures on the Christian idea of reconciliation.[33] There Aulén outlines what he calls "the classical reconciliation motive", oriented to a dualistic fundamental view, where Christ appears as victor, *Christus Victor*. When the lectures were published in printed form the work had no bibliography and the footnotes were few and sporadic, but there should be no doubt that Aulén had read the above quoted essay. In the *Festschrift* which was published on Aulén's 60th birthday in 1939, Fridrichsen was one of the contributors with his essay on "Människosonen och Israel", where he dealt with ideas, which he already had touched upon in his inauguration lecture on "Det nya testamentets tanker om religiös mottagelighet og uimottagelighet".[34] Following Aulén's installation as bishop in the diocese of Strängnäs in 1933, Fridrichsen was often invited to speak in priests' meetings and seminars. A number of such lectures have been published in *Södermanlands Bibelsällskaps Årsbok.*[35] During such days of study Fridrichsen often encouraged the priests to apply themselves to renewed and deeper exegetical study, and it can be said confidently that Fridrichsen inspired many a priest to take up his Novum Testamentum and go deeper into the Greek text, something that set its mark on their preaching.

At this jucture I have reached a point, where I think, we could summarize Anton Fridrichsen's significance for Swedish church life. I believe that in the first place we could and should state that Anton Fridrichsen was impelled by a deep consciousness that he in his capacity of teacher at a theological faculty, whose task was to educate priests and teachers of Christianity, had to also make a contribution to the service of the Church. In an obituary on Anton Fridrichsen in the Christmas Book of the Archdiocese for 1954[36] Gösta Lindeskog related that one of Fridrichsen's Norwegian friends had stated that at first Fridrichsen had no intention of staying in Sweden, but was toying with the thought of settling down in a Norwegian parsonage. The Norwegian parsonage was, to be sure, the environment of his childhood. But nothing came of it. Fridrichsen was quite happy with his academic life in Uppsala, where he soon had interested students and large numbers of friends – Fridrichsen was by nature a master at

---

[32] Anton Fridrichsen, "Jesu kamp mot de urene ånder",*STK*, 5, 1929, pp. 199ff. [in Norwegian; i.e. "The Conflict of Jesus with the Unclean Spirits", included in the present volume. (Tr.)].

[33] Gustaf Aulén, *Den kristna försoningstanken*, Lund 1930.

[34] Anton Fridrichsen, *Det nye testamentets tanker om religiös mottagelighet og uimottagelighet, NTT* (1929), pp. 1ff.

[35] E.g. Anton Fridrichsen, "Bibelns verklighetsåskådning och livssyn", *Södermanlands Bibelsällskaps Årsskrift* 1936, pp. 3ff.

[36] Gösta Lindeskog, "Anton Fridrichsen", *Julhälsning till församlingarna i Ärkestiftet* 1954, pp. 23ff.

making friends. But even as professor he regarded himself as being in the service of the Church. He has given us his own account of how he looked upon his own work in the "Epilogue" which he wrote in the *Svensk Exegetisk Årsbok* 1948, when he relinquished the office of editor to other hands – this, by the way, actually turned out to be the very last of Fridrichsen's publications in this series, which to such a high degree bore his insignia.[37] There he sketched out his plans – Fridrichsen always had plans! – for his last years as professor. He was going to write commentaries on the Gospel of Mark and on the Acts of the Apostles. His foremost project was going to be a commentary on *Den Svenska Evangelieboken.*[38] His ambitious plan with this work is ascertained by the "Sample Booklet" which he published. In this he speaks of his interest in the relation between theology and church, and writes: "These works I wish to leave as a valedictory gift to the Church of Sweden, which ultimately I have sought to serve with my work in the Theological Faculty of Uppsala".[39]

These plans never materialized. Illness broke Fridrichsen down in his last years as professor, and he died soon after his retirement. Of the planned commentary on Mark only the Introduction was published[40] and the Sample Booklet on the commentary on the Svenska Evangelieboken was the only one that saw the light of day. Birger Gerhardsson, however, gathered together all of Fridrichsen's expositional treatments of [biblical] texts with great deligence and published them in the large collection volume *Fyrahanda sädesåker.*[41] Through this collection we get a good idea of how to interpret texts, which Fridrichsen considered should be the basis of preaching. It would seem that few books have been studied as intensively as this in Swedish parsonages.

There we sat, therefore – we, Fridrichsen's students – in our parsonages. What had we taken with us of his teaching? We had learned a basic requirement. When we wrote our sermons we would have Novum Testamentum open before us. Every treatment of a New Testament problem, not least of all when it concerned the sermon, must have its point of departure in a careful study of the text. What stands in the text? The text we had read, we had also learned to place in the larger context of the entire Bible. We had learned that the Bible – in spite of the plural form *Biblia* – made up *one* book. That which had created this unity of the Bible was Jesus and his Messianic consciousness. The Old Testament pointed forward to Jesus, who is the fulfilment. We learned that when we studied the Old Testament we were to take Jesus as the point of departure, to read the Scriptures as he read them and as the early Church read them, cf. Lk 24:25–27. In the light which fell from Jesus we could read the Old Testament

---

[37] Anton Fridrichsen, "Epilogue", *SEÅ* 13 (1948), pp. 116ff.

[38] [I.e. *The Swedish Gospel Book,* (Tr.)].

[39] *SEÅ* 13 (1948), p.117.

[40] Anton Fridrichsen, *Markusevangeliet,* Lund 1952.

[41] Anton Fridrichsen, *Fyrahanda sädesåker,* Motala 1958.

with its multifarious aspects and perspectives. The words of the prophets were not static utterances, but were joined in the dynamic context of revelation, where God's actions constantly open new vistas and give new keys of interpretation. I believe that the priests of the Church of Sweden not least of all now, when we have a complete series of Old Testament texts, have every reason to actualize those impulses, which came from Fridrichsen's teaching and biblical interpretation.

This experience of the unity of Scriptures, however, had to do primarily with the New Testament. When we commenced our studies – this applied at any rate to those of us who were older – we felt that we stood helpless before the gap, which seemed to go through the New Testament itself. On the one hand, there was Jesus' Gospel concerning the kingdom of God, and on the other, the early Christian Gospel concerning Christ. The gap between Jesus and Paul seemed to be so wide that it was impossible to bridge. In early Christianity we met the Hellenization of the Christian message and far out in that wing stood John. What made the matter very difficult was that John's portrait of Christ came to us in the form of a Gospel – and from this Gospel a whole array of church sermon texts were chosen. In comparison with the Synoptic portrait of Jesus, the Johannine portrait seemed to lack a historical basis. This created a difficult homiletical problem. What we learned from Anton Fridrichsen, which was felt as a great liberation, was that the whole New Testament with its witness to Christ is a living unity, having originated in the Church's living faith in Christ. "The early Church lived on and in a tradition, a narrative, liturgical, catechetical substance, which in various forms and shapes saturated and gave nourishment to the whole Church. The written fixed forms of the New Testament books represent, of course, only a part of the mass of tradition, and this only in some of the forms, which took shape in the great, leading churches. This insight is of great consequence for the study of the New Testament writings, especially in understanding the internal relationship between them. But even the picture of early Christianity itself is transformed and becomes alive, when one is freed from the rigid, literary idea regarding the creation of the New Testament"[42].

So, there we sat with our *Novum Testamentum*. We had the text before us. Fridrichsen had taught us how to read it. It would seem that there are few theological essays, which have been studied so intensively and been discussed in such detail in priests' meetings as the programmatic article which Fridrichsen wrote in the first issue of the *Svensk Exegetisk Årsbok.*[43] In order to understand

[42] Anton Fridrichsen, "Epilog", *SEÅ* 13 (1948), p. 123. On the question of the unity of the New Testament, see Anton Fridrichsen, "Jesus, Johannes och Paulus," *En bok om Bibeln*, Lund 1947, pp. 148ff.

[43] Anton Fridrichsen, "Realistisk bibelutläggning", *SEÅ* 1 (1936), pp. 20ff. [I.e. "Realistic Interpretation of the Bible", published in this volume (Tr.)]. On this programmatic article see Harald Riesenfeld, "En framtidssyn i backspegeln. Realistisk bibelutläggning efter 50 år", *STK* 63 (1987).

the deepest significance of what it was all about, however, one should take the sub-title of the essay seriously: "A scientific demand and a practical desideratum". Fridrichsen was educated as a classical philologist. He had had reason to ponder over the problems of interpretation in general, not only in connection with New Testament texts. The requirements which he put forward in his essay concerned the interpretation of a text from Plato just as much as of a text from Paul. The truth to which Göran Schildt gave expression in a review of a work by Henrik Zilliacus is applicable here and very much to the point: "However profitable the historical research of sources may be, and however important the demand for factual basis remains, still interpretating and relating to a living now is the historian's basic task".[44] Biblical interpretation should be *realistic*. What this demand implies has been declared by Fridrichsen himself. When in his "Epilog", he looks back on his work as professor and as editor of *Svensk Exegetisk Årsbok* and on that occasion he returns to the essay about the realistic biblical interpretation. He writes: "The program which is intimated there, I have thereafter sought to implement – I hope with growing insight in the matter *(res)*" – the Italics are Fridrichsen's.[45] This implied that Fridrichsen was not *one* person when he wrote exquisite philological essays or scientific articles, and then *another,* when he wrote expositions of texts for priestly journals.

All text-interpretation demands insight in the matter, in the text at hand and what it purports to communicate. It was self-evident to Fridrichsen that one could not be careless in the study of a text. It was important to penetrate into the text, but this also meant that one must listen to what the text had to say. I believe that in order to understand Fridrichsen's interpretation of texts it is important that this is made quite clear. In an essay in *Svensk Teologisk Kvartalskrift,* Karl Josef Sundberg has examined methodologically Fridrichsen's biblical interpretation.[46] He writes there: "The task is to get hold of the pulse of the biblical texts. What we meet there is the life of faith, and this is what needs to be taken hold of. This cannot be grasped merely in a intellectual way. What is required here is a way of acquiring understanding which in classical hermeneutics is called empathy".[47] The author distinguishes clearly between the interpretation which can be attained only intellectually, and that, in which the interpretation flows from some kind of empathy. I think that for Fridrichsen this was an absolutely foreign distinction. For him it was never a question of some kind of intuition, which, as it were, was to be found side by side with the text and by means of which one could get a better understanding into the meaning of the text. The text as such was the object of research, and when it came to interpret-

[44] *Svenska Dagbladet* 13 March 1988. [I.e. A Stockholm daily newspaper, (Tr.)].

[45] *SEÅ* 13 (1948), p. 117.

[46] Karl Josef Sundberg, "Anton Fridrichsens bibelutläggning. En metodstudie", *STK* 61 (1985), pp. 24ff.

[47] Ib. p. 27.

ing the text, the scholar had to use not only his philological knowledge, but also his knowledge of the historical, cultural and religious environment, in which the text had originated and which the text sought to elucidate. But all such work with the text must rest upon a strictly scientific basis, and the more knowledgeable the scholar is in that area, the greater possibility he has to experience empathy in what the text wanted to say. The text is always the object, and for Fridrichsen it was never a question of "playing the Semitist" – to quote an almost classical taunt. In addition, Fridrichsen was too deeply rooted in his own time, and the kind of text-treatment which Fridrichsen demanded sprang up from the questions raised by the times. Fridrichsen was always sensitive to whatever was happening. Especially the problem of interpretation pressed hard on him. Karl Barth's Commentary on Romans fell like a bomb on him. Rudolf Bultmann – with whom Fridrichsen had a personal friendship – led by his results of a radically critical and skeptical research had taken his refuge in a text-interpretation characterized by the existential philosophy, which in principle was independent of historical research. On the Continent the demand was raised for a "pneumatic exegesis". It was in this international debate, of which we were hardly conscious in Sweden, that Fridrichsen engaged with his programmatic essay, and one can only express regret that it wasn't published in one of the major languages of culture. For him it was in no way a question of "playing the Semitist". However, Fridrichsen posed to himself another question. One of his favourite expressions was "perception of reality". He was aware of the fact that these texts had originated in a different perception of reality than ours, and that therefore one never arrives at their core, when one views them from our perspective, which is characterized by historicism and relativism. Here lay a great problem for Fridrichsen.

He takes up these questions in a newspaper article in 1933 on "The world-view of the resurrection faith".[48] The Church's proclamation of the ressurrection of Christ becomes meaningful only if it is rooted in a perception of reality which corresponds with that of the New Testament. When it comes to getting to grips with that, Fridrichsen makes as his point of departure – perhaps surprisingly – the Book of Revelation and its view of reality. "The polar forces of this reality, which release their power in history, lie, according to the New Testament, outside the world of men. This is found in a power field determined by the terrible opposition between God and the Devil. We have here the mythical expression of a thousand-year long religious experience, which would have taught us to interpret history and its events in the light of faith in the living God and in the conviction of the demonic world power of evil. This is the context of the early Church's Messianic faith and of the Gospel concerning the ressurrec-

[48] Anton Fridrichsen, "Uppståndelsetrons världsåskådning", *Svenska Dagbladet* 16 April 1933.

tion. Against this background Jesus' person grows to assume cosmic dimensions, and his death becomes the redemption of the world, his resurrection the irruption of the new Age, the triumph of the kingdom of God. Apart from this background, Jesus' person shrinks into becoming a Jewish wisdom teacher, his death becomes a Jewish martyr story, and the resurrection becomes a fanatic illusion. The Gospel then at its best can become a valuable historical contribution to the development of culture, but certainly not an immovable foundation for the Christian Church, which has stood through the centuries".

Fridrichsen has been reproached for taking the miracle texts too lightly in his realistic biblical interpretation, while pushing the question of history aside.[49] To this it must be said that according to Fridrichsen's way of looking at the matter, these texts are not "historical" texts in the sense that they seek to give actual information about a certain course of events. As we meet them in the Gospels they are part of the early Church's witness to and confession of Christ. When a priest preaches from a miracle text, the eventual demonstration of the historicity of the event can be of no help to him whatsoever. Looked at from the point of view of "the question of facticity", Jesus becomes merely one of all the wonder workers and *theioi andres* of ancient literature. Starting with the New Testament collection, both the scientist and the priest must ask the question: What do these texts purport to say about Jesus? If one asks such a question – that is, about the *res* of the texts, their material content – one sees that they speak of Jesus' fight with the demonic powers as a part in the establishment of the kingdom of God, whose powers are active wherever Jesus goes.

That which was important for Fridrichsen, which gave the interpretative key to the New Testament texts, was that they grew up *in the Church,* among the people of the Messiah. This he had learned purely scientifically from the form critical school, whose scientific methods he mastered in a supreme way. The life of the church with the worship of the Risen Lord, constituted the *Sitz im Leben* of these texts. They are all expressions of a confession of Christ; this applies to all of the New Testament writings. All of them, each in its own way and with its linguistic means, seek to give an answer to the questions: "Who is Jesus? What did he want?" *"Everything in the Bible emanates from the reality of Christ.* Thereby, its absolute character of revelation is given and explicit. But in that the Bible is *a witness to and an interpretation of the Christ event,* it is also a human word, conditioned and determined by historical, sociological, psychological circumstances. So, in the Bible we have the absolute in the relative. It is precisely the Spirit's work to make the word of man in the Bible into God's absolute word to us ... It is precisely in its concreteness that the word of the Spirit is made into an inner word, an absolute message from God

[49] *Bibelsyn och Bibelbruk.* Utgiven av Biskopsmötets bibelkommission, Lund 1970, pp. 56f.

here and now. It is the word in its historical context of meaning and content, that becomes God's word."[50] This outlook has for Fridrichsen an important hermeneutic consequence. Only in the spiritual atmosphere, which church fellowship constitutes, does one come most deeply into the biblical intent: "We must teach people to *approach the Bible as members of the Church of Christ.*"[51]

In his research Anton Fridrichsen had come to the conviction that the New Testament writings had grown out of the life of the early Church – *"the early Church"* was one of Fridrichsen's favourite expressions. If one did not take this insight seriously, one would never be able to grasp their meaning and message. This applied equally well to the New Testament scholar as to the priest. But while the scholar could stop when he had arrived at and grasped this confession of Christ, it was the priest's duty to relate this message to people in a new time and in a wholly different cultural situation. He was placed in a living process. Even as a scholar, however, Fridrichsen felt that in his interpretation of Scripture he was placed in a similar process. He was always open for new ideas. In a review of Axel Smith's book about Fridrichsen, Birger Gerhardsson points out that during Fridrichsen's final years interesting things were happening.[52] Fridrichsen lived intensively with his contemporaries. We should remember that many of his exegetical friends were Germans. Then came Nazism and the Second World War. His own country, Norway, was occupied by the Germans. Chaos came after the War – I know what anguish he had about the fate of Ernst Lohmeyer, who during one of the early years of the War still had the chance to lecture at Uppsala. All of this contributed to colouring Fridrichsen's view of European culture and its possibilities. Then illness broke out in his life. He tried more and more not only to become better acquainted with the New Testament understanding of reality, but this came also to colour his own outlook on existence. I might perhaps be allowed a personal recollection bearing on that. Only about a month before his death, I had the chance to visit him. He sat there marked by illness. I have never quite understood Paul, he said, but now I am beginning to have an idea of the secret of his person. I am beginning to have an idea of what he meant when he wrote: "My grace is sufficient for you" – "For my power is made perfect in weakness", 2 Cor 12:8. And so, he added: "Now I wish that I had the strength to write about Paul." – There was an existential feature in Fridrichsen's research. He was constantly alert for new ideas. I have a feeling that the New Testament view of reality, of which he spoke so often, became more and more his own.

---

[50] *Bibelsyn och Bibelbruk*, p. 70.
[51] Ib. p. 77.
[52] *STK* 54 (1978), p. 35.

Realistic Interpretation of the Bible

A Scientific Demand and a Practical Desideratum

(1936)

It is noteworthy that during recent years questions of *method* within the domain of exegesis have awakened to life and become the object of lively debate. After being consigned to obscurity for a long time, hermeneutics has come again into the focus of scientific interest. This is the case not only with biblical exegesis; also within philology and literature these methodological questions press to the foreground, these problems, which could be summarized in the great question: What is the scientific task in relation to the literary documents of past times?

In general, it may be said that the task is to *understand* these documents. Understanding is the object of all interpretation, and consequently also its *raison d' être. But what does 'to understand' mean?* – It is precisely this that has become a problem for our generation in contrast to earlier times. Within the domain of hermeneutics we experience many of the great changes, which on the whole characterize the intellectual life of our times. In the case of interpretation, however, one has to break with tradition, the great and glorious tradition, and to passionately demand to be allowed to walk along other paths. What is this all about?

If we turn our eyes toward the discipline that lies closest to biblical exegesis, sc. classical philology, we note that during the second half of the nineteenth century and the early part of our century, it experienced unparalleled prosperity. The classical languages, ancient history and archeology, textual criticism and literary criticism, – all were cultivated with an erudition, an acuteness, a diligence and a success, which are unmatched in the history of learning, and which have laid the solid foundation for all future research. Nevertheless, the present situation demands a new understanding, a new interpretation of antiquity. In spite of one's admiration for this great philological era, one is not quite satisfied with its interpretation of the classical documents. There was no real understanding. It is a strange fact, too, that the great era of classical philology coincided with a cultural period, during which classsical education – the humanities – definitely lost its old position of dominance in the West.

We are confronted with a similar development in biblical research. Never before has the exegetical study of the biblical writings experienced such a high watermark scientifically, as during the period from Strauss and Baur to Wellhausen, Holtzmann, Jülicher and Harnack. Both quantitatively and qualitatively the exegetical achievement of these past hundred years is really extraordinary. And yet the Church today reverberates with the cry for a new interpretation. Here also the strange fact meets us, that this immense boom in biblical science coincides exactly with the period during which the Bible lost its dominant position in the West. This is the situation in which we find ourselves at present and to which we must devote much attention. It is obvious that the parallel in the crisis of interpretation in both humanities and theology points to something common, something generally applicable to the situation. However, the latter issue has its own particular form and is fraught with its own peculiar problems within the sphere of the Church and theology.

What is going on? All around us we experience the reaction against rationalism. The philological interpretation, in so far as it went beyond textual criticism, philological facts and linguistic commentary, came readily to a halt at a cold, purely historico-psychological reflection, a strictly objective analysis of motives and literary forms, which in themselves were interesting and sufficiently arresting, but which had very little meaning for today's problematization. This was all right as long as this problematization was relatively tame and quite. But when it was seriously aroused and people were flung into serious crises, they began to make different demands even with regards to the interpretation of Plato, Greek tragedy, Horace and Tacitus.

The theological situation presents the same picture. Even here we see how the explosively advancing problematization raises the demand for a new biblical interpretation. The demand is formulated in various ways: 'theological' exegesis, 'pneumatic' exegesis, 'realistic' interpretation. However, one no longer meets *pure biblicism*. This is dead and the way to it is abandoned. Biblicistic theology was built on an illusion, namely, on the idea that the Bible was a literary and dogmatic unity. This idea was unhistorical, contrary to the factual nature of the Bible. As a product of genuine history the Bible exhibits a great diversity both as a literary and as a religious document. If it really were of such a nature as the biblicists thought, one would indeed have reason to suspect that it was a forgery, not an historical collection of documents. To seek to find in the Bible a connected salvation history and in connection with it, a revealed dogmatics, as *J. T. Beck* (or to a certain extent *von Hofmann*) sought to do, is nowadays, when the Scriptures' real character has become clear, impossible.

These insights, to which historico-critical biblical research has led, could very well be corrected at many points; but they are in themselves inescapable. For example, the picture which we have already obtained of the formation of the Old Testament, of its various component parts and their chronology, of the redactions, the reworkings, the expansions, can never be shaken to its foundations. The same applies to the tradition material and the literary redaction of the Synoptics, the distinctive character of John's Gospel, the development of early Christian legend, the various stages and motives of the history of the canon – to mention only a few concrete examples. Biblicism is definitely surrendered, just like verbal inspiration and fundamentalism.

It is in the face of such facts that the demand for a revolution in biblical interpretation has been raised. The man, who succeeded in speaking in such a way that the whole church and theology listened and paid attention to what he said, was Karl Barth, who 17 years ago both demanded a new exegesis and presented such an exegesis in his famous commentary on the Epistle to the Romans. The significant thing about Barth's contribution is not so much his method – it has been rejected almost unanimously and is now considered even by himself as a mere contribution for discussion – as his motives. This can be formulated in one word: one cannot preach the Gospel on the basis of liberal exegesis. This kind of interpretation leads the preacher into perpetual difficulties: Is this narrative historical or legendary? Is this word authentic or inauthentic? Do we have here to do with a direct biblical conception, or are we confronted with a religio-historical loan, an idea that belongs to the "history of the times"? To put it briefly: Is the word of the Bible the word of *God*, the speech of the Eternal One to us? According to liberal exegesis everywhere we turn we stumble on that which has come into being and is conditioned historically, the thoughts and literary activity of men. What has become then of the Gospel, which must be preached to the Church and save souls?

The opposition against the traditional interpretation arises from practice. And since theology, in the final analysis, seeks to serve the Church, rather then be an end in itself, it is quite clear, that the opposition must be heeded, it must be taken seriously. Especially if one is of the opinion that the theological interpretation of the Bible is of vital importance for practical preaching.

We must proceed from the problem facing the proclamation, – Karl Barth is absolutely right here. Can Christian preaching build on traditional critical exegesis?

Anyone who has listened a little to modern preaching and thereby paid attention to its relationship to the biblical text, ought to have often reflected upon the unsatisfactory character of this relationship. Not infrequently modern preaching is characterized by a certain embarrassment. One can observe a preacher's flight from the text to general Christian thoughts and meditations. Or, the text only serves as a springboard for a train of thought, which then follows its own inner logic. On the other hand, where real faithfulness to the text is sought, the result is often twisted, distorted and unbiblical. An edifying, genuinely biblical exposition of Scripture is not all that usual. The explanation for this cannot be merely that the sermon texts are badly chosen and arranged, or that preachers lack homiletical skillfulness. For the embarassment is quite common. Does the fault perhaps lie with the prevailing interpretation?

On this important question we must take a position. What is clear is that critical biblical research must go its own way, guided by well-tested issues and methods without regard for homiletical difficulties. Moreover, it is also clear that no theologically educated preacher can be spared these difficulties, which, besides, have been felt for as long as there has been a scientific biblical scholarship. Every theologian engaged in practical service ought to meet these difficulties with courage and confidence, conscious of what his exegetical education offers him. It has, to be sure, given him access to the biblical world, created order, clarity, coherence, chronology, perspective in it. It has given the prerequisites for understanding the language and thought of a time which is so distant from us, its life both on weekdays and Sundays; it has elucidated an extensive comparative material from the culture and religion of the ancient Orient and the Greco-Roman world; in short, it has made the Bible intelligible, accessible, real to us, who would read and cogitate on it today. One should not be unfair and ungrateful if exegesis does not give *everything*. Yes, even if one sometimes sighs with regards to one's critical training and thinks that it makes the religious authority of the Bible problematic, one should remember that this training has created innumerable bonds between the theologian and his Bible. The latter always says something to him, it is not an obscure, dumb hieroglyphic to him; it addresses him from the life, the faith, the hope, which bore up Israel, the Jews and the early Church.

Thereby exegesis has done the preacher an altogether indispensable service. It cannot do more, for it is a historical discipline and can only really be of any benefit by keeping strictly to its task and that within its bounds. If, besides offering the theologian a historical understanding of the Bible, it causes him at the same time a certain difficulty by relativizing revelation and putting a number of critical question-marks in the margin of the Holy Scriptures, it is only carrying out its obligation. It can have a good conscience toward the Church, for only he who is acquainted with the problems, text-critical, literary, and historical, which are associated with the biblical books, is suitable to be a priest[1] in the Christian Church of our time.

Thus far exegesis should be able to bear the Church's criticism with an equanimity arising from a good conscience. It should not turn a deaf ear, however, to the Church's grievance, but rather be driven by it to constant self-examination. It must ask whether traditional exegesis does not create unnecessarily great difficulties for the preacher by stopping somewhat short of the goal,

---

[1] [In Sweden the minister in the Lutheran State Church (Tr.)].

which is called "understanding", that is, by leaving its *scientific* task in part and on one essential point unfinished. Perhaps the preacher's complaint does contain, after all, a message for the scientific conscience of exegetes.

Exegetical research can and may never be directly edificational, its only aim is historical truth, no other consideration is valid. But in order to attain this truth, biblical science must not only strain all its powers, it must also radically deny all its dogmas, favourite thoughts or ideals and devote itself to the material unselfishly and intensively. This is real objectivity. This is the only possible way to understand a bygone time and to come in contact with it. Thus exegesis cannot fulfil its task by merely discovering the facts, the context, the development, the contrasting positions, and the innovations to the extent that this is possible. It is also under obligation to understand and interpret religion itself, *the faith.*. Of course, liberal interpretation has never thought of denying this; but it has devoted most, as well as the best, of its powers to critical work with the text, the language, the literary criticism, and the historical background. In these areas there was an immense amount of work to be done, so it may appear excusable, if this type of exegesis to a not inconsiderable extent stopped at the preliminaries. But this explanation is not wholly satisfactory. For there exist sufficient samples of the interpretation of biblical religion from this phase of exegetical work, to enable us to see that the retarding element was actually a *repelling one:* a critical, repudiating attitude towards the very religion, which one had as one's task to understand. This is what contributed greatly to the feeling that liberal exegesis had so little to offer, indeed, that it proved so paralyzing to the theologian when preparing his sermon. As has already been pointed out, much of this evaluation was unfair. What was justified about it, however, was not merely that the preacher found in his commentaries only the material for one particular interpretation of the text, but that he there did not find the immediate empathy with the biblical word, the empathy that would put him in touch with the text. It was looked at from the outside, not from the inside. In other words, there was a real scientific shortcoming, which had to have particularly dreadful consequences for the practical homilist.

The attitude of liberal exegesis to the religion of the New Testament comes to light clearly and characteristically on a particular, central point, namely, *the picture of Jesus*. Precisely here it becomes apparent that the pretended objectivity is a disguised subjectivity. How did this interpretative trend actually delineate the picture of Jesus? It did it in such a way that everyone now sees that this Jesus is nothing other than an incarnation of the religious ideal of personality current at the turn of the century. Thus, when it comes to objectively and positively grasping and presenting the core of New Testament religion, modern rationalism does it in such a way that it sets up its own picture in the sanctuary and declares it to be the historical Jesus. Measured by such a figure the New Testament naturally came to appear quite strange, a mixture of eschatological fanaticism, apocalyptic fantasy, gnostic speculation and coarse popular superstition.

With such a view of the New Testament it was naturally difficult for the theologically-minded preacher to preach on his texts. He felt bewildered, uncertain, perplexed. What could he do with all this 2.000 year old speculation and superstition?

One thing is, however, clear. The temporal distance – i. e. the historical and cultural gap – cannot and should not be conjured away by any kind of interpretation; the gap, the perspective, is surely an essential presupposition for a historical understanding. But the gap can and must *be overcome,* if one wants to understand the past from within – and only this deserves the designation "understanding".

For biblical science the way to such an understanding from within was paved by the *history of religions* school. At first this religio-historical interpretation supplied chiefly liberal exegesis with material for its "historical background" reductions of biblical religion. But at the same time it also called for a positive understanding and evaluation of it, and that precisely because of what to us is strange and peculiar. When Gunkel coined the expression "Primitive Christianity is a syncretistic religion", on his lips this meant not only that the New Testament contains all kinds of structural components, deriving from various religions, but also that it must be read and interpreted as a real, living religion, not as a product of decay, a corruption of Jesus' simple teaching. This demand was for Gunkel and his generation primarily motivated by aesthetico-intellectual considerations; they still looked upon ancient religions with the naive, narrow-minded superiority of a nineteenth century bourgeois mentality. Developments within the history of religions in general, however, have led to placing much more stringent demands on the researcher for taking the religion he studies seriously, that is, if he really wants to get acquainted with it and not to paint a caricature picture of it. Precisely the *comparative* point of departure has increasingly sharpened the mind of the historian of religions with regard to the characteristics and the coherence of the particular religion. In the light of the modern interpretation of religions, the older, superficial, rationalistic history of religions school stands out as the originator of terribly distorted images. The scientific pathos characterizing the modern history of religions school is a passionate will and an unlimited willingness to listen to the heartbeat of every religion. This must have certain consequences even for biblical research.

These consequences already made themselves felt on a central point a generation ago, namely with respect to the Jesus of liberalism. The protest arose already at the turn of the century and proceeded from a religio-historical motif: eschatology. At least so much was clear: the eschatological element in the Gospel tradition revealed a Jesus who had a totally different temperament than the liberal picture of him had indicated, a figure who defies every comparison with our own human type and psychological experience. The wandering Messianic prophet, *the Son of Man with the Kingdom of God*, is an absolute *mystery as an individual personality*. On the other hand, we can understand with full clarity and certainty his *claims*, his *message*, his *offer*, his *demands*. But what he claimed to be and wanted to accomplish is of such a nature that only an *unbiased,* strictly objective *realism* can penetrate, see its inner coherence, perceive and interpret the enormous, religious power-complex, which meets us here.

In its endeavour to understand and to describe this historical phenomenon, a self-righteous and self-complacent cultural consciousness cannot but fall short before it. Only a self-forgetting realistic interpretation can come in contact with and mediate contact with that which has actually been. And it is precisely this that constitutes the purpose and ground of existence of biblical science.

This scientific viewpoint converges with the practical-ecclesiastical point of view. Without doubt the liberal interpretation of the Bible has been a great blessing to many people in modern times. It has brought a great relief to many people, who would gladly be Christian, but who found in the Bible much that is strange, incomprehensible, offensive. That which was offensive disappeared and became natural, when it was seen in its context within a distant past, an ancient or primitive culture. Thereby the way was opened for that which was immediately accessible, attractive and convincing in the Bible. The significance of this may not be understimated. On the other hand, we may not be blinded to the fact, that the persons here in view constitute a little ethically-aesthetically-intellectually pronounced group of elite. There are many other people with other temperaments and other needs. Moreover, from its inception Christianity has been a religion of the *people*, and must remain such, if it is to be faithful to its history and to retain or regain its world-significance.

Something of the liberating quality about biblical criticism, in its many-faceted arrangement, explanation of facts and psychologically illuminating operation, is naturally experienced by every modern man interested in religion. He cannot be sufficiently grateful for this; for without such help he would experience almost insuperable difficulties with his Bible. However, an interpretation which dissolves *every* offense found in the historical motives and factors, is misdirected and misleading. If, for example, the "scandal" of the Son of Man is given the stamp of "church dogmatics" and is thereby eliminated, then one is cheated on the truth and is enticed to lay hold of shadows. One neither understands nor experiences either Jesus or the early Church in this way. Here one has left the solid ground of history, of reality, precisely where the *offense* presents itself as the characteristic criterion of reality.

Consequently, scientific realism demands that theological interpretation expounds the New Testament and early Christianity in all its massive faith-inspired strength. And practical, every day life demands that Christianity, the

Gospel, be preached in all its New Testament massivity to "the crowd" as well as to the cultured elite. Here we see how exegetical method and homiletical needs approach each other, – yet without ever coinciding. Historical interpretation and homiletical exposition must always be kept apart. No scientific exegesis can free the preacher, faced with an historically interpreted text, from the task of wrestling with the problem: *quid hæc ad nos?* But a realistic exegesis can prepare the way for the answer by showing *quid hæc ad illos*. If the past is allowed to appear as authentic life, then it will be easier for the homiletic meditation to find the fruitful connections between the historical document and current existential questions.

The starting-point and the foundation of all theological interpretation must be the early Christian kerygma, the message and the confession: Jesus is Lord, *Kyrios Jesus!* This confession is the key to the world of the New Testament, it is the way to understanding its documents. In other words, it is a confession, not an opinion. It is a testimony which appears with the absolute demand made by revelation and which must be interpreted and understood in accordance with it. Of course, there is nothing to prevent one from analysing psychologically and comparatively the religious ideas and outlooks which are part of this kerygma, or which form its general presuppositions. But one may not confuse this analysis – which is an indispensable scientific preliminary – with understanding itself. The analysis orients us only with regard to the historical scene, it shows us where we stand, it assures us that we have a solid ground of reality under our feet. Jesus, John and Paul are no projections of fantasy but facts, rooted and placed in their historical milieu. The issue now, however, is to understand them, to attain an intimate fellowship with them, strictly scientifically methodically and at the same time with intense empathy and identification in experience and thought. This is an overwhelmingly great and difficult task. He who imagines that he has overheard the secrets of these religious giants by means of a few psychological or theological formulations, is thoroughly deluded. To solve the problem we are in need of all the means which philology, history and psychology place at our disposal. But these are only means of assistance. Understanding itself is attained only by seizing and interpreting the biblical word on its own claims and its own spirit, absolutely Christologically. All other interpretations stop a long way short of the goal, or more correctly miss the goal.

If one has such a view of the supreme purpose of interpretation, then it is clear that all exegesis can fulfil its task only approximately. The full insight will come first with the clear light of eternity. The important thing, however, is that there is *movement* and *direction* towards the goal; for then there is something of the biblical reality's own mystical spark of life as well in the interpretation, which makes it to a certain extent become a *revelation*. For the supreme demand which objectivity makes on interpretation, is that in its strict matter-of-fact procedure it shall reveal the life, the spirit, the secret of its object. This can only be achieved in the higher unity of critical analysis and personal empathy.

Such an interpretation of the Bible understands and gives understanding, it is scientific. Should anyone want to interpret the New Testament starting with other presuppositions than its own, by another spirit than its own, i.e. from another viewpoint than the absolute viewpoint of the kerygma of Christ, let it be. But in that case, one should both see, admit and confess that this is a *re*-interpretation in modern style. Even such an interpretation has its rightful place, but not in theological scholarship, where strict realism and an unconditional sense of reality must be demanded. It is a scientific demand which cannot be lowered; it is also a practical desideratum, which cannot be suppressed.

Part One

The Synoptic Gospels

The Logion concerning "to carry one's cross"

A Critical-exegetical Study

(1922)

In Mark 8:34–38 we find some of the logia of Jesus which are collected under a distinct heading: Without suffering there is no salvation. The seriousness in this commitment is heightened through the reference to judgement (v. 38). The larger context of our logia is important: Peter's Messianic confession (8:27–30) is contrasted to the prediction of suffering (8:31) in a striking way, followed by the protest from the very same Peter and his rebuke by Jesus (8:32f.), a rebuke which ends with the words οὐ φρονεῖς τὰ τοῦ θεοῦ, ἀλλὰ τὰ τῶν ἀνθρώπων. To these logia the paradoxical words about self-denial as well as concerning the saving and losing of one's life are very appropriately added. Here we find τὰ τοῦ θεοῦ contrasted with τὰ τῶν ἀνθρώπων.

This well composed passage has been taken over without any changes in Matt. 16 and Luke 9. In addition, Luke gives the saying about the cross once again (14:27) in another combination of logia contrasting what is divine and what is human. In his great composition of sayings in chap. 10, Matthew produces a series of logia that have parallels in Luke 14 as well as in Mark 8 (10:37–39).

We are thus confronted with the source-critical problem of Synoptic doublets. We cannot discuss this problem here in its totality, rather we must limit ourselves to the example mentioned above.

1. Luke 14:27 and Matt. 10:37–39

Most scholars look upon the so-called Lucan "travel narrative" (9:51–18:14) as freely composed. Luke divides his material into three periods: the Galilean (most distant from his own interests), the journey to Jerusalem, and the period in Jerusalem. He puts everything that does not fit into either of the other two periods into the second period. Now and then he tries to maintain the fiction of a long continuous wandering (9:57, 10:1, 38, 13:22, 33, 17:1), but not consistently, however (cf. von Dobschütz in *Zeitschrift für wissenschaftliche Theologie*

(1912), pp. 366ff., Jülicher, *Einleitung,* 6th edition, p. 293, E. Klostermann, *Das Lukasevangelium* (1919), p. 472, J. Moffatt, *Introduction,* 3rd edition (1918), pp. 273f.). The principle that he has followed in arranging his material is not clear, and scholars have not succeeded in proving that Luke follows a continuous source (thus, e. g., Burton and B. Weiss). It may be necessary to state that the "travel narrative" is a conglomerate of material from various sources, where Luke himself to a large degree has tried to create a certain continuity with the help of introductory notes about chronology and the situation (see the in-depth treatment of this theme in K. L. Schmidt, *Der Rahmen der Geschichte Jesu* (1919), pp. 246–71).

In any case, it is fairly clear that the passage in 14:25–35 has been composed by Luke from different sources in order to throw light upon and emphasize a thought that is particularly important to him. Immediately preceding this passage he has placed the parable of the great banquet that ends with the words: "not one of those men who were invited will get a taste of my banquet." The message that Luke finds in this parable is evidently this one: The people are dependent upon worldly things and thus cannot receive their share in the kingdom of God (cf. 14:18–20). Thus a speech by Jesus follows which points to the necessity of making oneself free from everything worldly, 14:25–35.

The composition of this passage is clearly revealed by the three-fold οὐ δύναταί μου εἶναι μαθητής, that functions as a refrain all through the text (vv. 26, 27, 33). The passage is based upon material of different kinds: 1) a pair of sentences (vv. 26, 27), 2) a pair of parables (vv. 28–32), 3) a gnome (vv. 34–35). Between 2) and 3) we find a conclusion introduced οὕτως οὖν (v. 33).

We are now interested in the pair of sentences (vv. 26–27) which are also to be found in Matt. 10:37f.:

Luke: Εἴ τις ἔρχεται πρός με
καὶ οὐ μισεῖ τὸν πατέρα ἑαυτοῦ καὶ τὴν μητέρα
καὶ τὴν γυναῖκα καὶ τὰ τέκνα
καὶ τοὺς ἀδελφοὺς καὶ τὰς ἀδελφάς,
ἔτι τε καὶ τὴν ἑαυτοῦ ψυχήν,
οὐ δύναταί μου εἶναι μαθητής.

ὅστις οὐ βαστάζει τὸν σταυρὸν ἑαυτοῦ
καὶ ἔρχεται ὀπίσω μου,
οὐ δύναταί μου εἶναι μαθητής.

Matt.: Ὁ φιλῶν πατέρα ἢ μητέρα ὑπὲρ ἐμὲ
οὐκ ἔστιν μου ἄξιος,
καὶ ὁ φιλῶν υἱὸν ἢ θυγατέρα ὑπὲρ ἐμὲ
οὐκ ἔστιν μου ἄξιος·

καὶ ὃς οὐ λαμβάνει τὸν σταυρὸν αὐτοῦ
καὶ ἀκολουθεῖ ὀπίσω μου,
οὐκ ἔστιν μου ἄξιος.

It is evident that these doublets are very close to each other in form as well as in content. The problem is whether it is possible to say something about their mutual relationship.

There is every reason to believe that Matthew offers us *an original source unity* in contradistinction to Luke. Matt. 10:37–42 is clearly made up of a number of logia which are constructed in a similar way (they all begin with an emphasized participle or a dependent relative). Luke, on the other hand, uses the double logion together with other stylistically heterogeneous entities to build up a longer passage that makes a natural unity. In addition, we find in Mark 8 the same passages as in Matt. 10:37ff. closely connected to each other, and it is thus quite natural to suppose that Matthew has taken 10:37–42 (or more) directly from a source. If this is the case, it follows without further argument that Matthew presents us with *a more original form of the tradition*, while Luke himself has reformulated the wording of the logia. This supposition is clearly supported by three observations: a) the choppy style, b) the long list of relatives, c) the phrase οὐ δύναταί μου εἶναι μαθητής added after the rest.

a) The logion in Matt. 10:37 is built by using strict parallelism. There are two parts which vary the same theme in a well known manner: "father or mother" corresponds to "son or daughter" in the second part. Both parts begin with ὁ φιλῶν and end with οὐκ ἔστιν μου ἄξιος. Luke combines all of this into a long, formless sentence which seems overloaded and is totally dominant over the short final phrase. One easily gets lost in the alternatives mentioned and the concentrated power of the logion is weakened. We find striking stylistic parallels to the wording of Matthew, thus, e.g., Mark 9:43:

ἐὰν σκανδαλίζῃ σε ἡ χείρ σου, ἀπόκοψον αὐτήν·
καλόν ἐστίν σε κυλλὸν εἰσελθεῖν εἰς τὴν ζωὴν κτλ.

καὶ ἐὰν ὁ πούς σου σκανδαλίζῃ σε, ἀπόκοψον αὐτόν.
καλόν ἐστίν σε εἰσελθεῖν εἰς τὴν ζωὴν χωλὸν κτλ.

καὶ ἐὰν ὁ ὀφθαλμός σου σκανδαλίζῃ σε, ἔκβαλε αὐτόν.
καλόν σέ ἐστιν μονόφθαλμον εἰσελθεῖν εἰς τὴν
βασιλείαν τοῦ θεοῦ κτλ.

The Lucan wording however, lacks style.

b) In Matthew the mentioning of relatives ("father or mother," "son or daughter") serves as poetic examples. Luke, on the other hand, takes the list most seriously and wants to include all possibilities. We find this lack of sense for what is formally correct in other similar passages, thus Luke 12:53 (= Matt. 10:35), where Luke in a similar way doubles the basic OT text (Micah 7:6) and uses all of the alternatives. His redaction of Mark 10:29 = Matt. 19:29 = Luke 18:29 is also striking. It is true that he deletes ἀγρούς – most of those disciples of Jesus whom he knew certainly were townspeople – but he adds instead ἢ γυναῖκα. Just as he writes the realistic τὰ τέκνα instead of the poetic υἱὸς ἢ θυγάτηρ in 14:26, he condenses in 18:29 μήτηρ and πατήρ to γονεῖς, the single word, and ἀδελφούς and ἀδελφάς to ἀδελφούς, covering both brothers and sisters.

c) If we pose the question as to what sounds most original in Jesus' mouth, either οὐ δύναταί μου εἶναι μαθητής (Luke) or οὐκ ἔστιν μου ἄξιος (Matt.), we cannot hesitate in answering, when we consider the fact that μαθητής is the typical designation for a "Christian" in Acts (cf. Harnack, *Entstehung und Entwickelung der Kirchenverfassung,* p. 7). The categorical οὐ δύναται certainly is well known in the Synoptic tradition (Mark 3:24ff., Matt. 5:14, 36, 6:24), but we may ask if the wording here is not determined by this linguistic usage (see below). In any case, Matthew's form οὐκ ἔστιν μου ἄξιος seems original both from the point of content and language. The word ἄξιος plays a certain role in Jesus' sayings, especially when characterizing the relationship of people to the kingdom of God (Matt. 10:11, 13, 22:8). Here it is given a remarkable power and sublimity in that it expresses the relationship to Jesus himself: His quiet Messianic self-consciousness is expressed in the words ἄξιός μου. We find a parallel in Wisd. 3:5:

ὁ θεὸς ἐπείρασεν αὐτούς,
καὶ εὗρεν αὐτοὺς ἀξίους ἑαυτοῦ.[1]

It is not a prophet who is speaking in the Lucan wording, but rather a zealous preacher, who wants to bring home the need for self-denial to his followers. – It is also clear for other reasons that we must ascribe this wording to Luke. Luke continues as follows: εἴ τις ἔρχεται πρός με καὶ οὐ μισεῖ κτλ. It is evident that the μισεῖν, which is spoken about here, cannot be advanced as a general requirement, but is valid only when someone stands at the point of a decision to follow Jesus (εἴ τις ἔρχεται πρός με ...). The words ἔρχεσθαι πρός and μισεῖν then represent, in their reciprocity *vis-à-vis* each other, the comparative element that Matthew expresses with ὑπὲρ ἐμέ. In Luke this has been heightened into a contrast: either – or, which is expressed through the sharp μισεῖν. In contrast to the idea that this pointed μισεῖ is original we may state that the cautiously thought through φιλεῖν ὑπέρ is much more important for the content.

We may also point to the motive that caused the creation of this μισεῖ. Thus we read in Luke 16:13:

Οὐδεὶς οἰκέτης δύναται δυσὶ κυρίοις δουλεύειν·
ἢ γὰρ τὸν ἕνα μισήσει καὶ τὸν ἕτερον ἀγαπήσει,
ἢ ἑνὸς ἀνθέξεται καὶ τοῦ ἑτέρου καταφρονήσει.
οὐ δύνασθε θεῷ δουλεύειν καὶ μαμωνᾷ.

---

[1] What Deissmann says in *Neue Bibelstudien* pp. 75 f. about a characteristic use of ἀξίως has nothing to do with the use of ἄξιος in our connection.

There is certainly a possibility that Luke in his version of the logion on the occasional breaking of the bonds of blood (14:25) is influenced by the logion on the impossibility to serving two lords. He may be influenced in two ways. On the one hand, the wording οὐ δύναταί μου εἶναι μαθητής in 14:25 may be caused by the categorical οὐδεὶς δύναται, οὐ δύνασθε in 16:13. On the other hand, the absolute contrast in 16:13 τὸν ἕνα μισήσει καὶ τὸν ἕτερον ἀγαπήσει may have caused him to sharpen the original φιλεῖν ὑπέρ (Matt. 10:37) to a request for μισεῖν. It is evident that 16:13 does not allow any differentiation in love. Only two alternatives are given: to love or to hate. Consequently, if someone wants to love Jesus and follow him, he must hate everything that competes with him.[2]

The effects of this reformulation may be traced even further, thus in John 12:25:

ὁ φιλῶν τὴν ψυχὴν αὐτοῦ ἀπολλύει αὐτήν. καὶ ὁ μισῶν τὴν ψυχὴν αὐτοῦ ἐν τῷ κόσμῳ τούτῳ εἰς ζωὴν αἰώνιον φυλάξει αὐτήν.

This is clearly the Johannine version of the logion on saving or losing one's life (Mark 8:35 with parallels). The starting point is probably Luke 14:27 καὶ οὐ μισεῖ ... ἔτι δὲ καὶ τὴν ἑαυτοῦ ψυχήν, according to a Synoptic stylistic pattern being made into a contrasting parallelism through the addition of φιλεῖν.

If we therefore have to conclude that Luke 14:26 is formulated by Luke himself, the same conclusion is valid for what follows about carrying one's cross in v. 27. Here Luke is closer to his source as regards the form and as a whole he is close to Matt. 10:38, but there are some differences. The variant ἔρχεται ὀπίσω μου compared to ὀπ. μου ἀκολουθεῖν in Matthew is of no importance. When rephrasing Mark 8:34, both Matthew and Luke write ὀπ. μου ἔρχεσθαι (ἐλθεῖν) instead of ἀκολουθεῖν, which may be a coincidence, as these two phrases evidently were often used synonymously. It is more important that Luke 14:27 writes (ὅστις οὐ) βαστάζει, while Matthew uses λαμβάνει. Λαμβάνω has a basically ingressive meaning and thus gives the same impression as the aorist ἀράτω in Mark 8:34. The Lucan βαστάζει, however, expresses a durative condition, which is consistent with his rewording of Mark (Luke 9:23), adding καθ' ἡμέραν to Mark's ἀράτω. Since we have shown earlier that the Lucan εἴ τις ἔρχεται ... καὶ οὐ μισεῖ is the Gospel author's own formulation, we can now conclude that Matt. 10:38 represents a more original form of the logion about carrying one's cross in the Q-source used by both Matthew and Luke. We thus can leave out Luke in our search for the earliest transmitted

[2] It is striking that Luke overstates the meaning of μισεῖν. In the logion about to serve two lords the word "hate" means to "disregard" or "not bother oneself about", Cf. Judg. 14:16 καὶ ἔκλαυσεν ἡ γυνὴ Σαμψὼν πρὸς αὐτὸν καὶ εἶπεν Πλὴν μεμίσηκάς με καὶ οὐκ ἠγάπησας με, ὅτι τὸ πρόβλημα ... οὐκ ἀπήγγειλας μοι. The Semites do not nuance the word for these feelings. But Luke understands "hate" in all its acuteness.

form of the saying about the cross. The next step will then be to compare the source used by Matthew (and Luke) with Mark.

2. Matt. 10:38 and Mark 8:34

A glance at these two traditions shows us that we stand before a relatively fixed complex of sayings in two different variants.

Matt.: 1. The one who confesses me 10:32f.
2. The conflict between relatives vv. 34ff.
3. The one who loves his father and mother v. 37
4. To carry one's cross v. 38
5. Saving and losing one's life v. 39

Mark: 1. To carry one's cross 8:34
2. Saving and losing one's life v. 35
3. What use has a man vv. 36f.
4. The one who is ashamed of me v. 38

We find that the last two parts in Matthew and the first two parts in Mark are coextensive, and that part 1 in Matthew corresponds to part 4 in Mark.

We conclude from Luke and the stylistic symmetry that Matthew follows his source and combines the sayings about choosing Christ instead of one's father and mother and about carrying one's cross. It is clear from the comparison with Mark that these two logia have been closely connected in the transmission process with the saying on the confession or the denial of Christ and on saving or losing one's life (cf. also John 12:24–26). In addition, it was easier for Matthew to be faithful to his source, since he includes the combined sayings into a long speech, while Mark on the other hand uses the sayings in a specific and characteristic historical setting and thus may have worked in a more eclectic way, choosing and combining the sayings as he found suitable. He does not offer the saying that Christ is more important than father and mother, because it does not fit into his context. He puts the saying on carrying one's cross at the very beginning (8:34), since it provides an excellent continuation of the prediction of suffering and the scene with Peter. Here we may also search for the explanation as to why he only uses half of the logion on confessing or denying Christ (8:38); what is important in this connection is the threat.

I have of late, been strengthened in my view of the literary character of the passage Mark 8:34ff., as I have found that it is basically consistent with those source analyses done more recently. Walter Haupt, *Worte Jesu und die Gemeindeüberlieferung* (1913), p. 120, therefore argues that Mark 8:31ff. has mainly been taken from Q and has been given its present place by Mark as "ein Einschub, der sich besonders gut dem Character der Erzählungsstücke (the Messianic confession etc.) anpasst." Mark 8:34–9:1 "ist eine zur Ankündigung des Leidensprogramms sorgsam ausgewählte Zusammenstellung von Sprüchen aus der Jüngerrede." – Ed. Meyer, *Ursprung und Anfänge des Christentums* 1 (1921), p. 117, phrases his view of Mark 8:34–9:1 with reference to the Messianic confession and the rebuke of Peter as follows: "Es ist selbstverständlich, dass das Evangelium jetzt die Lehre vom Messias entwickelt und Jesus in den Mund legt, wie sie das Christentum gestaltet hat und verkündet ... Dieser ganze Abschnitt ist dem ursprünglichen, wirklich aus dem Leben Jesu stammenden Tradition gegenüber sekundär – was natürlich nicht ausschliesst, dass dabei einzelne wirklich von ihm gesprochene Worte (vv. 35, 36) benutzt sein können." – And R. Bultmann, *Die Geschichte der synoptischen Tradition* (1921), pp. 48, 200 ff., describes the passage as a combination of logia for which this was considered to be a suitable situation in the life of Jesus.

It can also be shown that Mark in this passage consistently gives the logia as secondary variants. We thus find a clear mission terminology in 8:35 "for me and for the gospel." When reading v. 38 "feel ashamed of me and my words" instead of "deny" the Messiah, we cannot resist the thought of Rom. 1:17 with the psychological situation that is taken for granted (cf. 2 Tim. 1:8, 12, 16 and 1 Pet. 4:16), when we read "is ashamed of me and of my words" instead of "denies" the Messiah in v. 38.

Having stated this we can hardly turn to the Marcan variant of the logion on carrying one's cross with much confidence.

Matt.: ὃς οὐ λαμβάνει τὸν σταυρὸν αὐτοῦ καὶ ἀκολουθεῖ ὀπίσω μου,
οὐκ ἔστιν μου ἄξιος

Mark: εἴ τις θέλει ὀπίσω μου ἀκολουθεῖν
ἀπαρνησάσθω ἑαυτὸν καὶ ἀράτω τὸν σταυρὸν αὐτοῦ καὶ ἀκολουθείτω μοι.

The Marcan recension is clearly *expanded,* thus with the words about self-denial, originally an independent logion, secondarily combined with the saying on carrying one's cross because of its spiritual proximity. The Marcan text is also *reshaped* in that following Jesus is no longer optional but *a necessary condition:* It is not written that one may follow Jesus, but that the one *who wants to follow him* (i. e. be a Christian) must do this or that. Here we evidently find a reshaping close to the one in Luke 14:26: "If any one comes to me ..." This change mirrors the situation. Here we do not encounter the question of joining Jesus, but we encounter a Christian parenesis: It is a matter of emphasizing for *those who already belong to the community* what they must do in order to be true Christians.

It may be doubtful from this perspective as to how to understand the concluding καὶ ἀκολουθείτω μοι. It is normally understood as a repetition of the introductory condition: "... and follow me." But if Mark has taken his starting point in a wording that talks about "following Jesus" already as a condition, we may pose the question if ἀκολουθ. μοι must not be understood together with the imperatives ἀπαρνησάσθω ἑαυτόν and ἀράτω τ. στ. αὐτ., thus as a – less than suitable – reminiscence of a more original version.

It is evident that we cannot depend upon the Marcan version if we want to reach back to the original logion. Neither can we use the variant in Matthew (or Luke) as self-evidently original. For here we find it combined with a strictly parallelistic logion, a firm unity in itself:

Ὁ φιλῶν πατέρα ἢ μητέρα ὑπὲρ ἐμὲ
οὐκ ἔστιν μου ἄξιος,
καὶ ὁ φιλῶν υἱὸν ἢ θυγατέρα ὑπὲρ ἐμὲ
οὐκ ἔστιν μου ἄξιος.

We can hardly doubt that the logion on carrying one's cross in its present context is an addition to an original gnome with two parallel parts. Consequently we must also admit that a *formal adjustment* has taken place between the double logion and the saying on the cross, self-evidently in such a way that the single logion was added and formally rephrased according to the already strictly formalized double gnome. This leads to the conclusion that the final οὐκ ἔστ. μ. ἄξιος cannot be an original part of the logion on carrying one's cross, and further that its character as a general religious statement may depend upon formalization. This means that we are not able to reconstruct any original logion that may be behind the tradition, and we must reckon with the possibility that it has been spoken in a situation about which we do not know anything concrete. We cannot rule out the possibility that it had its place in a purely individualistic exhortation or call like: "Take your cross and follow me!"

Is it conceivable that Jesus has expressed himself like this, and what then may be the meaning of such an expression?

3. To carry one's cross

Early biblical exegesis quite clearly considered this saying to be spoken by Jesus with reference to the death that he predicted. It was, however, quite natural for later critical exegesis to consider the logion as phrased *ex eventu*. This has been argued from the role which the cross plays for Paul as a symbol for how the Christian dies to the world, thus Loisy: *"se considérer comme crucifié avec Jésus, voué comme lui aux souffrances et à la mort pour la vie éternelle."* In addition, it is emphasized that the way in which Jesus died made the cross the most pregnant expression of *martyrdom:* the Christian must be prepared for this; only the martyr is a real Christian (J. Weiss, H.I. Holtzmann, H. Lietzmann among others). Wellhausen says: "Diese metaphorische Verwendung der noch nicht geschehenen Kreuzigung Jesu befremdet aufs äusserste in seinem eigenen Munde, da sie den Hörern völlig unverstanden bleiben musste.

Das Kreuz tritt schon hier als Symbol des Christentums auf."[3] And Harnack (*Sprüche und Reden Jesu,* p. 150) notes that here "liegt warscheinlich ein Hysteron-Proteron vor, aber gewiss ein uraltes." With Reinach he also adds the possibility that the death of the righteous one on the cross was a widely distributed idea, influenced by well-known passages like Plato, *Rep.* 362 and Psalm 22.[4]

There are those however, who maintain that Jesus may have used "the cross" as a symbol for martyrdom without directly thinking of his own death, taking for granted that the disciples would understand the expression without reference to his death on the cross. They refer to the fact that crucifixion was a very well known punishment in Palestine during the Roman era (Lagrange,[5] B. Weiss, Zahn: "dass er – der Jünger – sich willig zeige, den Kreuzestod zu erleiden ... Exemplifizierende Veranschaulichung der Gesinnung, welche Jesus fordert"), and they also assume that the wording may be proverbial.

It has not been possible to find any proof for this last-mentioned idea. For the time being, I can only refer to one passage which seems to indicate that crucifixion has been used proverbially – Epictet, *Diss.* 2.2,20. The philosopher preaches about ἀταραξία, but warns at the same time of an aggressive behaviour against the authorities, especially the court εἰ μήτι καιρός ἐστιν

[3] Against this view Bultmann (*Geschichte der synoptischen Tradition* (1921), p. 98) rightly points out that we are not to expect (τὸν σταυρὸν) ἑαυτοῦ but only τὸν σταυρόν. This very individualization of the carrying of one's cross argues against an original typical-symbolical meaning of the logion.

[4] The patristic interpretation finds in this saying both that willingness to become a martyr is requested (οὐδὲ σωθῆναι δυνήσῃ ἐὰν μὴ αὐτὸς εἰς τὸ ἀποθανεῖν ᾖς παρεσκευασμένος διαπαντός ... οὐδὲ γὰρ ἁπλῶς εἶπεν, ὅτι πρὸς θάνατον δεῖ παρατετάχθαι, ἀλλ' ὅτι καὶ πρὸς θάνατον βίαιον καὶ οὐ πρὸς θάνατον βίαιον μόνον, ἀλλὰ καὶ ἐπονείδιστον, Chrysostom) and the rather symbolical concept of an inner death away from the world (the one who denies himself, thus repents from his old life and becomes a witness for Christ ὁ τοιοῦτος Χριστῷ συνεσταύρωται καὶ ἄρας τὸν σταυρὸν ἑαυτοῦ ἀκολουθεῖ τῷ δι' ἡμᾶς βαστάζοντι τὸν ἑαυτοῦ σταυρόν, Origen). – F. Spitta has voiced a strange idea (*Streitfragen der Geschichte Jesu* (1907), pp. 109f., *Die synoptische Grundschrift* (1912), pp. 230f.). He states that φορτίον or something similar is original instead of σταυρός: "Wenn Jesus in früheren, besseren Zeiten seinen Aposteln verboten hatte, Gepäck auf ihren Missionsreisen mitzunehmen, da sie sich auf die Gastfreundschaft der Leute verlassen konnten (vgl. Luk. 9,3; Mark 6,8), so sieht er sich für die spätere Zeit der Feindschaft gegen ihn zu entgegengesetzter Praxis veranlasst: Luk. 22,36: ἀλλὰ νῦν ὁ ἔχων βαλλάντιον ἀράτω, ὁμοίως καὶ πήραν."

[5] Lagrange (*L'évangile selon St. Marc* 1911, p. 210) gives a number of examples from Josephus. It is striking which role crucifixion plays in Artemidorus' book on dreams (*Oneirocritica,* ed. Hercher). Dreams are consistently about crucifixions, and dreams predict this death, cf. pp. 7,19, 152,4, 231,14, 270,14. We also read (p. 159,19): τοὺς γὰρ ἀλιτηρίους κολάζομεν πολλάκις καὶ διὰ σταυροῦ. I also mention in passing that crucifixion and *exaltation* repeatedly are mentioned together in Artemidorus (cf. John 3:14, 8:28), e. g., p. 231,14ff. οἷον ἔδοξέ τις ἐσταυρῶσθαι, σημαίνοντος τοῦ δοκεῖν ἐσταυρῶσθαι δόξαν καὶ εὐπορίαν. δόξαν μὲν τὸ ὑψηλότατον εἶναι τὸν ἐσταυρωμένον ... cf. p. 69,11, 152,7. Perhaps ὑπερύψωσεν in Phil. 2:9 has something to do with this concept?

ἐπίτηδες ἐρεθίσαι τοὺς δικαστὰς ὡς Σωκράτει. καὶ σὺ εἶ τοιοῦτον ἐπίλογον παρασκευάζῃ, τί ἀναβαίνεις, τί ὑπακούεις; εἰ γὰρ σταυρωθῆναι θέλεις, ἔκδεξαι καὶ ἔρχεται ὁ σταυρός. Since Socrates, who emptied the cup of poison, could not direct people's thoughts to the death on the cross, it is more reasonable to suppose that this is a *locus communis,* at home in popular philosophy. It is probably Plato's famous ὁ δίκαιος ... πάντα κακὰ παθὼν ἀνασχινδυλευθήσεται which returns in the bold "Just wait, and the cross will come!" of the popular diatribe. We may also mention a passage in Artemidorus (*Oneirocritica* 4.32) who talks of the outcome of a dream about the philosopher Alexander and then mentions that he was sentenced to death, but on his prayer *escaped from the cross.* To judge from this passage, crucifixion seems to have been the self-evident or normal capital punishment for philosophers (Plato's "righteous").

It is, however, doubtful that the solution is to be found in this direction, since it is not death itself on the cross that is pointed out, but rather the way to the place of execution. This indicates that the metaphor is not about a single event (the martyr's death) but rather a lasting condition, a *battle of life.* This is also suggested by the verbs αἴρειν and λαμβάνειν which both point to the *beginning* (cf. the monologue by a Cynic philosopher to be when he describes his future life, Epictet, *Diss.* 3. 22,10 ... πηρίδιον προσλήμψομαι καὶ ξύλον καὶ περιερχόμενος αἰτεῖν ἄρξομαι τοὺς ἀπαντῶντας, λοιδορεῖν), Luke 9:3, 22:36, Epictet, *Diss.* 1. 24,11: Τί ποιεῖς, ἐκ πλοίου ὅταν ἐξίῃς; μή τι τὸ πηδάλιον αἴρεις, μή τι τὰς κώπας; τί οὖν αἴρεις; τὰ σά, τὴν λήκυθον, τὴν πήραν. The expression is frequently combined with the words καὶ ἀκολουθεῖ ὀπίσω μου, with the clear meaning: to become one of the disciples of Jesus, to begin to accompany him (cf. Matt. 4:19, Mark 1:20, John 12:19, ἔρχεσθαι ὀπίσω τοῦ Ἰ.).

Thus, to accompany Jesus is to dare to live a life as burdensome as the last journey of the one sentenced to death. What makes this journey so bitter in this connection is not primarily the knowledge of what is waiting at the end of the journey – even if that motive certainly is also present[6] – but the feeling *of being a social outcast* and the experience of *being the object of hatred and contempt of the masses,* the weight of *the people's judgement.* Crowds, on both sides, shouting and screaming invectives and curses – what a terrible gauntlet. Anyone sentenced to death was treated like that by the general public of the period just as by mobs all throughout history. The man of antiquity was so dependent on his environment that the whole terror of the situation was made still more frightful through the isolation and the judgement from the general public: it undermined the whole spiritual existence of the individual. Against this back-

[6] Cf. *Bereshit Rabba* to Gen. 22:6: "And Abraham took the wood for the sacrifice as one who carries his cross on his shoulders."

ground we can understand why the Stoics worked so energetically to help the individual to think and act independently and to preach against the popular view of human fate and judgements, cf. Seneca, *De prov.* 2,9: "*ecce spectaculum dignum, ad quod respiciat deus, ecce par deo dignum, vir fortis cum fortuna male compositus; ... non video, inquam, quid habeat in terris Juppiter pulchrius, quam ut spectet Catonem iam partibus non semel fractis stantem nihilo minus inter ruinas publicas rectum.*" – For a moment Paul gives voice to this dependence upon the environment that was so typical for the society of antiquity, thus in 1 Cor. 4:9: δοκῶ γάρ, ὁ θεὸς ἡμᾶς τοὺς ἀποστόλους ἐσχάτους ἀπέδειξεν ὡς ἐπιθανατίους, ὅτι θέατρον ἐγενήθημεν τῷ κόσμῳ καὶ ἀγγέλοις καὶ ἀνθρώποις. This is in reality the best commentary to the saying on carrying one's cross. The "cross" is not mainly an instrument of torture and execution, but rather the visible sign of the position of the one judged, the sign of shame that made him the object of everyone's contempt and rejection.

It was a generally accepted practice that the one sentenced to death carried his own cross by himself, cf. Artemidorus, *Oneirocritica,* ed. Hercher p. 153, 22ff. (II, 56): ὁ μέλλων αὐτῷ (sc. τῷ σταυρῷ) προσηλοῦσθαι πρότερον αὐτὸν βαστάζει, and Plutarch, *De ser. num. vind.* 554 A: καὶ τῷ μὲν σώματι τῶν κολαζομένων ἕκαστος κακούργων ἐκφέρει τὸν αὐτοῦ σταυρόν. We know from, e.g., Chariton's novel about Chaireas and Kallirrhoe (*Erotici scriptores graeci,* ed. Hercher II, pp. 72, 76) that the path to the place of execution was considered a terrible part of the punishment. There we read that the hero and his friend Polycharmos while on their way to find Kallirrhoe, are sold as slaves and innocently sentenced to death, – self-evidently crucifixion: Προήχθησαν οὖν πόδας τε καὶ τραχήλους συνδεδεμένοι, καὶ ἕκαστος αὐτῶν τὸν σταυρὸν ἔφερε. τῇ δὲ ἀναγκαίᾳ τιμωρίᾳ καὶ τὴν ἔξωθεν φαντασίαν σκυθρωπὴν προσέθηκαν οἱ κολάζοντες εἰς φόβον παράδειγμα τοῖς ὁμοίοις ... Πολύχαρμος δὲ τὸν σταυρὸν βαστάζων 'διὰ σέ', φησίν, 'ὦ Καλλιρρόη, ταῦτα πάσχομεν. Σὺ πάντων ἡμῖν τῶν κακῶν αἰτία'. Their innocence, however, is finally ascertained and they escape their fate at the last moment. At the same time Chaireas comes to know about Kallirrhoe's (presumed) unfaithfulness and starts complaining: "Ἄπιστε Καλλιρρόη καὶ πασῶν ἀσεβεστάτη γυναικῶν, ἐγὼ μὲν ἐπράθην διὰ σέ, καὶ ἔσκαψα καὶ σταυρὸν ἐβάστασα καὶ δημίου χερσὶ παρεδόθην ..." Evidently the carrying of the cross is an independent part of the defamation and suffering.

As far as I can see, we have reason to base our understanding of the metaphorical saying about carrying one's cross on the *social* experience that characterized such a situation: the disciple of Jesus is expelled from the established society, he will encounter total rejection everywhere, from all sides clenched fists, invectives, mortal hatred. He becomes a θέατρον, a *spectaculum*. The passages that are immediately connected in the tradition with our logion show this to be its earliest interpretation.

"Do not suppose that I have come to bring peace to the earth;
I did not come to bring peace, but a sword.
For I have come
to turn a man against his father, a daughter against her mother,
and a daughter-in-law against her mother-in-law – a man's enemies
will be the members of his own household.
Anyone who loves his father and mother more than me
is not worthy of me;
anyone who loves his son or daughter more than me
is not worthy of me;
and anyone who does not take his cross and follow me
is not worthy of me." [Matt. 10:34–38, Q (Tr.)]

In the same way in Mark:

"If anyone would come after me,
he *must deny himself* and take up his cross
and follow me." (Mark 8:34)

From this point of view it is possible, even probable, that the logion is created by Jesus. It is a logion which in its creative power is fully worthy of him. The question, however, is whether Jesus has really phrased himself in such an extremely drastic way about the consequences of following him. The answer is partly dependent upon how we in general judge a whole group of Jesus' sayings which point in the same direction (Matt. 8:20, 10:34f., Mark 13:12 etc.). Some of them are certainly created *post eventum,* but all of them? Even if we are not inclined to ascribe such general statements to Jesus, we cannot rule out that a specific situation may have given rise to an extremely pointed statement, full of dynamics: To follow me is to become like a criminal, dishonoured and rejected. We remember another logion, also heightened into the extreme: "Foxes have holes and birds of the air have nests, but the Son of Man has no place to lay his head" (Matt. 8:20).

Regardless of the origin of the logion on bearing one's cross, we can be certain that those who wrote down the Gospel tradition have seen it in the light of Jesus' death. It is the crucified, but also resurrected Lord who speaks through it to his community. We have found that it has been combined in Q with other statements which put the stress on suffering and the willingness to suffer as something unavoidable and necessary for a disciple, that even the loss of life is a gain of life. In this connection, the saying concerning the cross by necessity directs one's thoughts to martyrdom (Matt. 10:39). Thus we can find here two tendencies as regards the meaning in the literary context.

We find the same situation in Mark, in his source carrying one's cross and the denial of oneself have been put together as two alternative concepts. He himself, however, puts the saying concerning the cross immediately after the prediction of suffering and thus shows unmistakably how he understands it.

Luke, however, who found the saying in both of his sources, Q and Mark, in a context about martyrdom, has sided unequivocally with the original meaning by the addition of καθ ἡμέραν (9:23) and the use of βαστάζει instead of λαμβάνει (14:27). He did this either because he knew the proverbial character of the expression or because this understanding dominated in his environment. He may have voiced his understanding in a certain conflict with his sources which aim at martyrdom. Luke, however, has not been able to disregard this idea totally. In 14:26 where he paraphrases the Q-logion on making a break, even with the family, he has the list of family members end with a (μισεῖ ...) ἔτι δὲ καὶ τὴν ἑαυτοῦ ψυχήν, which certainly directs the thought to death as a martyr. Τὴν ψυχήν here cannot be identical with ἑαυτόν (cf. ἀπαρνήσασθαι ἑαυτόν 9:23; and 9:25 where Luke writes ἀπολέσει ἑαυτόν instead of ζημιωθῆναι τὴν ψυχήν), but must refer to the bodily life, with μισεῖν voicing a quiet contrast to ἀγαπᾶν. This last word is used in the early Church to refer to clinging to life while rejecting Jesus, cf. 2 Tim. 4:10, Rev. 12:11, Did. 2:7, Barn. 1:4.

We receive an indirect witness to the fact that our understanding of the original meaning of the metaphorical word is correct from John, who tells us in contrast to the rest of the Gospel tradition that Jesus himself carried his own cross (19:17). The Johannine note is certainly not caused by the idea that Christ did not need any help, but that by his own free will he took all suffering upon himself. Neither is it caused by any antidocetic tendency nor by any secondary influence from the saying on following Jesus by carrying one's cross, but quite simply by the tendency to stress the high points of the suffering and the derision: Jesus was not spared this *spectaculum*.

The expression ἀκολουθεῖν ὀπίσω μου has had a strange fate. The thought of the imitation of Christ, so important later on, has developed from it. In the Q-version, ἀκ. ὀπίσω (to carry one's cross and follow Jesus) means to join him openly as his μαθητής. Logically one might expect the two parts to be mentioned in the opposite order: to join Jesus and then carry the negative consequences of it. The emphasis, however, is put on the defying of these negative consequences, thus they are mentioned first. But from the point of view of the community, to "follow Jesus" will have a deeper and richer meaning than the concrete and original: to go the way the Lord himself went, "imitatio Christi." The idea of following the Lord's example and sharing his fate is basic for the very idea of discipleship (Lyder Brun, *Jesu Evangelium,* pp. 565 ff.). This motive, however, could develop fully only after the Lord's destiny was fulfilled and the totality of his life had been fixed by tradition (see J. Weiss, *Die Nachfolge Christi* (1895); R. Seeberg, *Aus Religion und Geschichte* (1906), pp. 1–41).

The Tripartite Formula in Matt. 28:19 and Baptism in the Three Names

(1922)

Our baptismal formula, which we share with all Christian churches, is taken from Matt. 28:19. We read as follows in the Great Commission of the resurrected Christ: βαπτίζοντες αὐτοὺς εἰς τὸ ὄνομα τοῦ πατρὸς καὶ τοῦ υἱοῦ καὶ τοῦ ἁγίου πνεύματος. Thus the Gospel author knows baptism as a baptism in three names. We know, however, that the earliest Christian baptism took place in the name of *Jesus* alone (1 Cor. 1:13, 6:11, Acts 2:38, 8:16, 10:48, 19:5, cf. Jas. 2:7 and the passages from Hermas, mentioned below). In the environment in which the author of the Gospel of Matthew was at home, however, baptism was done in the three names. Later on we find this custom in Didache 7 and Justin *Apol.* 61. Trinitarian baptism has thus developed in some parts of the Church in the 60's-80's. Gregory of Nyssa (4th century) brought about its acceptance as the only valid baptism in the Orient (*Ep. ad Sebast.* 2). In the West, however, the validity of baptism in Jesus' name alone was asserted time and time again, until the Council of Trent established the trinitarian formula for the Roman Catholic Church. Luther and Zwingli declared baptism in Jesus' name fully valid (cf., e.g., *De captivitate babyl.* 5.61), but baptism in the three names remained the rule in the Protestant churches.

Matt. 28:19 is not a baptismal formula in the strict sense, that is to say no word for word report of what was said over the baptismal candidate, but it characterizes the act of baptism. This is to be done in the three names. It is important to see what the phrase εἰς τὸ ὄνομα means. Scholars now seem to agree that the expression must be understood from the perspective given by Hellenism. At most, it may be disputed whether εἰς τὸ ὄνομα should be understood to mean "while mentioning" the name in question or more moderately "on behalf of". (See W. Heitmüller, *Im Namen Jesu* (1903) for the first view and J. Lindblom, *Jesu missionsoch dopbefallning* (1919), pp. 159ff. for the second view). In the end there is little difference, since the mentioning of the Diety's name over the baptismal candidate according to ancient thinking makes him the possession of the Divinity. As for the baptism itself, we may conjecture that the one who administered the baptism, at some occasion pronounced

Jesus' name or the three names over the one who was baptized (cf. Jas. 2:7 τὸ καλὸν ὄνομα τὸ ἐπικληθὲν ἐφ' ὑμᾶς, and Herm *Vis.* 3.7,3, *Sim.* 9.14,3, 8.1,1, 8.6,4). Justin says that it is ὁ τὸν λουσόμενον ἄγων ἐπὶ τὸ λουτρόν who pronounces the names (*Apol.* 61). Didache 7 mentions the choice between immersion and sprinkling and states that the latter shall take place three times, evidently once for each name. – The early Church did not have a baptismal formula like ours "I baptize you ...". We do not know for certain when and where they began to use Matt. 28:19 and thus *mentioned not only the names but also the purpose of the act.* It must have taken place during the second century, thus Tertullian (cf. *Adv. Prax.* 26).[1]

Thus the baptismal command in Matt. 28:19 became important for the future. It not only helped trinitarian baptism to a total victory, it gave the Church its baptismal formula as well. The passage is itself a part of the liturgical and terminological development, a part that influenced future history decisively. Here we encounter a double historical question: a liturgical question on how baptism in the three names suppressed baptism in the name of Jesus, and a terminological question on the creation of the trinitarian formulas themselves. And what about the formula in Matt. 28:19? – It is to be anticipated as probable that there is an inner connection between these two questions.

We must point here to the fact that our formula has exerted an enormous influence as well on the development of *dogma:* it is the foundation of the Trinitarian and the Christological dogmas. We know quite well the battles and the conflicts that accompanied this development, and we ask: Is all this subtle speculation, based upon the trinitarian formula, really consonant with its original intentions and meaning? The way we answer this question is important for our whole view of the history of dogma. – Our formula, however, is also of great importance for the *history of the symbols.* Research on the Apostolic Creed has been almost non-existent for some twenty years, but has now received great impetus in recent years through the works of Haussleiter, Holl and Lietzmann. It has been shown that the early Roman symbol, that later developed into our symbol, has two roots, both going back to the first century: the Trinitarian formulas and the Christological confession. If we manage to analyse these two basic elements and show what led to their combination in Rome at around A.D. 200, historical research on the Apostles' Creed will be firmly based in a manner we have not previously seen. Against this background in the history of dogma and the history of symbols, we will now turn to the question of the emergence of Trinitarian baptism and the Trinitarian formula.

---

[1] Since Cyprian the formula *in nomine patris* etc. was used in the West (= ἐν τῷ ὀνόματι, Acts 10:48, 1 Cor. 6:11), the wording εἰς τὸ ὄνομα being difficult to translate into Latin. The phrase "in the name of the Father etc." was understood to carry the meaning "on behalf of the Divinity", "with the authority of the Divinity."

Twenty years ago Usener tried to solve the problem of the emergence of the Christian Trinity with the help of comparative religion or rather the psychology of religion (*Dreiheit, Rhein. Mus.* 1903). He gathered a lot of examples of divine triads from various religions, primitive as well as higher, and traced them all to a psychological law stating that the number three has a dominating role in the human consciousness as such, it more or less being a rhythmical law for feeling, thought, imagination and speech. There are even primitive peoples for whom three is the highest number, and a group of three stands for something perfect, something complete. Here we will find the root of the divine triads, including the Christian Trinity.

Söderblom has discussed this theory critically in his book *Vater, Sohn und Geist unter den heiligen Dreiheiten* (Tübingen 1909) and, rightly as I think, rejected it. The only justifiable and correct method, when dealing with a historical religion like Christianity, is to show the religious *motives* that may lie behind such a trinity. It is another matter that a general psychological tendency towards trinities may have facilitated the development and led to the early emergence of fixed formulas. We must do justice both to the religious and the strictly psychological motives, and it is not enough to limit one's view to just one motive.

We may also mention a relatively recent attempt to throw light on our topic from the point of view of comparative religion. I am thinking of Ditlef Nielsen's work *Der dreieinige Gott in religionsgeschichtlicher Beleuchtung* (Gyldendal 1922). Nielsen concentrates on the Semitic ideas of a divine triad *Father – Son – Mother,* which he considers as the kernel of all Semitic religion. It corresponds to the role played by *family life* in the Semitic culture. He goes through the history of this concept and wants to show how the emphasis in the end is put on the Son, the Lord and the Saviour, who unites himself with mankind in the mystery cults, while the sexual element which is connected with the mother is suppressed and replaced by the Spirit or Wisdom. Thus early Christianity on Hellenistic ground is nothing but a variant of this Semitic mystery religion. In reality Jesus was just an ordinary human being, a pious Jewish teacher, but he is now identified with the Son of God and becomes the Lord. Thus the triad *the Father – the Son – the Spirit* existed in the very beginning, and the Trinitarian and Christological dogmas of the Church become the last offshoot of the Semitic myth of a divine family.

I am not able to say whether such a Semitic family myth of a triadic type has ever existed. That may be the case. We must state, however, for the early Church that an explanation taken strictly from comparative religion can be defended only when there is no other possible explanation. This explanation, taken from comparative religion, may be right on many points. The tradition about Jesus has made use of legendary and mythological elements. In Christian Hellenistic piety, concepts of faith and cult have been strongly influenced by the religious environment. But the fact cannot be denied that the Christian Faith goes back to the impression given by the historical Jesus and to his statements about himself and that it is the living relationship to him and the experience of the Easter events that are the foundation of early Christianity. Certainly there are unsolved historical riddles here, riddles that probably can never be solved, but this cannot nullify the historical connections that can in part be seen. We may also say that the hypothesis, developed from a strictly comparative religious perspective, is likewise confronted with many obscure and impenetrable questions. For the time being we therefore bypass the points of view developed from the perspective of comparative religion and psychology of religion and pose our questions about Trinitarian baptism and the triadic formula to early Christianity itself, to the New Testament.

As for the *locus classicus* Matt. 28:19, the conservative and apologetic view that emphasizes the mainly historical character of the text has found its most modern expression in R. Seeberg's well-known paper *Evangelium quadraginta dierum* in *Neue kirchliche Zeitschrift* 1905 (also in *Aus Religion und Geschichte,* pp. 42ff.; cf. *Lehrbuch der Dogmengeschichte* I, 2nd ed. 1908, pp. 60–63). Here Seeberg wants to show that the teaching shared by the early Church as a whole can be derived from that which the resurrected Christ taught during the forty days between his resurrection and his ascension. This included the instructions on mission and thus Christian baptism as well. We are not, however, to read Matthew's words on this part of the teaching of the Resurrected One as a word for word report. Jesus has characterized baptism in a general way as an admission into the community of the Trinitarian Divinity, Father, Son and Holy Spirit. The wording of Matt. 28:19 is from liturgical language (cf. *Dogmengeschichte,* p. 62, note 1: "Ich halte es für verkehrt, die Echtheit des Matthäusschlusses anzufechten; freilich ein Herrenwort im eigentlichen Sinn ist er auch nicht, sondern er ist ein zusammenfassendes Referat über das, was die Jünger in jenen Tagen an dem auferstandenen Herrn erlebt und von ihm gelernt haben, wie der Vergleich mit Lukas zeigt. Als Taufformel ist das Wort zunächst wohl nicht gemeint gewesen, sowenig Mt. 3,11 Christus zum Täufer machen soll"). Riggenbach indicates a similar view in his *Der trinitarische Taufbefehl* 1903, pp. 97f. with reference to Haupt, *Zum Verständnis des Apostolats,* 1886, pp. 38ff.[2]

Clearly these scholars have not been able to resist the impression that Jesus talks in an ecclesiastical and liturgical style in Matt. 28. The attempt to save the historicity of the tradition in spite of this idea is a makeshift solution that does not tempt the more realistic scholar. (The monograph by J. Lindblom, men-

---

[2] See also S. Odland, "Daaben i det nye testamente," *Norsk Teologisk Tidsskrift* 1900, pp. 1ff.

tioned above, is also of an apologetic character, which regrettably reduces the scholarly value of this broad, careful and learned work to a great extent.) We must admit that Matt. 28 sanctions the later mission custom by bringing it back to the Lord himself.[3] Since we cannot, however, reckon with a positive commandment given by Jesus, we must go on to ask for the *intrinsic* motives behind the Trinitarian complex.

I cannot share the views which Harnack voices in an appendix to his work *Entstehung und Entwickelung der Kirchenverfassung* etc. (1910), where he explains the creation of the formula in Matt. 28:19 against the background of the disagreement between those who believed in Christ and the Jews. The earliest stage of the formula was binitarian: God and Christ. The Christians replaced *Moses,* the great authority of the Jews, with *the Lord:* "For the Law was given through Moses; grace and truth came through Jesus Christ" (John 1:17). God however, stands behind Jesus: "Now this is eternal life: that they may know you, the only true God, and Jesus Christ, whom you have sent" (John 17:3). The Spirit was necessarily added to these two, because the gift of the Spirit legitimized the early Christians *vis-à-vis* the Jews according to the prophetic word in Joel 3. The Jews on their part referred to Scripture and tradition. – The fact, however, that the formula does not read "God – Christ – Spirit" but "*Father – Son* – Spirit" is dependent upon "God's Son" being the most disputed title for Christ. The Jews opposed this title most fiercely. The believers stressed it all the more until *the Son* became the dominant Christological title. It followed naturally that God was called *the Father* in this formula.

Against such an argument I would like to state that it is questionable to suppose that such a formula is brought about by negative, apologetic and polemical conditions. It is certainly more probable that positive interests and values were expressed. – Furthermore, it is not clear how Harnack conceives of the relationship between the terminological and the liturgical development. He seems to think that a polemical, tripartite slogan was applied to the newly created baptism in the three names. It is certainly more credible that the formula was in some way created in connection with liturgical praxis.

Can we now point to positive religious motives in the early Church that, liturgically and terminologically, led in a Trinitarian direction? And can we point to special prerequisites for the origin of a formula like the one in Matt. 28:19?

We must be conscious of the fact that we do not need to limit our field of vision to Jewish Christianity or to Palestine only because we find the Trinitarian formula in Matthew. This Gospel, as we have it today, is probably a product of

[3] This does not necessarily mean that the world mission (and the custom of baptism) was intended or established by Jesus. That is a question which is independent of Matt. 28 and which cannot be answered with full certainty.

the Church in Syria, just the place where Palestinian tradition met with Hellenism. In addition, the time that had passed between the beginning of the mission and the redaction of the Gospel was long enough for the Hellenistic mission to reinfluence Palestinian spiritually. We may also remember that we are in the time after the destruction of Jerusalem, a catastrophe that ended all future influence of Jewish Christianity and to a high degree caused the centre of gravity to move to Gentile Christianity.

The first and basic point in the mission among Gentiles was self-evidently *monotheism:* to break with the veneration of images and to believe in the one true God. Thus we read in our earliest mission text: "how you turned to God from idols to serve the living and true God" (1 Thess. 1:9), and in 1 Cor. 8:5–6 the gnosis of the Corinthians is worded as follows: "(as indeed there are many 'gods' and many 'lords'), yet for us there is one God, the Father". Christian mission here followed in the footsteps of Jewish propaganda.

If we look more closely at the two passages quoted above, however, we will find that Christ on both occasions is mentioned in close connection with God: "how you turned to *God* from idols to serve the living and true God, and to wait for his *Son* from heaven, whom he raised from the dead – Jesus, who rescues us from the coming wrath." And: "for us there is one *God,* the Father ... and one *Lord,* Jesus Christ." Monotheism and belief in Christ were the two main characteristics of the early Christians, the colours under which they sailed. This situation must have been fertile soil for binitarian formulas. Their religious faith centered around two points: the one true God and Christ, the Saviour, the judge to come. The relationship between these two was conceived metaphorically with Christ *sharing God's throne* (Rev. 5:6, 7:9, 22:1, Acts 2:33 etc.; Rom. 8:34). It is a dynamic binitarianism, not a static metaphysical one.

When we now try to imagine how more or less fixed binitarian formulas developed, we must distinguish between motives and presuppositions. Having pointed out the strong motive that was hidden in the religious situation of the missionary Church itself, we must add a reference to *the liturgy,* being a presupposition for the development of binitarian formulas. The two names must have been mentioned constantly side by side in prayers, psalms and invocations. It is here that we will find the earliest fixed formulaic clusters of words. Thus the Pauline formula "Grace and peace to you from God our Father and from the Lord Jesus Christ" (Rom. 1:7, 1 Cor. 1:3, 2 Cor. 1:2 etc.) turns up time and time again and is probably influenced by "liturgical" language. – Paul's epistles use a great variety of phrases which combine God and Christ: "To the church of the Thessalonians in God the Father and the Lord Jesus Christ" (1 Thess. 1:1), "remember before our God and Father your ... endurance inspired by hope in our Lord Jesus Christ" (1 Thess. 1:3), Timothy is "God's fellow-worker in spreading the gospel of Christ" (1 Thess. 3:2), "may our God and Father himself and our Lord Jesus, clear the way to you (1 Thess.

3:11) etc. – The Apostle is not only guided by a fixed phraseology, but also by his religious faith. As firmly as he ponders and distinguishes between the two and subordinates Christ, the Lord, under God the Father, he also feels the necessity to view them together and mention them side by side. If he has mentioned God as the source of all life and all salvation, he adds a reference to Christ as the mediator; and his thoughts proceed from Christ to God as the last and highest goal. Only in him do they come to rest. It sometimes occurs that he forgets about the difference and places them on the same level (von Dobschütz, *Kristustro og kristenliv* (Kristiania 1922, p. 27). – We certainly find tendencies toward Christological speculation in Paul (2 Cor. 4:4, Phil. 2, 1 Cor. 15, Col. 1 etc.), but he is still moving within the Jewish – Hellenistic theology of *hypostaseis,* and he does not yet have a feeling concerning all the speculations that came to dominate the *logos*-Christology of the early Church.

It is, however, not a binitarian but a trinitarian formula that we are dealing with. *The Holy Spirit* has been added to God and Christ as the third part of the formula. We find this also in Paul *in statu nascendi:* "May the grace of the Lord Jesus Christ, and the love of God, and the fellowship of the Holy Spirit be with you all" (2 Cor. 13:14, cf. 1 Cor. 12:1, 6:11, 2 Cor. 1:21f., Rom. 15:16–30). – If we ask for religious motives that may push the thought of the Spirit strongly into the foreground, we will easily find them. We know that the Spirit played an even greater role in the consciousness of the Gentile Christians than for the Jewish Christians. When it was necessary to break totally with the earlier life and throw away all old authorities, the principle of the new life, the Holy Spirit, was bound to be still more important. Not only the reception of the salvific mystery and the possession of eternal and immortal life was derived from the divine πνεῦμα, but the ability to do practical work in the life of the Church was also a χάρισμα (1 Cor. 12 and 14). Behind τὰ πνευματικά, the spiritual gifts in all their variety, we catch a glimpse of τὸ πνεῦμα. This πνεῦμα was an independent being who now and then revealed the qualities of Jesus, but then again stood out for the Christians as a being apart from Jesus and the Father: he calls out (Gal. 4:6), he "searches all things" (1 Cor. 2:10,13), apportions spiritual gifts (1 Cor. 12:11), he intercedes for us (Rom. 8:26f.) etc. When Paul allows himself such brave personifications, we can be certain that popular Christian ideas about the Spirit were still more concrete.

If it is against this background that we search for the presuppositions in the life of the Church which made the Spirit a person on the same level as God and Christ and thus became a part in Trinitarian formulas, we need only briefly point to factors in *comparative religion* and *the psychology of religion.* The concepts of *Sophia* and *Logos,* at home both in late Judaism and in a totally Hellenistic environment, show exactly the same ambiguity between an impersonal power and a hypostatic personification as the Spirit in the early Church.

Such a conception, something in between a myth and an abstraction, was evidently natural for the religious and philosophical consciousness of that age. – In addition, we will also find rich material in the New Testament showing that a *tendency towards a Trinity* was also at work in the language of the early Christians. This is evident everywhere: In the words of Jesus (Matt. 7:7f., 5:38f., Luke 6:20f., 7:24f., 9:58 etc., cf. von Dobschütz, *Paarung und Dreiung in der evangelischen Ueberlieferung,* Festschrift für G. Heinrici 1914), not only in the parables (the three kinds of farmland in Mark 4, priest, Levite and Samaritan in Luke 10, three times servants are sent to the workers in the vineyard in Mark 12, three parables about growth in Mark 4, three about what was lost and found again in Luke 15, three years the fig tree disappoints the Lord in Luke 13:7, the lord who goes abroad divides his money among three servants in Matt. 25), but also in the Gospel stories in a popular style (Peter's denial and the cock crowing three times, the question "do you love me" asked three times in John 21, three views about Jesus are referred to in Mark 8:28, the centurion illustrates his authority with three commandments in Matt. 8:9 etc.). Paul, who exhibits both a creative power that does not bother about forms and a careful feeling for literary style, gives us many examples of triads: Faith, love and hope (1 Cor. 13:13, cf. 1 Thess. 1:3; "from him and through him and to him" (Rom. 11:36), "spirit, soul and body" (1 Thess. 5:23) etc. It is strange that he mentions explicitly that he prayed three times to the Lord that he would deliver him from his suffering (2 Cor. 12:8).

We also find triadic combinations of heavenly beings (cf. Mark 13:32: "No one knows about that day or that hour, not even *the angels* in heaven, nor *the Son,* but only *the Father"* – and Luke 9:26 "when he (the Son of Man) comes in *his* glory and in the glory *of the Father* and of the holy *angels"* – and 1 Tim. 5:21 "I charge you in the sight of *God* and *Christ Jesus* and the elect *angels")* of which God, Christ and the Spirit finally stood out as the victorious combination. We find an intermediate stage in Rev. 1:4f. concerning God, *the seven spirits* and Jesus Christ. Justin provides the list: God, the Son, the angels and the Spirit, *Apol.* 1.6.

Triads like these were fixed and became the possession of people through liturgical use. Christianity entered a world with a rich cultic tradition and a highly developed liturgical feeling. Very soon Christian liturgy, what was said and what was sung, received its form and was fixed. Sadly, we are not able to follow the creation and the development of a Christian liturgical language in any detail. As could be expected, the sources fall short, but we do get glimpses, especially in *the Revelation of St. John.* It is evident that the insights into the heavenly world, described by the seer, are a transcendental correspondence to the cultic gatherings of the congregation. Thus the heavenly hymns of this book give us an impression of the prayers, hymns and songs that could be heard in the early Christian churches (cf. J. Kroll, *Die christliche Hymnodik bis zu Klemens von Alexandria.* Progr. Braunsberg 1921). In this very book we find a lot of formulaic expressions in two, three and even four parts. The greeting in 1:4 is from 1) a. ὁ ὤν b. καὶ ὁ ἦν c. καὶ ὁ ἐρχόμενος 2) καὶ ἀπὸ τῶν ἑπτὰ πνευμάτων ἃ ἐνώπιον τοῦ θρόνου αὐτοῦ 3) καὶ ἀπὸ Ἰησοῦ Χριστοῦ a. ὁ μάρτυς ὁ πιστός b. ὁ πρωτότοκος τῶν νεκρῶν c. καὶ ὁ ἄρχων τῶν βασιλέων τῆς γῆς. In this triad the first and the third parts are subdivided into three parts. We may also read formulas like ὁ πρῶτος καὶ ὁ ἔσχατος καὶ ὁ ζῶν 1:17f. and ὁ ἀμήν, ὁ μάρτυς ὁ πιστὸς καὶ ἀληθινός, ἡ ἀρχὴ τῆς κτίσεως τοῦ θεοῦ 3:14. These are just a few examples.

We thus find that the law of triads is active in the mind of the Messianic preacher as well as of the writing Apostle, in the popular story and in the liturgical prayer and hymn. But this general impression is not sufficient when we study the victory of our Trinitarian formula and the development of a baptism in the three names. We must search for the most concrete possible connection to the life of the Church as it appeared in those days. Then it is most natural to look at *the baptismal teaching.* If this teaching was patterned in some way after a trinity (the doctrine concerning God, the Lord and the new life) and caused the creation of triadic catechetical summaries or credal formulas, we will have a good explanation for the development of a baptism in the three names and of firmly fixed triadic formulas with *the Spirit* as the third part, because *the Spirit and baptism belong together*.

It is in vain that we will search for a systematically developed teaching about baptism in the New Testament. We find only that a number of ideas were combined with this cultic act in the earliest Church: the forgiveness of sins, justification, sanctification (purification from the contamination of evil spirits and communion with God), rebirth, death, burial and resurrection with Christ, spiritual circumcision, putting on of Christ etc. The most predominant element, however, is that the Holy Spirit is active in the baptismal water. It would be a methodological mistake to try to systematize. It is more reasonable to pose the question whether the New Testament mirrors various steps or different stages concerning the nature and effect of baptism. This certainly is the case. We have, however, no reason to discuss this here in any detail. It is sufficient to point out that both in Acts and in Paul, baptism and the Spirit are closely connected with each other.

Paul does not combine the gift of the Spirit with baptism by way of principle, but with the reception of the Gospel by faith (cf. Gal. 3:2 and his statement about baptismal activity in 1 Cor. 1:17). We can see however, that baptism and *pneuma* belonged together for Christians generally, because the Apostle now and then uses this view as the starting point for his parenesis (cf. 1 Cor. 6:11, 12:13). Water and Spirit are the two elements of baptism in John 3:6 (Tit. 3:5). – We will find in Acts both that the Spirit falls upon people independently of baptism (10:44) – this being the original view, and that it is given through baptism (2:38). Not only this, but also that the gift of the Spirit is a privilege of some people, given through the laying on of hands (8:16ff.), regularly in connection with the act of baptism (Acts 19:6; cf. Heb. 6:2). Here we find the different stages side by side: the original free enthusiasm, the fixed praxis of mission and even the hierarchical viewpoint. These two last mentioned views show a close combination of baptism and the gift of the Spirit. This is consistent with the tradition that Jesus received his Messianic Spirit at his baptism (Mark 1).

We may presume against this background that the Spirit also played at least some role in *baptismal teaching*. This can hardly be more than a spectulative supposition, since our sources do not give us much insight into this side of the missionary work. With great energy and boldness Alfred Seeberg has tried in several works (e.g., *Katechismus des Urchristentums* 1903) to describe early Christian baptismal praxis, arguing from the few and ambiguous notes that can be found in the New Testament. His main results have been rejected as having too weak an exegetical basis (cf. F.M. Rendtorff, *Die Taufe im Urchristentum* 1905). He must still be credited however, with the emphasis upon the doctrinal and formularic character of the tradition of the New Testament which points back to a side of the earliest mission seldom mentioned. It is, however, necessary to argue much more carefully than Seeberg did. In addition, later concepts like the Christ kerygma itself have been considered in quite a different light than that of Seeberg (cf. H. Lietzmann in Festschrift for Harnack 1921, pp. 226ff.).

Of course the baptismal teaching of the earliest period was very different depending on the background of those recently converted. Often baptism would have followed very quickly after the basic mission teaching. After a few decades however, during which the mission developed its strongholds in the various congregations, a relatively firm praxis would have developed, certainly influenced by the teaching of proselytes within Judaism.[4] Monotheism was self-evidently emphasized, and salvation through Christ was explained. But we must also suppose that some *teaching* was given *on the imminent baptism*,[5] its gift and task, thus including the Holy Spirit. We can take for granted that this

[4] In Matt. 28:19f. μαθητεύσατε ... βαπτίζοντες ... διδάσκοντες the word μαθητεύειν seems to have the general meaning "to make Christian," and it includes the proclamation of the gospel (and the elementary teaching). But the two elements of baptism and teaching in the Christian faith are singled out as the most important missionary tasks. The Gospel author does not stand in the very beginning but in an established community.

[5] In Heb. 6:1f. we read about the elementary teaching about repentance from dead (sinfull) works, faith toward God, instruction about βαπτισμοί, the laying on of hands, the resurrection of the dead, and eternal judgment. The plural of the word βαπτισμοί is striking, but it can hardly be understood in any other way than referring to the Christian baptism. Didache 7:1 (ταῦτα πάντα προειπόντες) seems to imply that the baptismal training included ethical teaching (cf. chaps. 1–6).

catechetical teaching led to the development of a number of summarizing, firmly fixed formulas, among them Trinitarian formulas. It is in addition tempting to suppose that such fixed formulas were used during *the baptismal act* itself in the form of short questions or confessions.[6] If this really was he case, it is easy to understand that the one name gave place to the three names at baptism. This change had hardly taken place in the mission among those circumcized, for there the salvation historical and the monotheistic background was self-evident from the very beginning. There certainly was however, a need against a Gentile background to mention all the basic motives of the Christian faith in the baptismal act. It was only in this way that a baptismal saying could satisfy the faith experience of the situation. Such a formula was ready at hand, – maybe even in the baptismal creed itself. The mentioning of Jesus' name was only replaced by the richer and more detailed complex formula mentioning the three names.

As mentioned above Matt. 28:19 is not a baptismal formula, but rather a summarizing characteristic of baptism in the three names. It is evident, however, that the words used are not created *ad hoc* but are taken from liturgical terminology. The triad "Father – Son – Holy Spirit" must have been a fixed unity for the author before he could use all three of them as a single *genitivus objectivus* to the single εἰς τὸ ὄνομα. How are we now to explain this specific wording? Hardly, as is stated by Harnack, as a polemic against the Jews who denied that the title "God's Son" could be used with reference to Jesus, but rather as created in the liturgical and catechetical praxis mentioned above. Here we certainly have a frequently used and thus refined, very condensed version of the most frequent trinitarian statements: if possible one word for each part. The Spirit however, can hardly lack the modifier "holy" to separate it from the *pneumata* that were at work in the world. It is a well known fact that a formula that is often used becomes refined and condensed.

If we now give attention to the titles which are used for the Divinity, we will find that we have reached a time when Christian vocabulary has begun to wear on the original meaning of the words and the nuances are disappearing. It is striking that the name which was decisive in the early baptism, *Jesus Christ,* is lacking and has been replaced by a title: *the Son.* It is astonishing that the name Jesus Christ has not been replaced by the title *the Lord* but by "the Son." We remember Paul's words: "Grace to you and peace from God *our Father* and from *the Lord* Jesus Christ." Baptism was first of all an incorporation into the heavenly Lord's sphere of power. The explanation must be that "the Father" as an absolute title for God in a finally fixed formula more or less necessitated the

[6] We are not able to say what is meant by "the good confession" in 1 Tim. 6:12 and by the ῥῆμα which accompanies the washing of water in Eph. 5:26.

title "the Son" for Jesus. It was natural that God received the modifier "The Father," ὁ θεός being a universal religious term, while ὁ πατήρ was specifically Christian, cf. 1 Cor. 8:6 "one God, the Father." Of course Gentiles now and then also addressed and spoke about their gods as "father." Zeus was thus "the father of all," "the father of gods and humans" (quotations from Homer). But in Christianity this was something important and a most holy inheritance – we need only think of the Lord's Prayer. ὁ κύριος however, would not sound organic next to the absolute ὁ πατήρ, cf. once again 1 Cor. 8:6 "one *God* ... and ... one *Lord* ..." It is only if *the Son* is combined with *the Father* in a formula that the inner organic connection between so closely connected terms is satisfied.

If this was the driving force behind the terminological development, it is evident that it is not possible to find any metaphysical speculative content in the formula in Matt. 28:19. It is also unnecessary to refer to a Semitic "family myth" in order to explain the combination of the Father and the Son.

There is an immediately perceived organic connection between the Father and the Son in the formulaic wording. In the same way the third part concerning the Holy Spirit functions organically on the pious consciousness, because the Spirit is the Father's best gift to his children (Luke 11:10). It is in the Spirit that we cry "Abba, Father" (Rom. 8:15), it was also the divine power operating in Jesus, the beloved Son (cf. the pericopes about Jesus' baptism), and Paul says "And because you are sons, God sent *the Spirit of his Son* into our hearts, the Spirit who calls out '*Abba! Father!*' " (Gal. 4:6), certainly because of a widely distributed conviction. Here we find the strictly fixed formula prefigured in a religious usage of a non-formalistic character.

The formula, created and then victorious in liturgical usage, must have influenced Christian vocabulary outside the liturgy also. We find traces of this in the New Testament. Thus it is quite natural to explain the strange wording in Mark 13:32 as an assimilation to a fixed wording, frequently used: "No one knows concerning that day or hour, not even the angels in heaven, nor *the Son,* but only *the Father.*" Here a triad of heavenly powers is mentioned, and nothing is more natural than the author being influenced by the triadic formula in common use.

The synoptic logion, unique in its kind, "No one knows *the Son* except *the Father*" (Matt. 11:27), points in the same direction; cf. the frequent Johannine vocabulary "the Father" and "the Son" in the absolute sense, both individually and combined (John 3:35f., 5:19 etc., 1 John 2:22ff. etc.). The instinctive feeling for an organic connection as expressed by the formula has now been consciously deepened as regards the real meaning of the relationship between the Father and the Son. The views however, are not yet those of the Trinitarian dogmatics of a later time.

The Parables in Recent Research

(1929)

Almost a generation has passed since the study of the Parables of Jesus received their basic scholarly treatment in *Die Gleichnisreden Jesu* by Adolf Jülicher (volume 1 was published in 1886, volume 2 in 1898, a second edition of volume 1 in 1899; both volumes were reprinted without any changes in 1910). This work has proved to be most important over the years and still has an enduring value. It is inconceivable that the exegesis of the parables will ever return to the methodologically arbitrary and vague situation which dominated the era before Jülicher.

This scholar, in many ways highly merited, has created a real monument for himself with his *Gleichnisreden,* which not only witnesses to his erudition and ingenuity, method and thoroughness, but is also, in its style and general point of view, strongly imprinted by his temperamental personality. Theology possesses in this book a work that is both fascinating and scholarly instructive. The first volume deals with the authenticity, the character, the object, the world and the literary transmission of the parables of Jesus, and gives an overview of the history of the interpretation of the parables in the Church. In volume 2, the various parables are interpreted according to the rules which have been found to be valid in the more general part of the work. We find discussions of "die Gleichnisse," i.e. the metaphorical speeches, and "die Parabeln," i.e. the parables proper,[1] and finally the four Lucan exemplary narratives (the good Samaritan, the Pharisee and the publican in the temple, the rich man and the poor man, Lazarus, and the rich farmer). For the first time in the history of exegesis we find a serious attempt to pursue a sound interpretation of the parables, an interpretation that builds upon the true character of the parables themselves and fits a realistic view of Jesus as a preacher, and which has replaced the fantastic conceptions of an earlier era about the enigmatic speeches by the divine man.

Thus the foundation was laid for all later exegesis of the parables. Every study of Jesus' parabolic speeches must take Jülicher's *Gleichnisreden* as its starting point.

---

[1] Jülicher reckons with 21 parables. Some of them rather belong to parable speeches, "lignelsessprogene."

Ten years after the work was published, Jülicher states in the preface to the second stereotyped edition, that he is fully conscious of the fact that recent research adds to his results on many points, and that the book no longer correctly mirrors his own view, but he lacks the time and strength to rework it and bring it up to date. He thinks however, that it still serves a purpose. He can certainly be assured that this is the case. No scholarly trained exegete can interpret the parables of Jesus with an allegorizing method any longer. The light that has been thrown upon the formal characteristics of the parables, as well as upon Jesus' message as a whole, is too bright. Neither can one disregard the vast number of pertinent exegetical observations to be found in Jülicher's interpretation of the individual parables. Thus it can only be a matter of modifying and making additions to some of Jülicher's views, as well as correcting his exegetical opinions about individual parables and his understanding of a number of details. Keeping this in mind we may now, one generation later, have a good opportunity to summarize the results of the parable research that builds upon and discusses Jülicher's basic work.[2]

As far as I can see, parable research during the last decades has basically followed four different lines:

1.

Most importantly, the main thesis in Jülicher's *Gleichnisreden* has been examined: *the demarcation of the parable against the allegory*. There were certainly those prior to Jülicher who tried to do so (H. Ewald, B. Weiss), but he has the merit of having done this with a strength and a clarity that was epochal in parable research. In close connection with Nygren, I characterize Jülicher's definition of a parable as follows: It is typical for the *parable* that, what is told in order to throw light upon a religious topic is an independent epic unity, which is illuminating as a whole and not in its individual parts. The metaphorical part (the narrative or description) and the spiritual reality are thus parallel to each other and must not be confused. In the *allegory,* on the other hand, every part is to be interpreted, every single motive in the metaphor has a hidden meaning. An allegory must thus be interpreted, while the parable is to be used. The allegory is an enigmatic speech. The parable is clear in itself and illuminating as

[2] The writing of this paper is mainly caused by Professor Nygren's thesis in *Svensk Teologisk Kvartalskrift* 1928:3: "Till förståelsen av Jesu liknelser." Cf. my own paper "Lignelsen om de onde vingartnere" in the following fascicle. Since I lectured about Jesus' parables in the last semester, and I intend to hold seminars on the same topic this semester, I could not resist the temptation to add some extra views to those taken up by Nygren. I also add some bibliographical notes which may be of some use for those interested.

a story, and the only question is: What does the speaker want to say with his story? What is the point?

If we use this definition of a parable and apply it strictly to the parables of Jesus as found in the Synoptic Gospels, we will find that it is basically valid. Most of the parables of Jesus, as we find them in the Gospels, fit the definition without any difficulty. Some of them, however, show a more or less clear allegorical character and must therefore either be considered secondary or looked upon as allegorically reworked. In the last case, it may be difficult to reconstruct the original form with any certainty.[3]

The view that Jülicher has created too rigorous a parable theory has gained strength. He has overemphasized that which is constitutive for the parable, but was not evident for earlier parable exegesis, which thus degenerated into arbitrary imagination. Jülicher, on the other hand, has abstracted his theory from multifaceted reality which cannot self-evidently be expected to use just pure literary categories, but rather must also be expected to include mixed forms. There is certainly a development in the Gospel transmission of the parables in an allegorical direction, that calls for a critical consciousness of the allegorical details in the transmitted parables themselves (thus in the interpretation of the parable of the sower, Mark 4:10–20, which has been made into a lesson about the four types of soil). But this cannot be decisive. Jesus was not, versed in literature, but rather a popular preacher, who in any reasonable assessment, did not use parables as a strict form. The parables of contemporaneous Judaism (as well as of the Old Testament) also show constant mergers of form. When we thus find merged forms in the Jesus' parables in the Gospels, this is what is to be expected and it cannot just be dismissed as secondary. We cannot give a general rule, but the question must be asked and discussed time and time again.[4]

In summary, we can say that the criticism directed against Jülicher has pointed more and more, and rightly so, to the necessity of a *greater realism* in the discussion of what is historically possible and reasonable. This realism includes not only comparative historical material (P. Fiebig, Chr. Aug. Bugge), but also a more careful study of the aesthetic laws of metaphorical speech and of its instruments as well as its different types (the metaphor, the comparison, language of parables, the parabolic narrative) and the various forms without strict boundaries in between. All of this does not annul the general presuppositions for parable exegesis as formulated by Jülicher, but it gives greater free-

[3] Jülicher here discusses the parables of the widow and the judge, the evil workers in the vineyard and the weeds in the wheat.

[4] Meinertz (*Die Gleichnisse Jesu,* pp. 21 f.) shows how what is metaphorical-allegorical goes together with what is parabolic-epic both in the Old Testament (thus, e.g., Nathan's story about the rich man who took the poor man's only lamb) and in the Greco-Roman literature.

dom and makes possible a more positive view of the stylistic genres that do exist.

We may especially point to the fact that we have obtained a sharper sense of the influence of the *metaphor* on the parable itself. If it has been usual to call God "Lord" and people his slaves, it is natural that these metaphorical expressions have been determinative for those parables where the actors are a lord and his slaves. The same is valid for many other metaphors (father and sons, wedding, groom etc.).[5]

In my paper on the evil workers in the vineyard (*Svensk Teologisk Kvartalskrift* 1928:4), I have also pointed out that the Old Testament parables, with which Jesus self-evidently was deeply familiar, do not support a strict parable form. We find the metaphors used by the prophets having a poetical fullness, metaphors and comparisons, enigmas and allegories are used together and cannot possibly have developed a puritanical feeling for style in the pious reader of the biblical texts. For this reason it must be more than reasonable that Jesus too, time and time again, has moved within these structures of thought, particularly in special situations.

This being the case, we cannot possibly declare as unauthentic everything that is not a pure parable. And when we explain Jesus' parabolic speeches, we must keep the possibility open that not everything is said with an eye to just one single point. Most scholars of today will probably accept what Wellhausen states (*Das Evangelium Marci* 1903, pp. 30f.): "It is certainly true that the Semitic parable very often has only one point and throws a bright light upon it, while everything else stays *hors de comparaison* and remains in darkness. But the parable may also fit several points in the topic that are the object for the comparison and thus comes close to an allegory. One is not permitted to judge all instances alike, but rather it is necessary to adjust to every single situation. The protest, however, against Philo and those like him who find allegory everywhere and in all ways is quite justified ..."

If matters are considered in this way, it follows that the exegetical possibilities become more numerous and consequently the uncertainty becomes greater. If we are to reckon with the possibility that a single detail in the whole metaphorical complex has an independent meaning, we must reckon not only with points, but with secondary points and even with double points, – well, we are soon in a quagmire, not at all what Jülicher imagined. Reality, however, makes its demands, and *in concreto* the uncertainty created in this way has little to say in comparison with the basic methodical clarity and stability that has been reached through Jülicher and his work on the parables.

[5] Thus also Weinel, *Die Gleichnisse Jesu,* 4th edition, 1918, p. 21. It can in many cases be doubted if the language is metaphorical or literal. Thus Bultmann wants to understand the weeds among the wheat as a plain parable, *Geschichte der synoptischen Tradition,* p. 110.

2.

Thus it is possible in one way to say that there is a conservative trend in recent parable research. But at the same time the criticism of the transmitted parables has become more acute, that is in relation to *form-critical* or *tradition-critical* Gospel research. This branch of exegesis puts heavy emphasis on the fact that each specific part of the Synoptic material has also had a history before it became fixed literarily, a history of tradition which the parables self-evidently have also had. If we accept this fact, we must necessarily conclude that many factors have influenced and reshaped the parabolic sayings from the moment when they left the preacher's lips for the first time to the moment when they received their final written form. It follows that the parables must be freed from their present literary context and looked upon as isolated transmitted entities, something that certainly poses new problems for their understanding.

There is surely no reason to harbour a radical scepticism *vis-à-vis* the transmission. It is generally accepted that the Synoptic metaphorical logia and parables have a distinctly Jewish-Aramaic character. They exhibit a strongly developed tendency and ability to use metaphors, very realistic and linguistically plastic metaphors, and these are used with an energy which often manifests itself in hyperbolical and paradoxical wordings, sometimes almost grotesque, (as the camel and the eye of the needle, the speck and the beam). This material as a whole must have its origin in a richly gifted and creative preacher. A form-historical analysis shows without any doubt however, that the parabolic material as we find it in the Synoptic Gospels has been reworked and modified many times during its oral transmission and literary reconstruction.

It is to be noticed immediately that the parables have been grouped according to systematic viewpoints during some stage of their history of transmission. Thus metaphorical sayings dealing with similar topics have been brought together, as in Mark 4 (three parables dealing with growth) and Luke 15 (three parables dealing with that which has been lost). We also find parables brought together under a common keyword such as "the kingdom of heaven is like ..." (Matt. 13). It is also evident that parables have frequently been included in literary contexts which are not original. Thus the exemplary story about the rich farmer, a warning against thoughtlessness, is told in a situation where Jesus warns against greed (Luke 12:15), and the story about the good Samaritan is combined with the question about the greatest commandment in the Law ("And who is my neighbour?"), while it is in reality an attack on Jewish self-righteousness. The question must be asked if any single one of the parables of Jesus has been given to us in its real historical situation, if not, all the existing contexts are just literary creations. This is supported by the observation that several parables have been given interpretations which are clearly secondary, including notes of morality added at the end (cf. the prudent steward, Luke

16:8–13), and points given in advance (e.g., the widow and the judge, Luke 18:1: "Then Jesus told his disciples a parable to show them that they should always pray and not give up"). Finally we have examples of a strictly allegorical interpretation, such as the parable of the sower, Mark 4, cf. Matt. 13:36ff.

It follows that in many cases we are hardly able to say, with a reasonable degree of certainty, what the original point of a parable was. Did the logion concerning the unpredictable children originally deal with the relation of the people to Jesus and John the Baptist? What about the metaphorical sayings about the man who built a tower and the king who made war, are they said with reference to the followers of Jesus? Was the parable about the sower originally intended to comfort those who preach God's Word? In what way was the shrewd manager meant to be illustrative? Were the sayings concerning the piece of unshrunk cloth and new wine said as a rejoinder in a discussion about fasting? etc. etc. We find that any interpretation which takes the critical notes seriously meets with great difficulties.

In addition, we must also reckon with important changes in, and reworkings of, as well as additions to, the original parabolic sayings and stories. Mark 2:20 is thus a clear addition to the saying on fasting and wedding. It also seems that the narrative of the rich man and the poor man, Lazarus has received a second point in addition to the original one (Luke 16:27–31). The question has also been asked whether or not some pairs of parables have come into being through the creation of secondary doublets (the mustard seed being a doublet to the leaven, the lost coin a doublet to the lost sheep).

We find an example where a parable has lost its metaphorical character and been changed into a logion in Matt. 5:25f. where the saying regarding reconciliation with one's adversary while on the way to the judge, originally was a metaphorical eschatological warning. It is also possible that the pericope about the widow's coin was a parable which was reshaped into a real event.

Tradition-historical criticism thus points to a number of difficulties which must be discussed in relation to the methodical-exegetical problems. Only when the individual metaphorical sayings and parabolic narratives have been studied independently of their secondary structures and liberated from later additions and when their earliest shape has been reconstructed as far as possible – only then can the foundation be laid for a discussion of the last and most important question: How did Jesus' metaphorical sayings function in his preaching?

3.

There is, however, one more element in the transmission of the parables to which we must pay attention, the *history of motives*. This is still in its early beginnings and can only be mentioned in passing. The task is to study the metaphors themselves in their wider and narrower contexts, historical as well as cultural. They must first of all be studied in relation to the Palestinian environment, but also against the background of the whole Oriental world of metaphors as we know it. Now and then the question will arise whether a Synoptic parable shows us a variant of a universally dispersed and commonly used metaphor. We have only a few studies on this topic, and really only one in-depth discussion, H. Gressmann's study of the narrative of the rich man and the poor man, Lazarus. Similar comparative material has been collected in relation to other parables: The rich farmer, the shrewd manager, the good Samaritan, the fig tree and the sower.

We can state generally that matters seem to be as could be expected, that is that the broad and varied Oriental background makes the Synoptic collection of metaphors stand out as relatively limited and restricted in itself. Taken together the motives witness to a common milieu of creation, even a common originator.

4.

Parable research is clearly moving toward a growing confidence in the originality of the transmitted parables, and also the originality of the form of the parables. As for the authenticity of the individual parables, we can especially trust those parabolic sayings which stand out as real parables (without any allegorical details) and which do not reveal any clear Christian (ecclesiastical) traits. And within these limits we can point to those parables which voice a clear contradiction to Jewish piety and morality, or which breathe a primitive eschatological atmosphere. Those parables that show these characteristics and do not reveal any clear secondary qualities may be the core collection for an historical study of those parabolic sayings which can be traced back to Jesus with any probability.

Based upon this material acquired through a critical sifting, a fourth problem, maybe even the most difficult one, must be tackled: How has Jesus used the metaphorical sayings? What did he want to do with them? What purpose would they serve in his preaching? This question is of basic importance for all exegesis of the parables, since the answer given will determine the direction for all parable research.

Professor Nygren has discussed the topic critically in this journal *vis-à-vis* Jülicher. The interesting points made by Nygren, both negative and positive, must be answered by exegetes, and I am happy to contribute some notes for this reason.

Nygren starts by analyzing Jülicher's theory concerning the parables. He states that it includes two different theses which do not necessarily belong together: 1. That Jesus' metaphorical sayings are real parables and not allegories, and 2. That Jesus always wanted to *prove* something with his parables. Nygren deals with both of these thoughts. As for the definition of parables, Nygren points out emphatically that what is important is not whether Jesus used pure parables, rather, what is of interest is whether the main tendency in Jesus' metaphorical sayings points in the direction of real parables and not allegories. About this there cannot be any doubt. I fully share this view, as is certainly evident from what I have written above on the topic. Being interested in exegetical details, however, I cannot play down the importance of the fact that Jülicher's definition of a parable has been softened in the way that Nygren has done it. For him the basic thoughts and tendencies in Jesus' message are more interesting.

As for Jülicher's second thesis, that the parable served as a proof for Jesus, we find that Nygren opposes this as energetically as he supports the first thesis. He thus protests against the idea that *all* parables serve as proofs. Nygren states that parabolic sayings can serve different purposes depending upon their various situations: they will prove, illustrate, clarify, make a truth stand out concretely, plastically, visible for the inner eye of the observer.

I cannot deny that I support Nygren on the whole in this case also, but not without some reservations as to how he conceives Jülicher's view of the parables and, in connection with this, about his understanding of the concept of "proof" and the two models of religion which he thinks that he can find in the praxis of parabolic sayings. Some supplemental notes on this will follow.

The objections to Jülicher's idea that the parables serve as proofs are not new. They were voiced at the same time as the attacks on his Aristotelian definition of parables. It was stated emphatically that the parables of Jesus are both argumentative and illustrative, depending upon the circumstances or the subject. Nygren, however, is certainly the one who has worded the criticism most sharply. He wants to derive the difference in the view of the parables from a deep contrast in the basic view of religion itself, the contrast between the "model of demonstration" and the "model of revelation." I am as willing to accept that which is justified and valuable in Nygren's positive view of the spiritual background of the parables as I am unwilling to look upon his criticism of Jülicher as wholly justified or to accept that he himself has really mastered the concrete nature and purpose of Jesus' parabolic sayings. As for the two models of religion, I do not think that they have any real foundation in exegesis.

If we want to understand Jülicher's extremely one-sided emphasis on proof, we must explain it by the lack of common sense which he had to fight against when interpreting the parables. All throughout the history of interpretation interpreters and preachers had worked with the idea that the parables were enigmatic hints at the multifarious secrets of the kingdom of God. They were partly revealing, partly concealing, made by a mystical being, an incarnated heavenly person. It is a line of thought, the seed of which we find already in Mark 4. The interpretation of the parables thus became a revelling in a more or less spiritual deciphering of enigmas. In contrast to this the aim was now to allow the bright light of history once and for all to illuminate this person and his parabolic sayings. At this juncture Jesus does not stand out as one who phrases enigmatic speeches with unfathomable possibilities of interpretation for coming generations of Christians, but as a popular preacher who desires to achieve something specific with that which he says and with those to whom he speaks, one who addresses his own age in its own language concerning current subjects. And these subjects are not dependent upon a static collection of dogmas, which Jesus has to explain through a series of parabolic sayings. No, the subjects are derived from the immediate situation, from questions posed to him, from objections, attacks, from a matter which requires an answer or a refutation, from the situation itself in countless ways. Thus the purpose of the parable is not to teach a distinct thesis; it is dependent upon the immediate situation and thus has a clear point. It is to drive off attacks, overcome opposition, and break through lethargy and apathy. All this is done through the power that is hidden in the parable genre itself. It necessarily follows that every parable contains something of a proof in itself, even if we, and I will soon return to the reasons for this, cannot speak about "proofs" in the strict sense of the word.

Thus it is self-evident that the argumentative power here need not be of a logical kind – and that the concept of "proof" is principally logical. The logical element is certainly not lacking in Jesus' parabolic sayings where he appeals to common sense, often pointing to what is self-contradictory in a statement or a viewpoint. The appeal to general experience is also closely related to logical proof. In the real parables, however, it is most often the *epical context,* the exciting story that stimulates the imagination, which serves as the proof or the *means of conviction.* If we think of the popular mind, we can safely state that a good story is as effective as a strict proof. It is better than a proof in the strict sense of that word, because it captivates the listeners with its magical power, so that they will say, "this is right!" whether they like it or not. Use a good parable at the right moment, and the battle is won.

Jülicher can certainly be criticized in that he understands the concept of proof too narrowly in a logical or matter-of-fact way and too little psychologically. He wants to find the irresistible power of the parable in the *typical and normal* character of the story being told instead of in its epical captivating power. Sometimes this biased view leads to what is a clear misunderstanding (thus in the parables of the workers in the vineyard and the prodigal son, cf. Nygren's pertinent criticism). The reason why Jülicher often shows this bias seems to be a certain lack of real psychological sense, lack of contact with popular patterns of imagination and thinking and its technique. But it is probably once again his opposition to allegorization which pushes him too far. Time and time again

Jülicher wants to drive home the point and emphasize that the parables of Jesus are not arbitrarily conceived narratives, created for a detailed interpretation, but that they give independent images of reality, complete in themselves, which will force the listeners to admit: "He is right!" thanks to their irresistible power and irrefutable inner logic.

The basic thought is correct, but Jülicher exaggerates it, when he does not respect the fact that it is not only that which is logical and typical, but also that which is epical that has a compelling force under certain psychological circumstances. In other words, he underestimates the secret of *artistry* for the effect of the parable. If one is open to this, one will see that a parabolic narrative can convince, that is in the popular sense, both when it describes something *typical*, what normally takes place (the sower), and when it describes what is the very *opposite* to the normal occurrence (the workers in the vineyard), or when it tells an *individual story*, which very well might have transpired in some other way (the father and the son who returned home). Jülicher's interpretation must be supplemented and corrected through an aesthetic-psychological evaluation of the parables and their individual details.

It is probably this lack of aesthetic-psychological sense for the power of the parable that has caused Nygren to find fault in the very religious basis of Jülicher and others like him, the attitude which Nygren calls "the model of demonstration." Nygren characterizes it as follows: "It takes its starting point in normal human life and tries to ascend from there to the religious life. It construes this life according to the rules that have been found valid in human life and the result that it desires to reach in this way is certain rationally based, general ethical and religious truth."

It is safe to call this a misunderstanding of Jülicher's view both of the parables of Jesus and his religion. He never conceived of things in that way. Jülicher also finds the background in Jesus' own relation to God, and this is expressed in his message. The parables are a medium for this message, but Jesus does not want to force a logical teaching about God on his listeners in this way. No, he wants to influence the popular mind, make it consonant with God and force it in a certain direction. This is in reality what Jülicher means with the word "proof," cf. chapter III in Jülicher about "Der Zweck der Gleichnisreden Jesu," where he talks more about "überführen" and "überzeugen" than about "beweisen." It strikes me that Nygren is guilty of confusing two things: He writes as if Jülicher considers the parables as a dialectical means to develop and ponder a dogmatic teaching, while Jülicher in reality views the parables as a pedagogical-rhetorical instrument to reach an immediate religious insight.

Nygren's comments concerning Luke 5:31 f.: "It is not the healthy who need a doctor, but the sick ..." show us how deeply he has misunderstood Jülicher's comments about "proofs." Nygren states that the truth of this passage cannot be denied and that it is immediately insightful. Nevertheless, it is not suitable as a proof that Jesus rightly turns to sinners. For why should Jesus compare himself to a physician? Wouldn't a judge be just as good? As a proof the sentence is a *circulus vitiosus*. If Jülicher had really used the word "proof" in this sense when discussing the parables of Jesus, then we must seriously doubt not only his scholarly intelligence but his common sense as well. We can certainly take for granted, however, that Jülicher is fully conscious of the difference between a proof in a strictly logical sense and the persuasive power of a metaphor as used by a popular speaker. Already in this last case, the fact that Jesus applies the metaphor to himself is psychologically sufficient to safeguard the argumentative effect of the self-illuminating truth of the logion. When Jülicher fails to define the popular rhetorical concept of "proof" explicitly, this is probably because he has found it superfluous.

Thus Nygren in his polemic makes a *metabasis eis allo genos* and consequently misses the target. As has already been said, however, there is something that is correct in his objection to Jülicher, although the fact is that what is wrong with Jülicher is not a faulty religious attitude but a lack of realism in his judgement of the psychological power of the parable genre.

Finally, this is the appropriate point to relate some notes with regards to Nygren's attempt to formulate a positive view of how to understand the parables of Jesus.

Nygren states that the parables of Jesus are not mainly a means of proof but a means of revelation. It is evident from what has been said above that I do not find any insoluble contradiction between these two viewpoints. That is if we consider the parable as revelation when viewed according to its prophetical and spiritual contents, but as proof, when viewed according to its rhetorical form, its pedagogical purpose and its psychological effect – proof not in a logical but rather in a popular and emotional meaning.

Nygren puts forth his view of the revelatory character of the parables in chapter IV of his treatise: *Bakgrunnen for Jesu lignelser*. Here he points out that it is only very seldom that we can obtain a reliable idea of the concrete background of the individual parables and their original historical situation, but we do know the *general* background, which is the main thing. Nygren reaches this general background through an analysis of the parable of the workers in the vineyard – in consistent polemic with Jülicher who, and this must be admitted, is unusually prosaic in his discussion of this very parable. What is revealed in this and other parables is the unmotivated sovereignty in God's relationship to mankind, in his love which does not distinguish between worthy and unworthy, which breaks through all moralizing and rationalizing boundaries that characterize the Jewish belief in God. This paradox in God's relationship to mankind is described metaphorically and illustrated in a number of parables.

Nygren expresses this thought in an extremely attractive way, and it cannot be doubted that he has stressed an important, correct and fruitful viewpoint: an understanding of the religious character of the parables, consonant with Jesus' words outside these parables. The question is, however, whether the parables themselves, those that are dealt with here, are aimed at making the listeners fully conscious of this unmotivated, sovereign paradox. Rather, is it not that this "revelation" is in the *background,* in the preacher's consciousness of God, and that the concrete parable intends to throw light upon God's relationship to mankind, even "self-evident." This is not at all to prove the statement *nihil rationabilius,* but it is to create a clear viewpoint in connection with a firm conviction. The paradoxical scope of the revelatory knowledge may very well be fully present even if the person does not consciously dwell on the paradox itself – the last-mentioned point is probably a typical modern attitude. This is still more probable when we consider the element of immanent polemic that is hidden in this very parable: A rational, moralizing, calculating and weighing concept of God is contrasted with a different one, not because of its paradoxical character but being the *self-evidently correct* one, the one that is *immediately convincing.*

If we consider the parables in this way, it is not sufficient to say that the parable is purely illustrative. It also has an argumentative power which is hidden in the metaphor itself, in the event recounted. It provides an emotional proof which is dependent upon its immediately illuminating character or upon the touching realism in the narrative.

Of course this is not to say that the parable has its persuasive power only through its psychological compulsion, its lucid, penetrating metaphorical character. The personality behind it is the real secret with regards to the power of the metaphorical sayings. This does not prevent us from admitting that the parable, the metaphorical saying as such has a certain independent persuasive power *vis-à-vis* the mind, just as a practical argument or a strictly logical proof stands on its own feet too, independently of the one who uses it.

When Jesus used metaphorical sayings in addition to other forms of speech, this was founded both in his own poetical tendency, his metaphorically creative compulsion, and in his experience of the power that this way of speaking had over the popular mind. But we may proceed one step further: We may believe that religious perception has burst through in Jesus himself at many points in connection with his all-pervasive impressions of the life of nature and humanity. Jesus certainly did not relate to the concrete reality which surrounded him like an observant artist who is searching for images, material that illustrates his ideas, or like an experienced preacher who is always hunting for good points. Still less did he draw logical conclusions regarding God's being from human conditions. It was rather that he, with his basic and original consciousness of God, lived with the concrete world in such a way that it became *sinnvoll,* it became *ein Hinweis auf Gott.* In his parabolic sayings he can thus go from the observations of daily life, his feelings and experiences, up to God, and draw his listeners with him in such a way that the illuminating, the "self-evident", came to express the paradoxical, the wonderful, that which had never arisen in the heart of any human being.

This can only succeed if the life of the preacher is characterized by religious originality, and if those listening have simple minds that are close to nature and sensitive to the metaphors. Here we find the *homiletical* problem of today as regards the parables, as we lack both such preachers and such listeners. It is very valuable in such a situation to analyse the general background of the parables. We must be observant of the fact however, that we now have left a naive relationship to the parabolic sayings and replaced it with a reflective view. There is hardly any other possibility. We must however, be cognizant as to the distance and the difference.

The Conflict of Jesus with the Unclean Spirits

(1931)

The Synoptic Gospels show Jesus to us not only as prophet, miracle worker, and teacher, but also as exorcist. In the earliest tradition the exorcisms play a great part,[1] but the attention paid to them by modern exegesis stands in no reasonable relation to the importance which the Primitive Church assigned to this side of Jesus' activity. True, the tradition on this point has never been seriously questioned; but it has been usual to treat the exorcisms of Jesus with a certain superiority, as a *zeitgeschichtlich* feature, as a form of superstition which Jesus shared with his time and which had no special importance for his conception of the task that confronted him.[2]

Modern scholarship is, however, characterized by a growing realism in regard to the history and teaching of Jesus, and his conflict with the unclean spirits has now begun to receive more serious consideration. It now appears that behind the exorcisms we may apprehend a deeper perspective; Jesus himself assigned to them a significance going far beyond the merely accidental, discerning in the background the mystery of spiritual evil; and the recognition of this fact can lead us towards a truer idea of his interpretation of his own mission.

I

First, then, let us notice the position of *demoniacal possession* and *exorcism* in Judaism at the time of Jesus. We have ample evidence; we know from Jewish sources that possession was a widespread phenomenon in Palestine at this time, and, consequently, that exorcism was a well-known practice.[3] This fact emerges

[1] Exorcism is absent from the Fourth Gospel. The reason for this will be suggested further down.

[2] G. Naumann, *Die Wertschätzung des Wunders im N.T.,* 1903; H. Monnier *La mission historique de Jésus,* Paris, 1906; F. Barth, *Die Hauptprobleme des Lebens Jesu,* 3 ed., 1907; R.A. Hoffmann, *Die Erlösergedanken des geschichtlichen Christus,* Königsberg, 1911. A more realistic view in M. Dibelius' *Geschichtliche und übergeschichtliche Religion,* 1925, p. 39ff.

[3] Josephus, *Antt.*, viii. 2, 5; L. Blau, *Das altjüdische Zauberwesen,* 2 ed., 1914; Strack-

also in the New Testament. We have the retort of Jesus to his accusers: "If I by Beelzebul cast out devils, by whom do your sons cast them out ?" (Matt. xii. 27); the narrative of the man who drove out demons by the name of Jesus, but did not belong to the circle of disciples (Mark ix. 38ff.); and the mention in Acts of "vagabond Jews, exorcists," among whom were the seven sons of Sceva the chief priest (xix. 13ff.). Lastly we find that, in this not very attractive field, Judaism made an important contribution to Hellenistic syncretism; Hellenistic magic abounds with Jewish magical formulæ and names – *e.g.*, Iao, Sabaoth, Adonai, Abraham, names of angels, and, above all, Solomon, the supreme conjurer of spirits.[4] The extraordinary frequency of Jewish magical names can only be explained on the assumption that the Jews were the great specialists in exorcistic practice.

Possession and exorcism, then, certainly came within the range of Jesus' experience and reflection; and when a series of the earliest and most original Synoptic narratives tell how he himself exorcised the possessed, this tradition suits the *milieu* very well.[5] The problem is simply to define the place of these episodes within the ministry of Jesus.[6] From the tradition one gets the impression that such occasions as a rule, at least in the early period of his ministry, came to him as unforeseen and startling experiences: he enters a synagogue, and immediately there is a possessed man who begins to utter loud cries. How are we to picture the inner causality in these cases ? One might point to the sensitiveness of persons with unbalanced or abnormal minds for unusual mental

Billerbeck, *Kommentar zum N.T. aus Talmud und Midrasch,* iv. 1, München, 1928, pp. 501–535, *Exkurs* 21: *Zur altjüdischen Dämonologie;* Taufik Canaan, *Dämonenglaube im Lande der Bibel,* Leipzig, 1929 *(Das Morgenland, H.* 21); M. Grünbaum, *Gesammelte Aufsätze,* 1901, p. 119ff.; I. Scheftelowitz, *Altpalästinischer Bauernglaube,* 1925; A. Kohut, *Angelologie und Dämonologie in ihrer Abhängigkeit vom Parsismus,* 1896; S. Daiches, *Babylonian Magic in the Talmud and in the Later Jewish Literature,* London, 1913; R.C. Thompson, *Semitic Magic, Its Origin and Development,* London, 1908; Otto Weber, *Dämonenbeschwörungen bei den Babyloniern und Assyrern. Der alte Orient,* VII., 4, Leipzig, 1904.

[4] Origen, *c. Cels.* IV., 33, Hippolyt. *Philos.* IV., 28, p. 547f. See Chester Mac-Cown, *The Testament of Solomon,* Leipzig,1922 (Untersuchungen zum N.T. herausgeg. von H. Windisch, 9). Rich material and literature in *Papyri Osloenses,* I., *Magical Papyri,* ed. S. Eitrem, Oslo, 1925; cf. *Ein christliches Amulett auf Papyrus,* von S. Eitrem; A. Fridrichsen, Oslo, 1921 (*Videnskapsselskapets forhandlinger,* 1921, 1), p. 9ff., F. Pfister, Art. *Epode* in Pauly–Wissowa–Krolls *Realencyklopädie Suppl., Bd.* IV., 323ff., C. Wessely, *Ephesia grammata,* Wien, 1886 *(Jahresber. des Frans-Josephs-Gymnasiums); Griechische Zauberpapyri von Paris und London,* Wien, 1888 *(Denkschriften der k. Akad. d. Wiss.).*

[5] The part played by exorcism in primitive Christianity points in the same direction.

[6] The mighty deeds of Jesus, especially the exorcisms, cannot possibly have been narrated merely in order to demonstrate the superiority of Jesus over the Baptist. Jesus' exorcisms gave his opponents reason for many dark accusations, which the Church for a long time had trouble to reject. This may have been one of the reasons why Jesus' exorcisms are not mentioned in the Fourth Gospel. The Baptist dwelt in the wilderness, and hence did not come in contact with the mass of the people; Jesus, on the contrary, was going round visiting towns and villages, and therefore of necessity was brought up against disease and possession continually.

states in others;[7] and if Jesus was generally known as a powerful teacher and miraculous healer – Galilee is small and rumour spreads fast – it is not strange that the atmosphere surrounding Jesus, the emotional wave following him wherever he went, should call forth a spontaneous reaction on the part of the possessed.

As regards the further interpretation of the narratives in question, it might be noted that they are, of course, modelled in a typical literary style. They are not mere reports of actual happenings – we must read them with a critical discernment of the elements of the tradition, and try to discover the type of material and the popular literary style which underlie them and have contributed to their formation.[8] The sudden, startling element belongs to the style of such anecdotes; but in this case, this feature is undoubtedly founded on reality. The same holds true of the loud cries accompanying the fits of the possessed.

But these cries are, in one part of the gospel tradition, not inarticulate; they contain a passionate address to the exorcist: "What hast thou to do with us, thou Jesus of Nazareth? Art thou come to destroy us? I know thee who thou art, the Holy One of God" (Mark i. 24). How are we to interpret these words of the demon, which cause Jesus to utter a severe and effective command of silence: "Be silent, and come out of him" (Mark i. 25)? Can we draw any conclusions with regard to the relation of Jesus to the possessed?

This problem has recently been treated at length by Otto Bauernfeind in his work *Die Worte der Dämonen im Markusevangelium.*[9] Bauernfeind's thesis is that the cries of the possessed at the approach of Jesus are an effort to drive away the exorcist by starting a counter-attack; an act of self-defence on the part of the demon. He founds this interesting view on material mainly drawn from Hellenistic magical formulæ, which may, however, be traced also in other sources. He takes as his starting-point the accusations against Jesus in the Fourth Gospel, of being possessed (John vii. 20, viii. 48, 52) and of being a Samaritan *(i. e.,* a pseudo-prophet, viii. 48). These accusations have in view the self-testimony of Jesus, which is taken to be on a par with the usual pseudo-prophetic-demoniacal dicta of the type "I am N. N." (God, the Power, Servant Spirit of God, etc.). This view is rejected in x. 21: "These are not the words of one that hath a devil." There was a definite type of demoniacal language, which

---

[7] *Vide* J. Tambornino, *De antiquorum dımonismo,* Giessen, 1909: J. Smit, *De dımoniacis in historia evangelica,* Rome, 1913; Th. Taczsak, *Dämonische Besessenheit,* Münster i. W. 1903; A. Titius, *Heilung von Dämonischen im N.T.* in *Festskrift for Bonwetsch,* Leipzig 1918; K. Oesterreich, *Die Besessenheit,* Langensalza, 1921; E. R. Micklem, *Miracles and the New Psychology,* Oxford, 1922; H. Rust, *Die Wunder der Bibel,* I., 1922 II., 1923, Pfullingen in Württemberg; A. von Harnack, *Mission und Ausbreitung,* 4th. ed., 1924, I., 152.

[8] M. Dibelius, *Die Formgeschichte des Evangeliums,* 1919, 36ff.; R. Bultmann, *Geschichte der synoptischen Tradition,* 1921, 129ff.

[9] Stuttgart, 1927, W. Kohlhammer (Beiträge zrm. Wissenschaft vom Alten und Neuen Testament, herausgeg. von R. Kittel, III., 8).

appears indirectly also in other Jewish literature – *e.g.*, Philo, *Quod Deus sit immutabilis,* § 138 (man's *dianoia* says to the Divine *Logos:* "O, man of God ! art thou come to me to call to remembrance my iniquity and my sin ?" *Cf.* 1 Kings xvii. 18). In Hellenistic magic we often find the exclamation: "I know thee! I know who thou art, N. N." This exclamation had a magical sound, and it served to obtain power over the spirit in question. The same applies to the exclamation: "Thou art N. N.!" Consequently, the demon who feels himself imperilled by the presence of the exorcist, tries to defend himself by a conjuring formula. But Jesus at once breaks his power by his command: "Be silent!" Bauernfeind, however, uses a very strange process of reasoning, to show that this, the demons' address to Jesus, is not a typification in the tradition, but actually corresponds to what happened at times at the exorcisms of Jesus (p. 94).

However interesting and valuable, from the point of view of comparative religion, the materials and conclusions of Bauernfeind may be, I do not think that his interpretation is valid. I still maintain the view that I have set forth more fully in my work *Le problème du miracle dans le Christianisme primitif* (Paris, 1925, p. 77), that in these exclamations we have to see a confession attributed to the demon and intended to defend Jesus from the accusation of being in alliance with Beelzebul: in his extreme need the demon testifies that he is standing face to face with "the Holy One of God," with the Messiah. Bauernfeind's demonstration that the demoniacal utterances take their form from the conjuration formulas retains its value also from this apologetic point of view. With regard, then, to the actual historical facts we get no more than certain principal features of these episodes – viz., the sudden cries of the possessed at the approach of the renowned miracle-worker, and then the command of Jesus: "Be silent, and come out of him !"

But we may, with complete certainty, assume that for Jesus himself the meeting with the demoniacs and the experience of his power over the unclean spirits must have been of great import. His other "mighty works," the healings, had always formed part of the endowments of a prophet, as direct manifestations of a power given by God. The power of exorcism was different. This was, in its very essence, closely associated with magical arts, and those who practised such arts were on the whole suspect, and enjoyed a dubious renown. When Jesus noticed this power in himself, he must have interpreted it from his own personal position and assigned a peculiar importance to his experiences in this field. He must have regarded his power over the unclean spirits as an important element in his proclamation of the nearness of the Kingdom of God: "If I, by the Spirit of God, cast out devils, then the Kingdom of God is come upon you" (Matt. xii. 28). But we possess direct evidence that he viewed his exorcisms in a wider connection; indeed, they became of essential importance for his interpretation of the situation. A distinct indication of this is to be found in the narrative that tells how Jesus had to defend himself against the accusation of being, as exorcist, allied with the demons with which he was apparently in combat.

II

In Mark iii. 22 it is narrated that the Scribes, who had come down from Jerusalem, said that he (Jesus) was possessed by Beelzebul and that it was by the aid of the prince of evil spirits that he cast out the demons. To this accusation, which, clearly, his opponents spread abroad wherever they went, Jesus gave answer (after "calling them unto him" – here the situation is plainly literary), in the well-known words about Satan driving out Satan, and the kingdom that, having fallen into internal war, is doomed to destruction.

I have elsewhere pointed to the strangeness of the accusation here brought against Jesus: with demonic help he casts out demons! I then considered as most probable that in the Christian tradition the accusation had been intentionally put in such a form as to make its absurdity immediately evident.[10] With this Bauernfeind, rightly, joins issue, suggesting that there might be here an idea of a "collusion" on the part of the demons: the one feigns casting out the other in order to inspire the onlookers with confidence in an exorcist who in reality is doing the demons' work: thus it is all no more than demonic humbug. And in this direction we have probably to see the correct interpretation. That a conjurer used his power over stronger spirits to drive out weaker ones, is a well-known idea in ancient magic. Here, however, it is said that Jesus is *possessed* by Beelzebul and expels evil spirits by his aid;[11] in this case, therefore, the principal demon is the master of Jesus and not his servant; Beelzebul's intention in driving out the lower demons must be to strengthen Jesus' renown as an exorcist, and create belief in him as the master over the demons, while in reality he is their passive and obedient tool.

Behind this idea lies the pluralism of popular demonology. The demons, it is true, form together a kingdom, a body of affiliated beings, divided into groups and classes with varying power and faculties; but there is no unity of will in this kingdom, nothing but planlessness, capriciousness, independent activity. It is the grotesque manifold of popular phantasy.

But the answer of Jesus: "How can Satan drive out Satan ?" reveals a different and a deeper view. Jesus does not consider the demons as more or less free and independent beings, but as *the servants of Satan:* it is his will they further, his commissions they perform. Therefore he did not regard his conflicts with the unclean spirits as isolated events according to the technical point of

[10] "Nachwort" zu S. Eitrem: *Die Versuchung Christi,* 1924, p. 33.

[11] Without doubt "Beelzebul", Mark iii. 22, is identical with "the Prince of the evil spirits."

view of the exorcist, but as single battles in the campaign against the prince of this world.[12] Satan, God's great enemy of old, hereby received an actuality which he did not possess in popular belief, where the Devil, like God, was a remote cosmic power, active principally in the oppressing empires and in the heathen cults. For Jesus he was "The Strong One" and the human world was his "house." Jesus actualized Satan, just as he actualized God. Just as he treated with full earnest the coming Divine Kingdom, so he treated also the present dominion of Satan. Jesus radicalized the concepts of religion on this as on all other points. The present situation, as a whole, bore for him a demonic aspect: the advent of the Divine Kingdom first and foremost signified that the prince of this world would be dethroned, fettered, and imprisoned. Therefore in each act of exorcism Jesus saw a defeat of Satan, a presage of the final triumph that was soon to come to pass.

III

It is now necessary to focus attention more closely on Jesus' view – the demonic aspect, the facts of the situation. He had a strong sense of the presence of a superhuman, evil power, hostile to God, with enormous resources, in continual warfare with him, and determined to work his destruction. Traces of this consciousness are to be found all through the gospel tradition. The narrative of the *temptation* at the opening of his Messianic activity strikes this note. Even if, as is probable, we have here a primitive Christian "myth" not directly connected with a historical event, it is, in any case, in keeping with Jesus' own judgment of the situation. Typical for the view found here – a view that certainly was Jesus' own – are Satan's words when from the high mountain he shows Jesus all the kingdoms of the world and the glory of them: "All this will I give thee ..." (Matt. iv. 9). St. Luke adds in the same spirit: "For that is delivered unto me, and to whomsoever I will I give it" (Luke iv. 6). The simile of the *birds* that pick up the seed sown on the wayside (Mark iv. 4) is interpreted as referring to Satan, coming and taking away the word sown in men (iv. 15). The interpretation of the parable is secondary; but it is illustrative of Jesus' own view of the restless activity of his great adversary. The parable of the *Tares among the Wheat* (Matt. xiii. 24–30) gives expression to a vivid consciousness of Satan's unresting enmity against the Divine Kingdom. In this case, also, the interpretation (xiii. 36–43) is probably of later origin than the parable itself, and the studied allegorical exposition of the details of the narrative (the Son of Man sows the seed, the enemy is the Devil, etc.) is a result of its homiletical use in the

[12] In the Fourth Gospel all demonism is condensed in the "Darkness," the "World"; there is here a thorough-going monism with regard to the activities of evil. This might be the main reason why all exorcisms have been removed in the Johannine redaction of the tradition.

primitive Christian preaching. But even apart from this, reading the narrative of the parable by itself,[13] one must admit that it implies the reality of a mysterious demonic power, active in the "tares."

From this point of view a surprising light is cast upon the otherwise difficult text (Mt. xi. 12): "From the days of John the Baptist until now the kingdom of heaven suffereth violence, and violent ones take it by force." If these βιασταί are taken to mean, not *men* but *spiritual powers,*[14] the meaning at once becomes simple and natural. The Baptist's appearance had been a presage for Satan's kingdom of the approach of the final day of reckoning: and it had been the signal for a feverish activity of the hosts of powerful and brutal assailants,[15] with the object of "taking the kingdom of heaven by force" – *i. e.,* of destroying the results of the preaching of the Baptist and of Jesus, and getting mankind in their power.[16]

Again, Jesus could only explain the spiritual unresponsiveness with which he met as a blindness caused by demonic agencies, which sought to paralyze men's power of understanding, so that even the most evident truths made no impression upon them, and even hardened them yet more. In this Jesus saw the efforts of his formidable adversary summoning all his helpers to maintain and strengthen his hold over the chosen people, and to prevent them from obeying the call to repentance and preparing themselves to receive the Divine Kingdom. But how did he judge the situation in detail ?

In his defence against the accusation of being allied with Beelzebul, Jesus says (Mark iii. 27): "No one can enter into the house of the Strong One and spoil his goods, except he first bind the Strong One." This is a general statement put forward as an argument in a particular situation; but the application lies so near at hand that undoubtedly it has moulded the simile and the form of expression.[17] Hence we may say that we meet here with a conviction in Jesus' mind that he was stronger than Satan; a conviction which seems not to have been founded exclusively on the experience of the exorcisms, but presupposes rather some experience which had signified a decisive victory over Satan himself. What this experience may have been we do not know. It is possible that the account of the temptation is a mythical echo of allusions which Jesus may have made to the experience in question. It would not be far-fetched to note also in this connection the saying "I beheld Satan as lightning fall from heaven" (Luke x. 18).

---

[13] *Vide* R. Bultmann, *Geschichte der synoptischen Tradition,* 1921, p. 110.

[14] *Vide* M. Dibelius, *Geschichtliche und übergeschichtliche Religion,* 1925, p. 39.

[15] If the βιασταί are demonic powers, then the term recalls the name of a special class of demons: *pega'im* ("assailants"). *Vide* Billerbeck, iv. 1, 501

[16] ἁρπάζειν, of demonic activity directed against the disciples of Jesus, John x. 28f.

[17] "The Strong One," Mark iii. 27, most certainly has a double meaning from the very first; purely figurative, but with an allusion to Satan. The translation "the strong *man,*" therefore, is not exact. The translation "men of violence," in Matt. xi. 12, makes the same mistake (in the English Bible as in the Swedish.–TR.)

But this defeat had not broken Satan's power over men. The judgment on him was indeed decreed; and against the Son of Man his falsehoods and his temptations could not prevail. But the judgment was not yet executed; only with the Parousia of the Son of Man would the end of evil arrive, and the intermediate period was marked by an increased activity of the hostile power.

This view was not held by Jesus only, but also by primitive Christianity as a whole. The traditional eschatological drama implied the idea that demonism attains to its greatest manifestation of power immediately before the final crisis (*cf.* the Apocalypse; 2 Thess. ii.). This increasing activity of Satan was noted by Jesus at the same time that he experienced his own victories over him and his subservient demons; he noted it not only in the lack of receptivity on the part of the people, but also in the growing hostility of their leaders, a hostility that he perceived would bring about his death. It would seem to be incontrovertible that behind this hostility Jesus saw the great Adversary, and that this conviction shaped his thoughts of his coming death. It took the form of the realization, both that his death was inevitable, and that it would mean deliverance and victory; Satan's triumph would be his, undoing.

This thought is clearly expressed in the Fourth Gospel. "The Prince of this world cometh..." (xiv. 30), he advances to the attack. But at the same time judgment is to be held on him, he is to be cast out (xii. 31, xvi. 11). The two aspects are united in the thought that Jesus' death is a "lifting-up" a "glorification." Death, it is true, puts him for a short while in Satan's power, but at the same time it forms the transition to the heavenly life with the Father, in which Jesus wlll be able to draw all men unto him. Death is assuredly death with all its horror; but it is also the means of transformation, of deliverance from Satan's power, and a "lifting-up" beyond the range of his activity.

This genuinely Johannine thought has no direct counterpart in the Synoptic tradition. Yet we might trace it in such an utterance as Luke xxiv. 26: "Ought not Christ to have suffered these things and to enter into his glory?" In Luke we find also the clearest expression of Jesus' consciousness of the demonism lying behind the enmity against him (xxii. 3, 31, 53). Of these sayings xxii. 31 perhaps gives the impression of being the most original: "Simon, Simon, behold, Satan hath desired to have you in order to sift you as wheat..." It is like a glimpse of what is going on behind the curtain, in the mysterious depths beneath the outward events: dark powers are on the march to annihilate the fruits of Jesus' messianic ministry. When to this we add the other allusions in this vein, it is no unfounded assumption that Jesus went to meet his death in the conviction that Satan was behind the enmity against him, and at the same time that only through his death could the Enemy's power over Israel be definitely broken. Therefore it was his Father's will that he performed in drinking the cup. The strange paradox that he, who was the stronger than Satan, should succumb to the power of evil and thereby break it – this paradox was involved in his situation as the Son of Man in lowliness, but having his high vocation, and all the while an instrument of God's will.

A direct expression of this conviction in the mind of Jesus can probably be found only in Mark x. 45: "The Son of Man is not come to be ministered unto but to minister, and to give his life a ransom for many " (λύτρον ἀντὶ πολλῶν).

The scepticism that has prevailed with regard to this passage, refusing to assign it to the oldest stratum of the tradition, is now beginning to give way to a readiness to accept it: and rightly. It was long considered as certain that it was no more than a Pauline variant of Luke xxii. 27; but now there is a growing tendency to assign it to the oldest Palestinian tradition. This is supported by the use of the term "Son of Man" and the phrase "for many," which in the Talmud means "the multitude," "the people." Nor has λύτρον any direct equivalent in the Pauline terminology, though we have there ἀντίλυτρον, λύτρωσις, ἀπολύτρωσις, and the terms based on the idea of purchase and price (ἀγοράζειν, etc.).[18] And the fact that this, the only interpretation given by Jesus of the meaning of his death (apart from the words uttered at the Last Supper), does not occur in the form of a dogmatic statement, but as part of a parenthesis, serves to support its authenticity.

But what does it mean? The saying clearly presupposes the Jewish conception of vicarious suffering (ἀντί). But that general idea can take various forms. It can have a cultic-sacral significance or else a more practical meaning; a historical element may also be involved.[19] Hence the question concerning the actual relation between the death and its redemptive effect, may be answered merely by pointing to the fact that those who heard the words found in them a coherent meaning. The problem then is to find the historically correct background for the redemptive act: what is the bondage from which the Son of Man is to ransom mankind by his ministering death? From bondage under the guilt of sin?[20] From the tyranny of death?[21] If, however, we seek an organic connection between this saying and Jesus' view of the situation that was leading on to his redemptive death, then it is fair to look for the historical meaning of the saying on the line of his conflict with Satan, as the continuation and the completion of that conflict.

On account of the scarcity of direct material on which to build, we must try to gain a correct historical view by noting that which precedes and that which

---

[18] *Vide* Martin Werner, *Der Einfluss paulinischer Theologie im Markusevangelium,* 1923, p. 69 ff.

[19] G. Hollmann, *Die Bedeutung des Todes Jesu,* 1901, p. 33; Lyder Brun, *Jesu evangelium,* 2nd ed., 1926, p. 487 ff. For Jewish ideas of the meaning of the martyrs for the nation, *cf.* E. Lohmeyer, *L'idée du martyre dans le Judaisme et dans le Christianisme primitif* in the volume dedicated to Loisy, 1928, ii., p. 121 ff.

[20] Thus, for instance, Zahn.

[21] J. Jeremias, *Das Evangelium nach Markus,* Chemnitz, 1928. Lyder Brun unites both views.

follows; that is to say, how did Jesus interpret the situation which was so rapidly and so plainly developing towards its awful issue? And what was the idea of this drama in primitive Christianity? If then the λύτρον passage fits in naturally, as a connecting link, between the answers to these two questions, then this interpretation will be to a certain extent confirmed.

The answer to the first question has been already given. Starting from Jesus' exorcisms, I have tried to show that in his Messianic ministry he felt himself pitted against a formidable adversary, who was seeking to undo the results of his teaching, and to bring to ruin him and his disciples.[22] True, he knew himself to be the stronger than Satan, and he had continual experience of his power over the unclean spirits, Satan's ministers. But the people as a whole were in the power of evil, stricken with blindness and hardened against truth, fettered by the iron chains of evil. How were they to be delivered from this bondage?[23]

One of the answers that the Primitive Church gave to this question was: Through the death of Jesus. Origen formulated this idea and rationalized it: the souls of men were in Satan's power on account of sin; Jesus gave his soul (life) up to death as a ransom, which Satan accepted for men's souls; but on Jesus' pure, sinless soul he could not retain his hold. The agreement, however, must stand, and thus the souls in Sheol and on earth were freed from Satan's power. This redemption is seen in its effects when Christian exorcists drive out demons in the name of Jesus.[24]

Origen in all probability here builds upon elements of popular belief, which had lived a subterranean, non-literary life, till the great theologian brought them into the light. We might trace these same ideas also in Irenaeus:[25] Christ, in virtue of his obedience and righteousness, which he showed also in his death has overcome sin, death, and the Devil, and delivered men from the bondage they incurred through the fall. The fallen angel, who deceived the first man, has been defeated by the Son of Man. Also in the Apologists[26] we meet with the idea that Christ's death delivered mankind from the demonic powers, just as the demons henceforth are expelled through the name of the Crucified.

The *Epistle to the Hebrews* (ii. 14) also expresses the idea that Jesus entered human life "that through death he might destroy him that had the power of death, that is, the devil." And in *Acts* ii. 24 we read that God raised up Christ, "having loosed the pains of death: because it was not possible that he (Jesus)

[22] Also in the storm on the sea Jesus seems to have recognized an attack from demons. Cf. the command: "Peace, be still !" (Mark iv. 39).

[23] Michaelis, *Täufer, Jesus, Urgemeinde,* 1928, p. 73,103, shows a remarkable superficiality and lack of realism in his treatment of this problem.

[24] *In Joh.* vi. 53; *c. Cels.* I., 31, chapters vii., viii., *passim.*

[25] Adv. Hœr., iii. 18, 7, etc.

[26] Justin, *Apol.*, ii. 6, 13; *Dial.*, 30.

should be holden of it (death)." In all these phrases there is revealed a very real conviction of an *activity* in Jesus' death: it is a victory over the devil and over death.

If now we return to the saying of Jesus in Mark x. 45, we perceive that the self-sacrifice of the Son of Man in giving himself up to death is there treated as part of his ministering work – indeed, as the completion of that work, hence as an activity. With this idea might very well be connected that of the death of the righteous as a purifying of the people, an expiation of its sins. This idea or complex of ideas was of old connected with martyrdom,[27] but when we seek to draw the direct connecting line between the ministering activity of Jesus, as described in the Synoptic tradition, and his death, we must take as our starting point Jesus' conflict with the great enemy, the Lord of the evil spirits. Jesus calls himself a λύτρον ἀντὶ πολλῶν, convinced that in going to death of his own free will he will bring to nought Satan's power on Satan's own ground.

If so, we are here within the same range of ideas which we found in the Fourth Gospel, with regard to Jesus' death; only that in this gospel the victory over the Prince of the World is characterized as a *judgment* on him, by force of which he is to be cast out. To this judgment on Satan corresponds the *justification* of Jesus, his exaltation to the triumph and majesty of "glory": the Paraclete shall convince the world of righteousness because Jesus goes to his Father, and of judgment because the Prince of this world is judged.[28]

The idea of resurrection and exaltation does not – so it seems – fall directly in with the idea of the λύτρον; it is death and Sheol that form the scene of the redemption. And it is probably the oldest interpretation of Jesus' death that the death is the victory; the resurrection (glorification) comes as the reward, the seal, the completion, the manifestation of the result.

The assurance of Jesus that in his death he would meet Satan in battle on Satan's own ground, sprang in the first instance from his own *experience,* from his interpretation of his own situation. But this interpretation coincided with the "mythical" view of the universe: death and evil were associated, and together they held mankind in bondage. This "mythical" view of the universe, as a background for the idea of redemption, can be traced also later, in the Church, particularly in Paul.[29] In the leading theologians and writers, however, other lines of thought, based upon personal-religious and ethical principles, take precedence.[30] But the idea of the victory over Satan and his hosts con-

---

[27] *E.g.,* Isa. liii.

[28] John xvi. 11f. The picture of the good shepherd who assails the wolf and surrenders his life for his sheep is also an "active" trait.

[29] Stressed by W. Wrede, *Paulus* (Rel-gesch. Volksbücher), 1904. *Cf.* E. Lohmeyer, *Kyrios Jesus,* 1928. One might point to such passages as 1 Cor. ii. 28; Gal. iv. 3ff.; Phil. ii. 6–11; Col. i. 13, ii. 15

[30] F. Karup *(Dansk Teol. Tidsskr.,* 1921) rightly emphasizes that also in these other lines of thought the *activte* side is easily under-rated.

tinued to live in the popular imagination, only appearing rarely in literature, but serving as the ground for the exorcistic practice of the Church. A variation of this popular conception may be detected in the idea of Jesus' victorious descent to Hades. It is a genuine popular dogma, which at an early time was linked up with various versions of an Oriental salvation myth.[31]

The Gospel tradition presents us with a continual balance of *actio* and *passio* in the life of Jesus. He is the object of temptations and trials (πειρασμοί) on the part of the Devil and his hosts, and finally he gives himself up, unresisting, into the hands of sinners, to be ill-treated, mocked, put to death. But he it is also who repels the attacks by God's word and his own irresistible wisdom. He speaks with an authority that moves men and strikes them with awe. He is the Stronger One who binds the Strong One and spoils his house.

The psychological problem arising here, the question of the development of Jesus' soul-life, his thoughts and feelings in his contradictory situation – a problem reaching its climax of difficulty in Jesus' death – this problem lies beyond the scope of the historian. It can only be stated that both the above-mentioned aspects are found in the tradition. The history of Jesus is not presented as a story of *martyrdom* exclusively, although the idea of martyrdom with its passivity has its place there. Still less does the tradition take the form exclusively of an *aretology,* a series of triumphs and glorious deeds, an epos of the Messianic hero; but this, too, is woven into the picture. The antinomy of these two sides is the antinomy of life itself, and it forms the very best demonstration of the truthfulness of the tradition. It is no product of a theory or reflection of an ideal. It is a transcript of historical fact.

It is fruitless to attempt to harmonize the two sides of the tradition by psychological construction. The spiritual history of the passion of Jesus is, and remains, a mystery. What we can get into touch with is the religious value of the wholeness of his personality, the self-consciousness of Jesus, and his reaction to outward reality.[32]

[31] 1 Pet. iii.18ff.; Eph. iii. 8ff.; Hermas, *Sim.,* ix. 16, 5ff.; Justin, *Dial.* 72 etc.; .J. Kroll, *Der descensus ad inferos,* Königsberg, 1922; W. Bousset, *Kyrios Christos,* 1913, 32–40; *Zeitschr. f. d. Neutestl. Wissenschaft,* 1926; Carl Schmidt, *Gespräche Jesu mit seinen Jüngern,* 1919, pp. 456–576.

[32] The two sides of the tradition concerning Jesus have been particularly stressed by Georg Bertram in his short but important article "Neues Testament und historische Methode" (Tübingen, 1928, *Sammlung gemeinverständlicher Vorträge,* No. 134). Bertram holds it to be removed beyond every possible doubt that both sides go back to Jesus himself. But at the same time he keeps to a strict *kultus-historisch* treatment of the sources. This is in keeping with his methodical view of the aim of historical scholarship: the object of history is not to reconstruct the historical personality – that would be a falsification of history, since the scholar's own rational view of the world must determine his reconstruction. The picture resulting from such a method – this holds true both of the idealistic and the materialistic historical schools – is dependent on the personal presuppositions of the scholar and highly arbitrary, and increasingly arbitrary in proportion to the scantiness of the sources. History in this way merely becomes a form of tradition, by the side of myth, legend, and fiction, yet of less value than these, since in

This self-consciousness of Jesus is revealed in a bright light by short episodes and pregnant sayings. The detailed interpretation of these episodes and sayings must of course be more or less hypothetical. But out of the scattered traits there arises a whole picture, which in its double-sidedness bears the mark of reality, the stamp of life.

This conclusion is confirmed by the fact that the same double-sidedness appears in the after-results of the life-work of Jesus. The primitive Church extolled martyrdom for Christ's sake, and presented Jesus as the great example of suffering patience, retaining as a living element in its consciousness the idea of the purifying, re-creative, expiatory power of suffering.[33] At the same time the earliest Christianity lived and moved in the conflict against Satan and the whole spiritual host of evil,[34] with the conviction that the power of demonism had been broken by Jesus' death. Thus the very *passio* of the martyrs was also an *actio*. In their great *peirasmos* they must hold steadfastly to their confession of faith, that they might share in Christ's victory.

---

such a rational reproduction of the past, reduced to strict causality, there is no room for the creative agencies of history, the great original personalities. From this it follows that the usual time "schema" for the description of the origin of Christianity must be dispensed with. What can and should be described, is the evidence we have of the religious life and conceptions of the primitive Christian congregations. The Synoptists, St. Paul, St. John, will then not appear one after the other as links in a chain of historical development, but rather stand side by side, as being all equally effects of Jesus' preaching, his life and death. To desire to get behind these testimonies to Jesus himself, is to attempt the impossible. Jesus can be grasped only in the results of his life-work, in the *Kristus-kultus,* the Christian religion. Starting from this methodical basis, Bertram discusses the Gospel tradition and finds there two types of narratives concerning Jesus: "Prophet legends," in which Jesus is the active, healing, demon-expelling man, and "ætiological cult-narratives," in which Jesus-Messiah-the Son of Man is the sufferer, the passive. Both aspects go back to the historical life of Jesus. But to unite them in a total view of the personality of Jesus is methodically inadmissible. With all his well-warranted reaction against "historicism" and his instructive emphasis on the *kultus-historisch* view, Bertram is guilty of a violent exaggeration and onesidedness in his fundamental conception of history and historical scholarship. History cannot possibly be viewed as consisting of mere complexes, motives, types; it must also be brought under the categories of time, space, and personality. But Bertram's reaction against the "historicism" and "psychologism," which have for a long time served to discredit the modern treatment of the history of Jesus, is quite comprehensible.

[33] Cf., e. g., 1 Pet. iv. 1.ff.

[34] 1 Thess. v. 8; Eph. vi. 11–18; 1 Pet. v. 8f.

Who Did Jesus Claim to Be?

The Historical Foundation of Faith in Christ According to Present Biblical Research

(1931)

The Problem

Who was Jesus of Nazareth? – this is a question to which no satisfactorily objective answer can be given. What we know of him is very little; only a few facts concerning his outward circumstances can be established with historical certainty. We know the name of his parents and of his home-town, a few disparate traits of an itinerant preaching ministry, a few unconnected and perplexing announcements concerning his death in Jerusalem during a Passover feast. As for the rest we are totally ignorant of his life story, both inwardly and outwardly. His "personality", his mental development and character are as much unkown to us as is his appearance. Measured by the measuring rod of historical biography, the Jesus tradition is an interesting but enigmatic bit of biography. Every attempt to draw a character picture, to describe the course of his life with the help of this tradition must necessarily be poetry, a picture of fantasy without scientific value.

Rather one ought to ask: *Who did Jesus claim to be?* If we phrase the question so, we might perhaps expect to get a clear answer from the Gospel tradition. For this shows us Jesus in the midst of a public ministry, which evidently created a strong sensation, provoking, on the one hand, an enthusiastic following, and on the other hand bitter opposition. With what claims then did Jesus make his appearance in this ministry of his?

But even though we put the question in this way, the answer is not so easy to obtain. Our knowledge of Jesus is not based on objective observations and critical announcements, but exclusively upon the witness concerning him which was produced in the circle of his disciples following his death. This was after faith in his resurrection from the dead had burst through and led to the creation of a Church, which with enthusiastic expectation looked forward to his return from heaven.

Is this testimony historically reliable?

The testimony is to the effect that Jesus claimed to be and that he actually was the Messiah. The picture which the Gospels present of his ministry is "Messianic", i.e. it has superhuman character. The words and acts of Jesus possess a power which witnesses to the fact that he has a special mission; he stands at the boundary between two ages, and in him the powers of the new epoch are concentrated and revealed. Jesus makes his appearance as the Messiah.

Messiah (in Aramaic מְשִׁיחָא, the anointed one, in Greek ὁ Χριστός) means "the king". This is how Jews in Jesus' time designated a saviour, who, they expected, would arise among the people and deliver them from all trouble. Many different ideas and hopes were connected with the figure of the Messiah. There was no fixed dogmatism about the Messiah. In its popular form the Messianic hope implied that the awaited scion of David would defeat and annihilate the heathen world power and establish in Israel a kingdom of happiness and righteousness. Bitter political hate, social need and old popular ideals of happiness were united here to create a religiously revolutionary atmosphere, which time and again broke out into wild, futile revolts, which in the end led to a total catastrophe for the whole Jewish Nation in Palestine. When the last messiah, Simon Bar Cochba, fell before the sword of the Roman attack-forces in the fortress of Better, south of Jerusalem, during the last days of August A.D. 135, the formerly populous Palestine was transformed into a desolate ruin. About 1,000 villages and cities were destroyed and more than one million people were killed. Following that the promised land was closed to Israel.

However, the idea of Messiah among the Jews had now assumed a higher aspect; it contained within it a genuine religious content, which in circles characterized by a deeper piety and a finer culture, took precedence over political passions and ousted them. In these circles the Messiah was seen first and foremost as the fulfilment of God's promises to his people, as the completion of salvation history, a history which had begun with the call of Abraham, and had continued with the wonderful deliverance from Egypt. In addition the kingdom which the Messiah was to establish, would, in the first place, be a kingdom of peace and righteousness, where all the evil elements, all the ungodly would be wiped out, and God's will would be the law and the delight of everyone.

But even this higher Messianic expectation contained a national-political element; and a gentle wind of the popular dreams of happiness even penetrated this spiritualized longing for God's kingdom.

Therefore, following Jesus' death when, the Christian Church, believing in his resurrection and return, made the proclamation: *Jesus is the Messiah!* – this implied that Jesus was the Saviour promised in the Holy Scriptures, he who ushers in the new age, God's kingdom. The content of these concepts: Messiah, kingdom of God, therefore had to undergo a thorough transformation as a result of Jesus' public preaching and of his death on the Cross. Nevertheless, the direct connection with Jewish faith and terminology is immediately clear. The question now is: Is this matter, namely, that Jesus is the Messiah, something new? Is it a conviction which was formed in the disciples *after* the emergence of faith in the resurrection (this is the opinion of e.g. W. Wrede in his well-known work *Das Messiasgeheimnis in den Evangelien,* 1901)? Or was this conviction older than faith in the resurrection and the presupposition for it?

Did Jesus claim to be the Messiah? This is an important question both for religion and science. Here we stand before *the problem of whether the Church's faith in Jesus as well as the Christ-cultus that is connected with this faith have their roots in Jesus's own self-consciousness,* or whether we have here a product of historical and psychological factors.

The question, as important as it is for practical religious life, must be investigated and answered in a scientific way. We stand before a historical problem, which demands a strictly objective solution, in so far as this is possible from the sources that are at our disposal. How does the question stand in modern Gospel research?

The following is what actually lies at the basis: A Jewish prophet and teacher from Galilee comes forward in the regions around his home town, proclaiming that the "kingdom of God" is near, and exhorts his compatriots to repent at the prospect of the judgment that is drawing near. He gathers around himself a group of disciples, who follow him in his journeys, during which he not only preaches, but also heals the sick and demon-possessed by word and laying on of hands. After a few months he is arrested immediately outside Jerusalem, where he has gone to keep the Passover. The arrest, set in motion by the Supreme Council, takes place in the darkness of night – one of the Galilean's own disciples showing the way. Following a hasty and tumultuous examination before the high priest, he is delivered to the Roman Procurator of Judea, Pontius Pilate, accused as a revolutionary, with plans for kingship. A brief, summary examination ends with his condemnation to death by crucifixion. The sentence is executed immediately.

So far there is nothing unusual or surprising in Jesus' history viewed at externally. Everything runs naturally, and no problems are raised other than those that depend upon our scant knowledge of the individual happenings in his life and its outer course of events.

But at this point something remarkable begins. We find his disciples – who, at the hour of danger, had fled – a few weeks later back in Jerusalem, convinced that their Master is risen from the dead and is exalted to a place at God's right hand. He will thence return to judge the living and the dead. This conviction soon spreads even outside the boundaries of Palestine. Churches are founded round about in the cities of the Mediterranean countries, churches which believe in Jesus Christ and salvation through his death and resurrection. They experience his presence with them through the gifts of the Spirit: prophecy, speaking in tongues, miracles, love, unspeakable joy, blessed peace. They enter into a mystic fellowship with the Lord through baptism and holy communion. His life, death, and resurrection are depicted in worship as a divine revelation. They seal their faith with their blood.

These are the historical *facts*. *The problem* is: What lies behind and beneath this strange and surprising development? It is the task of historical research to find clarity in this situation. It is a difficult task, however, difficult already in itself, but doubly difficult to solve, seeing that the Gospels supply us with only scanty and unclear information. For one hundred years the problem has been the object of restless and penetrating research, and the answer to this great question has been far from unanimous. But lately the situation seems to have become gradually clearer. The scientific understanding of the Messianic problem in Jesus' life has begun consolidating itself.

Messiah?

The first thing we need to make clear, is this: What does the *New Testament itself* have to say about the origin of faith in Christ and the Christ-cultus? How is the inner coherence of this unique epoch of religious history presented there?

The question is an easy one to answer. According to the New Testament, Jesus of Nazareth considered himself to be God's messenger to his people in the last days. He believed that he was God's anointed ("Messiah"), the king of the coming kingdom of God. Through his death he would deliver mankind from sin, death, and the power of Satan, and establish a new covenant of grace and love between God and his people. As the risen and glorified Messiah, he would return in judgment and salvation.

At first, the disciples did not understand the import of these words of Jesus, and when he fell into the hands of his enemies, they left him in the lurch. A few days later, however, Jesus appeared to them, the women found the tomb empty, faith broke through. Now, for the first time, they understood what Jesus had said; they formed a congregation, the true Israel, which gathered around its as yet invisible Master: the Lord at God's right hand; they awaited his return while they were united in brotherly love and mutual help. Faith in Christ and the worship of Christ had taken on their fundamental features, and they provoked an eager missionary activity, at first among Jews, and later among Gentiles.

This presentation of the New Testament must naturally be treated critically by science. This is the duty of scholarship. The latter must ask whether what is related here is in consonance with historical reality. For the stories and the witness of the New Testament are not the result of historical research, but the utterances of fighting and triumphant faith. There is, accordingly, a real possibility that the historical course of events has been stylized, re-sketched and brought under the influence of pious composition.

Certain features of the New Testament tradition are beyond scientific control: *the resurrection of Jesus* is by its very nature a mystery into which we cannot penetrate with our observation and experience. Therefore, it must be left aside, which, however, does not imply that one cannot critically examine the *resurrection* narratives and compare them with one other. But the resurrection itself as an eventually historical event cannot be approached in this way.

What we have to go by is the experience of the disciples, the resurrection *faith.* That it was genuine and honest is a fact that stands above all criticism. How should we, humanly speaking, explain its origin?

It is important to note right at the outset, that the conviction regarding Jesus' resurrection arose within a very short time and altogether suddenly as a momentary breakthrough, which even surprised the disciples themselves. Our task then is to ascertain the historical and psychological presuppositions for such a breakthrough.

In the first place we must reckon with the indelible impression of the Master's personality, his wisdom, his loftiness and purity, permeated as he was in fellowship with God, strong and authoritative, tender and lovingly self-sacrificing. That he should now be subdued by his enemies, by the Devil and death, and be banished to the shadowy land of Hades' realm, was an unbearable thought. He must have been taken up to God, just as were Enoch, the patriarchs, the prophets, the martyrs in earlier times! This conviction burst forth with increasing strength on account of the mental reaction against the terrible drama of the Cross and the disciples' inner collapse under it. The greater their fear, anguish, and despair had been, the stronger the reaction became: so strong that the beloved figure appeared like a mirage before them, as one who stood living in front of them. This occurred at first to a certain individual, then, through mutual suggestion, to the whole circle. And now many different age-old oriental ideas about a saviour arose, a god in human form, who had been saved himself; one who through his death defeated death and through his resurrection to new life created the possibility of life for his worshippers.

This is approximately how one may and must argue from the scientific point of view. But a number of difficulties are attached to this explanation. First of all: How could such a faith in Jesus as the risen Messiah arise within the disciples if there had been nothing in Jesus' own life and words to which such a faith could relate? How could such a victorious and creative conviction be established if it had not been founded by Jesus himself?

For, even if it is conceivable that the disciples in their need clutched at the idea of Jesus' *resurrection* from the dead, without Jesus ever having implied anything of the kind and thereby preparing the way for the resurrection faith, this still does not explain the fact that they now considered him to be the *Messiah*. For resurrection did not necessarily imply messianism. We observe that many believed that Jesus was John the Baptist, who had returned from Hades, without, for that matter, being regarded by the people as the Messiah (Mk 6:14; 8:28).

Therefore, it is probable that Jesus had given his disciples reason to connect him with the concept of Messiah. Another reflexion points in the same direction: it is obvious that Jesus' death proved to be a brutal blow to the disciples, which for a short while caused them to entertain doubts about Jesus' cause. Now if Jesus had only claimed to be a prophet and a teacher, then this shock would have been incomprehensible, for it was an old experience in Israel, that a prophet who told his people the truth, must be prepared to be paid back with *martyrdom:* "O Jerusalem, Jerusalem, you who kill the prophets and stone those sent to you ...!" On the other hand, we understand quite well the disappointment and perplexity of the disciples, if during their wanderings with the Master they had received the impression that he was and claimed to be the one "who was going to redeem Israel" (Lk 24:21). If Jesus had spoken in that connection of his imminent fate, then, in their dreams about the kingdom of God, they must have misunderstood the implications of his utterances. They had not paid the slightest attention to these words of the Master, otherwise they would have constituted a counterweight against the overwhelming impression of the catastrophe. These words now appeared to be so much stronger when calmness had returned, their thoughts began to clear up and the memory began to speak. Now, that which Jesus had hinted in pictures and symbolic actions: "That Christ had to suffer these things and then enter his glory" gradually dawned on them

This is the result to which we are led by the historical argument. But what do the sources say, in so far as they can stand a critical evaluation? *Did Jesus claim to be the Messiah?* – this is the question with which this whole line of thought stands or falls. As has already been pointed out, the evangelists are of this opinion. But are they right in this? Are they not projecting Christian dogma back to Jesus, in conflict with historical reality?

As it has already been stated, it is difficult to imagine that this dogma about Jesus as the risen Messiah would have been able to arise and to establish itself if it had been something totally new and had not been rooted in Jesus' own self-consciousness and his own words. It is still more difficult to get away from the unanimous witness of the Gospels, even if one disregards the redactional passages and the more recent components.

In actual fact, those scholars who deny that Jesus in some way connected the idea of Messiahship with himself are very few. The great majority take it for granted that he did so. They emphasize, however, that this idea *did not play any decisive role for Jesus himself*. He was a prophet who heralded the coming kingdom of God, and he was a teacher who taught God's will for Israel. If he considered himself to be the promised Messiah, which he probably did, then he found in this only an expression for his consciousness of a unique call, a supreme task in God's service. He rejected all national dreams of happiness, which were connected with the Messianic expectation. According to these scholars, he directed a covert attack against the chauvinistic messianic title "Son of David", when he at one point posed the question: "How is it that the teachers of the law say that the Christ is the son of David? David himself, speaking by the Holy Spirit, declared:

> 'The Lord said to my Lord:
> Sit at my right hand
> until I put your enemies
> under your feet'

David himself calls him 'Lord'. How then can he be his son?"! (Mk 12:35–37).

In other words, Jesus considered himself to be the Messiah, but he mounted a vigorous attack against the national idea of Messiaship, and, in addition, he attributed to his own messiahship no decisive importance. For him the important thing was to awaken his people and to teach them the will of God.

This view, which is quite common among scholars, does not seem to be correct. Jesus' attitude to messiahship ought to be understood differently. Indeed it is quite certain that throughout his ministry among the people there is no mention of Jesus ever referring to himself as Messiah. On the other hand, however, it is inescapable that at decisive points in his life he professed that title. Before the high priest, who asked him: "Are you the Messiah, the Son of the Blessed One?" Jesus explained: "I am, and you will see the Son of Man sitting at the right hand of the Mighty One and coming on the clouds of heaven" (Mk 14:61). When Pilate asked him: "Are you the king of the Jews?" he answered: "Yes, it is as you say" (Mk 15:2). A superscription on the cross stated his crime with the phrase: "King of the Jews" (Mk 15:26).

On the whole, it appears to be above suspicion, that Jesus was delivered to the Roman procurator under the accusation of hatching politico-religious revolt plans, and that he was condemned to death as a Messianic pretender to the throne of Israel. The presupposition for this is again that Jesus' preaching and his other ministry actually did touch on Messianic notes and hopes among the people, above all during his appearance at the feast in Jerusalem. Among his disciples was a "zealot", i.e. a Messianic revolutionary, and his arrival at the city of David took the form of a large scale Messianic demonstration. As for himself, he arranged his procession into Jerusalem in such a way as to correspond to the prophecy:

"Say to the daughter of Zion,
'see, your king comes to you,
gentle and riding on a donkey...'"
(Zech 9:9)[1]

It is not a coincidence either that he gathered around himself a band of twelve disciples. This is evidently symbolical: he is surrounded by the twelve tribes, the holy, chosen people. He is the Messiah in the midst of Israel.

The Gospel stories concerning the motives which impelled Jesus' enemies, and the measures which they took to rid themselves of him, must be read critically. We can easily see that these stories are inspired by a pronounced and strong anti-Jewish tone, while the Roman procurator, who pronounced the death sentence, is portrayed with relative indulgence: he is weak rather than wicked; only reluctantly does he give in to the pressure from the Jewish leaders and of the masses which they fanaticized. Under these circumstances we must reckon with the possibility that what dictated the intervention of the Jewish authorities against Jesus, was not exclusively religious repugnance and personal hatred, but, in the first place, political considerations. Surely leading circles had watched with concern the popular movement around the Galilean prophet. When he now appeared in the capital itself during the feast, provoking an outburst of messianic feelings in the large and easily inflammed crowds of pilgrims there, the time was considered ripe to prevent an explosion of religious revolutionary fervor by a quick and drastic intervention.

Herodes had already thought of cutting short Jesus' ministry in Galilee (Lk 13:31), and Jesus knew that the situation there was becoming threatening. But he did not flinch at danger, on the contrary, he went with his disciples to Jerusalem with the premonition that the decisive battle would take place there. He rode into Jerusalem under the thunderous cheerings of the pilgrim crowds and immediately acted with the utmost severity against the Jewish authorities. Like the old prophets of judgment he announced Jerusalem's fall and the destruction of the tempel, and in the sanctuary itself he proceeded with violence against offensive abuses.

Here we have the background to the Sanhedrin's measures against Jesus. During the great feasts Jerusalem was a source of constant concern for both the Jewish and the Roman authorities. The religious fanaticism of the Jews was always ready to burst out in flames; but during Passover, when the city was filled to the brim with huge masses of pilgrims in religious festive intoxication, the risk for an outbreak was particularly great. The city was like a keg of gunpowder, one single spark could bring about an explosion, creating serious problems both for the Jewish authorities, which would thereby be held responsible, and for the representatives of the Roman power. Thus, the Sanhedrin did

[1] [The Author actually gives the wording of Mt 21:5 (Tr.)].

not dare let the renowned and increasingly aggresive popular preacher's ministry continue undisturbed. He was arrested in the night and was delivered to the Romans. And with that his destiny was sealed.

In view of all this there can be no doubt about the Messianic character of Jesus' ministry. The panic which seized Jesus' disciples when their Master was arrested, condemned to death, and crucified, as well as the sudden flaming up of enthusiastic faith in his resurrection from the dead, can only be explained, if the Gospels are correct, in Jesus' having – directly or indirectly – inspired his followers with the conviction that he was the Messiah, and having told them that through his death he would go to glory and establish the kingdom of God.

However, here we are faced with a certain difficulty! Jesus could not possibly have presented himself to the people in his public ministry as the Messiah, for in that case restless Galilee would soon have been in flames, and the fate of Bar Cochba would have struck the prophet from Nazareth already at the outset of his career. Jesus must have strictly avoided the dangerous title as well as obvious messianic actions of the popular style. As for his entrance into Jerusalem with its allusion to Zechariah's prophetic word, no one other than himself must have understood its import: it was a Messianic act in camouflage.

Yet he awakened a strong Messianic stir among the people. This was naturally connected with his preaching about the kingdom of God and his personal relationship to his message. This personal relationship was clearly and decisively marked, and for this reason the future hope swelled vigorously and powerfully around him, but without actually taking on revolutionary tendencies. That Jesus in no way wanted to call forth any political movement is self-evident, this would have stood in the sharpest possible contradiction to the whole nature of his message and ministry. It is clearly already understood from this consideration that he did not designate himself as the Messiah. It would, however, be wrong to think that his position concerning the title of Messiah derived exclusively from practical, opportunistic considerations. Quite certainly Jesus' restraint towards the use of the title of Messiah had its explanation in the feeling that this title, as well as the ideas connected with it, did not contain or express the innermost secret in his consciousness regarding his personal relation to his message. The title of Messiah was loaded with altogether too strong political, national, material hopes and ideas, to serve as the characteristic word on Jesus' lips for that which he claimed to be.

On the other hand, Jesus could not completely avoid this title. The title of Messiah was indissolubly connected with the kingdom of God, which Jesus knew he had been called to proclaim and to prepare the way for. For this reason he had to place both himself and his work under the Messianic outlook, which, as we have already seen, implied certain characteristic, outward expressions.

It is in this double attitude, both positive and negative, to the idea of Messiah, that the explanation of Jesus' strange position on this point certainly lies. When

Peter on his, as well as the other disciples' behalf, uttered the confession: "You are the Christ" (the Messiah), Jesus forbad them strictly to mention this to anyone (Mk 8:30). And when the two brothers, James and John, requested as a favour to sit nearest him at his glory, he did not reject the idea that was being divulged here, but explained that it was not up to him to grant these positions (Mk 10:40). It is first before his earthly judges that he overtly and clearly confesses to the exalted, dangerous title. Now there were no more apprehensions, the time for words was gone, the time for acting and suffering had come. The only way to profess to his work in this situation was to confess himself as the Messiah. An evasive answer to the question asked at this juncture would have simply been denial, treason.

But even at an earlier phase Jesus had somewhat distanced himself from the title of Messiah. It did not fit in with the nature of his message and the innermost core of his self-consciousness. For this reason he calls himself not the Messiah, but *the Son of Man. This title reveals his self-consciousness. What lay behind this self-designation?*

Before attempting to answer this question, we must take a look at the historical presuppositions closest to Jesus' appearance, as well as at the nature and significance of his message. Against this background we will be in a better position to understand what lies in the self-designation "The Son of Man".

John

In the Gospels we get a glimpse of a figure behind Jesus, who evidently has played a large role in Jesus' life and has had a decisive religious influence over him. It is John, the son of Zacharias, the priest, usually called "the Baptist". This person, together with the movement which he started, gives us the key to the spiritual state which brought Jesus of Nazareth onto the scene. If we did not possess the scanty information about the Baptist that we do, Jesus and his mission would have been without context, an enigmatic hieroglyph in the saga of the Jewish people. To be sure, the Gospel tradition about John bears the clear stamp of the Christian church's evaluation of him, but even in this form the tradition has preserved certain important characteristics of the history, which is Jesus' nearest historical background.

We find the son of the priest, from Judea's mountainous countryside, in the desert near the Jordan River, where he has gathered a band of disciples around himself, and where large numbers of people have journeyed to hear him preach. He has started a revival among his people. The echo of his words was so strong, that the Galilean prince, Herodes Antipas' apprehensions were awakened, and he ordered first that the prophet be put in jail, and then that he be killed. Popular legend told a fantastic story, how he became the victim of princess Herodias' implacable hatred (Mk 6:17 ff.); in reality it was fear that this purely religious movement would have political consequences that dictated the measures which the prince took against John.

One must see the Baptist's behaviour in connection with the painfully oppressive situation in Palestine. Ever since Syrian times the history of the people had been just one series of wars, battles, revolts, carnage, plunder and deeds of violence. The large masses in the over-populated and primitively cultivated land lived in constant anxiety and in utter poverty. The Romans' iron grip controlled the holy land, pagans populated the cities and became rich at the expense of the peasantry. All this, together with the religious claims of the people, created a harrowed mentality, a mood characterized generally by despair, in spite of exaltation and fanaticism; the spiritual equilibrium was gone, and a *general mood of crisis and catastrophe* prevailed.

Since times of old *prophecy* belonged to such circumstances in Israel: in the face of collapse the prophets raised their voices, uttering portents, threats, prophecies and warnings. Jochanan bar Zachariah, John the Baptist, was such a prophet at this time of crisis and in the face of catastrophe. His life story is altogether unknown to us, though his birth and childhood are described in the New Testament legend. What drove him out to the desert and made him a prophet we do not know. We only know that he preached God's imminent judgment over his people and exhorted them to repent in order to escape the coming wrath.

John apparently had the same view of the people's religious condition as the prophets of old, whom he also imitated in his outward appearance: Israel as a whole had fallen away from her God and was now threatened by destruction, annihilation. The only way out was to repent and "bear fruit worthy of repentance". So far John moves in the Old Testament prophets' way of thinking. But we see from certain characteristic features in his preaching and ministry that he belongs to another, new time.

It is above all important that judgment over Israel not be executed by human authorities, by kings, the state and the people, but by a superhuman person whom John calls with a mysterious innuendo *"The Coming One"*:

> "After me will come one
> more powerful than I,
> the thongs of whose sandals
> I am not worthy to stoop down and untie.
> I baptise you with water,
> but he will baptise you with fire.
> His winnowing fork is in his hand,
> and he will clear his threshing-floor,

gathering his wheat into the barn
and burning up the chaff with unquenchable fire."[2]

This indicates that he did not move within the thought patterns of the old future hope. Rather he shared the view and the expectation, which at that time was widespread in Judaism, that this world, this aeon is on its way to destruction, on its way to a catastrophe, which will bring in an new aeon, a Paradise, a heavenly world, eternal and blessed. This is especially important as a background to Jesus' preaching of the kingdom of God.

At the transition between the two worlds stands "the Coming One", a historical figure, who appears as a human being among human beings, but who in God's hour is revealed as the judge of the world. This is once again an important feature in the historical presuppositions of Jesus.

John apparently belonged to the so-called *'apocalyptic' religious movement within Judaism*, which occupied itself earnestly with speculations about life beyond the grave and calculations about the coming world. But with John the apocalyptic conviction was centered on practical prophecy, on calling out for repentance [*bot* [3]], on the ethical demand. The spirit of prophecy in old Israel had in him been united with the new ideas about time and eternity, about the world, the kingdom of God, and the Messiah.

That John belonged to a new environment, characterized by apocalyptic mysticism, is made obvious even by his *baptismal practice*. This was so characteristic of him that he got his name from it: he was called "The Baptist". He baptized those who repented [*bot(färdiga)*], who confessed [*biktade*[4]] their sins, in the Jordan River, and he apparently ascribed purificational power to this baptism which made it possible to abide the judgment and to flee from wrath. Here John is certainly influenced by a religious movement widely diffused in the Near East, which ascribed saving power to washings "in living water", in rivers and springs.

The Baptist thus reveals a strange union of Old Testament piety, apocalyptic view of the world and Messianic expectation, as well as oriental sacramental mysticism. The heart of it all was the Old Testament demand for repentance.[5]

---

[2] [A combination of Mk 1:7–8 and Mt 3:11–12 (Tr.)].

[3] [On the meaning of this word, see below (Tr.)].

[4] [This is a technical word for "confessing to the priest" (Tr.)].

[5] [The Swedish original for "repentance" here has two words: *bot* and *bättring*. The Swedish Bible (1917), which the Author uses, renders μετάνοια everywhere in the NT with *bättring* = "betterment" or "improvement". In addition to this the Author also uses *bot* (Germ. *Buße*, Dutch *boete*) = "penance", "expiation", "satisfaction", though the word may sometimes occur with the more general idea of repentance, i.e. without the idea of 'satisfaction' being prominent. The significance which the Author puts in these words comes out in the beginning of the next section: "Israel must humble herself before God, lament, weep for her sins and make a radical improvement in her life" (*Israel måste ödmjuka sig inför Gud, klaga, begråta sina synder och göra radikal bättring i sitt leverne)*. Faced with this terminological and conceptual problem, I have chosen the course of rendering both *bot* and *bättring* with

But the new, that which was added to it, made him into a personal exponent of the genuine religious content in the then prevailing religious state within Palestinian Judaism.

Jesus was arrested by John's message and was baptized by him. In all probability he became one of his disciples, those who constantly surrounded him and formed an apocalyptic gathering with a certain organization, regulated order of life, fasting, prayers, etc. Together with them Jesus, the son of Joseph from Nazareth, prepared himself under strict asceticism to meet the judgment and the Judge, to stand before the terrible, all-seeing eye of "The Coming One".

Soon, however, we find that Jesus has separated himself from the Baptist and his circle. He has gathered around himself a little band of disciples around him, who, like himself, had earlier belonged to the Baptist's circle. For a time Jesus, too, and his disciples baptize in the Jordan, and we catch a glimpse of a certain competition between the followers of the two prophets (Jn 3:22–26). Jesus however, leaves the desert banks of the Jordan and moves on to the densely populated districts of Galilee, where he begins restlessly to move about from city to city and from village to village to *preach the Gospel.*

What has happened? Jesus, awakened and inspired by John, has burst the Baptist's framework of thought and has freed himself from his spiritual master, whom he afterwards called "the greatest of those born of women" (Mt 11:11). On which points does Jesus show his connection with John, and in what respects does he surpass him?

With John he shares the apocalyptic view of the two aeons and of the world-judgment, as well as the prophetic demand for repentance [*bot (och) bättring*]. On two points, however, he goes farther than John: he has another view of the coming kingdom of God and he has formed the conviction that he is himself "The Coming One", the Son of Man.

His time with John had ended, as well as his desert sojourn. From now on his work was to be among the people, his task was to preach the gospel to the poor.

The Kingdom of God

Jesus' message to his people is summarized in Mk 1:15 in the following words: "The time has come, the rule of God (the kingdom of God) is near. Repent [*gören bot* [6]] and believe the gospel!"

In this we see that Jesus, like the Baptist, was convinced that he stood before a cosmic catastrophe, before the destruction and renewal of the world. "The time

'repentance' rather than 'penance' and 'improvement' respectively – especially since it is a question of NT μετάνοια– while indicating the Author's own choice of expression within brackets (Tr.)].

[6] [I.e. "do penance". The Author here departs from the Swed. tr., which renders μετανοεῖτε with "Do better" or "make improvement" (Tr.)].

is fulfilled" – i.e. the measure of time which God, the eternal creator, has ordained for the existence of this world will soon be filled, and then the great, all-encompassing upheaval must take place. In this expression we recognize the 'apocalyptic' thought, that the course of the world runs as a series of periods of a certain length, which succeed one another in accordance with an eternally conceived divine plan. The destruction of the world also entails the last judgment on men, it determines their everlasting fate.

Before this imminent, inevitable crisis Jesus, like John, exhorts to repentance [*bot*]. Israel must humble herself before God, lament, weep for her sins and make a radical improvement in her life. On this Jesus and the Baptist are in agreement as well.

But Jesus evidently has *given up the baptism of repentance [bot];* there is not a trace of such activity in the tradition of his public ministry among the populace of Galilee. This was surely not only due to his having left the Jordan, thus being unable to baptize those who were penitent [*botfärdiga*] in the holy river, but it had to do with a different position he took with respect to reality, *the Rule of God,* a position that governed the Baptist's and his own thought and preaching. John saw in this the revelation of God's annihilating judgment over a sinful world. Jesus designates his message "The kingdom of God is near!" as a *gospel,* and exhorts not only to repentance [*bot*] but also to *faith.*

Thereby Jesus characterizes himself in the first place as a salvation preacher, as a bearer of the message of God's gracious and wonderful help to his people. The word "gospel" betrays an inner relation between Jesus and the unknown prophet, who speaks in "the book of comfort", Isaiah 40–55:

> "Comfort, comfort my people,
> says your God.
> Speak tenderly to Jerusalem,
> and proclaim to her
> that her hard service has been completed,
> that her sin has been paid for,
> that she has received from the Lord's hand
> double for all her sins".

Jesus reopened a living spiritual spring in his people by proclaiming afresh the "good news", that which had been the heart of Israel's religion during its classical time. During the time of the kings the gospel had its place in the temple-cult, where the high point of the great New Year's Festival was the exulting, triumphant cry: "Yahweh has become king!" In these holy moments Israel's gathered people experienced the great renewal of the world and of life, in that it solemnly proclaimed that Yahweh had defeated his enemies and was again seated on his throne as world ruler, he had re-established the rule of God. In the people's most dire need, in captivity, Second Isaiah proclaims this gospel to Israel as an *imminent* salvation.

> "How beautiful on the mountains
> are the feet of those who bring good news,
> who proclaim peace, who bring good tidings,
> who proclaim salvation,
> who say to Zion,
> 'Your God reigns!'
> ...
> Burst into songs of joy together,
> you ruins of Jerusalem,
> for the Lord has comforted his people,
> he has redeemed Jerusalem.
> The Lord will lay bare his holy arm
> in the sight of all the nations,
> and all the ends of the earth will see
> the salvation of our God".

Here the gospel has received the character of future hope, it appeals to faith, faith that God intends soon to create the new future for Israel.

Jesus knew and felt himself to be God's *"bringer of joy"* to his people. How he had gotten that conviction, is his own personal secret. But it is quite clear that the moment he understood that the message about the kingdom of God was a message of joy, and that he himself was the messenger of joy, that very moment he was through with his life in the community of John's disciples. John's preaching of repentance [*bot*] was surely a word of truth from God: John came teaching the way of righteousness ... (Mt 21:32). But Jesus had another, higher task to perform: it was to go out and proclaim the joyful message of the rule of God. What does the rule of God mean on Jesus' lips?

As it has already been hinted, the message: "Yahweh rules!" was the gospel in Israel since times immemorial. But during the different periods and circumstances different ideas were connected with the holy proclamation. At first it triggered the Israelite people's creative sense of the victory of life and order over chaos and annihilation; later it became the prophetic promise of the coming miracle, through which God created the new age for Israel. At the beginning of our era Judaism lived in the hope of the establishment of God's rule, or as was often said: the rule (kingdom) of heaven. It was a hope that united all the people, but one which appeared in rather wide variations and on different spiritual levels. The popular expectation to a large extent had a politico-revolutionary touch. Before their eyes the mirage of the old Israelite ideal of happiness appeared, according to which one could sit in safety and peace under one's vine and fig tree. In the apocalyptic circles, on the other hand, one was given to unearthly fantasies about a heavenly world in the eternal light of God's glory. And still others, considered the full realization of the ideal of righteousness within Law piety as the core of the new situation.

This thoroughly eschatological movement within Judaism may easily appear to us as a selfish dream of national happiness. But this would be to judge the Jewish hope of the future wrongly. Jewish eschatology is a necessary consequence of faith in God. God must show himself as the highest, as the only power in the world. And while God and Israel are historically united over against the rest of the world, God's self-revelation must be at the same time Israel's salvation, redemption, comfort and triumph. Therefore when Israel in faith and hope fought for her self-preservation, she fought for her God and her religious task in the world. It was not cultural and national values that were at stake, but faith in God and God's holy will. That is why Israel must hope in her redemption, in the kingdom of God. Otherwise truth and righteousness would be an illusion, chaos would swallow up life.

At the same time as the establishment of God's kingdom spelled redemption and blessedness for Israel as a whole, for the individual it spelled *judgment* over his life. This lent a deep gravity to the hope of the future. And it was this gravity that the Baptist emphasized with prophetic one-sidedness and vigour:

> "The axe is already at the root of the trees,
> and every tree that does not produce good fruit,
> will be cut down and thrown into the fire!"

This was the theme of John's proclamation. For Jesus this seriousness was self-evident. But the important thing for Jesus was the *possibility* which the kingdom of God afforded to him who accepts it, the blessed gift, which was thereby offered to man. That he put the emphasis here was not owing to his attaching less weight to God's holiness, or to his understanding of the possiblity of lostness as less frightful than the Baptist's. It was owing to his having his eyes opened for *God's fatherly will of salvation as the innermost driving force in and intention behind the establishment of God's rule,* and he knew and felt himself called to preach this gospel, and mediate to God's people the riches, which he possessed and administered. He came with *the fulfilment;* John was the precursor, Elijah, who would prepare the way for God's messenger, for the bringer of joy.

How then did Jesus understand the rule of God, the kingdom of God?

It is easy to see that Jesus shared the eschatological thinking of his contemporaries: the kingdom of God is *near,* i. e. it is a state that will be established by a great miracle of God, through which this world is to be succeeded by another one. The new world lies on another plane than the old one: men are there as God's angels; gathered around the holy patriarchs they live in blessed delight as the guests of the Messiah in God's immediate proximity, they are the sons of the Most High, they see God. Without question Jesus' gospel is eschatological, i. e. it proclaims the coming kingdom of God, it exhorts to prepare oneself with the joy of faith to be part of it.

The immediate nearness of the kingdom of God, however, puts its characteristic mark on the present, the hour that is now. The situation is highly critical, here and now the roads are parted. At the balances stands Jesus with his message; the position one takes *vis-à-vis* him is decisive. In what light does Jesus and his message appear against this background?

The *prophetic* character of his ministry lies in full daylight. He announces a message by divine commission without motivation, without proof. The word itself bears its convincing power. Where it is announced, it creates faith or defiance. The prophetic element in Jesus' actions sets its typical mark on his words and even on his outward circumstances. Without home and family, without a bourgeois occupation, without any fixed plan he walks around with his disciples, he appears first here and then there, he comes suddenly and disappears just as hastily.

But he is also a *teacher*. The disciples called him *rabbi;* time and time again we read in the Gospels that he "taught" in the synagogues or in the open air. And the greatest part of those words of Jesus which are found in the Gospels, originated from his teaching on the kingdom of God and true righteousness. Even these passages of the Gospel tradition exhibit typical *forms*, above all the use of pictures and parables and furthermore in general the plastic graphicness, which goes hand in hand with the brief, classical formulation so full of expression.

Moreover, that which is characteristic of Jesus as a teacher, is the independence, the authority, with which he acts and teaches. He does not appeal to authorities, nor does he spin his thoughts from the word and letter of Scripture. On the contrary, he sets his "But I say to you" over against that which "was said to the people long ago". He interprets the Scripture with supreme authority, he illuminates its letter with great, structural, leading ideas, and when the letter in consequence of it sometimes comes in a critical light, it does not worry him.

The prophetic teacher, however, exhibits such an understanding of the situation and such self-consciousness, that it demands a more careful characterization.

Jesus proclaimed that the present world was about to be destroyed. The rule of God was near. Thereby, he was intimating that another rule was about to disappear, that which was being exercised then: *the rule of Satan. It is an important feature of Jesus' outlook on life, that he saw a great mystery in life, the terrible mystery of evil.* In the world created by God there is an evil spiritual power at work, a demonic world-power. Spiritual dullness, temptation and sin, sickness and misfortune come primarily from him; the distress and oppression of the holy people is a visible manifestation of the rule of Satan in this age.

This mystery of life, this demonic mystery was not hidden for Jesus' contemporaries either. But Jesus felt it and experienced it with greater sharpness and more painful intensity than others. It is first in this connection that full light is thrown on the idea of the kingdom of God and his personal attitude to his own message.

Normative Jewish religion considered that the terrible might of the Devil must be checked by the strict practice of the Law in all situations of life; only by regulating their lives down to the least detail in accordance with God's Law could the holy people defend themselves against spiritual dissolution, against destruction. The people, the broad layers of the masses, however, entertained the fanatical conviction that one day the Messiah would reveal himself and mobilize his people for a struggle against Rome and the Devil, and lead them to victory and happiness. What they were trusting in was the *Law* and the *sword*.

Here Jesus goes his own way. For him the law is not an instrument for defence, nor the sword a weapon for attack. He sees and feels a *double mystery* under the surface of the world. Another power too has begun to stir in secret: *the kingdom of God*. Impossible to resist, it presses forward in spite of desperate opposition from the powers of evil, and at the horizon the mirage of victory's great day appears with the new world and God's rule. John the Baptist was the first visible sign of the awakening activity of the kingdom of God. And now it is being revealed in Jesus' own words and in his "miracles", his works of healing and the driving out of demons.[7] Yes, in the small group of disciples, who had gathered around him, the people of God is a tangible reality, the nucleus in the coming kingdom of God is already formed. Jesus himself is full of the miraculous power of the kingdom of God, and he is its organizing center.

In this way Jesus has already taken his stand towards the world, life and existence. He stands in the midst of the superhuman, enormous rapture of the cosmic powers. He represents in word and deed the irruption of the kingdom of God. Wherever he goes the demons are driven out of the ones possessed with strong cries and violent convulsions, the sick arise from their beds of pain, the blind, deaf, and lame receive once again the use of their senses and limbs. The kimgdom of God presses on victoriously with Jesus.

It is of extraordinary importance to note how Jesus, with this eschatological view of the situation, defines man's religious and ethical mission in life. We meet the strange situation that this prophet of the end of the world, this opponent of Satan and conqueror of demons, is in his *teaching* manner calm, composed and clear. The true righteousness which he demands and teaches, consists of childlike faith in God and obedience, in the peacefulness and unselfish love of a humble heart. One may ask, how this ties together with a mentality which waits for the destruction of the world to take place at any time, which fights against demons, and in a moment of triumph exclaims: "I saw Satan fall from heaven like lightning!"

To a superficial observer there may seem to exist an yawning chasm between the one warning of a storm, the miracle man, and the almost terrible figure

---

[7] Cf. B. Gadelius, *Om besatthet* (Verdandis småskrifter 153), where the problems of demon possession and healing are seen in the light of modern psychology.

standing at the boundary between time and eternity – between him and the great interpreter of God's will, the teacher of wisdom, the one who cared for souls. But the fact is that both of these apparently so different mentalities are fused into an organic unity in the person of Jesus. It must be remembered that even before the OT prophets the demand for righteousness which was made concerning Israel, had a deep, mysterious background in Yahweh's judicial rule of the world. Even in their view there existed an inner connection between the cosmic harmony and Israel's exercise of justice and mercy. With Jesus this deep background opened up in his personal life: under the strictly realistic, thoroughly practically oriented piety, lay the intensive feeling of life's terrible contrasts, under the calmness there exists an awful tension. It was this that gave to Jesus' teaching, as simple and concrete as it was, oriented to everyday practical concerns, a tremendous earnestness and an immeasurable depth. Every demand, every commandment sprang up from the depths of eternity and placed man before the question of his religious or non-religious existence, before life's decision.

What makes Jesus' words about true righteousness not only have this touching earnestness, this unconditional character, but also gives him his winsome and immediately convincing power, is that the tension in the eternal background of life's teaching rests deep down on the assurance of victory. The conviction of representing *the kingdom of God* in its irresistible advance was the nerve of Jesus' consiousness and the conquering power of his proclamation. The consequence of this was that his life's teaching, even where it appears as commandments with unbounded demands on men's faith, devotion and sacrifice, is still good news: the commandments spring forth from an overflowing, victorious, happy life, which presses on from within, seeking to form reality. This life is summarized by Jesus in the word *"love"*, and it is quite significant that he makes love an object for a commandment: "Thou shallt love!" It lets us see that in Jesus' life's teaching the commandment is only a reflection of the blessedness, which the gospel of God's kingdom creates in the soul. This is how the child of God *must* look upon life, such are the demands one *must* make on oneself. For the religious consciousness it appears that this is God's self-evident will and commandment, this is the righteousness of the kingdom of God.

This nexus between the kingdom of God and righteousness, between gospel and commandment, the gift of God and its effect on the creation of life, has been illuminated by Jesus himself in two short parables:

"The kingdom of heaven is like a treasure hidden in a field. When a man found it, he hid it again, and then in his joy went and sold all he had and bought that field.

Again, the kingdom of heaven is like a merchant looking for fine pearls. When he found one of great value, he went away and sold everything he had and bought it". (Mt 13:44–46)

Joy is the mighty note in Jesus message' and teaching, even where the message is about the destruction of the world and judgment, and even where his teaching mercilessly crushes the natural forms of life, condemns the human, well-tried wisdom of life, and strikes at the center of the immediate instinct of self-preservation. Joy saturated those who surrounded Jesus and walked with him, and made of those who were different and usually unimportant people, a vanguard for the kingdom of God, which would conquer the world. When Jesus was asked once why his disciples did not fast like John's disciples, for whom fasting was an important element of repentance [*botgörandet* [8]] wherewith they prepared themselves to stand the test of judgment fire, he answered with a question – again a picture:

"How can the guests of the bridegroom fast while he is with them?"

Consequently, from the glimpses we get of the spirit in Jesus' ministry among the people and the atmosphere in the circle of his disciples, we may gain certain ideas on the important question about the relation between the *present* and the *future* in Jesus' idea of the kingdom of God and his life's teaching. The kingdom of God is near, it belongs to the future. But it is also present here and now: in the Gospel, in the faith and joy which this Gospel creates, in the victories over Satan, in the Messianic community surrounding the messenger of joy with the creative and convincing word and with mighty works. This life here and now within the sphere of the kingdom of God has its blessedness in itself, but it is also passionately forward-oriented, it longs with burning desire for perfection, for God's full revelation. The first words in the prayer which Jesus taught his disciples, are therefore the following:

> "Father,
> hallowed be your name,
> your kingdom come!"

Life in the sphere of the kingdom of God here and now is wholly filled with its own tasks, which arise in every practical relation and claim man completely. But these tasks are not an end in themselves, they would not extend, promote, establish an earthly form of life, a historical stratum of society, nor would they develop the individual into an ethical "personality". It is instead a continuously repeated formation of life, an uninterrupted achievement by the powers of the kingdom of God on a never-resting existence, which restlessly surges over man and advances through his soul. Therefore, though man is constantly one with his activity and in it experiences existence as a whole, life as a totality becomes a patch work, the soul longs for the perfect new creation, for the perfected totality of life. At the same time as man trembles in the face of judgment, which at the end will try the thoughts, words and actions of the finished course of one's

[8] [*Bot* compounded with the verb *göra* 'to do', expresses "the doing of penance" (Tr.)].

life, whether they have borne the mark of the kingdom of God. *Longing* and the *sense of responsibility* unite with grateful, victorious *joy* and with it make up a complex, which spurs one on and gives peace, comforts and causes anxiety.

Present and future stand together in Jesus' idea of the kingdom of God. That which holds them together is *the miracle*. This is typical for the Messianic time of transition. It is the kingdom of God, which constantly breaks in at different points and thereby presages the great, definitive irruption, the future which is completely a miracle, when everything is swallowed up by God's own revelation in his heavenly splendour and glory. One stands confounded before the Gospel tradition if one does not clearly reckon with the Messianic, the demonic elements in Jesus' view of reality. This understanding was grounded in the consciousness of living at "the end-time". This time is the definitive *time of decision*. Now the line is drawn between those who are receptive and those who are impervious, for the judgment is already completed. With inexorable severity Jesus proclaims that whoever cannot interpret the signs of the times, is eternally lost: "Once the owner of the house gets up and closes the door, you will stand outside knocking and pleading, 'Sir, open the door for us.' But he will answer, 'I don't know you or where you come from!'." In this time of miracles and decision before the great cosmic miracle, the last judgment, the present receives its characteristic mark from the future without losing its concrete character of being the present. The assurance of being elected to the coming kingdom of God already gives now to life a special mark of fulfilment, feast, rejoicing and vitality. Sometimes we should take it for granted that among the disciples this kind of mood gave vent to thunderous, enthusiastic applause. We can only get a faint idea of what was experienced there at the high points of communal life, especially during the common meals, where they were already the guests of the Messiah. Here the celestial future projected itself into the present in the form of a common cultic experience. In this enthusiastic atmosphere miracle and unlimited faith are natural. The new righteousness has its place here; when the heart is full of an expectation of this kind, such a gratitude, then the commandments of the Sermon on the Mount are no problem, but self-evident laws of life: this is the way to live at the threshold of eternity.

After all this, how should we characterize Jesus' idea of the kingdom of God, his gospel?

The best characterization is given by Jesus himself in two parables:

"The kingdom of heaven is like a mustard seed, which a man took and planted in his field. Though it is the smallest of all your seeds, yet when it grows, it is the largest of garden plants and becomes a tree, so that the birds of the air come and perch in its branches.

The kingdom of heaven is like yeast that a woman took and mixed into a large amount of flour until it worked all through the dough".

These two pictures, which would have been thoroughly intelligible and striking to those who first heard them, require some commentary if they are not to be misunderstood by modern listeners. With our biological way of thinking we are liable to import foreign ideas into Jesus' pictorial speech: in these parables we would like to find the idea of a gradual development and growth, which at the end, without leaps and breaks, brings us to the finished product. These pictorial words say something different to the Oriental: they illustrate a *mystery*, which is being perfected in secret. Man can only see certain glimpses of this mystery, and highly surprising glimpses at that: at first a very little seed, sometime later a big tree; the woman leaves her newly kneaded, lifeless dough, and when she returns, it is leavened, it rises and is expanding. This receives an even clearer expression in the related parable in Mk 4:26f.:

"This is what the kingdom of God is like. A man scatters seed on the ground. Night and day, whether he sleeps or gets up, the seed sprouts and grows, though he does not know how. All by itself the soil produces corn – first the stalk, then the ear, then the full grain in the ear. As soon as the grain is ripe, he puts the sickle to it, because the harvest has come".

The idea of the progress of the kingdom of God is clearly present here. This progress is, however, neither something quantitative nor conceived as a continuous development. The various stages are different revelations of the miraculous power at work in the world, and the fully-formed wheat is the last act of God's revelation. With this the end of all history suddenly comes. The various stages are interconnected only by a mysterious nexus of power.

Jesus knew that he stood in the midst of this nexus of power; yes, it was concentrated in him, it revealed itself in his person, it discharged itself through his words and Messianic actions. The mystery of the kingdom of God was one with him.

It was thus certain that he could not apply a rational measure to his life. It was not a question of planning, preparing, intentionally performing, securing and consolidating and there was no place here for the thought of making a contribution of abiding value and influence in society and within the framework of its order of life. His only task was to perform his restless work as the bearer of the secrets of God's kingdom. It was in this light that he saw his existence; he must interpret his activity and his fate in the light of the world-encompassing will of the almighty and all-wise Father. The conditions of life, personal relations, friendship and enmity, life and death must be subordinated to this point of view. Through all this the Eternal One fulfilled his plan for the world.

We cannot possibly adequately imagine the crises and upheavals which this attitude brought about in Jesus' life. It is clear however, that when a man ascribes such a unique significance to his own person and work, then the conflicts with his outward circumstances and practical experiences would have destroyed one who was not solidly grounded in a strong and continuous fellowship with God and who did not possess an unerringly ethical judgment. How Jesus wrestled with reality in thought and prayer on the lonely mountain-tops under the night sky of Galilee, is a sealed chapter of his life-story for us. We can only know those words, which reflect his maturing self-consciousness. Here the significant word is *not Messiah,* as already hinted, and we now understand more clearly why Jesus did not use that name, although he did not reject it. An old theocratic cliché like the title "Messiah" did not fit his idea of the kingdom of God, or his task and personal relation to it. He needed a new self-designation, and he found it in "The Son of Man".

The Son of Man

What we mean by "human being" the Oriental expressed in his sonorous language by "Son of Man". Son of man thus means simply a *human being.* When pious Jews, who "waited for the consolation of Israel" and looked forward to the coming age with longing, spoke about the "Son of Man" and his day, they referred to a definite human being, the *heavenly man,* who would reveal himself as the Saviour at the end of time. This expectation of a heavenly saviour in human form appears to have had its origin in Iran, but for the rest it is still unresolved historically. Outside of the New Testament we have only a few traces of this complex of apocalyptic ideas. Best known and for Jesus certainly of great significance is a passage in the Book of Daniel, an apocalypse written about 150 B.C. during the Syrian era of martyrdom. Here we read in the seventh chapter the description of a vision, which Daniel received one night in his camp.

First he sees four beasts arise up from the sea – they are the four world empires, the Babylonian, the Median, the Persian and the Syrian-Greek. Furthermore, he beholds a figure of awe-inspiring age, in snow-white raiment sitting on a throne of flames, from which a river of fire went forth, and surrounded by innumerable servants. The beasts are partly killed, and partly deprived of their power. Thereafter he sees,

> "One like a son of man,
> coming with the clouds of heaven.
> He approached the Ancient of Days
> and was led into his presence.
> He was given authority, glory and sovereign power;
> all peoples, nations and men of every language
> worshipped him.
> His dominion is an everlasting dominion,

that will not pass away,
and his kingdom is one that will never be destroyed".

From this passage we see to what sector of Jewish piety the "Son of Man" belongs. It is the speculations and visions, which deal with the judgment of the world and the new aeon, that form the framework around this figure. Here we find ourselves in a different sphere than that of the old Jewish future hope.

This gives us the historical background for John the Baptist's announcement of "The Coming One", the great judge with the shovel in his hand. And when Jesus speaks of the "Son of Man", it is evidently first and foremost in an apocalyptic sense that he speaks it, it is that human figure who will come on the clouds at the end of time as judge and Saviour in heavenly splendor, surrounded by his angels.

Jesus speaks of the "Son of Man" in the third person: "You will see the Son of Man sitting at the right hand of the Mighty One and coming on the clouds of heaven." But thereby he refers to himself, just like the Johannine Christ calls himself the "Son". This solemn expression betrays Jesus' feeling that his human personality was the bearer of a superhuman task, that his individual I was a vessel which contained a supra-individual content. He stood, so to speak, at a certain distance from himself as God's chosen servant at the final time, as the revelation of the kingdom of God in the world.

The apocalyptic Saviour-title the "Son of Man" was for Jesus not merely a traditional label. The meaning of the word itself and its import of "human being" had a deep significance for him. Jesus found in this designation the secret which he bore in his own being: that the divine Saviour and Judge, the Revealer of the new heavenly aeon was a human being, and in particular one of "the little ones", the "poor ones". This secret found its significative expression and thereby its higher illumination in the apocalyptic tradition and the holy prophet's designation, "The Son of Man".

Here we stand before a highly remarkable historical phenomenon. A man without social and political influence, an itinerant teacher, possesses this unheard of self-consciousness, which surpasses all human measures. *At the same time* his personality and teaching are destitute of all exaltation. He proclaims and interprets the will of God with sober clarity and unerring certainty. In his innermost being authority and humility are united, a tenderness that sacrifices everything and an inexorable severity. The secret of this person is great and unfathomable. We can only establish the fact and elucidate the historical presuppositions. The deepest foundations of Jesus' conviction of his high calling lie hidden from our sight; they rest in the inaccessible sanctuary of personal fellowship with God.

But if we ask about the historical presuppositions for Jesus' distinctive self-consciousness, then we need to pay attention above all to the self-understanding of Judaism, its consciousness of being *the chosen people* – even as the little, oppressed, poor and powerless nation they were. This idea is already found already in the poet-prophet, who has written Isaiah 40–55. Ever since his time the law of paradox prevails in the Jewish religious thinking: the thoughts and actions of God are contrary to all human values and aspirations. The definitive revelation of God therefore consists in his abolishing everything that is of man and changing it to its opposite. The first become last, and the last become first.

Furthermore, we find the idea widespread not only in Judaism, but also in the entire oriental-Greek world, that it is precisely the "poor", the little ones, that are heirs to the kingdom of God; the one who is despised, the unappreciated, indeed, the rejected human being becomes the instrument for God's revelation. We see here the result of an old contrast between the primitive and genuine oriental worship of *the ruler*, the chief, the holy, radiant king and priest on the one hand, and on the other, the prophet, the man of the people, the shepherd, the peasant, the craftsman, who is seized irresistibly by the Spirit of God and is driven by an inner compulsion away from his usual occupation, in order to appear, despite all piety and old custom, even at the sanctuary or the palace, flinging his prophecies and passionate speeches of punishment at the face of dynasts. In this battle the prophet triumphed and with him the thought that God chooses his messengers among those who are not esteemed in the eyes of the world. Gradually the figure of the prophet is refined through *martyrdom:* God reveals himself and works through the tormented, suffering man. We also meet this conviction in Second Isaiah, in the songs of the Suffering Servant of the Lord.

We also find these thoughts in Jesus, though deeper and more purified: without any grudge and without being connected with personal or national dreams of happiness. They spring up out of his consciousness of being called by God to serve God and people, his brothers, in a very special way.

The contrast between present humility and future glorification, the contrast which forms the inner tension in the idea of the Son of Man, was accordingly a holy legacy which Jesus received from the deepest experience of his people. In his original way he hints at this idea in his question: the Messiah is according to David's own inspired words his lord; how then can he be David's son? In this question there was certainly no hidden polemic against the conviction that the Messiah would belong to the old royal dynasty. Nor did it entail any sting against the traditional Messianic hope. What we see here is something of that which went on in Jesus' mind with respect to his task and his destiny, namely the question: why must he who represents the rule of God, be David's son, a son of man? His opponents owed him an answer concerning this point. He himself was quite clear about it: the messenger of God was the "Son of Man", the man among men, but chosen from among all men to serve the kingdom of God.

This service also included *sacrifice of life:*

> "The Son of Man did not come
> to be served,
> but to serve,
> and to give his life as a ransom for many."

The road to perfection goes through death, the most terrible of all crises, where the "servant" goes under, and from whom the heavenly man emerges in glory. But death does not merely mean this radical transformation of the Son of Man's personal existence. His death is simultaneously "a ransom for many", an expiation, a purification of the sinful people (= "the many" according to the Jewish expression) and a victory over death and the demonic power of the world.

That such was the Father's will gradually became Jesus' firm conviction. The thought of death was not far away from the One who considered himself chosen to be the "Son of Man". Persecution and martyrdom had of course been the lot of the prophets in Israel since times immemorial. In the book of Second Isaiah the Lord's suffering and executed servant is the moving figure behind the time of happiness that is ushered. The bloody destiny of John the Baptist cast its gloomy shadow over the start of Jesus' ministry. In the bitter attacks of legalistic pharisaism, he was not slow to read his own condemnation, and he knew that the ever distrustful, unscrupulous prince of Tiberias had sent his spies out after him. For this reason he warned his disciples: "Watch out for the yeast of the Pharisees and that of Herodes!" He himself did not take any precautionary measures, because he was quite clear about what must come to pass. When they said to him: "Leave this place and go somewhere else. Herodes wants to kill you!" he answered:

> "Go tell that fox, 'I will drive out demons and heal people today and tomorrow, and on the third day I will reach my goal. In any case, I must keep going today and tomorrow and the next day – for surely no prophet can die outside Jerusalem'."

When the Passover feast drew near, and the people of Galilee prepared to go up to Jerusalem, Jesus also set out with his disciples to go there. What was it that drove him to present himself in the Holy City at the great feast among the enormous multitudes of pilgrims, and appear at the headquarters of the enemy? According to the Gospels he went to Jerusalem to meet his death:

> "We are going up to Jerusalem,
> and the Son of Man will be betrayed to the chief
> priests and teachers of the law.
> They will condemn him to death
> and will hand him over to the Gentiles,
> who will mock him and spit on him,
> flog him and kill him.
> Three days later he will rise."

It need not be doubted that Jesus took this step because he knew that the decisive time had drawn near, the time had come. The Gospel had been proclaimed to the poor in all Galilee, the disciples had confessed their faith in him, revolutionary fanatics threatend to light the fire of revolt among the people, apathy met him on one side, hate on the other, secret strings were being pulled around him to ensnare him. In all this Jesus traced the activity of the great Enemy: the more powerfully the kingdom of God went forth in word and deed, the more intensive the activities from the other side became. Faced with its annihilation, Satan's kingdom made its last, desperate efforts to check its doom. It was the Enemy who had sown apathy in the minds of the crowds and put murderous thoughts in the heart of his earthly opponents. But now the time had come to meet him on his own ground and destroy his power over the world and God's holy people.

In Jerusalem Jesus makes his appearance in a way that shows that he intentionally called forth the catastrophe. His frame of mind during this time is revealed by the violent scene at the temple, where he made a whip out of cords and drove all those who sold sacrificial animals away from the temple presincts, and overturned the tables of the money changers. This was a Messianic act, which prophetically foreshadowed the great judgment. He also preached in the sharpest possible tone against the pharisees and the scribes, whom he accused of hypocrisy, greed, and pride. He predicted the destruction of the temple and the cult that was connected with it; Jerusalem was to be laid in ruin and Israel to be rejected. He himself would erect a new temple in a wondrous way, and another people would take over the Lord's vineyard.

This "people" consisted of his *disciples,* the people of the Messiah. He had appointed Simon bar Jona as their leader, to whom he gave the name Kephas, that rock (in Greek *petra,* of which *Petros),* in that he said: "On this rock I will build my church". He would now leave this little community but only for a very brief time: "the third day", i.e. immediately he would return to them with the kingdom of God "in power". Just before the feast began, he had a farewell supper with his disciples, during which he spoke prophetically of his imminent death in terms of establishing a new covenant based on the remission of sins. He explained that the next time they gathered for a common meal with him, it would be in the new world:

> "I tell you the truth,
> I will not drink again
> of the fruit of the vine
> until that day when I drink it anew
> in the kingdom of God".

Immediately thereafter he went out to the Mount of Olives, where in a garden, Gethsemane, he was arrested and brought to the palace of the high priest, and later to the procurator. During both interrogations Jesus admitted to being the Messiah. The disciples left him and fled.

The Lord

One of Jesus' last words to his disciples was this: "I will go ahead of you to Galilee", i.e. Jesus explained that when he had gone through the crisis of death, he would meet his disciples again and lead them to Galilee, where the kingdom of God would be revealed in all its splendour and power. This word was decisive for the disciples as soon as they recovered from their initial shock. They returned to Galilee under the leadership of the Invisible Master, and there at the lake, where once they had received their call, they now received the revelations. A certain tradition of the first appearance of the Risen One in Galilee lies behind the narrative of John 21.

At the same time, however, revelations were given to Jesus' disciples in Judea, as we see in the narrative about the Emmaus disciples in Luke 24. These events resulted in the gathering of Jesus' followers in Jerusalem surely in order to await the parousia (i.e. the revelation of the Messiah with the kingdom of God). During this time together, characterized by tension and expectation, on the day of Pentecost, a mighty eruption of religious enthusiasm took place, which produced the first public confession of Jesus and at the same time introduced the formation of a Christian church and missionary activity.

In this church the conviction of the immediate nearness of the kingdom of God was alive in the form of a burning expectation of Jesus' revelation from heaven ("parousia"). The designation "The Son of Man" in these circumstances quickly lost its current interest; it was too reminiscent of Jesus' humility and degradation during his earthly life. In its place the term "Messiah" came to the foreground as the biblically-based designation of the risen Jesus, seated on God's right hand.

But even the title of Messiah was gradually pushed aside, or more correctly "Christ" (the Greek equivalent of Messiah) became a proper name, with the result that Jesus now had a double name – which was very usual at that time – namely, Jesus Christ or Christ Jesus. His title now became *"the Lord"* (in Greek: *kyrios*). This new title reflects the position which the risen Jesus Messiah assumed in his Church: he is the divine Helper and the absolute authority – both ideas are found in the title "the Lord". The disciples' experience of Jesus' will to save, of the power and authority of his person, now appear in the form of a *faith,* it appears as an unshakeable conviction of his almightiness and love and as an unconditional and unlimited subjection under his will. That which was historically given and experienced is now lifted to the sphere of the absolute.

Religious life in the primitive Church, faith and hope, was borne from the outset, not by the individual, but by the experience and confession of the community. For this reason it had its center and its source of strength in *worship,* and this again, concentrated itself around *the holy supper*. At this point we see perhaps clearer than anywhere else how that which is historically conditioned is sublimated in the cult. The Holy Communion was a continuation of the common meals of Jesus with his disciples, which undoubtedly had had a Messianic character and were characterized by a consciousness of the presence of the kingdom of God in the Son of Man and its imminent break-through in power. When therefore, following the Messiah's resurrection from the dead, the faithful sat around the table in remembrance of him, this evoked Jesus' cultic presence. The Lord was there present invisibly and united himself with his own by his spirit. Gradually the supper was ritually and dogmatically expanded under the influence of all kinds of Jewish and Hellenistic motifs.

Inseparably united with the Lord was the *Spirit,* who worked visibly and perceptibly in the church through prophecy, works of power, ecstasy, heroism, etc. This Spirit was sent by the risen Lord, who in his earthly existence and activities had had the Spirit without measure and now gave it to his confessors. Also at this point we can discern the line which leads back to Jesus. The spiritual and supernatural experiences, which the disciples had while following him, had pre-conditioned and prepared them for the effects of the Spirit in the Church, and led them to conceive of the Lord and the Spirit as one.

This close union of the Lord and the Spirit is very important for the development of faith in Christ and for Christian dogma. The historical picture of Jesus and the infinite experience of the Spirit have been united. The historical picture is thus lifted high above this world. At the same time it sets the characteristic mark of a personality on what is otherwise incomprehensible and metaphysical.

Thus Christian dogma has its roots in Jesus' own consciousness and the disciples' personal experience in following him. It has thereafter proceeded from the Church's common experience and confession, from the cultus. The point of departure for the formation of doctrine is the enthusiastic confession: *Jesus is Lord!* The confession could even take the form of an enumeration of the salvation-historical events, which constitute the historical basis of the faith and fill it with concrete content. Such a presentation did not have dogmatic, but cultic character. In their being proclaimed and enumerated, these events fulfilled themselves afresh and achieved salvation here and now. The oldest confession of this kind that we have is found in Paul, in 1 Cor 15, presented as the confession of the whole church:

> "For what I received I passed on to you as of first importance,
> that Christ died for our sins according to the Scriptures,
> that he was buried,

> that he was raised on the third day according to the Scriptures,
> and that he appeared to Peter, and then to the Twelve".

The sense of the immediate reality of this was so strong that the ideas, cosmic and theological, which very soon were added to this confession, were not understood or felt to be a human theory but an inspired superior insight, a pneumatic gnosis. How marginally theoretical this gnosis was, we see from the fact that it sometimes appears as poetry, in the form of a hymn, as e.g. in the epistle to the Philippians, where we have a very old christological hymn of clearly oriental-Semitic stamp:

> "Christ Jesus
> Who, being in the very nature of God,
> did not consider equality with God
> something to be grasped,
>
> But made himself nothing,
> taking the very nature of a servant,
> being made in human likeness.
>
> And being found in appearance as a man,
> he humbled himself
> and became obedient to death – even the death on a cross.
>
> Therefore God exalted him to the highest place
> and gave him the name
> that is above every name,
>
> That at the name of Jesus
> every knee should bow,
> in heaven and on earth and under the earth,
>
> And every tongue confess that
> Jesus Christ is Lord,
> to the glory of God the Father."

Faith in Christ and the worship of Christ have their historical presuppositions in the spiritual atmosphere which developed in the community of Jesus' disciples. The conviction concerning the Master's Messianic place in the kingdom of God which he proclaimed, and the experience of his wisdom, love, and authority gave to the disciples the common ground for rising up after the collapse they had experienced, and for continuing their life together under the Master's invisible guidance.

But this conviction and resilience of the disciples *vis-à-vis* the catastrophe, had its ultimate and basic presupposition in Jesus' own self-consciousness and his personal conduct. Therefore, the secret of the Church's faith in Christ ultimately goes back to the secret of Jesus' personality, which found its expression in the self-designation "The Son of Man".

Sensing the contradiction between his outward appearance and his position in the kingdom of God, Jesus kept referring to himself by this designation and at one point said: "Blessed is the man who is not offended on account of me!" This offence, which was inherent in the historical Jesus, was intensified to the utmost through his death on the Cross. With reference to his preaching of a crucified Messiah, Paul says that it is "a stumbling block to Jews and foolishness to Gentiles". The intimate fellowship with God and the immense ethical power, which bore Jesus up through the tension between the reality of time and the world of eternity, as well as through martyrdom, was at the same time sufficiently intimate and strong to clear away that which constituted an offence to his disciples and to generate a living and conquering faith. Paul, the first theologian of the Church, found in the paradox of Christ the revelation of God's wisdom (1 Cor 1:18–31). We meet the same line of thought on Jesus' lips according to the Gospel tradition (Mt 11:25–27):

> "I praise you, Father,
> Lord of heaven and earth,
> because you have hidden these things
> from the wise and learned,
> and revealed them
> to little children.
> Yes, Father, for this was your good pleasure!"

And further down:

> "All things have been committed to me by my Father.
> No-one knows the Son except the Father,
> and no-one knows the Father except the Son
> and those to whom the Son chooses to reveal him".

These words – the last ones may or may not have been said by Jesus – reveal Jesus' innermost thought to give us an authentic hint, as to who he claimed to be.

Literature

The above sketch of Jesus is closely related to the following works:

A. Schweitzer, *Geschichte der Leben-Jesu-Forschung,* 2nd ed. 1913
L. Brun, *Jesu evangelium,* 2nd ed. Oslo 1926
L. Brun, *Jesus i ljuset av historisk forskning,* Stockholm 1919
L. Brun, *Jesu billede*, Oslo 1910
P. Wernle, *Jesus,* 1916
E. Aurelius, *Jesu messiasmedvetande,* 1918
E. Aurelius, *Jesu tankar om sitt lidande och sin död,* 1919
E. von Dobschütz, *Kristustro og kristenliv i lyset av det nye testamente,* Oslo 1922
The Barthian interpretation of Jesus has received a splendid presentation by R. Bultmann, *Jesus,* 1928 (Swed. tr.)

The liberal portrait of Jesus is drawn by A. Harnack's famous *The Essence of Christianity,* 1900 and is to be found in:

A. B. Drachmann, *Christendommens oprindelse,* Köpenhamn 1919
D. Nielsen, *Den historiske Jesus,* Köpenhamn 1924
K. Schjelderup, *Vem Jesus var och vad kyrkan har gjort honom till,* Stockholm 1928

Radical criticism of the gospel tradition is to be found in:

W. Wrede, *Das Messiasgeheimnis in den Evangelien,* 2nd ed. 1907
W. Bousset, *Jesus* (in Religionshistoriska folkböcker), Stockholm

Excepta fornicationis causa

(1944)

"Anyone who divorces his wife, *except for marital unfaithfulness* (παρεκτὸς λόγου πορνείας), causes her to become an adulteress" (Mt 5:32). The words in italics are considered by many to be secondary. Originally Jesus prohibited every kind of divorce without exception. The exception which the traditional text prescribes, smacks – so it is said – of Church laws and is not in harmony with the unconditional, uncompromising way in which Jesus formulates his commandments. Whatever the case may be in this regard, we are also under obligation to determine the meaning of such an eventually secondary addition. This moreover, to be sure, must be expected to have a specially stringent, well-defined character, if it is an expression of the legal practice of the early Church.[1]

What is strange, however, is that the words in question cause significant difficulties. *Firstly,* it is striking that the text speaks of πορνεία, harlotry, fornication, in a context which has to do with marriage, μοιχεία. *Secondly,* adultery (i.e. the relation of a married woman with a man other than her husband – the relation of a married man with an unmarried woman or a woman not engaged to any man was reckoned as harlotry) was punishable by death (Dt 22:22f.). For this reason divorce in such cases could hardly come into question, since the marriage was now dissolved in a much more drastic way.

The latter difficulty could perhaps be disregarded. It is not quite certain that the rigorous practice prescribed by the law was applicable in Jesus' time. And if it were applicable, it is conceivable that the execution was preceded by a formal divorce procedure.

The terminological problem, however, remains: the text says πορνεία rather than μοιχεία.[2] It is hardly credible that a text like the Gospel of Matthew, which

[1] For literature on this question see W. Bauer on ἀπολύω (col. 161), as well as Falck-Hansen, *Skilmisse,* Oslo 1931, and J. Sickenberger, "Unzuchtklausel im Matthäusevangelium", *Theol. Quartalsschrift* Vol. 123 (1942), pp. 189–206; K. Staab, *Z. f. kath. Theol.* 67 (1943), pp. 36ff.

[2] The distinction between μοιχεία *(adulterium)* and πορνεία *(stuprum)* is maintained throughout ancient times. If the verb πορνεύειν is used of a *married* woman, it does not mean that on one or more occasions she has violated her marriage, but that she practices regular fornication as a harlot. Cf. Hos 2:2ff. ἐξεπόρνευσεν ἡ μήτηρ αὐτῶν, Sir. 23:23: ἐν πορνείᾳ

has been subjected to Church editing, would express itself carelessly on such an important point as divorce. In the face of such a difficulty it may perhaps be worth considering a new interpretation of the words παρεκτὸς λόγου πορνείας, namely, that the expression does not refer to illegitimate sexual intercourse on the part of the woman *within* marriage, but to fornication committed before marriage. The man discovers immediately after the wedding that his newly-wed wife is not a virgin (cf. Dt 22:13ff.), or he finds out sooner or later that his betrothed is pregnant, and that the pregnancy goes back to a time before he married her. She is a πόρνη (which, however, does not *necessarily* mean that she is a harlot). In this case he can divorce her. In the light of this train of thought the story of Joseph and Mary receives illustrative significance. After Mary had been betrothed to Joseph she was found pregnant. But Joseph, who was a righteous man, did not want to bring dishonor on her, and decided to divorce her secretly (Mt 1:18f.). We should certainly suppose that Mary's pregnancy was discovered shortly after her betrothal to Joseph, that its beginning must date to a time before the betrothal (in other words, differently from Lk 1:27), otherwise there would apparently be a case of adultery here, which could hardly be treated as mildly as Joseph treated it.[3]

If the above interpretation of Mt 5:32 is correct, it then perhaps explains why the death penalty, ordained by the Law, is not heeded. For if a woman, after coming to live with her husband was proved to have committed fornication before her betrothal, that would not qualify for any punishment. But the husband had, of course, the right to divorce her if he wanted. This right is expressly decreed by Mt 5:32. The words should be understood, however, as a *concession,* not as a decree. It is not prescribed that the man in such cases shall unconditionally divorce his wife. But he *can* do it, in which case the marriage is anulled before God as well, so that if the woman then marries again, her first husband will not be guilty of having caused adultery.

The thesis that the clause παρεκτὸς λόγου πορνείας does not refer to adultery appears to me to be supported by the following reflection. If the wife in a family within the Jewish-Christian Palestinian Church was taken in the act or proved guilty of adultery, if she was not a baptized member of the Church, the situation that had arisen was the Christian husband's private business. He could simply divorce his unfaithful wife. But it is unlikely that he, as a Christian, felt bound by the Deuteronomic regulations on punishment. He belonged to "Israel

ἐμοιχεύθη, and Dio Cassius 60:60 (about Messalina): ἐμοιχεύετο καὶ ἐπορνεύετο. It is, however, out of the question that παρεκτὸς λόγου πορνείας should mean: "except in cases where the wife happens to be a harlot"!

[3] Legal proceedings were to be taken unconditionally against adultery, cf. the Mishnah tractate *Sota* iv-v. The purity and holiness of Israel demanded this.

according to the Spirit" and interpreted the Scriptures from this point of view. However, if the woman herself was a Christian, then adultery on her side came under church discipline, in which case the situation that had arisen could not be solved by the simple formula of divorce. The woman had committed a sin unto death – this was the Christian interpretation of Dt 22 – and the Church had to intervene through its elders and excommunicate the adulteress. Such an abomination must be wiped out from the ekklesia of the saints. This naturally involved the dissolution of a marriage; but is it conceivable that a Church *auctor* in formulating the divorce command *would have reckoned at all with such a terrible eventuality as the adultery of a Christian woman?* And would he have reckoned therewith with such a situation as a matter of course, so as to calmly include within the command, for the sake of such cases – in a clause, so to speak – a few words designating adultery within Christian marriage as a ground for divorce? It appears highly incredible. That the *auctor* would have had in mind "mixed" marriages when he formulated the regulations, is not probable either. For it must have been very rare that in a Christian home the wife, too, did not belong to the Church.

If we think of cases where the wife, following marriage or betrothal proves to have committed πορνεία earlier (before marriage, not as betrothed), it would naturally be a serious matter warranting divorce, but it would not be nearly as serious a catastrophe as adultery. In this case it would not be necessary to engage church discipline. Thus far Mt 5:32 could be understood as an instance of early Church practice in such cases. But one may again ask: Could such a regulation as that of Mt 5:32 – interpreted according to my suggestion – have any wide applicability in the oldest Jewish-Christian Church? Christian men, who were not bound by a marriage contracted in their pre-Christian state, certainly married only Christian women within the Church. And if such a bride had lost her virginity or was simply an earlier harlot, this matter had been cleared up and dealt with by baptism and the remission of sins, and could not therefore come as an unexpected discovery later.

However one may look at that which is referred to in Mt 5:32, whether it is adultery or the wife's (fiancée's) pre-marital fornication – in either case we arrive at he same result, viz. that this regulation cannot be naturally explained as evidence of the early Church's application of ecclesiastical law. The words παρεκτὸς λόγου πορνείας should then be understood either as a purely *academic gloss,* inserted in the absolute command on divorce, or as a *pre-Church* regulation, formulated by Jesus himself as a rule applicable to his disciples in Galilee and Judea. The regulation must have come into being before the Christian Church of Palestine had separated from the Synagogue and had developed its own independent ecclesiastical laws and ecclesiastical discipline. That Jesus regulated his disciples' personal and mutual relations on important points through authoritative regulations ought to be self-evident, even if it were not clearly attested.[4] An example of such Messianic legislation concerning the Church is the command regarding divorce in Mt 5:32. It can only be understood within the context of Jesus' life. Marriage was not yet Christianized, and it might turn out that a μαθητής found that his betrothed or newly-wed wife was stained by πορνεία. Jesus then concedes divorce in such cases. Among the many Jewish grounds for divorce he chooses and approves of the most flagrant one. No disciple should be *obliged* to continue in marriage with a woman who has stained herself with whoredom.[5] If one accepts that Jesus actually legislated for his disciples, then there is nothing surprising about such a regulation.

[4] The clearest example of pre-Church discipleship order is the regulations for treating an erring brother in Mt 18. There is no reason to doubt that these regulations go back to Jesus himself, although in their present form they have been "ecclesiasticized" (*ecclesia*).

[5] That Jesus considered adultery as a sin unto death is evident; it leads to Gehenna. Even fornication which did not require punishment, was a transgression of God's command and will. Jesus did not want to bind a disciple to a woman of this kind. This attitude is not in conflict with the fact that Jesus opened the kingdom of God for the harlot and that he was displeased when people anticipated God's judgment on the woman taken in adultery (Jn 7:53ff.).

Neutestamentliche Wortforschung

Zu Matth. 11,11–15

(1946)

Die Boten des gefangenen Täufers sind mit der Antwort Jesu fortgezogen, und Jesus spricht nun zum Volk über ihn. Zunächst tadelt er die wegen ihres Verhaltens zu Johannes, den sie einst als einen großen ὄχλοι Propheten gefeiert, jetzt aber – das ist der indirekte Tadel – total vergessen haben (V. 7–10).[1] Die Fortsetzung folgt in den ironischen Worten V. 16–18, die die völlige Haltungslosigkeit des Volkes gegenüber sowohl Johannes als Jesus brandmarken. Dazwischen schiebt sich aber ein Redestück ein (V. 11–15), das die Unterlegenheit des Johannes am Himmelreich gemessen betont. Johannes ist zwar der Größte unter denen, die von Frauen geboren sind, aber der Kleinste im Himmelreich ist (kraft seiner Anteilnahme am Messiasreich) größer als er. Die folgenden Worte, die von den βιασταί reden, die das Himmelreich "rauben", können m. E. nur auf *die Täufergemeinde* zielen. Diese sieht in Johannes den Messias und will selbst die messianische Gemeinde der Endzeit sein. Das ist aber eine gewaltsame Usurpation. Der messianische Anspruch der Täufergemeinde steht im Widerspruch zum Gesetz und zu den Propheten, denn (γάρ) diese weissagten alle mit Bezug auf Johannes (ἕως Ἰωάννου), nämlich, daß er der kommende Elias (nicht der Messias!) ist. Die Worte εἰ θέλετε δέξασθαι sollen zwischen zwei Kommata stehen und richten sich in Wirklichkeit an die Täufergemeinde. Erst im Zusammenhang der Matthäus-Rede haben sie eine Adresse ans Volk bekommen. – Das eben angedeutete Verständnis der Verse 12–15 erheischt einige verdeutlichende Bemerkungen. V. 12: Durch den Anspruch der Täufergemeinde auf den Besitz des Reiches Gottes oder auf dessen Antwartschaft wird dem Himmelreich Gewalt angetan. Βιάζεται ist passiv, und der Satz ἡ βασιλεία τῶν οὐρανῶν βιάζεται bildet mit dem folgenden καὶ βιασταὶ ἁρπάζουσιν αὐτήν einen echt semitischen, synonymen Parallelismus.[2] Johannes selbst wird nicht für das

[1] Zu diesen Versen vgl. *meinen* Aufsatz in *Coniectanea Neotestamentica* IV, 1940, S. 9f. und F. Overbeck, *Das Johannes-Evangelium,* 1941, S. 419ff.; O. hält, mit Recht, Joh. 5,35 für einen Ausläufer synoptischer Tradition.

[2] Im *ThWBzNT* hat G. Schrenk Matth, 11,12 behandelt (I, S. 608ff.). Er kommt zu dem

Verhalten seiner Jünger verantwortlich gemacht, vgl. die unpersönliche Formulierung ἀπὸ τῶν ἡμερῶν Ἰωάννου τοῦ βαπτιστοῦ Johannes hat ja auch vom Gefängnis aus Jesus befragen lassen: "Bist du der Kommende?" Er ist am βιάζεσθαι des Himmelreiches unschuldig. Die Worte ἕως ἄρτι zeigen, daß die Täufergemeinde, allem Widerspruch zum Trotz, hartnäckig an ihrem Anspruch festhält. Eine Umkehr ist nicht geschehen. – V. 13: Dieser Satz ist zu übersetzen: Die Weissagung des Gesetzes und der Propheten geht einstimmig (πάντες) darauf aus, daß er der kommende Elias ist. Der Inhalt der Weissagung folgt in V. 14: Die Einführung des Objektsatzes durch ein καί nach verba sentiendi und declarandi ist im Spätgriechischen eine wohlbekannte Erscheinung.[3] Ein charakteristisches Beispiel haben wir Mark. 6,14: ἤκουσεν ὁ βασιλεὺς Ἡρῴδης ... καὶ (= ὅτι) ἔλεγον ὅτι Ἰωάννης ὁ βαπτίζων ἐγήγερται ἐκ νεκρῶν ...[4] Αὐτός ist nicht betont *(ipse,* "gerade er"), sondern unbetontes Subjekt für ἐστίν.[5] Daß Johannes nach dem Zeugnis der ganzen Schrift nicht der Messias, sondern (nur) Elias ist, muß natürlich für die Täufergemeinde eine bittere Wahrheit sein. Es bedarf der Mahnung: ὁ ἔχων ὦτα ἀκουέτω – Die hier vorgelegte Deutung von V. 11–15 könnte zu weitläufigen literarkritischen und formgeschichtlichen Betrachtungen Anlaß geben, aber ich begnüge mich einstweilen mit dem schon Gesagten. Vielleicht kann die vorgeschlagene Auslegung des vielumstrittenen Abschnittes für der Diskussion wert befunden werden.

Ergebnis, daß die βιασταί (dämonische) Feindesgewalten sind, die das Himmelreich den Menschen wegraffen wollen. Aber βίᾳ ἁρπάζειν, βιάζεσθαι καὶ ἁρπάζειν geschieht gewöhnlich im eigenen Interesse (vgl. H. Almqvist, *Plutarch und das Neue Testament* [Acta Seminarii Neotestamentici Upsaliensis XV, 1946, S. 38]), und die βιασταί Matth. 11,12 werden keine Ausnahme davon machen.

[3] Zahlreiche Belege bei H. Ljungvik, *Beiträge zur Syntax der spät-griechischen Volkssprache* (Skrifter utgivna av K. Humanistiska Vetenskapssamfundet i Uppsala, 27, 3, 1932), S. 80ff.; vgl. *P. Grenf.* I, 53 γράφει ψανῆς στρατιώτης καὶ ἀπόνοιαν φορεῖς "der Soldat Psanes schreibt, daß du dich unsinnig benimmst".

[4] Vgl. Ljungvik, *ZNW* 35 (1934), S. 90ff.

[5] Unbetontes αὐτός als Verbalsubjekt z. B. Luk. 4,15; 15,14; 17,13; 24,14; G. Bonaccorsi, *Primi saggi di filologia neotestamentaria* I, Torino 1933 zu Matth. 5,4 (S. 5) und Luk. 5,1 (S. 192): "καὶ αὐτός = *et ille,* non *et ipse,* ... di solito l'αὐτός non ha alcuna enfasi o appena percettibile." – Zu Mark. 4,27 (ὡς οὐκ οἶδεν αὐτός = "ohne daß er es bemerkt" vgl. P. Jouon, *L'Evangile de Notre Seigneur Jésus-Christ* (*Verbum Salutis* V), Paris 1930, S. 204.

Part Two

The Fourth Gospel

Jesus' Farewell Discourse in the Fourth Gospel

An Introduction to the Johannine Question

(1938)

All four Evangelists describe how Jesus spent his last evening together with his Disciples, and for all of them this event has the character of a supper. The details of the scene in the Synoptics (= Syn), however, are very different from those in John (= Jn). While the former relate only what Jesus did and said at the end of the meal when he divided the bread and the wine to the Disciples, that is, a very brief pericope, the Fourth Gospel (= FG) gives us a detailed description that includes the washing of feet as well as a fairly long discourse by Jesus with certain dialogical elements by the Disciples (13–16). This leads to a prayer to the Father (17). Common to both the Syn and the FG, in addition to the situation itself (the meal), are only the words about the traitor, Judas Iscariot. A somewhat middle position is taken by the Gospel of Luke, which, following the pericope about the Last Supper (22:14–23), communicates a number of sayings of Jesus, which are partly concerned with the farewell words in Jn (e.g. service in the circle of disciples, Jesus intercession for Peter, prediction of Peter's denial).

This agreement between Lk and the FG implies the existence of a richer tradition on the Last Supper than merely the pericope on the Eucharist. In the nature of the case much more must have been said at this juncture than the brief words we have about the traitor or at the giving of the bread and the wine. We can assume, however, with certainty that the gist of the words of Jesus during the last evening could be narrated: there was a tradition. This tradition, to be sure, is identical neither with Lk 22:14–23 nor Jn 13–17. In both cases we have reworking, selection, or expansion of the traditional material about which we can only have a general idea. This redactional shaping has much greater dimensions and an immensely more thorough character in the FG than in Lk. The Johannine farewell discourses are not merely a few logia freely joined together as in the third Gospel, they form a rather long speech with varying motives and certain redactional details that break up the monological uniformity. As the speech progresses a hightening of the intensity becomes unmistakable, the culmination is reached with the high-pitched, monumental final prayer.

Nevertheless, we can see that even in the FG the passage in question is not a free construction. The Evangelist was *bound by certain material,* to which he had to give literary form. This implied that the boundaries for his redactional activity were sharply drawn. The clearest and most noticeable evidence for this is 14:30f., where Jesus underscores the end of his speech and even suggests that they depart: "Come now, let us leave!", whereupon in 15:1 he goes on into a new line of thought. It is obvious here that 13:31 marks the end of a tradition complex, which the Evangelist supplements with other traditions, without abolishing the disturbing final exhortation, which presumably he interpreted spiritually about the severing of the heart from the world and its going to the Father in imitation of and fellowship with the Son. Here we have a palpable testimony to the dependence of the Evangelist on the material at his disposal.

This dependence appears also in the details of the composition itself. In the Johannine farewell discourses, we stand exactly before the same phenomenon that is found in the Synoptic speeches of Jesus (e.g. the Sermon on the Mount), namely, that related sayings of Jesus have been assembled into larger complexes, to what in a way are connected speeches. On closer inspection, these are seen to be conglomerates or perhaps, better, agglomerates of Jesus's words, which have been lined up or are barely held together in a very simple means. The redactional technique is surely more developed in the FG, but even there the simple principle of composition is unmistakable: we meet constantly repetitions and variations of the same thought, hurried transitions and leaps in the train of thought, which meander their way forward without a clearly logical progress. This has been explained and somewhat excused by the idea that the Apostle was very old when he wrote his Gospel, so that he could not give a connected presentation. These simplistic attempts to save John's authorial prestige, of course, have only curiosity interest, showing what one may achieve with quasi-pious apologetic. All one achieves is to make ridiculous what one wishes to defend. The author of the FG does not need to excuse himself for his work. On the contrary, he can lay claims to recognition and gratitude. For he has arranged quite piously the Jesus tradition that was at his disposal in a literary framework. This is what gives to his Gospel such a high religious and historical value.

The historical investigation therefore faces exactly the same fundamental problem with regard to the FG as when it addresses the Synoptic material. In Synoptic research the analysis of the material has been conducted with extraordinary vigour and significant success throughout a whole century. The most recent era, the "form-critical", has brought to the foreground certain viewpoints that have given a great impulse to the research of tradition in this and other areas. However, the Synoptics seem to have absorbed all the resources for Gospel study. In this respect the FG has been unfairly treated, but one need not be a prophet in order to divine that sooner or later exegesis is going to cast itself with burning interest upon *the Johannine tradition.* The dogma about the wholly secondary, structured character of the FG on the one hand, and the obvious unreasonableness of a fossilized apologetic on the other have placed the FG in obscurity, while the generally recognized more immediate proximity of the Synoptics to Jesus has allowed the three older Gospels to exert such an irresistible magnetism on the mind of scholars. This interest, however, will gradually stretch also to the FG, and then it will certainly place this Gospel writing in a historically truer light, lifting it above the battle between conservative apologetics and the radical denial of its apostolicity. Scholarship is already on the way, the truth is on the march. Confidence on the apostolic tradition-source behind the FG is growing. The conviction that the progressive formation and literary shape of the tradition has proceeded on an organic line and is becoming constantly stronger. It is increasingly becoming clear that the FG cannot possibly be regarded as a free construction. From beginning to end the writing is anchored in the apostolic witness with its points of departure in Jesus' own word and the experience of the Disciples.

The question about the *Johannine tradition,* its church formation and literary shape, – which is the heart of the so-called "Johannine question" – will not be taken up for immediate treatment. We will approach it by means of a survey of the motives of the farewell discourse. These speeches, more than any other part of the FG, are suitable as an introduction to the Johannine problem, at which we will look more closely in the next volume of the Yearbook. Here only so much will be mentioned as is necessary to indicate the angle from which the problem of the FG ought to be considered. The solution to the question of tradition is a distant goal. The important thing is that we see the unbroken connection of the words with the historical primitive factor, with the Son himself and with the primitive word from his mouth.

1. The first group of farewell sayings 13:31–14:31

The external presupposition that must be fulfilled before Jesus can begin to communicate his testament to his Disciples is that the traitor has gone to his work. Thereby, on the one hand, the chain of events issuing in death has been triggered off, and on the other, the circle around Jesus is purified from its heterogeneous element. Jesus' first words after Judas' departure interpret *the nature and significance of the hour* (13:31–32): the Son of Man now stands before his glorification in which God glorifies himself through him. This is John's well-known fundamental view of Jesus' entire work and especially of his death. This special and present element is marked off by εὐθύς *cum fut.* vs. 32. The glorification is the basic chord which the farewell discourses strikes; similarly in the final prayer of 17:1. This is a leading theological (which does not mean "theoretical") viewpoint with John, and it is connected with the immense paradox of *the Son of Man idea* in Jesus himself.

Accordingly, having interpreted the significance of the hour, Jesus proclaims the immediately imminent *divorce* (v. 33): the Disciples will find themselves in the same situation as the Jews, Jesus is away and beyond reach. Even here we meet a specifically Johannine term: "go away" (ὑπάγω), which later recurs frequently.

Together with this *introduction* (13:31–33) *the final words* (14:27–31) form the framework around the first group of sayings. The final words begin with a genuine Johannine variation of the farewell salutation itself: εἰρήνη שָׁלוֹם = farewell), which is contrasted with the anxiety, ταράσσεσθαι (v. 27). The content and purpose of the previous discourse is summarized (v. 28–29): it will preserve the Disciples' faith in the face of the catastrophe. But now the end has come, "the prince of the world" is advancing; "but he has no hold on me" (ἐν ἐμοὶ ἔχει οὐδέν) he cannot do anything to me (v. 30). Love to the Father, obedience to Him, is the most decisive motives (31). When Jesus is now about to depart (v. 31), he does it in the eyes of the world (ὁ κόσμος); since the world is the scene and the object of the Son's work in the FG.

The *framework* which bears the clear impress of "John" (13:31–33; 14:27–31) encloses a series of the sayings of Jesus, chiefly admonitions and promises, and in addition a number of monumental utterances about himself. The first motive, the most important concern at the hour of farewell, is *the new commandment* (13:34–35), the Church's constitution and foundation. It has its correspondence in the Lucan saying about service (Lk 22:25ff.). The prediction of *Peter's denial* (36–38) also has its firm place in the tradition (Lk 22:31ff.). But in addition to that, in the FG there is the promise about the Spirit (ὁ παράκλητος) as a substantial element in the farewell sayings: 14:15–17, 25–26. – The chief motives are joined together by utterances concerning the Disciples (= the Church's) situation and possibilities following Jesus' departure. These utterances, which in part are in dialogue form (Thomas 14:4; Philip v. 8; Judas v. 22), are organized throughout around certain main sayings: "In my Father's house are many rooms" (14:2); "I am the way and the truth and the life" (14:6); "Anyone who has seen me has seen the Father" (14:9); "I will do whatever you ask in my name" (14:13); "If anyone loves me, he will obey my teaching" (14:23). Around these great principal sayings threads have been spun which clarify, interpret, vary the main thought. This has certainly occurred already in the *pre-literary* stage, in teaching and preaching and quite certainly the Evangelist has been more of a redactor than an author. We can observe the result of the pre-literary process everywhere in the farewell discourses, which following an analysis, can be broken into several groups of such interpretative comments and variations about an original saying. To give an immediate example, take the saying on the new commandment (13:34f.):

A new command I give you: Love one another
(1) As I have loved you, so you must love one another.
(2) By this all men will know that you are my disciples, if you love one another.

The saying about the Father's house (14:2) is given within the framework of a comforting encouragement to show complete confidence in God and Jesus (14:1) as well as of an assurance that Jesus will return and take them to be with him (14:3):

In my Father's house are many rooms,
if it were not so, I would have told you.

"The father's house" (בַּיִת) is the world, where the Disciples will find a place even after Jesus' departure, while Jesus goes away to prepare a place for them and then return to take them to be with him. Naturally, this return does not refer to the parousia, but to the new religious situation which has come about through Jesus' glorification and exaltation. This situation is the "place" (τόπος), which Jesus is preparing; in this "he returns" and "takes them to be with him", so that where he is, there they, too, may be.

The two great sayings:
I am the way, the truth and the life (14:6)
Anyone who has seen me has seen the Father (14:9)

are joined together through the explanatory clauses: "No one comes to the Father except through me" etc. (6b–7) as well as Philip's petition and Jesus' answer (8f.) To this connect vv. 9c ff. – a somewhat longer form of the theme *Jesus and the Father* – centered around the concept of *Jesus' works* (ἔϱγα, מַעֲשׂוֹת), which leads to the thought of the believers' own ἔϱγα and the unconditional *answer to prayer.* 14:18–24 is composed of sayings about Jesus' continuing to be in touch with his own, under the condition that they keep his commandment in love to him. Here it becomes quite clear that Jesus' (and the Father's) "coming" (ἔϱχεσθαι) to the Church is of a spiritual nature, cf. vv. 18, 21 and 23b; "on that day" (vs. 20) is a solemn, biblical expression for the new situation following Jesus' departure. Judas' question, why Jesus is about to reveal himself only to the disciples but not to the world (22) calls forth an answer on Jesus' part, which is a variation on a principal saying that was uttered earlier (cf. 4, 15) and which calls to mind the thought of vs. 21b: "He who loves me will be loved by my Father". Here we can see clearly that through Judas' question the Evangelist is able to combine several variants of tradition. From the literary point of view the result is not particularly successful, since Jesus' answer (23) is hardly a real answer to Judas' question. Through this procedure, however, the Evangelists has preserved for us a number of variant sayings, which is particularly praiseworthy.

2. The second group of farewell sayings 15:1–16:23

This second group lacks an introduction. This was unnecessary, since the section appears as a continuation of the previous sayings. On the other hand, the end, as expected, is marked off by a *final section* (16:29–33) which is prepared for by 16:28 "now I am leaving the world and going back to the Father". The final section recalls 14:27ff. in so far as the intention of the discourse is recapitulated (ταῦτα λελάληκα ὑμῖν ἵνα), and the whole is rounded off in the εἰρήνη of the farewell greeting. Otherwise the passion, which is now really commencing, puts its mark on what is said in the end: the Disciples' confession of Jesus and his harsh reply (31f.) and finally the majestic: "But take heart! I have overcome the world".

The main literary arrangement is clear: fellowship with Christ and the Christian life (15:1–17); the hate of the world and the problem of unbelief (15:18–16:4a); the work of the Spirit in the world (16:4b–15); farewell and reunion (16:16–32). In these sections we find words and motifs which we already know from the first group. Above all we find the *command to love* in several variants and connections of thought, the promise of the *Paraclete* as well as the unlimited *answer to prayer.* Special farewell motifs run through the whole like the characteristic "a little while" (cf. 16:16ff.). A new element is the *world's hate* towards the Church; since Jesus' own passion is now approaching, the time has come to prepare the Disciples for what is awaiting them, too. The matter is, however, already hinted at in the words to Peter about discipleship, 13:36ff.

Particularly instructive for studying the Evangelist's procedure is the section about Jesus' friends (15:13–17). The command "love each other as I have loved you" (15:13) receives the comment "greater love has no one than this, that he lay down his life for his friends" (ὑπὲρ τῶν φίλων). Through the comment, the command to love in this context receives its center of gravity in the second part: "as I have loved you". Jesus is presented as the example of sacrificial love. The last saying in the clause (ὑπὲρ τῶν φίλων) supplies the point of departure for an excursus or parenthesis concerning the title given to the Disciples, *"Jesus' friends"* (vv. 14ff.). We have here a characteristic connection of key words of a kind that we know so well from e.g. the Epistle of James. In actual fact this connection of key words is a compositional principle that is used frequently by most biblical authors. We also have a good example of the way in which the farewell discourses of the FG are saturated with the thought and terminology of the Church. Among the many appelations, which were formed early to designate the believers in Christ, this one was included also: Jesus' friends (φίλοι Ἰησοῦ). Perhaps it existed already in Jesus' time as a term among the Disciples. At any rate it now receives its Johannine definition. The presupposition for being a "friend of Jesus" is keeping his commands (vs. 14) and the implication of Jesus' friendship is that he initiates the Disciples into everything that he has heard from the Father (vs. 15). The heart of friendship is therefore *intimate spiritual fellowship.* However, immediately afterwards Jesus' *sovereignty* is underscored: as Jesus's friends the Disciples are chosen by him and appointed by him to bear fruit. Their own initiative had no say in this (vs. 16). With this latter element John preserves the connection with the original significance of the appelation. For originally "Jesus's friends" must have been those whom he chose, took into his friendship, those who stood under his protection and with whom he identifies. The intimate Johannine interpretation allows the inner side of the relation to be seen in connection with the term "friend". There is certainly something *personal* in this as we often sense in the FG. This personal, inner element corresponds with the linguistic form, the Greek, in which the Evangelist meets us. The opposition between friend and slave is understood purely by *way of principle;* for in actual fact there were innumerable examples of slaves who were trusted by their Masters, and that one was careful in what one confided to a "friend". It is the *concepts* themselves that are being contrasted, – and this seems to be Greek in character. To a friend are communicated all the thoughts and intentions of the other friend (cf. πάντα ... ἐγνώρισα ὑμῖν vs. 15), while the slave is ignorant of the Master's doings (οὐκ οἶδεν τί ποιεῖ αὐτοῦ ὁ κύριος does not mean: "he does not know what his Master does", but: "he has no idea what his Master is up to", what he is considering doing, cf. Theophrastus, *Characteres* I 4:41 μηδὲν ὧν πράττει ὁμολογῆσαι, "he never divulges what he is about to do"). Such an abstract operation with the concepts of "slave" and "friend" reveals a development in thought which has taken account of the difference between the usual appelation for the members of a cultic fellowship (עֶבֶד, δοῦλος) and the genuinely Christian appelation.

We meet a similar Johannine interpretation of traditional terms in Jesus' saying about the *Paraclete* (16:8–11). When he comes he will convict the world of guilt in regards to *sin* and *righteousness* and *judgment.* The Spirit will clarify the situation in such a way that no one will be able to deny or dispute it; though unwillingly the world must confess it. The triad "sin-righteousness-judgment" is clearly very old in Christianity, evidently going back to Jesus himself as are the other three words too (Mt 23:23): justice, mercy and faithfulness. Sin and righteousness are also chief motives in the missionary preaching of the early Church with its eschatological perspective (the judgment). John comments on this basic faithfulness to concepts by way of a regular interpretation: περὶ ἁμαρτίας μὲν ὅτι ..., περὶ δικαιοσύνης δὲ ὅτι ..., περὶ δὲ κρίσεως ὅτι ... Sin is unbelief towards Jesus, the attitude taken towards him is the decisive thing for one's standing before God. Righteousness is not a product of men's pious endeavours, but a fruit of Jesus' salvific work, which is completed when he goes to the Father. It thereby follows that the judgment has already taken place, in that Satan is judged, defeated, dethroned by Jesus' exaltation. This intensification, this spiritualization of the inherited concepts, surely has no polemic purpose. In a positive way it brings to expression the Johannine church's religious insight and experience under the Spirit's guidance through the use of terms that have been handed down. Time and time again we observe the three stages of development: tradition, interpretation, redaction.

This observation is clearly confirmed and illustrated by the first paragraph of the second group of farewell sayings: the figure of the *vine* (15:1 ff.). It is easy to see that vs. 3 is an interpertative comment on vs. 2 in connection with the word "prune": "you are already clean" etc. Moreover, it is obvious that the whole figure occurs in a homiletically developed form, since the figure is immediately interpreted and applied: "I am the true vine, and my Father is the gardener" (15:1); "I am the vine, you are the branches" (vs. 5). That the parable in the last analysis derives from Jesus, there is no reason to doubt. However, the allegorical interpretation is the work of the Church. Also a genuine word of Jesus is the figure of the *woman giving birth* (16:21), which Jesus must have used originally of himself in the face of death, just like the figures of "baptism" and "the cup" (Mk 10:39). The figure of the woman giving birth is combined in the farewell discourses with the saying about "a little while" (16:16). That we have here an original saying that has been handed down, is made clear by the detailed deliberation that is joined to it (16:17f.). This μικρόν was difficult to interpret at the time of the Evangelist. He therefore lets Jesus himself interpret it: μικρὸν καὶ ὄψεσθέ με refers not to the parousia, but to the great uppheaval which will occur when Jesus, as the One exalted through death, visits his Church again and turns sadness to joy (cf. πάλιν ὄψομαι ὑμᾶς, 16:22).

3. Principal motifs in the two groups of sayings

A comparison between the two groups of sayings shows that there is a marked parallelism in the main lines, while there are many dissimilarities in the details. A detailed investigation, which is naturally out of the question here, would show that for the section of 15:1 ff. the Evangelist has had a fuller parallel tradition at his disposal. But what is of immediate interest here, are the common main motives, above all *love, Spirit, prayer* as well as *joy,* which surface now and then in the farewell discourses. Common features are also the expressions *Christ-fellowship* and *God-fellowship.*

The command to love occurs in the FG in the form: love *each other* (ἀγαπᾶτε ἀλλήλους) in distinction from the Syn, where the object of love is *the neighbour* (ὁ πλησίον). With this corresponds the fact that the "brother" in the Syn is the fellow-Israelite (cf. e. g. Mt 5:22; 7:2) but in the FG it is the fellow-Christian (Jn 21:23) and for this reason the Johannine Christ does not speak at all of "the brother". We meet this term by contrast much more often in 1 John. Surely

Jesus himself stands behind the particularization of love to reciprocal love among the disciples; to him should also be attributed the saying about "the new command", which does not mean that the command had not existed earlier. It was, of course, found in the Bible, in the law of Moses; but the command is "new" because it received a new significance and motivation through Jesus (cf. 1 Jn 2:8 "because the darkness is passing and the true light is already shining"). "Love each other as I have loved you" – this idea runs through the farewell discourses and takes on numerous forms. This "as" (καθώς, 17 times in Jn 13–17) marks not only the prototype, but also the motive (cf. Jn 13:15 καθὼς ἐγὼ ἐποίησα ὑμῖν καὶ ὑμεῖς ποιῆτε = you should follow my example). In addition to the new command, mention is made constantly of the necessity of keeping Jesus' commands in the plural (τηρεῖν τὰς ἐντολάς), cf. 15:10ff. plur. and 15:12 sing. (ἡ ἐντολὴ ἡ ἐμή). The plural certainly refers to the various concrete situations, where it is important to keep the one, great and new command.[1]

The Spirit, the Holy Spirit, the Spirit of truth, "the Counsellor", is one of the most characteristic elements of the Johannine farewell discourses. Jesus' utterances about the Paraclete reflect the Church's experience of the Spirit. He is "with and in" the Disciples (14:16f.); he teaches on the basis of Jesus' words (14:26), naturally through the Spirit-gifted *teachers;* he witnesses about Jesus (15:26), that is, through the *missionaries.* He exposes the world's spiritual predicament (16:7, 11) through the Christian *preacher,* who, with the help of the Spirit, convicts the world of sin, righteousness, and judgment. In short, the Paraclete makes the entire spiritual reality accessible to the Church in organic continuation of Jesus' historical work (16:13–15). In the last mentioned passage we sense a light breeze from the pneumatic complex of problems in the early Church: "he will not speak on his own; he will speak *only* what he hears" (vs. 13).[2] Therefore no prophecy or teaching may occur, which goes its own way, the way of the spirits of falsehood and of heretics. The pneumatic is strictly bound to that which Jesus has created and founded: "he will bring glory to me by taking from what is mine and making known to you (vs. 14). The saying "All that belongs to the Father is mine. That is why I said the Spirit will take from what is mine and make it known to you" must be understood in such a way that if in the Church's prophecy or teaching there occur things that are legitimate, but which do not have any direct and immediate connection with Jesus' historic work and words, these, too, belong to Jesus and serve his glorification. They are part of the divine reality, and "all that belongs to the Father is mine". The name "Counsellor" (ὁ παράκλητος) must have been given to the Spirit originally in his capacity of helper *(advocatus)* of the Disciples at court during

[1] The question of "Jesus' words" (λόγος, ῥήματα) and "commands" in the FG will be investigated in a dissertation by Åke V. Ström.

[2] This is how ὅσα ἀκούει 16:13 must be rendered with.

persecution (Mk 13:11, cf. Jn 15:20ff.; 16:1ff.). Afterwards the appelation came to include all of the Spirit's functions. Already the pre-Christian Jewish *paracleta* appears to have had a many-sided and comprehensive meaning: helper, witness, guide, intercessor etc.[3] The Spirit has certainly been a main element of Jesus' eschatological picture of the future; in the fully established kingdom of God the Spirit of God is all prevailing, following his definitive annihilation of demonism (Mt 12:28).[4] Here lies the point of departure for this motive in the Johannine farewell discourses, where Jesus designates the Paraclete as his substitute with the Disciples, i.e. in the Church (ἄλλος παράκλητος Jn 14:16) and characterizes him according to his most important functions. Among these the function of foretelling that which is to come also belongs (16:13): τὰ ἐρχόμενα ἀναγγελεῖ ὑμῖν. The Johannine Church knew and appreciated prophets of this kind (cf. Agabos, Acts 11:28; 21:10f.).

Prayer in Jesus's name and its *answer* (14:13–14; 15:7, 16; 16:23–26) are an essential element in the new situation which is brought about as a result of Jesus' going to the Father. Now the Disciples can pray "in Jesus' name", which earlier had not been possible ("until now you have not asked for anything in my name" 16:24). The prayer situation has now, through the completion of Jesus' work in his exaltation, become quite different from what it was before. The various formulations of this thought, which meet us in the farewell discourses, show that this new prayer situation has not been without its problems for the Johannine Church, cf. especially 16:26: "I am not saying that I will ask the Father on your behalf. No, the Father himself loves you ..." At all events, however, prayer in the name of Jesus is such an essential matter to the Church, that it cannot be missing from Jesus' testament to his Disciples. Points of contact with the primitive tradition are not lacking.[5]

Joy must be the Christian Church's insignia: "I will see you again" (ὄψομαι = visit), and you will rejoice, and no one can take away your joy (in translation αἴρει needs a modal auxiliary verb: "can"), 16:22. The traditional thought of the blessedness and joy of the coming Messianic kingdom here has become deeper by being connected with Jesus' destiny, his suffering, death and triumph over death: "your grief will turn to joy" (16:20), and by being connected with the answer to prayer: "ask and you will receive, and your joy will be complete" (16:24). Jesus speaks also of "my joy" (ἡ χαρὰ ἡ ἐμή,15:11; 17:13), which will be the Disciples' joy in full measure. The expression ἵνα ἡ χαρὰ ὑμῶν (ἡμῶν) ᾖ πεπληρωμένη is found also in 1 Jn 1:4; 2 Jn 12, cf. the expression on the Baptist's lips Jn 3:29. It seems to be somewhat formula-like, nevertheless it witnesses to the basic mentality in the Church: the perfect joy, Jesus' own joy

[3] An excellent investigation of this by S. Mowinckel is *Zeitschr. für die neutestl. Wissenschaft* 1933, pp. 97ff.

[4] Cf. H. Windisch in *Studies in Early Christianity,* 1930.

[5] Prayer in the FG will be treated in a dissertation by pastor Helge Persson.

and blessedness, which he has won through his death and exaltation. It is not merely, as in Judaism and heathenism, a few brief, more or less intensive festive moments; here everything is joy. Moreover, we are given to understand that this Church's joy in Jesus is not a resting state, a possession which is at the Church's disposal, but joy must constantly win its perfection with Jesus' help, it must be renewed all the time through answer to prayer (16:24), through the word of Jesus in proclamation and worship (15:11; 17:13), through the renewal of Christian fellowship (1 Jn 1:4; 2 Jn 12). Joy must constantly assert itself afresh and take its sovereign place in the Christian life.[6]

4. The Church and Tradition

The subject of the Johannine farewell discourses is *the Church,* the Church which was to be the fruit of Jesus' work. At the farewell hour the One about to depart allows his Disciples to get a glimpse of the coming situation when Jesus has gone to the Father and through his Spirit he guides and helps the Disciples. One could say that according to the FG Jesus founds and constitutes the Church in that at the last night, even though the word ἐκκλησία never occurs, just as little as the word ἀπόστολος (13:16 is a proverbial saying : "nor is a messenger greater than the one who sent him"). On the other hand, ἀποστέλλω occurs in a technical sense in 17:18. The FG has substantially developed and expanded the primitive tradition in the light of the current state of the Church, but without breaking the connection with this tradition. At all points he is firmly anchored in it.

Clearly behind the literarily fixed Gospel writing stands the living apostolic word, the primitive apostolic witness. The Disciple of Jesus who was the bearer of this word and witness, has obviously imprinted his stamp on the thought and language of his Church. And the FG has most likely come into existence in order to replace his living word with the written one, after the Apostle had been harvested by death. The addition to the FG in ch. 21 allows us to guess the context: Peter has died as a martyr and the Beloved Disciple, too, has been called away, although some had believed that the Lord had designed him to experience the parousia. It was in this situation that the Fourth Evangelist felt called to write down the witness of the deceased one to Christ. This witness has a strong personal colour, but for this very reason it is so valuable, both religiously and historically; it paints Jesus' portrait reflected in a deep and great soul.

---

[6] The first monograph treatment of joy in the early Church has been given by E. Gulin, *Die Freude im N.T. II Das Johannesevangelium.* Helsinki 1936. This work will be reviewed in the next volume of the Yearbook [i. e. Svensk Exegetisk Årsbok (Tr.)].

The Johannine farewell discourses clearly reveal the Church's strong consciousness of being Jesus' own creation. The foundation of love, the Spirit's activity, prayer and answer to prayer, joy, and fellowship with Christ and the Father, – all this has been Jesus' will and work. Yes, he has expressly placed it in prospect when taking his farewell from his own. His departure, which to the Disciples was a harrowing catastrophe, was the necessary presupposition for the establishment of the Church on earth, for "Unless I go away, the Counsellor will not come to you; but if I go, I will send him to you" (16:7). Through his departure to the Father, that which Jesus had founded during his ministry on earth could come to full development and maturity. It could be achieved only by the Spirit's work in the Church, after Jesus had crushed the power of "the prince of this world", returned to glory and "prepared a place" in the Father's house. Then he can "draw all men to himself". Then the barriers to his historical work in Israel will have fallen down, the way will now be free for the Christian faith, the Christian word, which the Son had planted on the earth, in his Disciples.

Jesus' work ἐν σαρκί is thus of basic and preparatory nature, – this is a basic viewpoint in the FG. It is not until he is the exalted, glorified victor over sin, death and the power of Satan that he can fully assert his authority, send the Spirit. First in the Church does it become obvious what he is and what he can do. This very prominent insight of the FG is the presupposition for the detailed form of the farewell discourses. *In the final analysis the Son came into the world in order to found the Christian Church.* This way of thinking, this conviction demands with inner necessity a programmatic saying, a spiritual testament, from Jesus, as he stands at the threshold of the other world; for now for the first time the results of his life and death will be revealed.

This programmatic saying, this spiritual testament we have in the Johannine farewell discourses. Historically speaking these are of exceptional interest as expressions of what went on in the Church of Asia Minor during the immediate post-apostolic age, when the apostolic tradition was still alive. The farewell discourses are composed of apostolic words and to a significant extent of Jesus' words in Johannine fashion and interpretation. Thus, the FG offers greater opportunities than any other New Testament writing for studying the context and development in the oldest period of the Church. The apostolic authority, the apostolic interpretation and commentary mediated the transitions, led the breaking of new ground, so that no break in continuity occurred. The organic connection was preserved in spite of continuous development both in Church and tradition. This is what we can observe particularly clearly in the FG. It binds the Church together with Jesus in a wholly historical, reliable way. The Disciple, who is the source for the Gospel, bound in his person and his word the past with the present and created some monumental, imperishable expressions for this unity. The Son of Man with his group of Disciples in Israel and the Son in glory leading his Church in the world through the Spirit are one and the same according to the apostolic consciousness and word. For this reason no one can thereafter successfully separate them. All such attempts are bound to shipwreck on John's words.

Bemerkungen zur Fußwaschung Joh 13

(1939)

Das Interesse des vierten Evangelisten an der Fußwaschung tritt offen zutage 13, 12ff., wo Jesus selbst den Sinn der Handlung ausführlich darlegt als ein ὑπόδειγμα zur Nachahmung der Jünger,– natürlich nicht nur im buchstäblichen Sinne[1]. Daneben verfolgt aber Johannes auch einen mehr negativen Zweck: Er nimmt die Gelegenheit wahr, einen Stoß zu führen gegen gewisse Tendenzen in der Kirche, die auf die Forderung ritueller Waschungen hinausgingen. Und zwar handelt es sich nicht in erster Linie um eine Mißdeutung der Fußwaschung selbst in ritueller Richtung, sondern u. a. um Waschungen der Hände (und des Kopfes) zum Zweck der Reinheit[2].

Wenn man bedenkt, welch gewaltige Rolle die Kathartik damals spielte, bei den Juden sowohl als bei den Heiden, muß man annehmen, daß die rituelle Reinheitsfrage die ältesten Christengemeinden vor große Probleme gestellt hat. Leider haben diese Probleme fast keine Spuren in unseren Quellen hinterlassen; wir können auch nicht das Aufkommen einer kultisch geregelten christlichen Kathartik verfolgen[3]. Aber die johanneische Fußwaschungsszene läßt uns einen Einblick tun in die ζητήσεις περὶ καθαρισμοῦ in der alten Kirche.

Nach[4] dem Essen schickt sich Jesus an, die Füße der Jünger zu waschen. Ein überraschendes Unternehmen, nicht nur weil der Herr diesen Sklavendienst[5] auf sich nimmt, sondern auch weil die Fußwaschung ja ihren natürlichen Platz vor dem Essen hat[6]. Durch die Verlegung der Handlung an den Schluß des Mahles erhält sie eine nachdrückliche Selbständigkeit als ὑπόδειγμα und kann außerdem als Ausgangspunkt der folgenden Belehrung dienen.

Der Dialog mit Simon Petrus soll ausschließlich dem schon gekennzeichne-

[1] 1 Tim 5, 10 zeugt jedoch von der Fußwaschung als Bestandteil des urchristlichen Liebesdienstes.

[2] Wellhausen spürt Polemik gegen die Wiederholung der Taufe.

[3] Joh 3, 22ff.; Act 18, 25f.; 19, 3ff.; Heb 6, 2; 10, 22.

[4] ἐκ τοῦ δείπνου = δειπνήσας vgl. Herod. I 50 ἐκ τῆς θυσίης, I 126 ἀπὸ δείπνου, Xen. *Anab.* IV 6, 21 ἐκ τοῦ ἀρίστου, ἐξ ἑορτῆς *Pap. greci et latini* IV 403 (Moult.-Millig, Vocab. 190).

[5] Zur niedrigen Art dieses Dienstes vgl. Plut. *Mul. virt.* 249 D διηκονοῦντο τοῖς ἄλλων γονεῦσι καὶ ἀδελφοῖς ἄχρι τοῦ καὶ τοὺς πόδας ἀπονίζειν.

[6] Vgl, Lc 7, 44 εἰσῆλθόν σου εἰς τὴν οἰκίαν. ὕδωρ μοι ἐπὶ τοὺς πόδας οὐκ ἔδωκας.

ten negativen Nebenzweck des Evangelisten dienen und birgt keine tieferen Geheimnisse in sich. Zunächst weigert sich Petrus zweimal, um das drittemal zur entgegengesetzten Übertreibung zu gehen[7]. Und eben darauf will der Evangelist hinaus. Die Worte Jesu, durch welche er den Widerstand seines Jüngers bricht (vv. 7 und 8b), werden also nicht allzu tiefsinnig zu deuten sein. Zunächst gibt Jesus das Seltsame und Unverständliche seines Handelns zu, verheißt aber spätere Einsicht[8]. Dann aber wird der Ton mehr drohend: Durch seine erneute Weigerung läuft Petrus Gefahr, aus seiner Gemeinschaft zu scheiden, es ist einfach Frage nach Gehorsam oder Ungehorsam, nicht nach irgendeiner mystisch-sakramentalen Realität, die mit der Fußwaschung verknüpft wäre, und der Petrus durch seine Widerspenstigkeit verlustig gehen könnte. Also: "Wenn ich nicht dich waschen darf[9], kann ich nichts mehr mit dir zu tun haben"[10]. Da begehrt nun Petrus auch noch die Hände- und Kopfwaschung, und so erreicht die Darstellung ihr *punctum saliens, die formelle Entscheidung Jesu:* ὁ λελουμένος οὐκ ἔχει χρείαν νίψασθαι[11].

Diese grundsätzliche Formulierung stammt ohne jeden Zweifel aus der jüdischen Reinheitslehre und enthält eine in derselben geltende Maxime: Unmittelbar nach einem Vollbad ist eine Waschung (etwa der Hände, vor dem Essen) überflüssig[12]. Wir wissen ja von den Juden zur Zeit Jesu: ἐὰν μὴ πυγμῇ νίψωνται τὰς χεῖρας οὐκ ἐσθίουσιν[13], ferner aber: ἀπ' ἀγορᾶς[14] ἐὰν μὴ βαπτίσωνται οὐκ ἐσθίουσιν[15]. Im letzten Falle fällt natürlich die Händewaschung weg. Diesen Grundsatz bringt der Evangelist hier zur Geltung, um die verständnislose Bitte des Petrus zurück- und zurechtzuweisen. Dabei setzt er als selbstverständlich voraus, daß die Jünger sich durch ein Bad zum Mahle vorbereitet haben. Es war ja ein spätabendliches δεῖπνον, zu dem Jesus und

---

[7] Das Gesetz der epischen Dreiung macht sich hier geltend ("Achtergewicht"), vgl. von Dobschütz, Paarung und Dreiung in *NTl. Stud · für Heinrici,* S. 92ff.

[8] Das Motiv der späteren Einsicht ist typisch für das Joh-Evangelium (2, 22; 14, 26).

[9] ἐὰν μὴ νίψω σε (13, 8) bedeutet: Wenn ich (durch deine Weigerung) nicht dazu komme, dich zu waschen...

[10] οὐκ ἔχεις μέρος μετ' ἐμοῦ = da scheiden sich unsere Wege, vgl. Mt 24, 51 τὸ μέρος αὐτοῦ μετὰ τῶν ὑποκριτῶν θήσει "du lässest ihn das Schicksal der Heuchler teilen".

[11] εἰ μὴ τοὺς πόδας ist offenbar sekundärer Einschub eines Lesers, der sonst die kategorische negative Formulierung nicht in Übereinstimmung bringen konnte mit der Tatsache der eben geschehenen Fußwaschung.

[12] Zum Unterschied zwischen λούεσθαι und νίπτεσθαι vgl. Plut. *Aqua an ignis util.* 10 (958 B): ὕδωρ ὠφέλιμον κατὰ θίξιν λουσαμένοις ἢ νιψαμένοις.

[13] Mc 7, 3f.

[14] ἀπ' ἀγορᾶς ("nach Heimkehr vom Markte") vgl. *Pap. graec. Holmiensis* ed. Lagercrantz (Uppsala 1913), S. 10, 26 μετὰ τὴν κάμινον ("nach Brennen im Ofen").

[15] Zu lesen ist βαπτίσωνται vgl. Lc 11, 38 ἐθαύμασεν ὅτι οὐ πρῶτον ἐβαπτίσθη πρὸ τοῦ ἀρίστου. Das ῥαντίσωνται von SB zeigt, daß man nicht ἀπ' ἀγορᾶς verstanden hat und an die Spülung mitgebrachter, gekaufter Eßwaren dachte (ἀπ' ἀγορᾶς = τὰ ἀπ' ἀγ. κεκομισμένα). Der Sachverhalt ist überzeugend dargelegt bei Brandt, *Jüdische Reinheitslehre* (Beih. z. *ZAW* XIX), 1910, S. 34ff.

seine Jünger sich versammelten, nachdem sie tagsüber sich im Volksgedränge der überfüllten Stadt bewegt hatten. Ein Vollbad war da vonnöten. Hier liegt auch die Voraussetzung dafür, daß der Evangelist die Fußwaschung am Schluß des Mahles anbringen kann, ohne dadurch die Vorstellung einer Doppelung von etwas schon Vollzogenem hervorzurufen.

Indem Jesus Petrus daran erinnert, daß er ja λελουμένος und also keines νίψασθαι bedürftig ist, *verneint er* eo ipso *auch jeden kathartischen Zweck der eben von ihm vollzogenen Fußwaschung. Als Reinigung* war ja dieselbe überflüssig, der Gebadete ist καθαρὸς ὅλος. Nun steht aber der Evangelist vor der Aufgabe, die antikathartische Spitze des Wortes Jesu über die konkrete jüdische Situation hinaus geltend zu machen, *und das geschieht durch die kategorische Erklärung Jesu:* καὶ ὑμεῖς καθαροί ἐστε. Damit ist das geschichtlich Bedingte und zeitlich Begrenzte der Szene durchbrochen, und die Jünger stehen als Reine da, – natürlich nicht als λελουμένοι im Sinne der jüdischen rituellen Reinheit, sondern Reine *kraft des Wortes Jesu* und ihrer Gemeinschaft mit ihm[16]. Für Judas muß natürlich eine Ausnahme gemacht werden (v. 10 Schluß und 11).

Der alte jüdische Grundsatz: ὁ λελουμένος οὐκ ἔχει χρείαν νίψασθαι erstrahlt so in einem neuen Lichte. Freilich, ob schon Johannes dabei ausdrücklich an die Taufe gedacht hat, muß sehr fraglich bleiben; wenigstens ist die Annahme nicht notwendig, geschweige denn zwingend.

---

[16] So mit Recht von Campenhausen (*ZNW* 1934, 269ff.) unter Hinweis auf Joh 15, 3; nur verkennt er den konkreten Sinn von λελουμένος in der geschichtlichen Situation.

The Shepherd Chapter

Jn 10

(1943)

The tenth chapter of the Fourth Gospel has always been felt as an especially difficult passage to interpret. Opinions about its correct intrepretation have differed widely and they still continue to do so. The modern debate about the Shepherd discourse was introduced about a generation ago by Wellhausen, who made a couple of critical contributions. These were followed, among others, by Spitta and Brun. In more recent times the debate has been renewed by Hirsch, Bultmann and Fascher, who presented some significant new points of view. It is therefore, hardly necessary to offer any justification for giving an account of the most important points that have emerged during these years, and which throw light upon this question. The literature that is to be considered in the first place is the following:

E. Schwarz in *Zeitschrift für die neutest. Wissenschaft (= ZNW)* 1906.
J. Wellhausen, *Erweiterungen und Änderungen im Vierten Evangelium,* 1907; *Das Evangelium Johannis,* 1909.
Fr. Spitta in *ZNW* 1909, cf. *Das Johannesevangelium,* 1910.
L. Brun in *Norsk Teologisk Tidsskrift* 1909.
E. Hirsch, *Studien zum vierten Evangelium,* 1936
R. Bultmann, *Das Evangelium des Johannes,* 1941.
E. Fascher in *Deutsche Theologie* 1941, pp. 37–66; 1942, pp. 33–57; 118–133.

1.

The Shepherd chapter is the only section in the Gospel of John in which imagery occurs to any appreciable extent. A large part of this section has the character of "mashal", calling to mind the Synoptic type of tradition. But the Johannine imagery occasions difficulties in interpretation chiefly for two reasons. Firstly, because the figurative elements occur in rapidly changing contexts, and secondly, because the whole is interwoven with theological reflections and predicates in I-form. Taken together, this implies that the intrepretation must move along the boundary between image (parable) and allegory. At many points we may even feel uncertain as to whether we are dealing with a systematized metaphorical utterance, whose constitutive elements need all be interpreted, or with a parable, where the situation described expresses a thought that gives the overall picture. The Evangelist himself defines vv. 1–5 as a *paroimia,* which, however, is not of much help, since the concept of *paroimia* in John is as undefined as the Jewish concept *mashal.* – And finally: What *comprehensive view* shall be based on this strange discourse with its heterogeneous elements?

It is altogether obvious that our chapter is a *literary composition* by the Evangelist, a composition with theological character. The Evangelist has brought together and fused disparate elements. The strange boundary path between allegory and parable, into which the exegete is forced, must be owing to the fact that the text had precisely such an origin. Therefore, to seek to reconstruct the Evangelist's "sources", as most of the recent commentators do, cannot be a correct procedure. At the basis of such attempts lies the conviction that whatever is really valuable is to be found in the sources, "the original writing", or whatever it is called. The Evangelist or the "Redactor" has simply destroyed it all with his insertions, glosses, rearrangements and other manipulations. He has thus brought about a terrible disorder, which we must now restore into order as best we can. Hirsch and Bultmann are still controlled by this idea. It is naturally most tempting to try to restore the original text of ch. 10, where an original, great figurative context (bildsammanhang) seems to have been shattered by an allegorizing redactional reworking. Here source-criticism operates with particularly great plerophory. However, it becomes obvious that even here the reconstructions follow quite different lines and that the results invite criticism. Above all, however, it must be emphasized that through these source-critical operations many of the theologically most significant utterances are rejected as glosses and interpolations, which disturb and distort the text. Quite correctly Fascher, and essentially Brun too, have rejected such a view of the man who lies behind the Gospel of John, and have argued that it is precisely *his* work that we are interested in understanding and interpreting. For it is he who has created from the elements of tradition this mighty totality which the Gospel presents, this unity, which gives the Johannine witness its theological and church-historical significance. It is John, the Evangelist, who has brought the different elements of the material to day-light and fused them into a single integrated outlook, where everything becomes organically coherent with its center in the Son.

From this point of view it is unnecesary to treat in greater detail the various critical analyses and attempts at reconstruction. However, Bultmann demands our attention on account of the great number of his interesting literary-critical, religio-historical, and theological standpoints. Nevertheless, the main thing must be to let Fascher have the word. According to our opinion he is on the right track towards understanding the Shepherd chapter, as well as the Johannine texts in general. His basic view is related to that of Brun, complementing the latter's work, which for its time was an especially admirable treatment of our text.

2. Wellhausen

According to Wellhausen, Jn 10 existed as an independent unit before it was inserted – in expanded form – in the Fourth Gospel (= FG): in other words, it did not belong to the basic material of the Gospel. Vv. 1–5 originally had its continuation in vs.7, where we should read: "I am the *shepherd* of the sheep (not "the gate"); and further in vv. 8 and 10 (vs. 9 is an interpolation). In this way we get (1–5, 7, 8, 10) a connected description of the contrast between the shepherd and the thief, i.e. between Jesus and the false Messianic pretenders. Thus, in Jn 10:1–10 we have a specimen of the Church's discussion with the synagogue about Jesus's Messiahship. – Vv. 11–18 are an addition (16 is a redactional interpolation), where the Johannine dogma of Jesus's voluntary death is developed in connection with the figure of the shepherd. This addition to the imagery of vv. 1–10 was made before the section was incorporated in the FG.

Already Blass, on the basis of the support of the Sahidic translation, wanted to read *poimen* instead of *thyra* in vs. 7. This support is, however, exceedingly weak; the Sahidic variant is a correction and does not have any text-critical value. When Wellhausen prefers in vs. 7 to read *poimen,* this is actually a mere conjecture. He is of the opinion that very early an original *poimen* in vs. 7 was altered to *thyra* as a consequence of the insertion of vs. 9 into the text by an interpolator. This procedure is, however, utterly improbable. The phrase "I am the door" repeated in vv. 7 and 9 also receives the support of the phrase "I am the good shepherd" which is repeated in vv. 11 and 14. Both Spitta and Bultmann use therefore other means in dealing with "door" in vv. 7 and 9.

Problematic for Wellhausen's thesis is also the circumstance that I- sayings with an historical perspective occur in vv. 7 and 8 in the midst of what, moreover, is a fundamental context, and by means of which the purity of the imagery is no longer intact. There is also a material objection. In vs. 8 it is said of the false messianic pretenders: "... but the sheep (= Israel) did not listen to them". Is this historically correct? Did not the messianic revolutionaries, too, have their following?

Spitta

Like Wellhausen, Spitta supposes that a Johannine "original writing" has been interpolated by later redactors, and he directs all his efforts to restore this original writing. Unlike Wellhausen, however, he reckons that the Shepherd chapter belongs to the original substance of the Gospel. In the original writing, ch. 10 was the continuation of the narrative about the healing of the blind man in ch. 9. When Jesus had heard that the Pharisees had driven the man away (9:35a), he uttered the words which follow in ch. 10 (9:35b–41 are interpolated). In this situation Jesus sets himself over against the Pharisees by describing the contrast between the shepherd and the thief (10:1–5) and between a true shepherd and a hireling (11b–15). The section about "the door" (7b–10) as well as the I-predication (11a) are secondary. Finally, Jesus applies the shepherd imagery to himself and to his relationship to his disciples in Jerusalem (14–15). Besides these, Jesus has other sheep, i. e. disciples outside Jerusalem, whom he must take under his leadership (vs. 16a) at the Father's command (18c). Vv. 16b–18b are an interpolation. The original shepherd discourse consisted of 1–5, 11b–13, 14–16a, 18c.

This reconstruction carries with it its own self-condemnation by means of its boundless arbitrariness and its mistaken leading principle: i. e. to try to produce a historical document that is of importance for Jesus' biography. It leads to such absurdities as the one according to which the "sheep that are not of this sheep pen" are disciples outside Jerusalem, and that the Father's "command" (*entole*) consists of Jesus' going away from the capital to the country!

Hirsch

Like Spitta, Hirsch thinks that Jn 10:1–21 belonged to the original Johannine writing (E) and that it consisted of 1–5, 7 (read: *poimen*), 10, 11a, 14b, 15, 17–21. Here Jesus is depicted as the true shepherd, the Christians as his sheep. A church redactor (R) then reworked the text with his own church situation as his point of departure and inserted vv. 9, 11b–14a, 16. Christ now becomes the door through which the Church's true teachers (the Apostles and their successors) enter in. From this ecclesiastical viewpoint the thief and the robbers are the gnostic heretics.

What we have here is only a new variant of the arbitrary procedure with reconstructions. Like Wellhausen (and Bultmann) Hirsch considers the Shepherd chapter as an isolated fragment without any connection to a historical situation. The connection with ch. 9 is a work of the R (Ev.). Conversely Spitta wants to establish an original connection between ch. 10 and the situation in ch. 9. But both of these positions are erroneous. To be sure, the connection between chs. 9 and 10 is undoubtedly created by the Evangelist; *but the Shepherd discourse is also his work and must, accordingly, be interpreted as an integrated thought complex and in its relation to ch. 9.* The "source" of the Evangelist, the Gospel's preliminary literary stage, is of no exegetical interest to us, – quite apart from the fact that we cannot reconstruct them with any degree of certainty.

This does not mean, however, that the question, where the Evangelist's material has come from, is or can be of no interest to us. That question must indeed be asked and, in so far as it is possible, also be answered. In that case, however, the purpose is not to produce a more original and more valuable stratum than that which is represented by the Gospel, but rather to create the best possible presuppositions in order to understand and evaluate the Evangelist's work and allow it to appear as a new spiritual unity, reflecting the Johannine church's life in Christ, represented by one of the greatest teachers of this as well as of the entire Christian Church.

Thus if one rejects source reconstructions as fictional, one must still keep one's eyes open for the origin of the material and its various elements. This naturally implies that the question about the connection of the various elements of this material with Jesus's historical proclamation and ministry receive its proper attention.

3. Bultmann

The most recent commentary on the FG goes about its task entirely along the lines of source analysis. Bultmann differentiates among *Source, Evangelist* and *Redactor*. The Evangelist has embodied the sources in his presentation and greatly reorganized, commented and annotated them. Finally, a redactor supplied the Evangelist's work, which had thus fallen into great confusion, with all kinds of insertions and additions. With respect to ch. 10 Bultmann finds that the original substance of the Shepherd discourse belongs to one of the main sources of the FG, the so-called "revelation source". In the context created by the Evangelist, the discourse is an answer to the Jews' appeal in 10:24: "If you are the Christ, tell us plainly!" Jesus' answer begins with 25–26 and continues with 11–13, 1–10, 14–18, 27–39. This is what the Evangelist's composition looked like. From this one must now peel off the *Source* by eliminating the interpretations and glosses which originated with the Evangelist and the Radactor. These are: 7, 9, 15b–18, 31–39. The source thus contained: 11–13, 1–5, 8, 10, 14–15a, 27–30. As one can see Bultmann breaks all records in analytic and reconstructive boldness. In spite of that his interpretation of the Shepherd discourse (pp. 272–298 in his commentary) is of great interest on account of the religio-historical views, which are there developed and which justify a somewhat more detailed presentation.

Bultmann interprets the meaning of *paroimia* in such a way that in the face of unbelief this indirect, paradoxical answer to the question of Messiahship is the only one possible. The Revealer cannot answer in any other way than by saying that only in the circle of those who are his own, can he be known and his essence be revealed. The paroimia is thus at the same time an invitation to enter this circle. The Shepherd discourse is the last revelatory discourse before the people. Here Jesus still speaks *of* the relation of the Revealer to his own. In the farewell discourses that will soon follow he speaks with this relation *as his point of departure;* the third person gives place to the second: "You and I".

Vv. 11–13. "I am the good shepherd" is not yet a paroimia, but real discourse: Jesus claims for himself the title of "Shepherd" (cf. I am the bread of life, etc.). The predicative "good" (*kalos*) contains partly the absolute (the true, real, *alethinos*), and partly also the shepherd's significance for the flock. He is the One whom the people need and seek. – Bultmann devotes a detailed excursus to the *shepherd imagery,* or more correctly: to the title Shepherd. In addition to the biblical material he also reviews the gnostic tradition (primarily the Mandaean). Bultmann finds in John a closer affinity with gnosis than with the Old Testament. In the FG the Shepherd is not a royal figure as in the OT, but the heavenly Redeemer, who loves and takes care of his sheep and protects them from the wolf. The shepherd concept is now claimed for Jesus. Vv. 11a and 11b–13 describe in a parable the genuine shepherd in contrast to the hired keeper of the flock, which naturally should not be interpreted of concrete persons; the comparison is purely a matter of principle.

In vv. 1–5 the parable continues in that the position of the real shepherd is depicted in contrast to that of the thief and the robber. The point is that only the shepherd has the right of ownership to the sheep; only he has the right to freely and without hindrance enter through the door. This exclusive right to ownership has its correspondence in the sheep's confidence, which no stranger can win. The sheep, i.e. all those who are of the truth, instinctively recognize the shepherd and follow him. The parable does not give the criterion by which the shepherd and the thief can be distinguished. The sheep are the shepherd's "own" (*idioi*) sheep, they belong to him and follow him willingly.

Bultmann has no doubt about the gnostic background of the Johannine shepherd imagery. What was originally referred to were the Saviour and the pre-existent souls, i.e. the particles of light scattered in darkness. In John the myth is demythologized. Here we are concerned with Jesus and human beings. It is first in the second place, and in a derivative sense, that the parable refers to Jesus and the Church. Even this latter, however, is "the flock", which must constantly realize who they are by following the voice of the shepherd.

The parable of the shepherd is now followed by an *interpretation,* v. 7ff., which first emphasizes the exclusiveness and absoluteness of the revelation (8, 19), then the certainty of faith (14, 15a, 27–30). From vs. 5 the thought goes on to vs. 8: "All who ever came before me were thieves and robbers" etc. From Bultmann's point of view the old, controversial alternatives in interpretation are dropped. The Revealer stands in opposition to all earlier revealers, all "Saviours", who have persuaded men to follow them. The clause is general and is given as a principle. Who the Evangelist was thinking of is not easy to determine, presumably he thought of the "Offenbarer und Heilande der hellenistisch-gnostischen Welt, deren Anhängerschaft in die Gegenwart hineinreicht". The word is eschatological, and the eschatological "now" sets in every time Jesus' word becomes effective: "Es sind alle angebliche Offenbarer aller Zeiten, die durch das im Glauben erfahrene 'Kommen' Jesu nunmehr erledigt sind". Originally the clause appears to have been gnostic: "Die Formulierung entspricht der gnostischen Überzeugung von der Überlegenheit des Offenbarers über alle Vorgänger".

It is superfluous to give a more detailed presentation of the interpretation of the rest of the reconstructed source (10, 14, 15a, 27–30); the train of thought is consistently carried out in accordance with what has already been said. However, something must be said of Bultmann's understanding of the saying about the *gate* (7, 9) as well as other interpolations (15b–18).

With respect to "the gate" in vv. 7 and 9, Bultmann is of the opinion that the Evangelist has placed these two glosses as an explanation of "the gate" in vs. 1. In that respect he took vs. 9, which is a genuine "I am" – clause, out of its source, but from a wholly different context than the shepherd discourse. Vs. 7, on the other hand, is formed by the Evangelist as a variant to vs. 9. In the source "the gate" was the entrance to salvation (in gnosis: to the world of light); but the Evangelist made of it "the gate for the sheep" (i.e. the gate by which the sheep enter) and supplied the entrance with the popular concept "exit" and with "pasture", by which the gate image becomes connected with the shepherd image, with which originally it had no connection. The purpose of and interest in the glosses is to emphasize still more Jesus' exclusive, absolute position.

Vs. 15b "I lay down my life for the sheep" should lead to the sayings about the meaning of Jesus' death in vv. 17–18. It is in this connection that the Redactor has placed vs. 16, the idea of the universal Church and universal mission. This central Johannine saying on mission thus appears as a redactional gloss inserted at random within a closed context, which is thereby broken.

Thus far Bultmann. We may here leave his theological reflections on the text aside (with a somewhat long excursus on 'the intolerance of revelation'), and limit ourselves to the purely exegetical issue.

Bultmann's analysis is carried out with brilliant acuity, but it falls to the ground already on account of its being improbable. The assumed large-scale rearrangement and annotation of source and Gospel is altogether incredible. Also the "gnostic" background against which Bultmann, carries out his interpretation with such great plerophory is to a high degree hypothetical. In

Bultmann's interpretation history disappears totally, and where in the text it appears in a tangible way, it is relegated to the lumber-yard of the glosses, as e.g. the saying on mission in 10:16. The old exegetical crux, in vs. 8, with its historical character is difficult to fit into Bultmann's system. We will return to this verse later on.

The question of the provenance of concepts and terms is naturally inescapable. Inescapable is also the fact that in the FG we have a main element which is neither Synoptic nor from the OT nor from Judaism. Even though we allow the exclusion of the specifically "mythical", however, it is not necessary for that matter to suppose that whole systems and whole literary complexes have been taken over and been Christianized in the FG. At any rate, such traditio-historical and source-critical operations must be the last expedient to be resorted to, and that only after an integrated interpretation of the present text within the whole framework of the Gospel has proved to be impossible to carry out. That such an interpretation is possible cannot be denied, at least for the present, even though it is fraught with great difficulties.

4. Brun and Fascher

When Brun, 34 years ago, treated the Shepherd chapter, he rejected all textual and source-critical interferences, and set as his goal to understand the text as it stands. Where he disagrees with Bultmann, he does it not least with respect to the text's being firmly anchored in history. The criterion for the correctness of the interpretation is whether it fits Jesus' situation, – or the Evangelist's. Brun regards the text as a composition of the Evangelist's, but he takes it back so close to Jesus that the two become practically identical. However, a certain one-sidedness is inherent in the treatment, in that the FG is rather forced into the historical framework. One wishes that Brun had gone deeper into the question of the origin of the Johannine tradition's elements and ideas.

Brun sees vv. 1–5 as the basic framework in the composition and considers 7–10 and 11–18 as "freer variations on related themes in a related imagery". In other words, in the last two sections he refuses to see "interpretations" of the basic paroimia (1–5), demanding that every individual section "be interpreted on its own terms, without hasty combinations". This demand may be justified as a reaction against the tendency to apply to the text certain apriori, formal theories. On the other hand, however, it becomes a hindrance to a deeper understanding of Johannine thought and composition. The three sections remain standing side by side rather unexpectedly. Thus, the unity and totality of the passage do not fully come to their right estate. It is also a little unfortunate that the investigation is limited to vv. 1–18, instead of including also 22–30. However, it is instructive to read this dissertation, which by its methodological stringency makes precisely the question of the *method of Johannine exegesis* of current interest for the modern reader.

According to Brun, the Shepherd discourse is dominated by *the question concerning the Messiah.* It was this question that occupied and stirred Jerusalem during these days. The narrative of the man born blind in ch. 9 fits well in this context. The contrast comes to expression in what happens with and concerning this man: the contrast between faith and unbelief, between genuine and false messianism. The Shepherd discourse interprets this situation with its contrasts in the form of its imagery. The Shepherd is Jesus, his sheep are the receptive Jews who are here represented by the blind man who is healed. The thief and the robber, who is the hireling, is the false messianic pretender, he who "comes in his own name" (5:43). Brun pays particular attention to 10:8: "All who ever came before me" etc. This saying must almost certainly refer to pseudo-Christs. Brun does not wish to deny that the imagery also contains a polemic against Israel's spiritual leaders, especially the Pharisees and their scribes, in other words "the Jews" in a technical sense (cf. the "strangers" at 10:5).

Fascher takes seriously the exegetical principle that our concern here must be to understand and interpret *the Gospel of John.* He thus applies a theological total approach upon the text and thus comes into closer contact with it than other interpreters have succeeded in doing. Fascher's controversy with earlier attempts, especially by Wellhausen and Bultmann, is very instructive. He shows that every attempt to tear off source fragments from the text and to reconstruct an older form of the text only leads to new difficulties and it raises new questions. It is not possible to tear the Johannine work to pieces. It is such a well thought-out and in every respect coherent unity, that if this unity is destroyed, it will raise a confusing diversity of alternatives for analysis, of which no one will be absolutely compelling and decisive. This does not mean that Fascher has closed his eyes to the religio-historical and literary-critical problems in the Gospel of John. He sees them and reflects on them, but only in order to better understand the text and the thought of John. This is the goal and object of his investigation. From this it follows that Fascher's interest is not directed in the first place towards elucidating the relationship of the historical Jesus to the Shepherd discourse; but he emphasizes strongly the "Synoptic" element in Jn 10. We will return to this below while here a brief presentation will be given of Fascher's interpretation of the Shepherd discourse.

That this discourse has its basis in Jesus and the early Church's historical situation, Fascher finds *inter alia* i vs. 8: "All who ever came before me" etc. Here an historical element (aorist) enters right in the midst of what is otherwise a general description which continuously keeps to present tense verb forms. The saying can thus only refer to all those persons, who at the time of Jesus and of the early Church appeared with a program which confused political with religious motives. This was the type of Messiah which the Pharisees basically approved of, though, officially they dissociated themselves from activistic tendencies. For them Jesus, with his strict submission to the Father's will, was incomprehensible (Jn 5:43). Fascher refers to a certain parallelism in Paul, 2 Cor 11:4, 20: men find it easier to understand the brutal force of will than the one who only wants to serve God. It is thus evident that the Shepherd discourse should be interpreted as an essential part of the dispute with Judaism, the dispute in which Jesus was deeply engaged and which became a legacy to the Apostolic Church. It is a question of the true, genuine Messiah. But in John this dispute is not an isolated element, that is limited to ch. 10. It goes through the entire Gospel and is especially applicable from ch. 9 on. Jn 10 points forward to and prepares for 18:28–38. Here, before Pilate, the same motive recurs, and it dominates the entire Johannine passion story.

Fascher emphasizes strongly that the main thought in this dispute lies in the following double idea: just as Jesus and the Father are one, so also Jesus, the Shepherd, is one with the sheep. Jesus' legitimization is based on this mutual and reciprocal relation. As Fascher himself correctly maintains, vv. 3–4 point forward to *vs.14;* here we have before us a conscious compositional order. There is also a clear connection between the imagery (bildtal) of vv. 1–5 and vv. 27–30, which summarize the significance of the imagery in a concluding formulation. The train of thought culminates in these verses, cf. the reaction of the Jews in vs. 31: they want to stone Jesus. That the external course of events before this is interrupted by vv. 19–21, and that by a new situational marker, vv. 22f., means nothing in particular. The Johannine plan certainly takes within its purview much more than the immediate context. Thus Fascher shows an intentional connection between vv. 3–5 and vs. 14. The idea of the unity between Jesus and the sheep in vs. 14, however, passes directly on to the idea of the unity between Jesus and the Father, vs. 15, precisely as the case is with vv. 27–31. Immediately following the saying about Jesus and his sheep, comes the saying about Jesus and the Father, issuing into: "I and the Father are one". The point therefore is not, as is often said, simply that the true Messiah dies for the flock. Even Judas, Theudas and Bar Cochba offered their life on behalf of their own followers. The main thought is that Jesus received his office from God and that in all his work he is one with the Father. It is for this reason that he can save the sheep by his death. For thanks to his *exousia* he can lay down his life and take it back. No one of the pseudo-Christs can do this, for they must remain in death, they have no exousia.

It is thus impossible to separate 10:1–5 from 14–18. The two groups of sayings have a mutual correspondence. The imagery receives its interpretation in vv. 14–18. From this light is thrown on the images. "The fold" is Israel as fenced by the Law and tradition. Only Jesus can appear here with legitimate authority; the watchmen of the Law are "strangers", outsiders and ill-disposed, thieves and robbers. Jesus is the good, the right shepherd. The Shepherd discourse belongs to the conflict with the Pharisees and their scribal learning, cf. ch. 9, where the man born blind – but not "the Jews", the Pharisees – hears Jesus' voice and follows him (9:40). They ask for the liberation of Barabbas, the insurrectionist (ληστής), the illegitimate representative of Israel's hope for the kingdom of God. Fascher holds together 10:1–13 with 18:40, without wishing to postulate an absolute correspondence between image and reality. The wolf is Rome, and a shepherd of the type of Barabbas gladly withdraws from the game, he flees if he can. It is quite different with Jesus as he gives himself up voluntarily to his enemies (18:8). The people who ask for the release of Barabbas, being incited and misguided by their leaders, mistake the hired hand for the shepherd.

According to Fascher we have found a firm connection between *10:1–5* and *14–18.* Now it becomes evident that vv. *11–13* also belongs together with vv. 14–18 at the same time as vs. 12 is in close relation to vv. 3–4. Therefore Fascher calls 11–13 and 14–18 "regelrechte Ausdeutungen von 10:1–5".

With regards to *10:7–10,* Fascher emphasizes that "the gate for the sheep" is the gate through which the sheep must pass in order to find life and nourishment. The flock is not Israel as a whole, but Jesus' "own", those Israelites who hear his voice and follow him. While the Pharisees and the scribes close the way to the kingdom of God for men, Jesus wants to open it. In the Shepherd discourse an OT motive can be perceived (Ps 23; 80 etc.), but the OT lacks the reciprocal, trustful relationship between the shepherd and his sheep. Fascher wants to see here a gnostic element. But the contrast with Pharisaism and scribal learning is "Synoptic".

Fascher is of the opinion that in vs. 7 John (the Evangelist) begins an interpretation of vv. 1–5 with special reference to vs. 2. John interprets the three concepts "shepherd", "gate" and "sheep" from his own standpoint. Vs. 16 is on the same line as vv. 1–5; the thought is about the boundaries of the "fold", but it does not include the whole cosmos. Only those who are out there in the world of men, who belong to Jesus, are included. Vs. 16 has therefore mission-historical significance, and allows us to see Jesus' situation. The point of departure is the faithful of Israel and Jesus' work there. Thus, the Johannine Shepherd is neither wholly rooted in the OT nor wholly gnostic; he has a Synoptic, historical foundation. This situation is reflected in the image of "the gate", which also unites the three elements in itself: Jewish, Jesus, gnosis[1].

[1] Fascher has collected a rich and valuable material to elucidate "door" and "gate" as religious terms in Judaism and the early Church. The essay on Jn 10:17–18 leads into the depths of Johannine thought and is very significant.

5. Corollary

The above-mentioned works occasion various reflections of a hermeneutical and exegetical nature. With regards to the reconstruction of sources, to the extent they propose to *replace* the present Gospel text, enough has already been said. This method is an expression of a kind of historicism, which is actually interested only in the primitive elements of the tradition and sees in their being committed to writing a product of tendentious, disorderly reworkings of these elements. This view implies a gross misunderstanding of the Evangelists and especially of John, who to an even greater degree than the Synoptics, has fused his sources to produce an integrated religious outlook. It ought to be unnecessary at this juncture to say more on this point. However, what still deserves to be touched upon is partly *the character of the Johannine imagery* partly *the relation of the Gospel of John to history* and partly, in conclusion, a few questions concerning *Jn 10:1–18.* Naturally, it can only be a question of a few brief and very incomplete remarks on all these points.

1. Bultmann and Brun have devoted considerable attention to the character of the Johannine imagery: is it a parable, an allegory or something else? This question has lately been treated by Ed. Schweizer, who in his important work "Ego eimi" (Göttingen 1939) discusses this problem in the section "Das Ziel der johanneischen Bildrede" (pp. 112–124) and works out the theological significance of the results obtained (pp. 124–140).[2] What is presented here relative to this question confirms the impression that the Johannine use of imagery cannot simply be assigned to the category of parable or allegory. Rather it appears to be the case that the presupposition for the imagery in John is an existing theological world of concepts in images, where image is the name of a certain religious reality, but which, of course, at the same time can also develop its associative significance like the parable or the metaphor. Behind the image lies a realism of concepts, which sees image and reality as one. Schweizer is fully correct in assuming that this realism of concepts is older than John's Gospel, for it is evident that the Johannine images have polemical significance: *I* – and no one else – am "The Good Shepherd", "The True Vine" etc. Thus, the use of the image is not determined primarily by the inner logic of the image and its associative power, but by *Jesus' absoluteness.* This is what is primary, the image is secondary. From this it follows that we cannot speak of allegory, even if the metaphorical element is pursued quite a long way as e.g. in the image of the vine in ch. 15. What this is all about is given beforehand, to be sure. The meaning does not come first at the end as the solution to a riddle.

Under these circumstances it should not surprise us that in Jn 10 the image

[2] Schweizer's "Einzelauslegung" of ch. 10 (pp. 141 ff.) works wholly along Bultmann's tracks and offers nothing of substantial interest.

changes suddenly (shepherd–gate–shepherd), or that now the one now the other image element is worked out in changing directions (Jesus goes through the gate, Jesus is the gate) as well as with different contrasts (the shepherd contra the thief and the robber on one side, contra the hired hand on the other). The images do not reveal reality, they illustrate it. Therefore the boundary line between image discourse and proper discourse is not sharp. Jesus can say to the Jews: "You are not of my sheep"; and the transition from the general depiction of the shepherd's behaviour to the concrete self-predication "I am the good shepherd", is easy and natural.

2. The question about the relation of the Fourth Gospel to history is not the same as the question to what extent the statements and narratives of the Gospel have a true historical reality-content, or whether the Johannine discourses of Jesus, to a greater or lesser extent, contain genuine words of Jesus. Rather the problem is to what degree and in what way the Fourth Evangelist stands in Jesus' situation and claims genuine Jesus motives for this situation. If one were to put the question in this way, then one must state outright that the Gospel of John is historical, *nota bene* in its present form. According to Bultmann and others this form is supposed to be the fruit of an "ecclesiastical" reworking of an older form. But is it credible that an ecclesiastical reworking would have wanted to or so confidently been able to place Jesus in the historical situation? No, that John's Gospel is "historical" in the above mentioned sense is owing to the fact that the strongest element in the Gospel is a genuine and unadulterated Jesus tradition, which to be sure, exists in "Johannized" form, but which has kept its connection with the historical reality unbroken. To try to peal off elements of primitive tradition from the Gospel of John is to no purpose. Here history and interpretation have been so inextricably fused together that they cannot be separated from one another. This situation is seen quite clearly in ch. 10. The situation and its meaning are genuinely historical and the sayings, the terms, the thoughts are typically Johannine.

3. Finally a few disparate notes on the Shepherd discourse. That vv. 7–10, 11–13 and 14–18 are to be considered as interpretations of or – what amounts to the same thing – paraphrases of the basic image in vv. 1–5, may be taken as certain. When John begins the series of comments with the saying about "the gate", this is quite simply owing to the fact that "the gate" is the first strongly emphasized concept (vs. 1,2). Thus, John connects his paraphrase primarily to this saying and that in such a way that "the gate" now does not express the legitimacy of the shepherd (as in vv. 1–2), but his absoluteness: *extra hanc januam nulla salus!* At any rate, it is striking that the idea of *legitimacy* and the idea of *power to save* are so closely interwoven in these verses. In the image of vv. 1–5 what stands out over against the legitimate shepherd is not primarily a neutral outsider, but the thief and the robber. The dominant thought, however, is not the damage which he causes, but the fact that the sheep do not follow him.

They do not recognize his voice, for them he is an ἀλλότριος. In vv. 7–10 on the other hand, the dominant idea is the *saving power*, and here the concepts of "thief" and "robber" are seen in their proper light: the thief comes only in order to steal, slaughter and destroy. Jesus, on the other hand, is the gate; he who enters through him is saved, he goes in and out and finds pasture. Nevertheless, even here the idea of legitimacy comes into play, namely, in the much-discussed vs. 8:

> All who ever came before me,
> were thieves and robbers,
> but the sheep did not listen to them.

I cannot see anything other than that κλέπται καὶ λησταί in this context is practically identical with ἀλλότριοι, unauthorized, illegitimate. First in vs. 10 "thief" receives its full material significance, and then by way of a development of that which lies in the concept itself (ὁ κλέπτης is generic). This should be heeded when interpreting vs. 8. We should not make too much of "thieves and robbers", but rather see these expressions as a designation for the lack of divine authorization of those concerned, cf. the continuation: but the sheep did not listen to them.

Who are then "all who ever came before me"? I think Fascher is right when he refuses to differentiate sharply between pseudo-Christs and Pharisees (scribes), but takes both of these categories together as a contrast to Jesus. Jesus rejects every messianic pretention and the entire scribal learning that was favourably disposed toward a national messiah. All such claims and aspirations have no divine sanction, rather they are only power politics in a religious apparel. Therefore I consider vs. 8 as a bracket, which holds together the interpretation of vv. 7–10 with the image of vv. 1–5 and constitutes a bridge between the two sections, before the theme about the "gate" is developed more closely.

With respect to the image material I concur with Fascher. In vv. 1–5 the "fold" is Israel as fenced by the Law. Only the legitimate shepherd comes with God's authorization (the door-keeper opens to him), and his sheep follow only him. τὰ ἴδια πρόβατα vv. 3f. stands in contrast to the other sheep, who do not follow the shepherd, that is, the unbelieving Israelites. That these other sheep should belong to some other flock in the fold and another (for them legitimate) shepherd, is an idea that lies outside the scope of the image. In vs. 16 "the fold" returns, Jesus has sheep that are not ἐκ τῆς αὐλῆς ταύτης, i.e. not Israelites; cf. my essay in SEÅ II, p. 144,[3] where, however, "this sheep pen" is identified with "the Apostolic Church in Israel". This is rather ἡ ποίμνη, the flock, which is to be enlarged with the sheep roaming outside Israel. When Jesus in vs. 15 speaks of giving his life for the sheep, a closer definition is demanded of the quite

[3] ["Missionstanken i Fjärde evangeliet", *SEÅ* 2 (1937), 137–148 (Tr.)].

undefined concept τὰ πρόβατα, and it comes in vs. 16: it is the universal church composed of Jews and Gentiles.

Jn 10:16 marks in the strongest possible way John's firm basis in history. On this verse strand all attempts to detach parts of the texts from the framework of the Gospel and arrive back at a pre-church textform. The mission saying of 10:16 mirrors Jesus's situation in a way that no later secondary formulation would have been able to copy. Wellhausen and Bultmann must excise this saying in order to be able to carry out their text-critical operations. Already this procedure carries with it the condemnation of their attempt.

In Jn 10 we stand in the midst of the controversy of the early Church with Judaism in continuation of Jesus' own struggle with it. Fascher is right in pointing out again and again the close relationship to the Synoptics: Jesus' self-consciousness, his utterances of judgment over the Pharisees and the scribes. To this is added in John the motive of the bond which so intimately unites the shepherd with his flock: "I know my sheep and my sheep know me". It is, of course, possible that a gnostic scheme lies behind this, but in that case it has become the bearer and expression of a historical reality: the relation of the Son of Man to his disciples, such as this was established in Galilee and was perfected through Easter and Pentecost.

Part Three

Paul

Zur Auslegung von Röm 1,19f.

(1916)

Paulus behauptet am Anfang des Römerbriefes eine Verantwortlichkeit Gott gegenüber auch bei den Heiden: διότι τὸ γνωστὸν τοῦ θεοῦ φανερόν ἐστιν ἐν αὐτοῖς· ὁ θεὸς γὰρ αὐτοῖς ἐφανέρωσε. τὰ γὰρ ἀόρατα αὐτοῦ ἀπὸ κτίσεως κόσμου τοῖς ποιήμασι νοούμενα καθορᾶται, ἥ τε ἀΐδιος αὐτοῦ δύναμις καὶ θειότης, εἰς τὸ εἶναι αὐτοὺς ἀναπολογήτους.

I

Der Sinn dieser Worte ist ja ganz unzweideutig: die Geschöpfe zeugen von dem Schöpfer, nicht nur daß er ist, sondern auch z. T. wie er ist. – Die Form aber, in welcher dieser damals geläufige Gedanke bei Paulus hervortritt, erfordert eine genauere Erörterung.

Man übersetzt gewöhnlich etwa: "Gottes unsichtbares Wesen, seine ewige Macht und Göttlichkeit, wird seit der Weltschöpfung gesehen, indem es an den Werken erfaßt wird."

Mit einer Reihe von Fragezeichen hat P.O. Schjött in dieser Ztschr. 1903 S. 75–79 diese Übersetzung versehen und auch eine Auslegung geliefert, die von den gewöhnlichen Auffassungen unserer Stelle abweicht. In kürzerer Form hat er dasselbe wiederholt in seiner Schrift "Romerbrevet" 1912 S. 47.

Es handelt sich um folgendes:

1. τὰ ἀόρατα τοῦ θεοῦ – wie ist das zu verstehen? Das Wesen Gottes ist doch eine Einheit, hier aber heißt es pluralisch τὰ ἀόρατα. Gibt's denn im Begriffe Gott Seiten, Qualitäten, die gesehen werden können?

2. νοούμενα – der Begriff καθορᾶται weist auf etwas Absolutes hin, das für keine weitere Ergänzung Platz übrigläßt. Eine ergänzende Erklärung wird aber bei der gewöhnlichen Auffassung von νοούμενα dem Begriff aufgezwungen. Das muß den Anschein erwecken, als wolle Paulus seine Worte entschuldigen und dadurch abschwächen.

3. Was soll das heißen, daß die unsichtbaren Dinge Gottes "ersehen werden von der Schöpfung der Welt her", also als der Mensch noch nicht da war?

4. Es geht nicht an, zu sagen, daß ein Ding mit den Augen gesehen wird, während es mit dem Gedanken erfaßt wurde.

Schjött schlägt dann vor, ἀόρατα mit νοούμενα zu verknüpfen; so komme ein philosophischer Gedanke heraus, der von Philo und den Neuplatonikern her bekannt sei: als νοούμενα kamen die unsichtbaren Qualitäten Gottes durch einen besonderen Prozeß (nämlich durch den Schöpfungsakt) zu sichtbarer Offenbarung. Es wird übersetzt: "Die unsichtbaren Gedanken Gottes, die von der Schöpfung der Welt her in seinen Werken hervortreten [realisiert sind], liegen offen zutage, sowohl seine ewige Macht als seine Gottheit."

Von diesen Einwänden gegen die bisherige Auslegung darf man sofort 1 und 3 als nicht zutreffend bezeichnen:

1. Τὰ ἀόρατα [τοῦ θεοῦ] läßt sich ungezwungen als die Summe des göttlichen Wesens verstehen, vgl. τὰ ὁρατὰ καὶ τὰ ἀόρατα Kol 1,16 = τὰ ἐν τοῖς οὐρανοῖς καὶ τὰ ἐπὶ τῆς γῆς Ign. *Trall.* 5, 2; Röm 5, 3; Joh 3, 12. Und τοῦ θεοῦ braucht ja nicht partitiv zu sein, vgl. τὸ χρηστὸν τοῦ θεοῦ Röm 2, 4; τὸ παραυτίκα καὶ ἐλαφρὸν τῆς θλίψεως ἡμῶν II Kor 4, 17. Dem ganzen Ausdruck entspricht, daß Gott ἀόρατος genannt wird Kol 1,15; I Tim 1,17. Man muß sich in der Tat fragen, wie anders Paulus den abstrakten Gedanken der Unsichtbarkeit Gottes hätte ausdrücken sollen.

3. Ἀπὸ κτίσεως κόσμου, das mit καθορᾶται zu verknüpfen ist, ist nicht anstößig; denn es ist ganz natürlich, daß der terminus a quo der Offenbarung Gottes in der Natur angegeben wird, der Zeitpunkt, wo der Unsichtbare aus seiner Verborgenheit heraustrat; besonders bei einem jüdischen Schriftsteller, der einen absoluten Anfang der Welt annimmt.

Aber die Worte [τὰ ἀόρατα αὐτοῦ ... τοῖς π.] νοούμενα καθορᾶται machen unleugbar den Eindruck einer ungewöhnlichen Redeweise. Jedoch liegt die Erklärung kaum in der von Schjött angewiesenen Richtung. Denn

1. Die Satzkonstruktion wird unerträglich hart, wenn man übersetzen soll: "Seine unsichtbaren Gedanken, die in den Dingen hervorgetreten (realisiert) sind." Man sollte erwarten, etwa τὰ ἀόρατα νοούμενα (ἐν) τοῖς π. φαινόμενα o. ähnl.

2. Kann man sagen, daß "die ewige Macht und Göttlichkeit Gottes" Gedanken sind, die durch die Weltschöpfung sich realisieren? Neuplatonisch ist das wenigstens nicht.

3. Ob das Wort νοούμενον, das ja bei Platon die ruhenden, unsichtbaren Ideen bezeichnet, in der neupythagoräisch-neuplatonischen Terminologie vorkommt, weiß ich nicht. Es scheint mir zweifelhaft, daß νοούμενα gleichbedeutend mit νοητά geworden wäre; wenn überhaupt, wird es sehr selten sein. – Auf jeden Fall aber würde der Sinn, den Schjött aus dem verhandelten Pauluswort herausbekommt, schlecht zu der neuplatonischen Denkweise passen. Denn dieser zufolge produzierte ja der göttliche νοῦς – nicht die Welt, sondern – den κόσμος νοητός, der unsichtbar ist; und erst nach diesem Vorbilde ist die

sichtbare Welt geschaffen worden, so daß sie nur eine schwache Vorstellung von der göttlichen Gedankenwelt gibt; vgl. Philo, *De op. mund.* 16ff., 25, 36 (Wendl.): Zuerst wird der κόσμος νοητός, ἀόρατος, ἀσώματος geschaffen, und dann als dessen μίμημα (πρὸς τὸ παράδειγμα αὐτοῦ) der κόσμος αἰσθητός, ὁρατός, σωματικός, – und Plut. *Mor.* 477 D: Die Welt, Sonne, Mond, Sterne, Flüsse usw. sind ἀγάλματα ... οἷα νοῦς θεῖος αἰσθητὰ νοητῶν μιμήματα ... ἔφηνεν. Deshalb haben die echten Neuplatoniker sich nie den Stoikern angeschlossen, wenn diese die Welt (das Geschaffene) als Grundlage der Erkenntnis Gottes (des Schöpfers) darstellen. Vgl. Philo, *Legg. All.* III, 100ff., der der stoischen Gotteserkenntnis διὰ σκιᾶς (s. u. sub II) als höhere Stufe die unmittelbare Schauung gegenüberstellt: Ἔστι δέ τις τελεώτερος καὶ μᾶλλον κεκαθαρμένος νοῦς τὰ μεγάλα μυστήρια μυηθείς, ὅστις οὐκ ἀπὸ τῶν γεγονότων τὸ αἴτιον γνωρίζει, ὡς ἀπὸ σκιᾶς τὸ μένον, ἀλλ' ὑπερκύψας τὸ γενητὸν ἔμφασιν ἐναργῆ τοῦ ἀγενήτου λαμβάνει, ὡς ἀπ' αὐτοῦ λαμβάνειν τὴν σκιάν.

II

Können wir also nicht der Lösung Schjötts beistimmen, so ist es kaum möglich, die Worte τοῖς ποιήμασι νοούμενα anders zu fassen wie als Parallele oder Näherbestimmung zu dem Oxymoron τὰ ἀόρατα ... καθορᾶται. Das Motiv, das bei dieser Ausführlichkeit der Ausdrucksweise wirksam gewesen ist, läßt sich gewiß aufdecken; sachlich ist das längst geschehen, mit besonderer Sorgfalt von v. Hofmann z. St.[1] Aber zur klareren und allseitigeren Beleuchtung empfiehlt es sich, einige Parallelstellen[2] heranzuziehen.

Vor allen Dingen ist es die Frage, ob sich Spuren einer eingebürgerten Ausdrucksweise aufzeigen lassen, wie bei einem so allgemeinen und häufig vorgetragenen Gedanken zu erwarten wäre.

Der (späte) Neuplatoniker Themistius fragt, ob der Anblick des Himmels und der Himmelskörper uns nur die ποιήματα kennen lehrt und nicht zugleich Gott, οὗ τάδε πάντα τὰ ἔργα τε καὶ ποιήματα; und er antwortet selbst: τὴν θεοῦ φύσιν τὰ ποιήματα ἐπιδείκνυσι. – Bei Epiktet finden wir häufig ähnliche Gedanken. Z. B. *Diss.* I 6, 6ff.: Wenn Schwert und Scheide zu einander passen, urteilen wir (ἀποφαίνεσθαι εἰώθαμεν), ὅτι τεχνίτου τινὸς πάντως τὸ ἔργον, οὐχὶ δ' εἰκῇ κατασκευασμένον. ἆρ' οὖν τούτων μὲν ἕκαστον ἐμφαίνει τὸν τεχνίτην, τὰ δ' ὁρατὰ καὶ ὅρασις καὶ φῶς οὐκ ἐμφαίνει; vgl. 16,8 u. ö. – Plutarch (*Mor.* 879 B) spricht von einem ἔννοιαν λαβεῖν θεοῦ durch die

[1] "... νοεῖν bezeichnet den Vorgang des Wahrnehmens, wo er seiner Natur nach ein sinnlich vermittelter ist, nach der Seite seiner Innerlichkeit." – "Der an sich selbst unsichtbare Gegenstand, von welchem hier die Rede ist, wird insofern wirklich mit den Augen gesehen, als das Sichtbare, welches seine Wahrnehmung vermittelt, dem Auge stetig gegenwärtig ist."

[2] Zum größten Teil schon von Wettstein gesammelt.

Beobachtung des Umlaufs der Himmelskörper, vgl. *Stoic. vett. frgm.* II 1009ff. denselben Ausdruck.

Diese ausgehobenen Redewendungen begegnen uns auch im hellenistischen Judentum:

Sap Sal 13, 1
καὶ ἐκ τῶν ὁρωμένων ἀγαθῶν οὐκ ἴσχυσαν εἰδέναι τὸν ὄντα,
οὔτε τοῖς ἔργοις προσέχοντες ἐπέγνωσαν τὸν τεχνίτην,

Bei Philo finden wir sie in reicher Fülle: *Legg. all.* III (97ff. Wendl.) sagt er: ἐζήτησαν οἱ πρῶτοι (sc. die Stoiker), πῶς ἐνοήσαμεν τὸ θεῖον˙ εἶθ' οἱ δοκοῦντες ἄριστα φιλοσοφεῖν ἔφασαν, ὅτι ἀπὸ τοῦ κόσμου καὶ τῶν μερῶν αὐτοῦ καὶ τῶν ἐνυπαρχουσῶν τούτοις δυνάμεων ἀντίληψιν ἐποιησάμεθα τοῦ αἰτίου˙ ὥσπερ γάρ, εἴ τις ἴδοι δεδημιουργημένην οἰκίαν ἐπιμελῶς ... ἔννοιαν λήψεται τοῦ τεχνίτου, ... οὕτως δὴ καὶ εἰσελθών τις τόνδε τὸν κόσμον ... καὶ θεασάμενος οὐρανὸν ... γῆν ... ζῷα ... φυτὰ ... λογιεῖται δήπου, ὅτι ταῦτα οὐκ ἄνευ τέχνης παντελοῦς δεδημιούργηται, ἀλλὰ καὶ ἦν καὶ ἔστιν ὁ τοῦδε τοῦ παντὸς δημιουργὸς ὁ θεός. – Οἱ δὲ οὕτως ἐπιλογιζόμενοι διὰ σκιᾶς τὸν θεὸν καταλαμβάνουσι, διὰ τῶν ἔργων τὸν τεχνίτην κατανοοῦντες. – Dasselbe Schema: θεασάμενος ... ἐννοεῖν, ἔννοιαν λαβεῖν ... (dreimal), ὑπολαμβάνειν, *de monarch.* 33–35; *de praem.* 41ff.

Die popularphilosophische Ausdrucksweise in bezug auf die Gotteserkenntnis setzt sich offenbar aus folgenden Elementen zusammen: 1. Dem Sehen (θεᾶσθαι sc. die Welt und ihre Einrichtungen). – 2. Dem Schließen (λογίζεσθαι, ἀποφαίνεσθαι) auf den τεχνίτης, ποιητής, δημιουργός – oder, anders ausgedrückt: 1. der Erkenntnisquelle (ἐκ, διά, ἀπὸ τῶν ἔργων, ποιημάτων, τοῦ κόσμου καὶ τῶν μερῶν αὐτοῦ usw.), und 2. der Erkenntnis, die gewöhnlich durch ἔννοιαν λαμβάνειν oder κατανοεῖν bezeichnet wird; daneben durch ἐννοεῖν, ἀντίληψιν ποιεῖσθαι, ὑπολαμβάνειν, καταλαμβάνειν, und auch νοεῖν.

Auch für Paulus sind die ποιήματα die Erkenntnisquelle; und auch er verknüpft das "Sehen" und "Erkennen", aber nicht in der geläufigen Weise: θεασάμενοι ... (κατα)νοοῦμεν, sondern umgekehrt νοούμενα καθορᾶται. – Das ist natürlich eine Folge davon, daß er den Gedanken als ein Oxymoron gestaltet: τὰ ἀόρατα καθορᾶται. Dazu haben wir die schöne Parallele Ps. Aristoteles *de mundo* 6 (ὁ θεός) πάσῃ θνητῇ φύσει γενόμενος ἀθεώρητος, ἀπ' αὐτῶν τῶν ἔργων θεωρεῖται. Im Verhältnis zu dieser Stelle ist die paradoxe Ausdrucksweise bei Paulus noch etwas schärfer gestaltet. Aber warum hat denn der Apostel diese Verschärfung dann wieder durch νοούμενα modifiziert?

Man könnte sich denken, daß ihm das nackte Oxymoron bedenklich vorkam, und es ihm wünschenswert schien, jegliches Mißverständnis zu verhüten. – Ferner läßt sich darauf hinweisen, daß (κατα-εν-)νοεῖν ein eingebürgerter terminus für die natürliche Gotteserkenntnis gewesen zu sein scheint und sich mit dem Gedanken im Bewußtsein hervordrängte.

Im ersten Falle haben wir also mit Rücksichten zu rechnen, die einem Juden mitten in der idolstrotzenden römischen Welt durchaus nicht fernliegend sein mochten.[3] Im zweiten liegt eine Vermischung zweier stereotyper Ausdrucksweisen vor. Es steht aber dem nichts im Wege, daß beide Motive zusammengewirkt haben. – Auf jeden Fall bleibt es ein offensichtiger stilistischer Schönheitsfehler;[4] hier kommt es aber auf das sachliche Verständnis an.

Wir gehen also zunächst von der Voraussetzung aus, Paulus habe in seinem Eifer, um die Unentschuldbarkeit der Heiden zu vergegenwärtigen, den populären Gedanken der natürlichen Gotteserkenntnis so scharf wie möglich formuliert; aber aus Rücksicht auf eventuelle Mißverständnisse und unter dem Zwange der gewöhnlichen Redeweise erklärend und vorbeugend "(τοῖς ποιήμασι) νοούμενα" in das einfache Satzgerippe "τὰ ἀόρατα αὐτοῦ ... καθορᾶται" eingefügt.

Die Möglichkeit dieser Auffassung wird von Schjött bestritten: "Es geht nicht an, zu sagen, daß ein Ding mit den Augen gesehen wird, während es mit dem Gedanken erfaßt wurde" – oder, wie er in "Romerbrevet" sagt: "νοέω bedeutet nicht 'bemerken'; ... es bedeutet 'denken', 'durch den Gedanken erfassen'." – Dieser Einwand ist nicht stichhaltig. Es handelt sich hier um ein Doppeltes, die sinnliche Wahrnehmung und das geistige Erkennen, beides in einem. Die beiden Momente lassen sich logisch trennen, psychologisch aber nicht. Das zeigt schon der Gebrauch von νοεῖν bei Homer. Allerdings schreibt er oft ἰδὼν ἐνόησε, das die beiden Vorgänge naiv nebeneinander stellt;[5] aber

---

[3] Bei den heidnischen Autoren finden wir oft eine genauere Umschreibung des Gedankens. Cic. *Tusc.* I 29 *Deum non vides, tamen ... Deum agnoscis ex operibus suis.* Philodem περὶ εὐσ. p. 71 Gomperz. Apuleius (Wettst.). – Xenoph. *Mem.* IV, 3 wird das gleichzeitige Verborgensein und Geoffenbartsein Gottes mit der Sonne verglichen, die, allen sichtbar, doch den Menschen ihren genauen Anblick verwehrt (vgl. Philo, *de mon.* 40), oder mit der Seele, die durch die Herrschaft, die sie in uns ausübt, kenntlich ist, aber selbst unsichtbar, vgl. Ps. Arist., *de mundo* 6 ψυχὴ ... ἀόρατος οὖσα τοῖς ἔργοις αὐτοῖς ὁρᾶται. – Einen prägnanten Gebrauch von θεᾶσθαι hat Epiktet, z.B. I 6, 22 ὁρᾶτε οὖν, μὴ ἀθεάτητοι τούτων (sc. des göttlichen Wesens, das sich in der Weltregierung betätigt) ἀποθάνητε. Aber 6,19 τὸν ἄνθρωπον θεατὴν εἰσήγαγεν (ὁ θεὸς) αὐτοῦ τε καὶ τῶν ἔργων αὐτοῦ, καὶ οὐ μόνον θεατήν, ἀλλὰ καὶ ἐξηγητὴν αὐτῶν, vgl. 6, 24 θεάσασθαι καὶ κατανοῆσαι (τὰ ἔργα). – Mit fast wissenschaftlicher Genauigkeit formuliert den Gedanken die Sap Sal 13, 5:

ἐκ γὰρ μεγέθους καὶ καλλονῆς κτισμάτων
ἀναλόγως ὁ γενεσιουργὸς αὐτῶν θεωρεῖται.

[4] Man darf wohl überhaupt urteilen, daß überall, wo Paulus überkommene Gedanken handhabt, die Darstellung vielfach Stringens und stilistische Geschlossenheit entbehrt. Nicht am wenigsten ist das der Fall im ersten Kap. des Römerbriefes (vgl. die Worte Wendlands, *Hell.-Röm. Kultur* 1. Aufl. S. 141–142; 2. Aufl. S. 245).

[5] Vgl. Marc. Ant., ed. Schenkl VI 30, 6 ... εὖ μάλα κατιδὼν καὶ σαφῶς νοήσας. – Danach und nach der allgemeinen Redeweise sollte man also bei Paulus eher erwarten τὰ ἀόρ. ... τοῖς π. ὁρωμένοις κατανοεῖται. Aber die Gestaltung des Gedankens ist in erster Linie von dem zugespitzten Begriffe der Sichtbarkeit des Unsichtbaren beherrscht.

daneben wird νοεῖν zusammenfassend für beides gesetzt, z.B. Δ 200 τὸν δ' ἐνόησεν ἑσταότα. Trotz der platonisch-philosophischen Spezialisierung hat sich die Beziehung des Wortes zur äußeren Wahrnehmung gehalten; vgl. Polyb I 49,8 'Ατάρβας ... νοήσας τὸν ἐπίπλουν τῶν ὑπεναντίων. Sir 41, 27 LXX hat κατανοεῖν geradezu die Bedeutung "sehen", "beobachten" angenommen; vgl. Jak 1, 23. 24 u.ö.i. NT. Es ist deshalb möglich, νοούμενα Röm 1, 20 als sachliche Parallele zu καθορᾶται zu verstehen und es mit τοῖς ποιήμασι zu verknüpfen (so die englische und die skandinavischen Kirchenübersetzungen; Luther). Für diese Auffassung kann man außer den sachlichen Erwägungen auch den oben erwähnten geläufigen Gebrauch von κατανοεῖν anführen, vgl. besonders Philo a.a.O. διὰ τῶν ἔργων τὸν τεχνίτην κατανοοῦντες; es ließe sich denken, daß Paulus νοούμενα statt κατανοούμενα schrieb wegen des folgenden καθορᾶται. Aber auch das bloße νοεῖν läßt sich nachweisen in der Bedeutung: "Auf Grund von etwas Gesehenem sich eine Vorstellung wovon machen"; vgl. Philo a. a. O. πῶς ἐνοήσαμεν τὸ θεῖον mit Stellen wie Epiktet ed. Schenkl frgm. 7,5: φαμὲν γὰρ τὸν εὐκαταφρόνητον νοεῖσθαι μὲν καὶ κατὰ τὸ ἀδύνατον εἶναι βλάψαι· ἀλλὰ πολὺ μᾶλλον νοεῖται κατὰ τὸ ἀδύνατον εἶναι ὠφελεῖν, sc. seine innere Art wird erkannt durch die Wahrnehmung seiner äußeren Haltung. Ähnlich Marc. Ant. ed. Schenkl IV 10,2. Hier ist auch zu erwähnen Sap Sal 13, 4[6]

εἰ δὲ δύναμιν καὶ ἐνέργειαν (sc. der Himmelskörper) ἐκπλαγέντες,
νοησάτωσαν ἀπ' αὐτῶν πόσῳ ὁ κατασκευάσας αὐτὰ δυνατώτερός ἐστιν.

III

Indessen wäre vielleicht noch eine andere Erklärung ins Auge zu fassen, die, wenn zutreffend, zwar sachlich auf genau dasselbe hinauskommt, aber doch der Aussage eine etwas andere Farbe verleiht – sie sozusagen ihrer kühnen Paradoxie entkleidet und in die Reihe der kunstgerechten religionsphilosophischen termini hineinstellt. Eine solche Redewendung findet sich z.B. bei Josephus *Antt.* Prooem. 19, eine Stelle, die hier nähere Beachtung verdienen dürfte: Μωϋσῆς ... πάντων ἀναγκαιότατον ἡγήσατο τῷ καὶ τὸν ἑαυτοῦ μέλλοντι βίον οἰκονομήσειν καλῶς καὶ τοῖς ἄλλοις νομοθετεῖν, θεοῦ πρῶτον φύσιν κατανοῆσαι καὶ τῶν ἔργων τῶν ἐκείνου θεατὴν τῷ νῷ γενόμενον ... πειρᾶσθαι κατακολουθεῖν. – θεᾶσθαι τῷ νῷ heißt hier augenscheinlich die geistig vertiefte Beobachtung. Die äußere Wahrnehmung bildet den Ausgangspunkt der inneren Überlegung, der intellektuellen und religiös-ethischen

---

[6] Zu diesen Ausführungen ist zu vergleichen Ed. Norden, *Agnostos Theos* 1913, S. 24ff.; 125ff. (woselbst Schjötts Aufsatz erwähnt und beurteilt S. 128 Anm. 1). – Die Frage, ob Röm 1 von Sap 13 direkt abhängig ist, kann noch nicht für entschieden gehalten werden; ich behandle deshalb unsere Stelle, ohne Rücksicht auf diese Frage zu nehmen.

Schlußfolgerung. Nur wenn das Sehen durch die geistige Verarbeitung des Gesehenen ergänzt wird, kommt eine richtige Erkenntnis zustande. Vgl. Plut 98F: καὶ νοῦς ὁρᾷ καὶ νοῦς ἀκούει, τὰ δ' ἄλλα κωφὰ καὶ τυφλά.[7]

Auf diesem Hintergrunde läßt sich auch die besprochene Ausdrucksweise bei Paulus erklären: [τὰ ἀόρατα τοῦ θεοῦ ... τοῖς ποιήμασι] νοούμενα καθορᾶται wäre in dem Falle gleich νῷ καθορῶμεν zu verstehen; vgl. die Übersetzung Lietzmanns: "Seine unsichtbaren Eigenschaften ... kann man ... an dem Geschaffenen mit (den Augen) der Vernunft erblicken", oder Jülicher: "... mit dem Auge des Geistes"; Weizsäcker: "... durch das Denken gesehen". – Das ungewöhnliche νοούμενα ließe sich vielleicht aus einer doppelten Einwirkung von seiten der umgebenden Worte erklären: einerseits mag die passivische Form καθορᾶται durch Assimilation dazu beigetragen haben, τῷ νῷ in das passivische νοούμενα zu entwickeln; andererseits kann man an eine Dissimilation denken in der Weise, daß der Sprachsinn des Verfassers die Nebeneinanderstellung zweier grammatisch kongruenter, aber inhaltlich verschiedener Konstruktionen (τοῖς ποιήμασι τῷ νῷ) vermeiden wollte.

Hält man dagegen an der im Abschnitt II befürworteten Auslegung fest, wird man eine Übersetzung ersinnen müssen, die das Paradoxe des Ausdrucks deutlich hervortreten läßt. Die glücklichste Formulierung scheint mir die Stages zu sein: "Sein unsichtbares Wesen ... wird seit Erschaffung der Welt dem denkenden Verstande in seinen Werken sichtbar." Um einerseits dem Oxymoron sein volles Gewicht zu lassen, andererseits aber der Modifikation, die in νοούμενα liegt, zu ihrem Recht zu verhelfen, ist es angemessen, mit Stage νοούμενα aus dem Passivischen ins Aktive umzusetzen, und zwar als Eigenschaft des logischen Subjekts.

IV

Schließlich verdient noch eine Schriftgruppe besonders erwähnt zu werden wegen ihres Reichtums an Gedanken, die mit den hier besprochenen eng verwandt sind: das Corpus Hermeticum. Dieses zeigt in charakteristischer Weise die neuplatonische Mischung von Dualismus und Pantheismus, von Mystik und Rationalismus. Es wird geschieden zwischen dem κόσμος νοητός und dem κόσμος αἰσθητός;[8] auf den ersteren haben sich die religiösen Bestrebungen zu richten. Hier vollzieht sich das mystische Gottschauen durch den νοῦς. Dies Schauen ist ein inneres Erlebnis,[9] das zuweilen als ekstatisch aufge-

[7] Dem νοῦς entspricht das stoische ἡγεμονικόν oder προαιρετικὴ δύναμις, vgl. Epikt. *Diss.* II, 23,9ff.: Die Augen sind blind und können nichts sehen als αὐτὰ τὰ ἔργα; sie werden geöffnet von der προαιρετικὴ δύναμις, αὐτὴ δὲ μόνη ὀξὺ βλέπει καὶ τὰς ἄλλας καθορᾷ κτλ.

[8] XVI (Reitzenstein); XIII 14 (Parthey).

[9] IV 6.11; VII 2; VIII 5; X 4.9.10; XI 19; XIII 6.15; XIV 3.

faßt zu sein scheint.[10] – Andererseits aber kann die νόησις auch durch die Außendinge angeregt werden,[11] und in diesem Sinne wird sogar von einem "Gott sehen" im Gegensatz zum "Gott begreifen" gesprochen.[12] Denn die sichtbare Welt ist von der göttlichen Energie durchdrungen und gestaltet und zeugt deshalb von Gott. Freilich ist sie keine voll genügende Grundlage der Gotteserkenntnis[13] (vgl. oben den ähnlichen Gedanken bei Philo).

Ein besonderes Interesse hat für uns Kap. V, das überschrieben ist: ὅτι ἀφανὴς ὁ θεὸς φανερώτατος ἐστιν: Gott ist ἀφανής, weil ewig. Denn πᾶν τὸ φαινόμενον γεννητόν. Gott bringt aber alles hervor: πάντα φανερὰ ποιεῖ. Daher kann man von Gott sagen: διὰ πάντων φαίνεται καὶ ἐν πᾶσι, καὶ μάλιστα οἷς ἂν βουληθῇ φανῆναι. – Das größte Gut nun ist νοῆσαι θεόν. νόησις γὰρ μόνον ὁρᾷ τὸ ἀφανές. Der Herr erscheint τοῖς τοῦ νοῦ (τῆς καρδίας) ὀφθαλμοῖς. Diese νόησις ist schließlich eine Gabe Gottes und betätigt sich in der unsichtbaren Welt; aber sie ist nicht ohne Beziehung zur sichtbaren Welt: εἰ δὲ θέλεις αὐτὸν (sc. τὸν θεὸν) ἰδεῖν, νόησον τὸν ἥλιον, νόησον τὸν τῆς σελήνης δρόμον, νόησον τῶν ἀστέρων τὴν τάξιν˙ τίς ὁ τὴν τάξιν τηρῶν; ... τίς ὁ ἑκάστῳ τὸν τρόπον καὶ τὸ μέγεθος τοῦ δρόμου ὁρίσας; ... τίς ὁ τῇ θαλάσσῃ τοὺς ὅρους περιβαλών; τίς ὁ τὴν γῆν ἑδράσας; es muß einen ποιητὴς καὶ δεσπότης τούτων πάντων geben. Wenn man die Kraft erhält, sich über der Teilerscheinungen Fülle emporzuheben und das Ganze zusammenzuschauen (ὑπὸ μίαν ῥοπὴν πάντα ταῦτα θεάσασθαι), da sieht man τὸν ἀκίνητον διακινούμενον καὶ τὸν ἀφανῆ φαινόμενον. – Die wohlbekannte, etwas grobe popularphilosophische Argumentation erscheint hier gewissermaßen verfeinert, spiritualisiert. Aber je länger, je mehr lenkt die Rede in die traditionellen Bahnen ein.[14] Es folgt eine Ausführung, die aus konventionellen Redewendungen aufgebaut ist: Wer hat die Augen, die Ohren usw. usw., wer das Kind im Mutterleib gebildet und alles wunderschön und harmonisch? Wer anders als μόνος ὁ ἀφανὴς θεὸς τῷ ἑαυτοῦ θελήματι πάντα δημιουργήσας. Und wenn man das alles sinnend schaut, kann gesprochen werden von einem θεάσασθαι τὸν δημιουργὸν καὶ διὰ τῶν θνητῶν. Schließlich wird zusammengefaßt: οὗτος ὁ θεὸς οὗτος ὁ ἀφανὴς, οὗτος ὁ φανερώτατος, ὁ τῷ νοΐ θεωρητός, οὗτος ὁ τοῖς ὀφθαλμοῖς ὁρατός.

In diesem letzten Satz tritt wieder der neuplatonische Spiritualismus hervor. Wenn Gott bezeichnet wird als ὁ τῷ νοΐ θεωρητός, so ist das eine andere Vorstellung als die bei Joseph. *Antt.* Praef. θεατὴν τῷ νῷ γενόμενον. Denn νοῦς im *Corp. Herm.* ist an dieser Stelle offenbar Organ der reinen Kontempla-

[10] X 5.6; XIII 10.

[11] IV 2; X 13; XI 6.12.21.

[12] XII 20.21.

[13] VI 4; VIII 5.

[14] V 8 fragt: Keiner behauptet, daß ein Kunstwerk ohne Künstler entstehen kann. Aber sollte denn dies großartige Werk (die Welt usw.) ohne δημιουργός geworden sein? ὢ τῆς πολλῆς τυφλότητος, ὢ τῆς πολλῆς ἀσεβείας· Vgl. Epict. *Diss.* I 16, 8.

tion bzw. der Ekstase. Ferner wird bewußtermaßen mit den Gegensätzen gespielt: ἀφανής – φανερώτατος, τῷ νοΐ θεωρητός – τοῖς ὀφθαλμοῖς ὁρατός. Die Denkweise des Paulus – wie des Josephus – liegt auf einem anderen Plan. Er findet in der Schöpfung Zeugnisse von dem Sein und Wesen des persönlichen, überweltlichen Gottes, und nur als verklausulierte Paradoxie wagt er die Behauptung: Wir sehen den Unsichtbaren. Auch der Stoizismus ist anders orientiert. Auch für den Stoizismus sind die Welt und ihre Einrichtungen schließlich Zeugnisse der göttlichen πρόνοια. Bei Paulus wie im Stoizismus ist deshalb die Gotteserkenntnis eine geistig-moralische Überzeugung. Im *Corp. Herm.* dagegen lebt die Vorstellung von der mystisch-realen Berührung mit der Gottheit, einem realen Schauen. Die gewöhnliche Psychologie wird von heterogenen Vorstellungen durchbrochen, Vorstellungen, die aus dem Gebiet der Intuition, der ästhetischen Anschauung und der Extase herstammen. Dann wird wieder sofort die eben entwickelte Gedankenreihe negiert, und der νοῦς als das einzige Organ für das Gottschauen erklärt.[15] – Solches war dem Paulus gänzlich fremd. Er hätte nie sagen können (ebensowenig als ein Stoiker): οὐδὲν γάρ ἐστιν ὃ οὐκ ἔστιν εἰκὼν τοῦ θεοῦ, vgl. *Corp. Herm.* XI,2. Auch nicht hätte er – wenn es anginge – davon sprechen können, daß die Gedanken, νοούμενα, Gottes geschaut werden in der geschaffenen Welt. – Andererseits war es dem Paulus (und den Stoikern) wirklich ernst um das "Gott sehen". In den Werken des Schöpfers offenbarte sich ihm wirklich etwas von dem unsichtbaren Wesen Gottes. Der neuplatonische, übergeistige Gottesbegriff lag ihm fern.

[15] In diesem Selbstwiderspruch offenbart sich die fundamentale Schwierigkeit des neuplatonischen Denkens: die Schwierigkeit, dualistisch-theistische und pantheistische Gedanken auszugleichen.

Die Apologie des Paulus Gal. 1

(1920)

Unter den vielen Schwierigkeiten, die die Auslegung des Galaterbriefes bedrücken, ist die nicht die kleinste, wie man sich die Gegnerschaft der Agitatoren in den galatischen Gemeinden denken soll. Denn nur wenn es gelingt, ein einigermaßen klares und einleuchtendes Bild der von Paulus vorausgesetzten und bekämpften Tätigkeit der Gegner zu gewinnen, treten die Aussagen des Kampfbriefes in die richtige Beleuchtung, enthüllen sie ihren vollen Inhalt. Ein solches Bild haben wir nicht; der Galaterbrief bietet immer noch genug der Fragezeichen, von denen wahrscheinlich viele nie getilgt werden können.

Müssen wir uns aber in manchen Fragen mit Vermutungen begnügen, so wird das Bestreben nie zur Ruhe kommen, den richtigen Sinn der Ausführungen Kap. 1–2 zu ermitteln. Denn hier stehen wir Ereignissen und Verhältnissen gegenüber, die für unsere Kunde vom Urchristentum von entscheidender Bedeutung sind, und zu deren Erkenntnis nur die richtige Interpretation der paulinischen Worte führen kann. Es soll im Folgenden der Versuch gemacht werden, zur Aufklärung eben dieses wichtigen Abschnittes etwas beizutragen, und zwar mit besonderer Rücksicht auf Kap. 1.

I

Daß Paulus Gal. 1 sich gegen gewisse, gegen ihn vorgebrachte Verleumdungen wendet, findet man meistens ohne Weiteres klar, – es fragt sich nur gegen welche. Das muß aus den Worten herausgelesen werden. Seine apologetische Hauptthese lautet: das von mir gepredigte Evangelium ist nicht κατὰ ἄνθρωπον (V. 11); und diese Behauptung wird sofort genauer präzisiert oder ergänzt V. 12: Mein Evangelium beruht nicht auf menschlicher παράδοσις noch διδαχή, sondern auf Christusoffenbarung. Dieser Satz wird dann, was die negative Seite betrifft, durch den geschichtlichen Überblick V. 13–24 gestützt.

Wenn wir hier durch die Worte des Paulus hindurch die Stimme der judaistischen Agitatoren in Galatien vernehmen, erfahren wir, daß sie ihm ein Doppeltes vorgeworfen haben: 1. Sein Evangelium sei menschlich, d. h. mit menschlichen Schwächen behaftet, und 2. er habe es von Menschen gelernt. Also eine

Beschuldigung des Irrtums und der Unselbständigkeit. Der sich an den Protest gegen diese Verleumdungen anschließende Abriß seines Lebenslaufes während der entscheidenden Jahre bezieht sich offenbar auf das zweite Moment, die behauptete Unselbständigkeit, und zwar, wie es scheint, Unselbständigkeit gegenüber den jerusalemischen Autoritäten (οἱ πρὸ ἐμοῦ ἀπόστολοι 1,17 vgl. 2, 6ff.). Dabei entsteht aber die Schwierigkeit, daß die beiden Momente sich ausschließen; denn wenn die Agitatoren Paulus als einen Schüler der Urapostel bezeichneten, konnten sie unmöglich in demselben Atemzuge sein Evangelium als einen Irrtum darstellen.

Um diesem Widerspruch auszuweichen, will Sieffert einen Bedeutungswechsel des Wortes "Evangelium" innerhalb der beiden Verse annehmen: Paulus habe "von früher bekehrten Christen, und besonders von den Uraposteln, den Inhalt und Auftrag seiner Verkündigung erhalten, nämlich insoweit dieselbe überhaupt mit der urapostolischen Lehre übereinstimme (während die paulinische Lehre von der christlichen Gesetzesfreiheit, wie aus Kap. 3 zu schließen ist, von den Judaisten als willkürlicher Zusatz des Paulus zur Überlieferung der Urapostel betrachtet sein muß)". Ähnlich Bousset (in den Schriften des N. T. usw. herausgeg. von Johannes Weiß): "Seine Gegner behaupteten – so dürfen wir schließen –, daß sein Evangelium in dem, was ihm eigentümlich, menschliche Erdichtung sei, und daß Paulus, was daran tauglich sei, von anderen empfangen habe."

Indessen, diese Auffassung ist gewiß unhaltbar. Denn vor allen Dingen läßt sich ein solcher Bedeutungswechsel von τὸ εὐαγγέλιον τὸ εὐαγγελισθὲν ὑπ' ἐμοῦ nicht annehmen. Sowohl in V. 11 als in V. 12 wird es sich um dieselbe Größe handeln: die Botschaft des Paulus an die Heiden. Man versteht unter diesen Voraussetzungen auch nicht recht, was Paulus mit seinem geschichtlichen Überblick erreichen will. Denn steht es fest, daß seine Lehre von der Gesetzesfreiheit originell ist, und daß er durch eine Christusoffenbarung berufen worden ist, da braucht er sich nicht aufzuregen, weil man ihm nachsagt, er habe dies oder jenes, wenn auch noch so bedeutsame, von den Uraposteln gelernt. Endlich läßt sich nicht leugnen, daß seine geschichtliche Apologie gar nicht zureicht, wenn es gilt, seine völlige Unabhängigkeit von den andern darzulegen.

Dieselben Einwände treffen auch die anderen Auslegungen unseres Abschnitts. Wenn man nicht eine doppelte Beschuldigung, der Fälschung und der Unselbständigkeit, in den Worten des Paulus vorausgesetzt finden will, sondern an der einheitlichen Bedeutung von τὸ εὐαγγέλιον festhält, muß man τὸ εὐαγγέλιον τὸ εὐαγγελισθὲν ὑπ' ἐμοῦ (= τὸ εὐαγγ. μου) im weitesten Sinne (als die christliche Heilsbotschaft überhaupt) fassen, und nicht, was doch am nächsten liegt, als die paulinische Botschaft an die Heiden. Das ist an sich unwahrscheinlich. Außerdem muß man sich fragen, was die Gegner mit einer solchen Beschuldigung erreichen wollten; es ist nicht einzusehen, wie ihm unter diesen Umständen ein Schülerverhältnis zu den Uraposteln zum Nachteil gereichen sollte. Ferner, innerhalb des von Paulus skizzierten Lebensganges bleibt Raum genug für Belehrung und Unterricht. Man hat denn auch verschiedene psychologische Erwägungen anstellen müssen, um zu zeigen, die kategorischen Worte des Apostels seien nicht ohne weiteres im absoluten Sinne zu nehmen. So sagt z.B. Lietzmann *(Handbuch):* "Das Ereignis von Damaskus hat das Leben des Paulus wie ein Blitzschlag getroffen und in seinen geheimsten Tiefen aufgewühlt und umgekehrt; alles was er an christlichem Besitz hat, vermag er nur im Lichte dieses Erlebnisses zu schauen und empfindet es als in dieser Stunde empfangen, in ihr vereinigt sich für sein Fühlen wie in einem Brennpunkt das Ergebnis einer wohl jahrelangen Entwickelung. Und dieser Überzeugung leiht er mit der ganzen impulsiven Stärke des religiösen Genius Worte. Der Philister freilich, der nur die billige Erfahrung des Alltagsmenschen gelten läßt, wird den Paulus der Übertreibung zeihen, und manch bedenklicher Exeget sieht zu, ob sich die Worte des Apostels nicht doch vielleicht anders, weniger absolut, deuten lassen. Aber auch wer die Auffassung des Paulus hier voll zu begreifen vermag, wird, falls er der historischen Kritik ihr Recht einräumt, zugeben, daß der Apostel sich hier faktisch über seine eigene Entwickelung täuscht ..." – Diese Überlegung hat ihr dauerndes Recht. Beim Rückblick verschieben sich die Linien, die Perspektive wird verkürzt, alles wird in einen geschlossenen Vorgang zusammengezogen. Jedoch kommt man mit solchen psychologischen Erwägungen hier nicht voll aus, denn Paulus will offenbar bestimmten Beschuldigungen entgegentreten, man muß deshalb voraussetzen, daß seine Apologie, was das konkret-negative betrifft, wirklich beweiskräftig ist.

Gegen die traditionelle Auffassung erheben sich also ernste Bedenken: 1. "Das von mir gepredigte Evangelium" muß in einem anderen Sinne als dem nächstliegenden und allein natürlichen verstanden werden. 2. Der Zweck und der Stachel der vorausgesetzten, gegen Paulus gerichteten Beschuldigung der Abhängigkeit von den Uraposteln ist nicht einleuchtend. 3. Der Gegenbeweis des Paulus genügt nicht. Dazu kommt 4. daß es fraglich scheinen muß, ob man V. 11 so übersetzen darf: Das von mir gepredigte Evangelium *stammt nicht von Menschen her;* denn κατὰ ἄνθρωπον wird sich auf die Art und den Inhalt der paulinischen Botschaft beziehen, und in dem Falle setzen die Worte nicht nur eine formale Leugnung seiner apostolischen Autorität, sondern eine reale Beanstandung seines Evangeliums voraus.

Zahn, der die schon hervorgehobenen Schwierigkeiten klar sieht, sucht einen Ausweg zu finden, dadurch daß er zwischen V. 11 und V. 12 scharf scheidet. In V. 11 erinnert Paulus die schwankenden Galater an die göttliche Art des von ihm gepredigten Evangeliums, das er soeben (V. 7–9) als das einzige bezeichnet hat. Wenn er dann die göttliche Ursprünglichkeit seines Evangeliums behauptet, ist das nicht eine genauere Ausführung von V. 11;

denn "der verneinende Satz V. 11 könnte auch dann zu Recht bestehen, wenn Paulus das Evangelium durch Vermittelung eines anderen Menschen empfangen hätte. Auch die Schüler der Apostel besitzen ja in ihrem Glauben das Evangelium Gottes und Christi, welches nicht menschlich von Art und Wesen ist. Paulus aber kann dies mit besonderer Zuversicht von sich behaupten, weil er, und zwar, wie das betonte ich sagen will, er im Unterschied von den meisten Christen, das Evangelium, das er predigt, nicht einmal durch Vermittelung eines Menschen, zu eigen bekommen hat, wodurch die Möglichkeit ausgeschlossen ist, daß er ein schon durch die Schuld seines Bekehrers entartetes und in üblem Sinne menschlich gewordenes Evangelium empfangen habe."

Paulus richtet sich somit hier nicht direkt gegen gegenteilige Behauptungen der Judaisten; er bemüht sich nur, die göttliche Art seines Evangeliums einzuschärfen und greift deshalb auf die Anfänge seines Christentums zurück: Nicht nur göttlich von Art ist sein Evangelium, sondern auch noch dazu direkt von Christus erhalten. – Allein, auch Zahn muß eine direkte Bezugnahme auf gegnerische Verleumdungen annehmen; diese hebt aber erst V. 16 an. Das stark betonte εὐθέως, das nur mit den negierten Verben (οὐ προσανεθέμην ..., οὐδὲ ἀνῆλθον ...) zu verknüpfen ist, zeigt, daß hier einer gegenteiligen Behauptung widersprochen werden soll: "Nur, wenn von gegnerischer Seite behauptet worden war, daß Paulus nicht gleich damals, in der nächsten Zeit nach seiner Bekehrung, sondern erst viel später sich der Befragung anderer Menschen enthalten und der Beratung und Anweisung von deren Seite entzogen habe, konnte sich Paulus gedrungen fühlen zu behaupten und weiterhin zu beweisen, daß er gleich damals die in dem Nichtbefragen von Menschen und Nichtbesuchen Jerusalems und der dort ansäßigen älteren Apostel sich darstellende Selbstgewißheit des Bewußtseins und Selbständigkeit des Handelns besessen und bewiesen habe." "Die Judaisten müssen also den Galatern eingeredet haben, Paulus habe in der ersten Zeit nach seiner Bekehrung, sei es jahre- oder monatelang, sich um Beziehungen zu den älteren Christen und besonders den zwölf Aposteln bemüht, um von ihnen Bestätigung seiner Bekehrung, Anerkennung seines Christentums und Rat und Weisung für die Ausübung seines Predigtberufes zu empfangen. Und später erst habe er sich in Lehren und Handeln eine Selbständigkeit angemaßt, welche ihm nicht gebühre, habe die Berührung mit den Autoritäten in Jerusalem gemieden und sei so zu einem falschen Evangelium, zu einer verkehrten Art der Heidenmission gekommen und in offenbaren Widerspruch mit der Muttergemeinde und den Häuptern der ganzen Christenheit geraten."

Es ist jedoch nicht möglich, sich bei dieser Lösung der Schwierigkeit zu beruhigen. Denn erstens kann man sich schwerlich dem Eindruck entziehen, daß schon (V. 11 und) 12 direkt gegen Äußerungen der judaistischen Agitatoren in Galatien gerichtet sind; und dann liegt es vor allen Dingen auf der Hand, daß V. 13–24 eine zusammenhängende und im Dienst eines und desselben

Interesses stehende geschichtliche Apologie ist. Der ganze Abschnitt bildet eine Einheit und ist von vornherein auf ein bestimmtes Ziel angelegt. Es ist deshalb untunlich, wie Zahn, eine direkte apologetische Tendenz erst mit V. 16 einsetzen zu lassen. Es muß der Versuch gemacht werden, einen anderen Ausweg aus dem Dilemma zu finden. Zuerst ist es aber geboten, auf die interessanten Anschauungen einzugehen, die W. Lütgert jüngst in einer Abhandlung über den Galaterbrief entwickelt hat (*Gesetz und Geist.* Eine Untersuchung zur Vorgeschichte des Galaterbriefs. Beiträge z.F. chr. Th. XXII 6).

II

Lütgerts Untersuchung wirft ein neues, überraschendes Licht auf den Galaterbrief. Kurz gesagt handelt es sich darum, daß er auch in Galatien (neben den Judaisten) eine gnostisch-antinomistische Richtung bezeugt finden will, und gegen diese letztere soll sich zum guten Teil die paulinische Apologie und Polemik richten, nicht am wenigsten in Kap. 1 u. 2.

Den Ausgangspunkt bietet Kap. 5, wo Lütgert sehr scharfe Gegensätze innerhalb der Gemeinden spürt (vgl. 5,15), und zwar spielt dabei eine pneumatische, antinomistische Partei eine Hauptrolle (vgl. 5,5ff..13; 6,1). Von diesen Leuten ist dem Paulus vorgeworfen worden, er predige die Beschneidung noch (5, 11), er richte das Gesetz wieder auf (2,17–21), er habe sein Evangelium von Menschen (1,11–24), er habe vor den Aposteln die Freiheit geleugnet und sich in Jerusalem die Predigt der Beschneidung zur Pflicht machen lassen (2,1–10). Paulus kämpft somit im Galaterbrief auf einer doppelten Front; die schon im Briefeingang sich dadurch heraushebt, daß er gleich von seinem Ausfall gegen das ἕτερον εὐαγγέλιον der Judaisten (1, 6. 7) sofort zu den gegen ihn von Seiten der Freiheitsmänner erhobenen Vorwürfen übergeht (1, 8ff.).

Es soll hier keine ausführliche Wiedergabe und kritische Beurteilung der Lütgert'schen Gesammtauffassung des Briefes gegeben werden; wir beschränken uns auf eine Untersuchung seiner Ansicht, soweit sie Kap. 1 betrifft.

Wie die Auslegung sonst läßt auch Lütgert die tadelnden Worte 1,6–7 gegen die judaistischen Neigungen in Galatien gerichtet sein: Mögen die judaistischen Agitatoren behaupten, sie (und die Apostel) verkündigen ein "anderes Evangelium" als er (Paulus), im Grunde ist ihr Evangelium kein anderes (ἄλλο) als das seine, sondern nur sein Evangelium in verdrehter Gestalt, ein Zerrbild, und somit ein ἕτερον εὐαγγέλιον. Es sieht aus als eine Ergänzung und Korrektur des paulinischen Evangeliums, ist aber in der Tat eine Verkehrung der Wahrheit in Lüge. – V. 8 aber dreht nun Paulus plötzlich den Spieß um und macht einen Ausfall gegen die Pneumatiker: Diese hatten die Berechtigung des Paulus gegen die Judaisten aufzutreten bestritten; er habe ja selbst sein ursprüngliches Evangelium fallen lassen und die Beschneidungspredigt aufgenommen. Das geht aus dem ἡμεῖς V. 8 hervor. Und wenn es ebendort heißt: Wenn ein Engel vom Himmel ein anderes Evangelium predigte usw., so setzt das voraus, "daß es Leute gab, die ein anderes Evangelium verkündigten und sich auf eine Offenbarung durch einen Engel vom Himmel beriefen".

Diese Auslegung wird nicht viele überzeugen und unterliegt schwerwiegenden Bedenken. Zunächst spricht ἀλλά V. 8 gegen sie, denn diese Konjunktion verknüpft die folgenden Worte aufs engste mit V. 7: Die Judaisten verdrehen das (von Paulus gepredigte) Evangelium Christi; ein solch falsches Evangelium aber dürfe nicht gepredigt werden, auch wenn Paulus selbst oder ein Engel vom Himmel es predigte. – Ferner, wehrte sich Paulus hier gegen die Beschuldigung, daß er sein ursprüngliches Evangelium hatte fallen lassen und später ein anderes gepredigt, hätte er kaum V. 8 (παρ' ὃ εὐηγγελισάμεθα) ὑμῖν geschrieben, sondern nur παρ' ὃ εὐηγγελισάμεθα. Da käme es ja nicht darauf an, daß er ursprünglich den Galatern das richtige Evangelium gepredigt, sondern nur darauf, daß er es gepredigt hatte. Das Interesse haftet aber nun eben daran, daß *die Galater* an dem ursprünglichen Evangelium festhalten, vgl. παρ' ὃ παρελάβετε V. 9. – Was das ἡμεῖς V. 8 betrifft, ist es allerdings wahr, daß man hier unwillkürlich an 5,11 denkt. Wenn aber hier ein Zusammenhang bestehen sollte, wird die Auslegung von 5,11 für die Erklärung von V.8 maßgebend. Das natürliche ist aber "wir selbst" und "ein Engel vom Himmel" als eine möglichst zugespitzte Ausdrucksweise zu verstehen. Daß der Engel mit pneumatischen Offenbarungsansprüchen etwas zu tun haben sollte, ist durchaus unwahrscheinlich, schon weil eine solche Zusammenpressung eines apologetischen (ἡμεῖς) und eines polemischen Momentes (Engeloffenbarung der Pneumatiker) in einer geschlossenen Aussage gegen jedes Stilgefühl streiten würde. – Und schließlich beweist die allgemeine Fassung desselben Gedankens V. 9 (εἴ τις κτλ.), daß die traditionelle Auffassung die einzig mögliche ist: Paulus verteidigt hier nicht sich selbst, sondern kämpft gegen den drohenden Abfall in Galatien.

Für eine pneumatische Gegnerschaft ist auch 1,11–24 kein Raum. Lütgerts Kritik der gewöhnlichen Auslegung dieses Abschnittes ist treffend, aber seine positiven Vorschläge lassen sich nicht aufrecht erhalten. Der Schlüssel zum Verständnis liegt nach Lütgert in 1,18. Paulus schreibt hier, er sei nach drei Jahren nach Jerusalem gereist, um mit Peter zusammenzukommen und sei bei ihm 15 Tage geblieben, während deren er keinen anderen von den Aposteln gesehen habe, sondern nur den Jakobus, den Bruder des Herrn. Das letzte beteuert er feierlich. Lütgert betont mit Recht, daß diese 15 Tage vollkommen ausreichen wurden, um dem Paulus das Evangelium des Peter zu vermitteln. Und wenn Paulus beschwört, er habe keinen anderen von den Aposteln gesehen als Peter und dazu noch Jakobus, so hat das gar keinen Sinn, wenn er dadurch beweisen will, daß er seine Unabhängigkeit gewahrt habe. "Schwört er aber, daß er gerade und nur diese beiden damals kennen gelernt habe, so muß ihm ein

Vorwurf gemacht worden sein, der mit dieser Tatsache widerlegt war, und der kann nur gelautet haben, daß er damals andere Leute kennen gelernt habe, von denen er sein Evangelium empfangen habe, Leute, die ihm ein anderes Evangelium überliefert hatten als das, welches Petrus und Jakobus vertraten. Im Munde der Judaisten wäre ja sein Verkehr mit Petrus und Jakobus und seine Abhängigkeit von ihnen auch gar kein Vorwurf gewesen." Es muß also dem Paulus nachgesagt worden sein, er habe sein (gesetzesfreies) Evangelium von einem von den andern Aposteln in Jerusalem, nicht aber durch Offenbarung. Eine solche Behauptung könnte aber nur von den Freigeistern in Galatien stammen, die ihre Enttäuschung über Paulus in der Weise Luft geben, daß sie ihn als nicht-inspirierten Prediger darstellen. Von wem sollte er abhängig sein? "Es wäre müßig zu raten, wer hiermit gemeint sein könne. Wenn man sich den uns bekannten Apostelkreis vergegenwärtigt, so kann man nur an Johannes denken ... Auch nach der Apostelgeschichte ist Paulus nicht der erste Vertreter des gesetzesfreien Evangeliums. Es gab schon eine freie Richtung in der Gemeinde, an die er sich anschloß. Nun erhob sich die Frage, woher hat er dieses Evangelium, wenn er doch kein Inspirierter ist? Den Gerüchten, die darüber in Umlauf gesetzt sind, setzt er entgegen, ich habe es aus Offenbarung, denn die beiden einzigen Menschen, welche ich damals sah, als ich es gelernt haben soll, waren gerade Petrus und Jakobus."

Lütgert betont stark, was auch eine notwendige Voraussetzung seiner Auslegung ist, daß Paulus sich nicht gegen eine Kritik seines Evangeliums wehrt, sondern gegen den Vorwurf, daß er es nicht von Gott habe. Es handelt sich um den Ursprung seines Evangeliums, nicht etwa um seinen Inhalt und seine Wahrheit. Somit gewinnt auch Lütgert kein richtiges Verhältnis zu 1,11: Mein Evangelium ist nicht κατὰ ἄνθρωπον. Mit den anderen Auslegern ist er in der Lage, daß er eine sachliche Beanstandung des paulinischen Evangeliums von Seiten der galatischen Gegner nicht annehmen kann ohne seine Auffassung des Abschnitts zu gefährden.

Ferner, wenn die Freiheitsleute den Paulus als nichtinspirierten Prediger darstellten, müßte ihre Meinung etwa die sein, wenn Paulus das freie Evangelium durch Offenbarung empfangen hätte, wäre er nicht später abgefallen; durch seinen Übertritt in die Reihe der Beschneidungsleute zeigt er, daß er nicht ein Gottbegnadeter ist. Ein solches Raisonnement läßt sich denken. Aber die Art der Entgegnung des Paulus ist unter diesen Voraussetzungen nicht recht verständlich. Denn seine eigentliche Aufgabe mußte ja bei dieser Lage der Dinge die sein, den Verdacht eines Abfalls zur Gesetzespredigt abzuwehren; was aber in dieser Richtung gedeutet werden kann, beschränkt sich auf einige wenige, schwer verständliche Andeutungen. So wie er seine Apologie gestaltet, bekommt man unbedingt den Eindruck, daß er seine Inspiration aus Rücksicht auf sein gesetzesfreies Evangelium und seine Mission unter den Heiden behauptet.

III

Können wir uns also keiner der früheren Auslegungen voll anschließen, stehen wir vor der Aufgabe, einen noch nicht beschrittenen Weg zur Lösung des Problems zu suchen. Uns scheint, daß einige ganz einfache Erwägungen auf einen solchen hindeuten, der zwar hypothetisch bleiben muß, jedoch nicht außerhalb des Bereichs der Möglichkeiten liegen dürfte.

Es ist davon auszugehen, daß τὸ εὐαγγέλιον τὸ εὐαγγελισθὲν ὑπ' ἐμοῦ V. 11 *die Missionsbotschaft des Paulus an die Heiden* bezeichnet, von der er sagt, sie sei nicht menschlicher Art, und er habe sie nicht von einem Menschen übernommen noch sei er darin unterrichtet worden, sondern verdanke sie einer Offenbarung Christi. – Ferner, daß er diese Behauptung gegen *judaistische* Agitatoren richtet, die also etwa gesagt haben, seine Botschaft an die Heiden sei eine menschliche Erfindung und sei ihm von Menschen beigebracht, habe keine göttliche Autorität. Mit anderen Worten, Paulus ist von seinen Gegnern in Galatien *als Irrlehrer und als unselbständiges Werkzeug oppositioneller palästinischer Kreise,* als Kreatur der dortigen Freiheitsleute geschildert worden. Sich selbst werden die Judaisten wiederum als Vertreter der legitimen Kirchenleitung vorgestellt haben.

Nun ist es aber offenbar, daß sie sich auch über das Verhältnis des Paulus zu den Uraposteln ausgesprochen haben, und zwar natürlich nicht zu seinem Vorteil (vgl. 1,17; 2,1ff.). Sie werden die behauptete Unselbständigkeit des Paulus bis zu vollkommener Haltungslosigkeit gesteigert haben: zur Rede gestellt von den Autoritäten in Jerusalem habe er nicht den Mut gehabt, seinen geistigen Vätern treu zu bleiben, sondern habe sich servil betragen und um die Gunst der Großen gebuhlt. So schwinge er zwischen zwei Polen, ein Bild der verächtlichsten Charakterschwäche.

Gegenüber diesem raffinierten Versuch, seine persönliche Achtung zu untergraben und damit seine Predigt zu diskreditieren, ist es nun die Aufgabe des Paulus, *einerseits die Originalität seines Evangeliums zu behaupten, anderseits seine konsequente feste Haltung zu erweisen.* –

Die erste und wichtigste Frage ist nun die, ob diese Auffassung in der Auslegung von Kap. 1 sich ungezwungen durchführen läßt. In zweiter Linie kommt die Frage, ob es eine oppositionelle Freiheitspartei in Palästina gegeben hat; auch wenn das sich nicht strikte beweisen läßt, behält unsere Ansicht ihre Möglichkeit. – Wir versuchen also zunächst, im Folgenden Kap. 1 unter dem oben angegebenen doppelten Gesichtspunkt zu betrachten.

IV

Schon gleich am Eingang des Briefes stoßen wir auf das gegensätzliche Begriffspaar ἄνθρωπος – θεός 1,1 vgl. 1,10–12 (2,6). Dieser Gegensatz, der, wie natürlich, dem Urchristentum geläufig war, (Act. 5, 29. 38f.; Joh. 5, 34. 41; 10, 33; 12, 43), gehört zum festen Bestand der paulinischen Begriffe und Termini, vgl. 1. Thess. 2,4. 6. 13; 4,8; 1. Kor. 1,25; Kol. 3,23; Röm. 2,29; 8,4. Und er deckt ein Gebiet, auf dem Paulus offenbar sehr empfindsam war. Schon im 1. Thess. verwahrt er sich mit allem Nachdruck dagegen, daß er Gunst und Ehre bei Menschen gesucht hätte, 2,4. 6 (ἀρέσκειν ἀνθρώποις, ζητεῖν ἐξ ἀνθρώπων δόξαν) vgl. Gal. 1,10. Und er betont, daß die Thessalonicher seine Predigt aufnahmen nicht als Menschenwort, sondern als das, was sie ist, Gottes Wort, und daß wer seine Weisungen verachtet, nicht einen Menschen verachtet, sondern Gott selbst, 2,6; 4,8 vgl. Gal. 1,11. Auch κατὰ ἄνθρωπον Gal. 1,11 findet sich sonst in charakteristischer Verwendung 1. Kor. 15,32 εἰ κατὰ ἄνθρωπον ἐθηριομάχησα ἐν Ἐφέσῳ; d.h. wäre es hier nach menschlichen Plänen und Berechnungen gegangen ... (vgl. Johs. Weiß z. St.).

Es ist also zu beachten, daß die Ausdrucksweise Gal. 1,1. 10–12 nicht *ad hoc* geschaffen wurde, sondern fertig vorlag. Somit können wir nicht direkt von den Aussagen des Paulus auf die Ausdrucksweise der Gegner schließen. Paulus bewegt sich in seinen eigenen Vorstellungsbahnen, seinem eigenen sprachlichen Schema. Er wird es deshalb sein, der den gegnerischen Vorwürfen die prinzipielle Wendung (göttlich-menschlich) verliehen hat.[1] So schon 1,1. Das

---

[1] Wenn man die ausgesprochen paulinische Formulierung betont, konnte man auf den radikalen Ausweg verfallen, Kap. 1 jede direkte Bezugnahme auf gegnerische Aussagen abzusprechen. Galatien war ein weites Gebiet, und es läßt sich denken, daß P. von dem Treiben der Judaisten und den Zuständen in den Gemeinden nur eine allgemeine Vorstellung hatte und nur wenige Nachrichten über konkrete Einzelheiten besaß. Er bewegt sich deshalb in allgemeinen Ausdrücken, und seine Phantasie arbeitet, von der Sorge angetrieben. Wir wissen vom 1. Thess. her, daß P. auch ohne positive Anhaltspunkte zu haben sich leicht Gefahren ausmalte, die sein persönliches Ansehen und damit seine Missionserfolge bedrohten: Ausführlich und eindringend erinnert er (Kap. 2) an die Lauterkeit seines Wandels unter ihnen (eben hier das Schema οὐκ – ἀλλά), obgleich gewiß keiner von den Gläubigen in Thessalonich daran dachte, ihn des geldgierigen Goëtentums zu zeihen. P. wußte aber, daß er von feindlicher (jüdischer) Seite solche Verleumdungen erwarten konnte, und regt sich nun beim Schreiben auf, als wären sie schon da. Auf ähnliche Weise können ihn in der Galaterfrage frühere bittere Erfahrungen beunruhigen und seine Worte apologetisch gestalten. So mag es ihm öfters passiert sein, dem Nachhall solcher feindlichen Behauptungen zu begegnen wie denen: Er habe sein Evangelium selbst erfunden; oder er sei von anderen großgezogen worden und von ihnen ausgesandt und bevollmächtigt, gebärde sich aber nun wie eine selbständige Autorität; oder er sei ein Opportunist, der sich den sich gegen das Gesetz sträubenden Heiden sowohl als den gesetzesstrengen Judenchristen anzupassen wisse. Wenn man diese verschiedenen Angriffe nicht einer bestimmten, einheitlichen historischen Lage und den selbigen Personen zuschreibt, heben sich die Widersprüche, an denen die traditionelle Auslegung leidet: Die einen huldigen dieser Taktik, die anderen jener; Paulus kennt das alles genau und nimmt seine Maßregeln. Sollte die Sache so stehen, braucht man in der

doppelte οὐκ ἀπ' ἀνθρώπων οὐδὲ δι' ἀνθρώπου könnte an sich so gedeutet werden, daß Paulus die Beschuldigung ablehnt, er sei von einem Kreis gesandt (ἀπ' ἀνθρώπων), aber von einem einzelnen Mann in diesem Kreis (etwa dem Führer) besonders beeinflußt (δι' ἀνθρώπου vgl. παρὰ ἀνθρώπου V. 12). Allein, wir haben hier gewiß nur die rhetorische Variation eines Schemas zu finden. Gesagt haben sie, er sei ein Werkzeug der Latitudinarier in Palästina; das hebt nun Paulus in das Licht des großen Gegensatzes Gott-Mensch empor. – Daß die Negation überall vorangeht (οὐκ - ἀλλά V. 1. 12. 16ff.), ist sachlich begründet in der apologetischen Tendenz, entspricht aber zugleich der paulinischen Stilgewohnheit (vgl. 1. Thess. 1,5; 2, 1; 3,4–8. 13; 4,7f.; 5,9; Gal.2,6f.; 3,12–16; 4,1. 7. 31; 5,6. 13; 6,13. 15)[2].

Der Gedankengang des Briefes bewegt sich zwischen dem persönlichen und dem sachlichen Interesse hin und her. Der Gruß 1,1 setzt schroff persönlich ein, es geht um Ehre und Vertrauen. Den Briefanfang 1,6 beherrscht natürlich der sachliche Gesichtspunkt, das wahre und das verdrehte Evangelium, aber bald wieder bricht die persönliche Empfindung hervor 1,10, und nun muß Paulus sich diese Angelegenheit vom Herzen schreiben. Von Kap. 3 an ist die sachliche Argumentation vorherrschend, nur hier und dort ein persönlicher Erguß (4,11ff.; 5,7ff.). Der Schluß ist wieder ganz persönlich (6,12–17).

1, 8. 9 steigert sich das Pathos des Paulus zu einem feierlichen Verdammungsurteil über jeden, der ein anderes Evangelium verkündigt. Eben auf diesem höchsten Punkte machen sich die Verleumdungen der Gegner im Bewußtsein geltend: Er, der er sich jetzt so absolut ausspricht, soll ja selbst ein

---

Auslegung nicht so streng logisch zu verfahren. Wenn P. V. 11 sagt, sein Evangelium sei nicht κατὰ ἄνθρωπον, denkt er an solche, die behaupten, er habe sich seine Botschaft selbst zurechtgemacht. V. 12 wiederum mag soviel heißen, als "ich bin nicht von anderen Menschen autorisiert, sondern vom Herrn", also zuerst ein Wort gegen sachliche Beanstandung und Verdächtigung seiner Verkündigung, dann gegen formale Herabsetzung seiner Autorität. Man darf dabei nicht die Identität von "mein Evangelium" in VV. 11 und 12 pressen, denn es ist denkbar, daß P. eine gegnerische Behauptung, "er ist ursprünglich von der Kirchenleitung ausgesandt worden", in seiner Sprache so wiedergibt: "Ich habe mein Evangelium nicht von einem Menschen übernommen". Dem entspricht es, daß er bei Erwähnung der ἀποκάλυψις seine Berufung zum Heidenmissionar hervorhebt (1,15). Ziel der Apologie wäre somit nicht, sein Fernsein von jeder christlichen Überlieferung darzutun, sondern seine Selbständigkeit im Handeln vom ersten Augenblick seines christlichen Daseins zu illustrieren (vgl. οὐ προσανεθέμην, was mehr ist als sich bekehren lassen): Er faßt sofort seinen Reisebeschluß, zieht nach Arabien, zurück nach Damaskus usw., kurz handelt mit der souveränen Selbständigkeit des göttlich Berufenen. Sogar seine eifrigen Bemühungen um die Klarlegung der Beziehungen zu Jerusalem und den Aposteln brauchten nicht direkt von den Verhältnissen in Galatien provoziert zu sein, sondern können durch anderweitige Erlebnisse hervorgerufen sein und mehr prophylaktische als unmittelbar apologetische Aufgabe haben; vielleicht haben wir Paulus' eigene innere Auseinandersetzung mit Jerusalem in dieser Form erhalten. – Als mehr als eine letzte Möglichkeit will ich jedoch nicht diese Auffassung hinstellen, verzichte deshalb auf eine Ausführung in Einzelheiten.

[2] Dieses Schema ist auch im 1. Petr. beliebt, vgl. 1,14–15. 18f. 23; 3,6. 21; 5,2f.

kläglicher Opportunist sein! Und so fragt er ἄρτι γὰρ ἀνθρώπους πείθω[3]. Diese Frage muß irgendwie mit der folgenden ἢ ζητῶ ἀνθρώποις ἀρέσκειν; sinnverwandt sein. In beiden Fragen haben wir charakteristische paulinische Formulierungen, nicht wörtliche Zitate der gegnerischen Vorwürfe. Die lauteten, Paulus habe nicht den Mut gehabt, sich gegenüber den Jerusalemischen Autoritäten zu behaupten; das fällt für Paulus unter den Begriff des ἀνθρώπους πείθειν, ἀνθρώποις ἀρέσκειν. – Aus 2. Kor. wissen wir, daß dem Apostel nachgesagt wurde, bei persönlicher Konfrontation fehle ihm der Mut, die feste Haltung (κατὰ πρόσωπον ταπεινός 10,1). Er tritt dem entgegen durch die Zusicherung, er werde bald selbst eintreffen und ohne Schonung Abrechnung halten, durch die Tat die Verleumder zu schanden machen. Im Gal. muß er sich, notgedrungen (4,20), mit dem Schreiben begnügen; er weist auf seine eben ausgesprochene Verurteilung der judaistischen Prediger hin und fragt: "Rede ich jetzt den Leuten nach dem Munde?" Das boshafte Wort der korinthischen Gegner (10,10): "Die Briefe sind freilich wuchtig und kraftvoll, aber sein persönliches Auftreten ist schwächlich und seine Rede nichts wert" hat er offenbar noch nicht gekannt. – Ferner bezeugt 2. Kor., man sage von Paulus, er bestrebe sich, sich zu insinuieren (ἑαυτὸν συνιστάνειν 3,1; 4,2), die Menschen für sich zu gewinnen πείθειν (5,11). Dieses πείθειν betrifft hier seine eigenen Gemeinden, und er läßt es gelten, indem er den Sinn des Wortes umbiegt: "In dem vollen Bewußtsein der Furcht des Herrn überreden wir Menschen, vor Gott aber sind wir klar erkannt: ich hoffe aber auch in eurem Gewissen klar erkannt zu sein." Den Galatern dagegen will man einreden, daß er gewußt habe, durch allerlei Konzessionen und Künste sich den Jerusalemern mundgerecht zu machen. Seine Antwort hierauf muß sein: Wenn ich noch um Menschengunst buhlte, wäre ich ein Sklave Christi nicht!

Diese Argumentation ist rein religiös: entgegen dem Vorwurf, daß er ein wetterwenderischer Gunstschleicher ist, hält er sein Bewußtsein, ein δοῦλος Χριστοῦ zu sein, – es ist ein unmittelbarer Erguß; erst 1,16 nimmt er die Sache auf, um sie mit Gründen endgültig abzutun. Nachdem er 1,10 sein Herz erleichtert hat, will er gründlich aufräumen und chronologisch verfahren; also setzt er zunächst bei dem Gerücht ein, er sei ein Jünger der Freiheitsleute in Judäa. Das feierliche γνωρίζω V. 11 zeigt, daß hier ein selbständiger Abschnitt anhebt (vgl. 1. Kor. 15,1; 2. Kor. 8,1), und wir brauchen somit dem überleitenden Partikel, ob δέ oder γάρ, kein tieferes Nachdenken zu widmen. Die These lautet: Das von mir gepredigte Evangelium ist nicht κατὰ ἄνθρωπον. Diese

[3] ἢ τὸν θεόν vermag ich nicht zu erklären. Man könnte versucht sein νὴ τὸν θεόν zu konjizieren (nachgestelltes νή bei Paulus vgl. 1. Kor. 15,31); aber wahrscheinlich sind die Worte eine Glosse, von dem durchgehenden Gegensatz Mensch–Gott hervorgerufen. – Oder sollte τὸν θεὸν πείθειν auf das Anathema V. 8f. Bezug nehmen? "Überrede ich jetzt Menschen, oder nicht vielmehr Gott?" d.h. das ἀνάθεμα ἔστω ist im Munde des Paulus eine effektive Herbeirufung der göttlichen Strafe. (Auf diese Möglichkeit machte mich L. Brun aufmerksam.)

Aussage, die *die Geltung* seines Evangeliums betrifft, bezieht sich auf die Folgerungen, die seine Gegner aus seiner angeblichen Jüngerschaft bei den Freiheitsleuten gezogen haben: Er hat sein Evangelium von halb häretischen Kreisen, also ist es eine Irrlehre ohne göttliche Autorität. In seiner Erwiderung geht Paulus natürlich den umgekehrten Weg: Zuerst das sachliche, die Geltung, und dann die Voraussetzung der Geltung V.12; οὐδὲ γάϱ ist gleich καὶ γὰϱ οὐ, und die Setzung von ἐγώ entspricht der Wucht der Aussage.

Die Behauptung nicht-menschlichen Ursprungs seines Evangeliums stützt er V. 13–24 durch einen kurzen Abriß seines Lebensganges, der zeigt, daß er keine Möglichkeit hatte, in Abhängigkeit von den palästinischen Oppositionsleuten zu geraten. In diese Ausführungen mischt sich aber auch die Rücksicht auf den anderen Anklagepunkt: seine Stellung zu den Aposteln. Das ist natürlich, eben weil er chronologisch verfährt. Indem er die Hauptlinien seines Lebens während dieser Jahre zieht, melden sich bei den verschiedenen Etappen die verschiedenen Beziehungen zur Sprache.

Die ausführliche Erinnerung an seinen bekannten anfänglichen Christenhaß V. 13f. könnte an sich die rationelle Erwägung hervorrufen wollen: Bei einem solchen Verhalten war jeder Verkehr mit Christusgläubigen ausgeschlossen. Eher steckt jedoch ein religiöser Gedanke darin. Einen solchen blutigen Fanatiker konnte nur Gott selbst bekehren. – Die Offenbarung Christi wird nur im Nebensatz erwähnt; die Beweisführung hat ein negatives Ziel. – Es ist nicht zu bezweifeln, daß Paulus 1,16 ursprünglich εὐθέως ἀπῆλθον εἰς τὴν 'Αϱαβίαν schreiben wollte. Zahn verknüpft εὐθέως mit den negierten Verben und erklärt: Sofort, vom ersten Anfang an wahrte ich meine Selbständigkeit und habe mich nicht erst später emanzipiert. Dabei wird aber nicht beachtet, daß die Negierung lediglich heraushebende Folie für die positive Aussage ist; das verbürgt die Beobachtung, daß wir hier das Schema οὐκ – ἀλλά haben. Εὐθέως muß daher zum positiven Hauptbegriff gehören. Indessen empfindet Paulus den Drang, den Gedanken, der durch ἀπῆλθον εἰς τὴν 'Α. verhütet werden soll, ausdrücklich auszusprechen und zu negieren: Er hat überhaupt keine Lehrmeister aufgesucht, weder legitime noch ketzerische, sondern ist sofort weggegangen. Zunächst gestaltet er den Gedanken ganz allgemein: οὐ πϱοσανεθέμην σαϱκὶ καὶ αἵματι.[4] Dann aber taucht vor seinem Blick die Gruppe auf, vor der er habe sich verbeugen sollen, die Apostel: Wenn je, hätte es jetzt dem Neubekehrten naheliegen müssen, Bestätigung und Belehrung bei diesen

[4] Es ist psychologisch völlig begreiflich, daß P. hier nicht daran denkt, daß er gleich nach seiner Bekehrung wenigstens eine kürzere Zeit lang mit den Gläubigen in Damaskus verkehrte und dort getauft wurde (auch in "Arabien" wird er kein Eremitenleben geführt haben). Das Pathos seiner Apologie, die großen, raschen Striche, das Bewußtsein von der Originalität seines Evangeliums verleihen seinen Worten den absoluten Ton; erst nachdem er auf palästinischen Boden angelangt ist, kümmert ihn das Detail.

Größen zu suchen; aber er hat es nicht getan,– schon in dieser psychologischen Situation manifestierte sich seine Selbständigkeit ihnen gegenüber.

Die nächste Phase (ἔπειτα V. 18) tritt ein nach drei Jahren, somit nach geraumer Zeit. Diese Zeitbestimmung ist notwendig, um dem früher berichteten Aufenthalt in Arabien und Damaskus das volle psychologische Gewicht zu verleihen, es war kein flüchtiger Besuch sondern ein längeres Verweilen. – Was er V. 17 ausdrücklich bezeugt, damals nicht getan zu haben, tut er jetzt, ἀνῆλθον εἰς Ἱεροσόλυμα. Jerusalem und Judäa sind die Gebiete, die in der galatischen Agitation eine Rolle spielen und sein Ansehen bedrohen; die beste Abwehr ist, ganz objektiv zu erzählen, was sich zugetragen hat, und die nackten Tatsachen wirken zu lassen. So kommt denn Paulus jedem Verdacht zuvor, indem er sofort die Absicht und den Charakter dieser Reise angibt: er wollte Bekanntschaft mit Peter schließen und ist bei ihm ein paar Wochen geblieben. Hier sollen die Leser zweierlei empfinden: Paulus hat selbst die Initiative genommen, und der Besuch war eine ganz privat-persönliche Sache ohne jeden offiziellen Anstrich. Das letztere wird aber ausdrücklich festgestellt durch die Versicherung, daß er sonst keinen von den Aposteln sah, sondern nur den Jakobus, den Herrenbruder. Daß bei dieser Sachlage intime und dauernde Beziehungen zu freisinnigen Kreisen hätten geknüpft werden können, ist völlig ausgeschlossen, wird nicht einmal in Betracht gezogen; das ganze Gewicht liegt auf der anderen Seite, auf dem Verkehr mit den Aposteln. Wenn Paulus feierlich den privaten, nicht-offiziellen Charakter seines Besuches beschwört, so müssen wir vermuten, daß etwas dahinter steckt. Ausgeschlossen ist es, daß der Liberalismus einen Vertreter im Apostelkollegium hätte haben sollen, mit dem Paulus nicht zusammengekommen sein will (Lütgert). Eher muß man sich die Sache so zurechtlegen, daß man annimmt, die Judaisten in Galatien haben überhaupt die Jerusalemreisen des Paulus gegen ihn ausgenutzt: er sei zu wiederholten Malen nach Jerusalem zitiert worden, und – *laudabiliter se subiecit*. Darauf erwidert nun Paulus, daß er das erste Mal (1,18) einen vierzehntägigen, ganz privaten Besuch bei Petrus machte und nicht von ferne in irgendwelche offizielle Beziehung zum Kirchenregiment trat: das nächste mal (2,1) war die Sache zwar offiziell, deshalb bekommen wir aber auch ein für uns allerdings wenig durchsichtiges Referat.[5]

Nach Beendigung des Besuches bei Petrus (ἔπειτα V. 21) ging Paulus in die

[5] Voraussetzung dieser Deutung von 1,18 ist, daß in Jerusalem eine feste, allgemein bekannte Praxis für die offiziellen Gemeindeverhandlungen sich herausgebildet hatte, etwa so, daß bei solchen Gelegenheiten ein Kollegium von mehreren Aposteln (und "Ältesten"?) bestehend teils für sich als leitender Ausschuß beriet, teils die Gemeindeversammlung leitete. Die Verhandlungen zwischen Peter, Johannes und Jacobus Gal. 2,6ff. waren privater Natur, hatten aber selbstverständlich ihre Bedeutung für die Haltung des führenden Kreises in der öffentlichen Gemeindeversammlung. – Will man sich in dieser schwierigen Frage anderen Vermutungen hingeben, könnte man annehmen, die Gegner hätten in Galatien erzählt, Paulus habe bei seinem Aufenthalt in Jerusalem einem bestimmten, näher bezeichneten

syrischen und kilikischen Gegenden. Die Nennung dieser Landschaften hat dieselbe Absicht wie die geographischen Angaben V. 17, es soll die Möglichkeit eines Verkehrs mit den liberalen Judenchristen abgeschnitten werden. Diesmal genügt es aber dem Paulus nicht, die Schlußfolgerung den Lesern zu überlassen, sondern er stellt ausdrücklich fest, daß er jene Reise nach Jerusalem machte, ohne zu den judäischen Gemeinden in persönliche Beziehung zu treten (V. 22). Daß er sich zu dieser Feststellung gedrungen fühlt, kommt natürlich daher, daß jetzt von seiner Berührung mit dem kompromittierenden Boden die Rede ist, da heißt es vorsichtig sein, um jedem Verdacht vorzubeugen. Die einzige Verbindung zwischen ihm und den Gemeinden in Judäa wurde vom Gerücht vermittelt, von der frohen Kunde, daß der frühere Verfolger nun ein Verkündiger des von ihm verfolgten Glaubens ist, und sie priesen Gott an ihm. Es ist nicht zu verkennen, daß der warme, erbauliche Ton V. 23f. einen wirkungsvollen Kontrast bildet zu den bösartigen Verleumdungen, denen hier entgegengetreten wird: was haben nicht jene Leute alles in das Verhältnis des Paulus zu den palästinischen Kreisen hineingelegt und hineingelogen! Das alles wird nun auf etwas ganz unschuldiges reduziert, ja, stellt sich als etwas schönes und herzergreifendes heraus: den Dank der Gläubigen bei der Kunde von der Bekehrung des Verfolgers. Statt des Flüsterns und Murrens, des intrigierenden Grolls erklingen die reinen Töne des Lobgesangs.

Vierzehn Jahre verstrichen, ehe Paulus wieder den palästinischen Boden betrat. Was diese Jahre in sich beschlossen, wußten die Galater genau: damals wurde die Weltmission gegründet, der sie selbst ihren Glauben und ihr Heil verdankten. Erst nach einer so langen und ausgedehnten selbständigen Wirksamkeit hat Paulus die Veranlassung gefunden, sein Evangelium den Jerusalemern vorzulegen.

Die Weise, in der er von diesem Ereignis erzählt (2,1ff.), bezeugt, ebenso wie die Versicherung 1,19f., daß auch diese Jerusalemfahrt feindlich ausgenutzt worden ist. Aber ebensowenig wie bei der Erwähnung des ersten Besuches wissen wir hier, wie die Gegner die Sache eigentlich dargestellt haben. Zwar ahnen wir bei diesen und jenen Worten, daß Paulus auf böswillige Verdrehungen der Wahrheit Bezug nimmt, aber der Schluß auf diese Verdrehungen wird durch seine eigentümliche Schreibweise sehr erschwert. Jedenfalls sieht man, die Tatsache der Anerkennung seiner Mission und Predigt von Seiten der Autoritäten in Jerusalem ist von ihnen verschleiert worden, sie haben es eher so aussehen lassen, daß Paulus in entscheidenden Fragen habe nachgeben müssen, ja, daß er gerade mit allen Mitteln um die Anerkennung und das Gefallen der Apostel geworben habe; in der Tat habe er in der Folgezeit in gewissen Gegenden die Beschneidung gepredigt.[6] Paulus wiederum behauptet, daß er in

---

Apostel gegenüber sein Evangelium verleugnet. Das ist unmöglich, sagt P., denn bei dieser Gelegenheit kam ich außer mit Peter mit keinem von den Aposteln zusammen.

[6] Gal. 5,11. Diese dunkle Stelle muß doch wohl so verstanden werden, daß Paulus (ganz wie

der Hauptsache, der Beschneidungsfrage, einen vollständigen Sieg gewonnen hat, Beweis: nicht einmal die Beschneidung des ihn begleitenden Titus konnten die Gesetzeseiferer durchsetzen, und die Säulen haben ihn persönlich anerkannt und einen Vertrag mit ihm geschlossen. Später, in Antiochia, hat er sogar die Haltlosigkeit eines der Größten, des Petrus, gerügt.

Wenn man die paulinische Apologie unter diesem Gesichtspunkt der doppelten Anklage liest, ebnen sich die Schwierigkeiten, die sich bisher jeder Auslegung entgegenstellten, und es ergibt sich ein guter Sinn.

Fragen wir nun zunächst nach der *inneren Wahrscheinlichkeit* der von uns angenommenen Art der antipaulinischen Agitation in Galatien, so ist zuzugeben, daß solche Reden den Judaisten naheliegend sein mußten. Am nächsten lag es natürlich, die großen Apostel gegen ihn auszuspielen, und zwar war es von höchster Wirkung, wenn sie nicht als Antipoden des Paulus, sondern als seine Zensoren und Richter, er aber als der Unterwürfige dargestellt wurden. Indessen konnte ja nicht geleugnet werden, daß Paulus weit und breit das gesetzesfreie Evangelium gepredigt hatte. Da zeigt sich eben seine Art: bald predigt er Beschneidung, bald Freiheit vom Gesetz, ein Meister der Skrupellosigkeit, des ἀνθρώπους πείθειν: dem entspricht es auch aufs beste, daß er sein Evangelium von anderen gelernt hat, er wird von anderen benutzt als Werkzeug ihrer Pläne.

Aber auch die *Gedankenfolge* Kap. 1–2 scheint unter diesen Voraussetzungen natürlich zu verlaufen. Die beiden Größen, denen gegenüber er seine Selbständigkeit darlegen will, sitzen auf palästinischem Boden; mithin empfiehlt sich von selbst ein geographisch-chronologisches Verfahren, – nur wenn sein Weg Judäa berührt, sind nähere Kommentare erforderlich, sonst sprechen die Angaben für sich selbst.

Es erübrigt noch, einige Worte über die *supponierte Freiheitspartei in Judäa* zu sagen.

V

Um das Problem befriedigend zu lösen, mußten wir mit einem unbekannten Faktor, einem x rechnen, mit einer Strömung in den jüdischen Gemeinden, die der Emanzipation vom Gesetz zuneigte. Von dieser Seite her sollte Paulus inspiriert sein. Dagegen hatten die Gegner offenbar nicht versucht, Paulus als abgefallenen Juden etwa unter Beeinflußung der Antiochenischen Gemeinde, was doch nahe liegen mußte, darzustellen. Das erklärt sich ungezwungen so,

1,8–10) mitten im heftigsten Ausfall gegen die Beschneidungspredigt und ihre Vertreter plötzlich an die gegen ihn selbst gerichtete Beschuldigung der Gesetzesverkündigung erinnert wird – eine leicht verständliche Kontrastwirkung – und auf die andauernden Verfolgungen hinweist, die das Entgegengesetzte bezeugen.

daß tatsächlich eben eine Opposition bestand, die den Bestrebungen des Paulus wohlwollend zusah und vielleicht gelegentlich auch ihre moralische Stütze lieh, und die deshalb leicht als den geistigen Nährboden des Paulinismus bezeichnet werden konnte.

Die Hypothese, daß es eine solche, lediglich auf dem Wege logisch-exegetischer Erwägungen erschlossene Richtung gegeben hat, mag etwas gewagt scheinen, schwebt jedoch nicht vollständig in der Luft. Daß wir nicht ausdrücklich von einer solchen Strömung etwas erfahren, ist nicht verwunderlich. Unsere einzigen Quellen für diese Zeit sind Paulus und Acta. Paulus aber schreibt an Wissende, deshalb sind seine Aussagen nur Andeutungen, und wir können nur mit Schwierigkeit seine kurzen, temperamentvollen, oft geradezu absichtlich dunkel gehaltenen Charakteristiken uns anschaulich machen: "Gewisse Leute, die euch verwirren...", "eingeschlichene Falschbrüder...", "die Geltenden...", "euer Verstörer wird die Strafe tragen, wer er auch sei", – man erhält nicht eben eine klare, scharf umrissene Vorstellung von den Gegnern. Dasselbe gilt in fast noch höherem Maß von den beiden Korintherbriefen. Es ist somit sehr wohl denkbar, daß hinter dem κατ' ἄνθρωπον, παρ' ἀνθρώπου, σὰρξ καὶ αἷμα usw. Kap. 1 eine freiheitliche Partei sich verbergen kann.

Die zweite Quelle aber ist Acta. Allein, wer die Art dieser Schrift richtig erkannt hat, wird von ihr keine Aufklärung über die Parteiverhältnisse in Palästina erwarten. Der Verfasser der Apostelgeschichte hat keine konkrete, historische Anschauung vom alten Judenchristentum. Zu seiner Zeit gehörte dieses der Vergangenheit an, und nur vereinzelte Traditionen über die Anfangszeit stehen ihm zu Gebote. Diese hindurchgeretteten Einzelüberlieferungen ermöglichen es uns, einige Züge der ältesten Entwickelung zu ahnen, aber auch nicht mehr. Ein wirkliches Bild dieser Zeit können wir uns nicht machen, ihre Geschichte können wir nicht schreiben. Der Verfasser der Apostelgeschichte hat eine sehr schematische Auffassung der Lage in Jerusalem. Den Anfang der Heidenmission läßt er durch den durch eine Offenbarung erleuchteten und angetriebenen Petrus gemacht werden; die Gläubigen in Jerusalem und Judäa entrüsten sich über die Taufe Unbeschnittener, lassen sich aber von Petrus beruhigen und preisen sogar Gott für diese Neuerung (10,18). Wie sehr dieser Vorgang vom Gesichtspunkt der späteren, heidenchristlichen Generation aus gesehen ist, zeigt sich in der Bezeichnung der Begleiter des Petrus und der judäischen Christen als οἱ ἐκ περιτομῆς (9,45; 10,2); als ob andere als beschnittene Gläubige überhaupt hätten in Frage kommen können. Ebenso in der Schilderung der Reibungen in Antiochia und der Verhandlungen in Jerusalem. Die Unruhen in Antiochia werden verursacht von τινὲς κατελθόντες ἀπὸ τῆς 'Ιουδαίας (15,1), und diese Leute sind offenbar gedacht als Vertreter der τινὲς τῶν ἀπὸ τῆς αἱρέσεως τῶν φαρισαίων πεπιστευκότες in Jerusalem (15,5). Also die bösen Pharisäer sind es, die wieder am Spiel sind; ihre Bestrebungen scheitern aber an der einmütigen Haltung der "Apostel und Presbyter", an die sich die Gemeinde schließt. Die Haltung der Gemeinde und ihrer Führer ist die ganze Zeit freisinnig und konsequent, nur einige bornierte Fanatiker stören gelegentlich die friedliche Entwickelung. Wer sich eine solche Vorstellung von den Verhältnissen macht, hat keine reale historische Anschauung.

Nun wissen wir aber von anderswo her, daß die Lage bedeutend verwickelter war, und daß der Widerstand gegen die Anerkennung der paulinischen Heidenmission viel ernster gewesen ist. Und die Apostelgeschichte selbst gibt uns Stoff für die Vermutung, daß anderseits eine Tendenz zur Brechung der Gesetzesherrschaft sich geltend machte. Das Vorhandensein eines hellenistischen Elements schon auf der ältesten Stufe der Jerusalemischen Gemeinde ist von der Apostelgeschichte unwidersprechlich bezeugt. Die hervorragendste Gestalt dieses Kreises, Stephanus, tritt klar hervor in seiner Opposition gegen den traditionellen Kultus, der nach seiner Meinung den sittlichen Gehalt des Gesetzes verdrängt hatte. Ihm waren die "lebendigen Worte des Mose" (7,30) die Hauptsache, und wir dürfen annehmen, daß er eine Richtung vertrat, die die ethischen Intentionen des Gesetzes mit der Predigt Jesu verschmelzen wollte, – ein echt jüdisch-hellenistisches Unternehmen. Dadurch trat er in einen gewissen Gegensatz zu dem eschatologisch-dogmatisch gerichteten palästinischen Judenchristentum. Während dieses Tempel und Ritus, die Kennzeichen des heiligen, berufenen Volkes, hochhielt, haftete die Aufmerksamkeit der Hellenisten eher an den schroff verurteilenden Worten Jesu gegen die theokratischen Institutionen. Was später aus diesem Kreise geworden ist, können wir nicht wissen. Wahrscheinlich sind sie nach dem Märtyrertod des Stephanus aus Jerusalem vertrieben worden und haben später den Mut oder die Gelegenheit zur Rückkehr nicht gefunden, – weder die Juden noch die gesetzesstrengen Gläubigen werden sich für diese freisinnigen Geister haben erwärmen können. Draußen aber, in der Provinz, in den Städten Judäas, können sie sich wohl erhalten haben, und zwar in geschlossenen Kreisen (vgl. die besonderen Synagogen der Libyer, Kyrenäer und Alexandriner, 6,9, die eine Neigung zu Zusammenhalt der Hellenisten in Palästina bezeugen). Ein Mann wie Barnabas mit seiner positiven Haltung zu dem aufsprossenden Heidenchristentum könnte von solchen Glaubensgenossen in Palästina beeinflußt sein. Der Evangelist Philippus hat wenigstens zu diesem Typus gehört, ebenso Mnason in Cäsarea.

Wahrscheinlich kann auch zu Gunsten unserer Annahme auf die Art der synoptischen Überlieferung hingewiesen werden. Zunächst zeugt die Sprachform von einem zweisprachigen Milieu; sodann aber verlangen viele von den überlieferten Worten Jesu, mögen sie echt sein oder späteren Ursprungs, ein von streng jüdischen Vorurteilen freies, auf das rein ethisch-geistige gerichtetes, kritisches Medium.

Der Gegensatz zwischen diesen freieren Kreisen und den Rigoristen mag sich zeitweilig zu Konflikten verschärft haben, und eben in oder gleich nach einer solchen Konfliktslage kann man sich denken, daß die judaistischen Agitatoren darauf gekommen sind, den Paulus dadurch herabzusetzen, daß sie ihn als Werkzeug dieser Empörer gegen Tradition und Autorität schilderten.

Der wahre Jude und sein Lob

Röm. 2, 28f.

(1922)

Aus Röm. 3:9 (προητιασάμεθα γὰρ Ἰουδαίους τε καὶ Ἕλληνας πάντας ὑφ' ἁμαρτίαν εἶναι) sehen wir, daß es dem Apostel vorschwebte, die sittliche Verdorbenheit und religiöse Schuld sowohl der Heidenwelt als der jüdischen Volksgemeinde in helles Licht zu stellen, und so sein Evangelium, das 1:16–17 thematisch angeschlagen, 3:21ff. definiert wird, auf dem allgemeinen Hintergrund der Heilsbedürftigkeit zu zeichnen.

Das Thema 1:16–17, die Gottesgerechtigkeit aus dem Glauben im Evangelium geoffenbart, wird wieder aufgenommen 3:21, jetzt aber unter genauerer Herausarbeitung des Moments, das schon 1:17 in ἐκ πίστεως lag, nämlich als Gegensatz zur Gesetzesgerechtigkeit: νυνὶ δὲ χωρὶς νόμου δικαιοσύνη θεοῦ πεφανέρωται. Dementsprechend sollte man erwarten, daß die dazwischenliegenden Ausführungen diese prinzipielle Aussage irgendwie vorbereiteten, etwa durch den Nachweis, daß die Gesetzesgerechtigkeit unerreichbar sei. Allein, das ist keineswegs der Fall. Der Apostel beschäftigt sich lediglich mit der *tatsächlichen* Ungerechtigkeit der Juden und der Heiden. Den ganzen Hintergrund der prinzipiellen Definition der Glaubensgerechtigkeit 3:21ff. bilden einzig und allein die Verse 3:19–20, die in keinem oder höchstens in einem sehr losen Zusammenhang mit dem Vorhergehenden stehen. – Das Thema, die Glaubensgerechtigkeit, ist von Paulus von vorn herein ins Auge gefaßt, darauf will er hinaus; aber andere, ihm längst geläufige Gedankenzüge bieten sich ihm dar als Vorstufen zur Hauptaussage, die aber nicht ans Ziel führen: deshalb muß er sich schließlich gewaltsam den Übergang zum eigentlichen Gegenstand des Briefes bahnen.

So schildert er zunächst die trostlose Lage der verwilderten und mit Gottes Zorn beladenen *Heidenwelt,* 1:18–32.

Der Inhalt setzt sich zusammen aus jüdisch gefärbter stoischer Polemik (1:19ff.) und Zügen aus der zeitgenössischen Sittenschilderung (1:26ff.); das ganze läuft in einen Lasterkatalog hinaus (1:29ff.). – Daß wir hier, in teilweise konventioneller Form, ein literarisches Gegenstück haben zu einem wichtigen Moment in der Missionspredigt des Apostels, ist sehr wahrscheinlich, vgl. A. Oepke, *Die Missionspredigt des Apostels Paulus,* 1920, 63ff., 82ff.; P. Wendland, *Griech.-röm. Kultur* ^{2}1912, 244f.; A. Fridrichsen, *Zeitschr. für d. nt. Wiss.* 1916, 159ff. – 1:18 ist sicher eine generelle Charakteristik des Heidentums und nicht zugleich der Juden. Wenn die Beziehung auf die Heiden nicht direkt ausgesprochen ist, sondern aus der Charakteristik erschlossen werden muß, ist es weil Paulus sich bestrebt, möglichst prinzipielle und umfassende Gesichtspunkte aufzustellen, vgl. πᾶς 1:16.18; 2:1.9f.; 3:9. – ἡ ἀλήθεια 1:18 ist der Monotheismus mit dessen ethischen Konsequenzen, vgl. 2:8: οἱ ἐξ ἐριθείας sind die Juden, οἱ ἀπειθοῦντες τῇ ἀληθείᾳ die Heiden; 2 Thess. 2:10.12f.; *Theol. Stud. u. Krit.* 1922, 76f.

2:1 ff. richtet dann Paulus einen plötzlichen Stoß gegen *den Juden,* den Typus des κρίνων.

Luthardt, von Hofmann, Zahn u. a. wollen auch 2:1 ff. Heiden finden, solche nämlich, die die Ruchlosigkeit ihrer Zeitgenossen tadeln. Aber 2:3 paßt nur auf den Juden; nur von ihm konnte in dieser Weise gesagt werden, daß er sich gegen das Gericht gefeit glaubt ohne Rücksicht auf sein sittliches Verhalten. – Daß 2:1 eine plötzliche, scharfe Schwenkung der Front stattfindet, ist unverkennbar. Die ersten Worte, διὸ ἀναπολόγητος εἶ, scheinen die vorausgehende Gedankenreihe weiterzuführen, vgl. εἰς τὸ εἶναι αὐτοὺς ἀναπολογήτους 1:20. Aber πᾶς ὁ κρίνων steht in offenbarem Gegensatz zu denen, die 1:32 als solche beschrieben werden, die Gottes Satzung kennen, nämlich daß wer solches tut, den Tod verdient, und dennoch nicht bloß selber das alles tun, sondern sogar die andern, die es tun, beloben. ὁ κρίνων muß somit die Kategorie derer sein, die von solchem Treiben Abstand nehmen. Zwar macht διό Schwierigkeit, und man nimmt gewöhnlich an, daß Paulus mitten im Satz den Spieß umdreht und so eine überraschende Wirkung erzielt: Er scheint die Schuld der bösen Heiden nochmals feststellen zu wollen, – und da sitzt plötzlich der Stoß im Herzen des selbstzufrieden dem Urteil zustimmenden Dritten! Allein, bei dem souveränen und freien Gebrauch der Partikeln, die wir in den paulinischen Briefen wahrnehmen, darf man die logisch oder sachlich begründende Kraft des διό nicht allzu hoch veranschlagen, vielmehr es hier als eine lose Verknüpfung des Folgenden mit dem Vorhergehenden beurteilen. – Übrigens kann man sich fragen, ob nicht in dem διό ein uralter Schreibfehler steckt, und wir statt seiner ein δὶς ἀναπολόγητος εἶ lesen sollen: *Doppelt* unentschuldbar bist du, o Mensch...! Paläographisch stehen ja ΔΙΟ und ΔΙC einander sehr nahe; und wenn auch eine Unentschuldbarkeit logisch besehen absolut ist und nicht gesteigert werden kann, dürfte doch eine emphatische Steigerung bei Paulus nicht befremden.

Auch 2:1 tritt eine allgemeine Charakteristik (πᾶς ὁ κρίνων) an die Stelle einer direkten Nennung, vgl. 1:18 (ἐπὶ πᾶσαν ἀσέβειαν κτλ.); und auch der Inhalt 2:1 ff. ist an sich allgemeiner Art: Das Bild des Sittenrichters, der selbst tut, was er an den andern tadelt, ist ein weit verbreiteter Topos in Satire und Moralpredigt. Dem entspricht gewissermaßen die aus der Diatribe stammende, wohlbekannte Anredeform, die eine gemeingiltige Wahrheit individualisiert und einprägt.

ὁ κρίνων in den Logia Jesu Mt. 7:1–5 (Splitter und Balken), vgl. Epiktet *Diss.* II 16, 45; Seneca *vit. beat.* c. 27; Horaz *sat.* I 3; Persius *sat.* 4; Plutarch *de curios.* p. 515 D; Babr. 66; Aesop. *fab.* 359; Phaedrus *fab.* IV; Catull. *carm.* XXII 21. – Zum Diatribenstil vgl. R. Bultmann, *Der Stil der paulinischen Predigt und die kynisch-stoische Diatribe,* 1910.

Diesen Topos gestaltet aber der Apostel durchaus selbständig: Mit der stärksten Emphase stellt er ihn unter den Gesichtspunkt des göttlichen Zorngerichts (τὸ κρῖμα τοῦ θεοῦ 2:2, ὀργή 2:5). – Daß Paulus nach der Abrechnung mit dem Heidentum sich an die Juden wendet, lag in seinem vorausgefaßten schriftstellerischen Plan. Es fragt sich nur, warum die Auseinandersetzung gerade diesen Verlauf nimmt: den plötzlichen, fast leidenschaftlichen Übergang 2:1; die Charakteristik des Juden als ὁ κρίνων und die auf diesen Begriff gestellte Polemik. Wir werden wohl nicht fehlgehen, wenn wir auch hier den literarischen Wiederhall praktischer Missionserfahrungen zu verspüren meinen. Indem Paulus von der Straße oder dem Markt in die Synagoge tritt, erfaßt ihn eine besondere Stimmung, taucht vor sein Bewußtsein ein charakteristisches Vorstellungskomplex auf: Die Selbstgerechtigkeit, der religiöse und moralische Dünkel eben des Diasporajuden (und des σεβόμενος, – denn nichts verbietet, vielmehr empfiehlt sich die Annahme, daß Paulus bei ὁ κρίνων auch an die in der Synagoge verkehrenden Griechen denkt), auf die er so oft gestoßen ist, und die der Heilsverkündigung so zähen Widerstand leistet.

Oft genug hat er dieses hohe Selbstbewußtsein bekämpfen müssen und es wohl meist unüberwindbar gefunden. So erklärt sich das Jähe und Schroffe seiner Gedankenbewegung: Doppelt unentschuldbar bist du, o Mensch, welcher ein κρίνων bist! Das ist ein spontaner, wuchtiger Keulenschlag gegen die feste Mauer, die zu brechen der Apostel so oft vergeblich versucht hat. – Als Brechstange gegen diese Mauer wird Paulus manchmal den *tatsächlichen* Nachweis schwerer sittlicher Schäden im Kreis der Juden und Proselyten benutzt haben. Diese konkrete Begründung mußte in der literarischen Gestaltung wegfallen; es bleibt das allgemeine Räsonnement, das sich dem bekannten Topos nähert aber offenbar nicht *in abstracto* gemeint ist, sondern auf die Juden überhaupt zielt: Sie wähnen sich über die Heiden erhaben, sind aber um kein Haar besser, in der Tat nur noch mehr kompromittiert als sie. In dieser allgemeinen Fassung schwebt die Argumentation in der Luft: Warum sollte es nicht unter den κρίνοντες etliche, ja viele sein, die den heidnischen Greueln innerlich wie äußerlich fern standen? Nimmt man die Worte 2:1–5 so wie sie stehen, geben sie eine schiefe und unhaltbare Vorstellung vom Diasporajudentum; erst wenn man ihre psychologischen Voraussetzungen in die Rechnung bringt, kann man sie gerecht beurteilen.

Die Behauptung, daß ὁ κρίνων, weil er selbst das Böse tut, dem Zorngericht entgegengeht, mündet in *den allgemeinen Gedanken der Vergeltung* aus, 2:6.

Dieser wird nach beiden Seiten hin ausgeführt, sowohl mit Bezug auf die Strafe als auf den Lohn, 2:7–8; obgleich der Zusammenhang streng genommen nur den Hinweis auf die *Strafe* als den letzten Gedanken forderte. – Hier macht sich wieder ein geläufiger religiöser Begriff geltend (2 Cor. 5:10 und bestimmt die Richtung der folgenden Gedankenführung: das ἕκαστος 2:6 führt von selbst auf eine genauere Bestimmung, und auch hier standen fertige Begriffe dem Apostel zu Gebote.

Im Zusammenhang des allgemeinen Vergeltungsgedankens vollzieht nun Paulus die von vorn herein beabsichtigte *Zusammenfassung* von Heiden und Juden unter einen gemeinsamen religiösen Gesichtspunkt, 2:9–10.

Aber dieser ist nicht der definitive: die Zusammenfassung ist eine ganz prinzipielle und beschließt in sich *beide* Aspekte: Heil und Verderben. Auf den letzteren Aspekt aber hat Paulus natürlich sein Augenmerk, und er führt zunächst die Parallele zwischen Juden und Heiden genauer aus mit Bezug auf ihre *Verantwortlichkeit,* 2:11–16, die er für die Heiden aus dem νόμος ἄγραφος in den Herzen herleitet, – wiederum eine allbekannte Vorstellung (R. Hirzel, Ἄγραφος νόμος in *Abhandl. d. sächs. Gesellsch. d. Wiss. phil.-hist. Kl.* XX 1, 1900; *Stoic. vett. frgm.* (Arnim) III 308–326; Ed. Norden, *Agnostos Theos,* 1913, 11. 122). – Es ist in der Gedankenführung begründet, daß hier nicht das frühere Interesse herrscht: Die Juden sind gleich schuldig wie die Heiden, sondern umgekehrt: Die Heiden sind gleich verantwortlich wie die Juden. Und die Verantwortung wird etwas anders formuliert als 1:19ff.: dort wurde ausschließlich *die religiöse Verschuldung* betont, hier *die moralische Zurechnungsfähigkeit* überhaupt.

Paulus hat den Punkt erreicht, wo in gleichem Maße Schuld und Verantwortlichkeit der Juden und der Heiden aufgezeigt ist. Aber es treibt ihn über diesen Punkt hinaus: die Juden haben doch schließlich eine Sonderstellung; ihr Verhalten ist doch ernster zu beurteilen, wenn man ihre Vorzüge und ihr stolzes Gebahren den Heiden gegenüber bedenkt. So kehrt er nochmals, und jetzt mit direkter Nennung des Namens, besonders zu *dem Juden* zurück und stellt wieder den Zwiespalt zwischen Ansprüche und Wirklichkeit ans Licht, 2:17–24. Wieder herrscht der Gesichtspunkt: der Jude ist um nichts besser als der Heide. Dieser letztere rückt dabei in ein immer günstigeres Licht; schließlich heißt es, daß der Heide, der das Gesetz erfüllt, den beschnittenen Gesetzesübertreter richten soll (2:27); ja, am Ende negiert Paulus überhaupt jede Bedeutung der äußeren theokratischen Stellung und löst den Begriff "Jude" auf, indem er ihn spiritualisiert: er zeichnet ein Bild *des wahren oder idealen Juden,* das ganz allgemein menschlich orientiert ist.

Polemischer Eifer und dialektische Neigung treiben Röm. 2:17–29 den Apostel weit über die Grenzen seiner wirklichen Anschauung hinaus. – Der Jude hat die größere Verantwortlichkeit (δὶς ἀναπολόγητος 2:1), – das ist der Grundgedanke der lebhaft rhetorisch gestalteten Apostrophierung des Juden 2:17ff., die mit dem vernichtenden Urteil schließt (2:24): "Gottes Name wird um euretwillen unter den Heiden gelästert, wie geschrieben steht!" Allein, Paulus fühlt sich noch nicht am Ziel: er muß den Gedanken bis in dessen äußerste Konsequenz verfolgen. So erklärt er 2:25, daß der beschnittene Gesetzesübertreter auf die Stufe des Heiden herabsinkt (ἡ περιτομή σου ἀκροβυστία γέγονεν); dann aber kehrt er 2:26 diesen Satz einfach um: der unbeschnittene Gesetzeserfüller ist gleichwertig dem Juden (ἡ ἀκροβυστία αὐτοῦ εἰς περιτομὴν λογισθήσεται). Voraussetzung der letzteren Formulierung ist der allgemeine Gedanke des περισσὸν τοῦ Ἰουδαίου (3:1 vgl. 2:25): Der Heide, der das Gesetz hält, ist in Gottes Urteil einem – das Gesetz haltenden – Juden gleichwertig; realiter wird aber durch diese Aussage der Vorzug des Juden aufgehoben: eine völlige Parität wird proklamiert, vgl. 2:28f., wo der theokratische Ehrenname Ἰουδαῖος verinnerlicht und vergeistigt wird.

Im Verfolg seiner Polemik gegen den auf seine Zugehörigkeit zum theokratischen Volke pochenden Juden hebt sich also der Apostel zum Begriff des wahren Juden empor. Angesichts dieser großartigen Formulierung darf nun nicht vergessen werden, daß Paulus hier einen konsequenten Radikalismus entwickelt, der keineswegs seinen Anschauungen *in concreto* entspricht. Wie nicht am wenigsten aus dem Römerbrief zu ersehen ist, bewertet er Israel als die religiöse Aristokratie der Welt, die Gott gegenüber eine Sonderstellung einnimmt. Anderseits, das Bild des gesetzerfüllenden Heiden ist ein nur gedachtes, ist ein dialektisches Moment in der Auseinandersetzung mit dem stolzen, selbstgerechten Juden.

Zur positiven Stellung des Paulus zur Theokratie vgl. A. von Harnack, *Beiträge z. Einleit. z. N. Test.* IV 1911, 21ff.; A. Jülicher, *Protest. Monatshefte* 1913, 1 rf.; F. Philippi, *Paulus und das Judentum,* 1916. – Zahn läßt den Apostel Röm. 2:14ff. letzten Grundes an Heiden*christen* denken, und 2:28f. soll der wiedergeborene Judenchrist geschildert sein. Das ist eine völlige Verkennung der besonderen Art dieser Ausführungen. – Es muß auch gegenüber Mißverständnissen betont werden, daß 2:28f. nicht der rechte Jude dem nur äußerlichen entgegengestellt werden soll, sondern Paulus meint überhaupt den Begriff "Jude" seines ethnographisch nationalen Charakters zu entkleiden. Es ist also zu paraphrasieren: Nicht wer es im äußeren ist, ist Jude (im wahren Sinn des Wortes), sondern wer im Verborgenen ein Jude ist, der ist – mag er äußerlich beschnitten sein oder nicht – ein wahrer Jude. – Bei diesem grundstürzenden Gedanken angelangt empfindet Paulus eine doppelte Notwendigkeit: sein abfälliges Urteil über die Theokratie zu modifizieren, und einen Rückweg zu gewinnen zum Thema, der Glaubensgerechtigkeit, von dem er weit abgekommen ist. So folgt eine Erwägung der jüdischen Vorzüge (hier Ἰουδαῖος wieder im eigentlichen Sinne) 3:1–8; diesen Gedankengang läßt er aber fallen, um aufs neue die Parität der Juden und der Heiden als Sünder – jetzt an der Hand der Schrift – zu behaupten, 3:9–18. Von diesem Nachweis der tatsächlichen allgemeinen Sündhaftigkeit gelangt Paulus durch eine überaus künstliche Schlußfolgerung zu einer Aussage (3:19–20), die dem Gesetz rettende Kraft abspricht und so der Definition der Glaubensgerechtigkeit 3:21ff. den Weg ebnet.

Der wahre Jude ist der, welcher im Verborgenen ein Jude ist. Somit wird Ἰουδαῖος hier als religiöser Ehrenname gebraucht, wie sonst Ἰσραηλίτης Röm. 9:4: u.ö., vgl. besonders Jo. 1:48 ἴδε ἀληθῶς Ἰσρ., ἐν ᾧ δόλος οὐκ ἔστιν: ein Mann nach dem Herzen Gottes, ein rechter Gottangehöriger, ein wahres Glied des Gottesvolkes (Paulus sagt: ein Glied des wahren Gottesvolkes; jedoch ohne die christliche Zuspitzung dieses Gedankens, die z.B. Röm. 9:6ff. begegnet). Dem entspricht, daß die wahre Beschneidung der äußerlichen im Fleisch entgegengestellt wird als "Beschneidung des Herzes durch den Geist, nicht durch den Buchstaben (d.h. durch Gesetzesgebot)". Der Gegensatz πνεῦμα – γράμμα ist ganz prinzipiell und entspricht dem gegensätzlichen Paare ἐν τῷ κρυπτῷ – ἐν τῷ φανερῷ (anders Röm. 7:6; 2 Cor. 3:6). – Diese kühne

Umdeutung und Vertiefung eines im allgemeinen Sprachgebrauch inhaltlich festgelegten Begriffes ist echt Paulinischer Art; und das hier verwandte Schema: Zuerst Negation, dann positive Ausführung (οὐκ . . . , ἀλλά . . .) findet sich sehr häufig bei Paulus.

Die Umdeutung eines nationalen Begriffes erinnert gewissermaßen an die Umwertung des sozialen Begriffes des ἐλεύθερος in der Stoa. Überhaupt rufen die Worte des Apostels, hier wie sonst so oft, eine Reihe von Äußerungen aus dem Neuen Testament und dessen Umgebung ins Gedächtnis, Äußerungen, die auf den Gegensatz zwischen äußerem Schein und innerem Sein Bezug nehmen.

Häufig getadelt wird die Discrepanz zwischen *Hören* und *Tun* oder zwischen *Worten* und *Praxis* (Mt. 7:26f.; Jc. 2; Epiktet *Ench.* c. 52; *Tab. Ceb.* c. 34; Mt. 7:21ff.; 23:3; 1 Jo. 3:16ff.). Besonders eindringlich predigt Epiktet die Notwendigkeit, nicht nur den *Namen* sondern auch die Lebenshaltung des Stoikers zu haben: *Diss.* II 19, 19ff.: . . . τί Στωικὸν ἔλεγες σεαυτόν; . . . Στωικὸν δὲ δείξατε μοι, εἴ τινα ἔχητε. ποῦ ἢ πῶς; ἀλλὰ τὰ λογάρια τὰ Στωικὰ λέγοντας μυρίους . . . τίς οὖν ἐστι Στωικὸς: ὡς λέγομεν ἀνδριάντα Φειδιακὸν τὸν τετυπωμένον κατὰ τὴν τέχνην τὴν Φειδίου, οὕτως τινά μοι δείξατε κατὰ τὰ δόγματα ἃ ἐλάλει τετυπωμένον. – III 7, 17 οὐδὲν διοίσεις ἡμῶν τῶν λεγομένων Στωικῶν˙ καὶ αὐτοὶ γὰρ ἄλλα λέγομεν, ἄλλα δὲ ποιοῦμεν. ἡμεῖς λέγομεν τὰ καλά, ποιοῦμεν τὰ αἰσχρά. III 24, 40 τί οὖν Στωικὸν σαυτὸν εἶναι λέγεις: vgl. Röm. 2:17 εἰ δὲ σὺ 'Ιουδαῖος ἐπονομάζῃ . . .

Neben der Forderung einer *Übereinstimmung* zwischen Theorie und Praxis steht die *Kontrastierung* des Inneren und des Äußeren. Diese Anschauung spricht sich aus in der bei den Stoikern üblichen Gegenstellung von εἶναι und δοκεῖν (vgl. die von mir *Theol. Stud. u. Krit.* 1922, 81f. zusammengestellten Beispiele). In den Logia Jesu lesen wir die bekannten Worte vom rechten Beten, Fasten und Almosengeben (vgl. ἐν τῷ κρυπτῷ (κρυφαίῳ) Mt. 6:4.6.18). Ähnlich rät der Stoiker dem Weisen, jeden Schein zu vermeiden: Euphrates bestrebte sich λανθάνειν φιλοσοφῶν. So wußte er nämlich, daß er das Gute tat um seiner selbst und Gottes willen, nicht mit Rücksicht auf die Zuschauer (οὐ διὰ τοὺς θεατὰς ἐποίουν, ἀλλὰ δι' ἐμαυτόν . . . πάντα ἐμαυτῷ καὶ θεῷ) Epiktet *Diss.* IV 8,17 vgl. *Ench.* 47; Marc. Ant. I 7.

Daß wir das Bild von dem Juden, der es im Verborgenen ist, als eine durchaus originelle Konzeption des Paulus anzusprechen haben, liegt auf der Hand. Die Vorstellung ist ganz und gar durch die geschichtlichen Verhältnisse bedingt, die dem Apostel in seiner Mission begegneten. Der Gegensatz Schein-Sein erhält in diesem Zusammenhang eine besondere Ausprägung in der Gestalt eines terminologischen Kunstgriffes: gegenüber dem Juden im *gewöhnlichen* Sinn stellt Paulus den Juden im *höheren* (und wahren) Sinn .

Anders orientiert ist das bekannte Wort Epikt. *Diss.* II 9, 19f.: τί οὖν Στωικὸν λέγεις σεαυτὸν; τί ἐξαπατᾷς τοὺς πολλούς, τί ὑποκρίνῃ 'Ιουδαῖον ὢν Ἕλλην; οὐχ ὁρᾷς, πῶς ἕκαστος λέγεται 'Ιουδαῖος . . . καὶ ὅταν τινὰ ἐπαμφοτερίζοντα ἴδωμεν, εἰώθαμεν λέγειν 'οὐκ ἔστιν Ἰουδαῖος, ἀλλ' ὑποκρίνεται.' ὅταν δ' ἀναλάβῃ τὸ πάθος τοῦ βεβαμένου καὶ ᾑρημένου, τότε καὶ ἔστιν τῷ ὄντι καὶ καλεῖται Ἰουδαῖος ... – Hier ist die Rede von der Harmonie zwischen Ansprüche und Lebenshaltung. Dazu gehört eben auch das äußere Hervortreten.

Dabei ist die innere Verwandschaft des paulinischen Gedankens Röm. 2:28f. mit den oben zitierten Worten unverkennbar, und es fragt sich, ob wir nicht an dieser Stelle einen leisen Einfluß jener Vorstellungen und Überzeugungen verspüren können, nämlich in dem abschließenden Satz οὗ ὁ ἔπαινος οὐκ ἐξ ἀνθρώπων ἀλλ' ἐκ τοῦ θεοῦ. An diesem Satz ist zweierlei auffallend: Das plötzliche Auftauchen der Vorstellung des ἔπαινος, und die relativische Verknüpfung mit dem Vorhergehenden. Schon dies letztere scheint auf Gewohnheit zu deuten (vgl. Phil. 4:3); und in der Tat, erst wenn sich nachweisen ließe, daß der Begriff des *Lobes* irgendwie mit dem wahren, inneren sittlichen Verhalten eng und allgemein verknüpft war, löst sich die Frage, wie Paulus hier auf den ἔπαινος zu sprechen kommt, nachdem er vorher die ganze Zeit nur vom *Richten* (κρίνειν, κρῖμα) geredet hat.

Die Kommentare gehen auf diese Frage wenig ein. Zahn trägt einen völlig fremden Gedanken ein, wenn er paraphrasiert: "dessen Lob stammt nicht von Menschen, am allerwenigsten von ihm selbst ..." – Jülicher: "... der Jude und die Beschneidung, die solche Ehrennamen von Gott zuerteilt erhalten, gleichwohl ob die Menschen es wissen und annehmen oder nicht ..." (ähnlich Kühl). Jülicher hat gesehen, daß die Erwähnung des Lobes mit dem Begriffe ἐν τῷ κρυπτῷ zusammenhängt und ihn ergänzt. Das ist eine richtige Erfassung des Gedankens; es fragt sich nur, warum eben der Begriff des ἔπαινος sich einstellt. Es soll unten versucht werden, das näher zu beleuchten.

Die Jesusworte Mt. 6:1ff. richten sich gegen die Heuchler, die ihre Gerechtigkeit tun, um von den Menschen gesehen zu werden: durch ein solches Motiv wird die Handlung entwertet, und der Mensch bringt sich selbst um die Hauptsache: *Gottes Anerkennung.* – In der Bergpredigt nun wird dieser Gesichtspunkt auf gewisse besondere Betätigungen der Frömmigkeit angelegt: Beten, Fasten, Almosengeben. Wir sehen ihn aber auch auf *das sittliche Leben als ganzes* bezogen, vgl. die schon erwähnte Epiktetstelle *Diss.* IV 8, 7: φιλοσοφεῖν διὰ τοὺς θεατάς ... πάντα ἐμαυτῷ καὶ θεῷ. Auf diesem allgemeinen Hintergrund ist es wohl verständlich, daß die Ablehnung des Menschenlobs im Hinblick auf die göttliche Anerkennung sich so zu sagen von selbst mit dem Begriff des wahren Juden verbindet; eine solche Näherbestimmung gehörte überhaupt zur Definition des wahren sittlichen Lebens.

Wenn Paulus das Ideal der Innerlichkeit in der Gestalt des wahren Juden zeichnet, stellt er sich auf einen überjüdischen Standpunkt, aber zugleich auf hellenistischen Boden. Das letztere bekundet sich im Begriff des ἔπαινος. Aus der hellenistischen Literatur ließe sich ein reiches Material herbeibringen, das dieses Wort beleuchtete. Hier soll nur ein einzelnes Moment besprochen werden, weil es auf die paulinische Terminologie hinführt.

Diss. III 12, 16 zollt Epiktet der körperlichen Übung (Abhärtung) eine gewisse Anerkennung, nämlich wenn sie der geistigen Zucht dient (εἴη καὶ αὐτὰ ἀσκητικά): ἂν δὲ πρὸς ἐπίδειξιν, ἔξω νενευκότος ἐστὶ καὶ ἄλλο τι θηρωμένου καὶ θεατὰς ζητοῦντος τοὺς ἐροῦντας ‘ὢ μεγάλου ἀνθρώπου’. Dieser Bewunderungsausruf ist eben ein ἔπαινος des vulgären Schlages. Dieselbe Lobsucht II 16, 5ff.: διὰ τί ὁ ῥήτωρ εἰδὼς ὅτι γέγραφε καλῶς ... ὅμως ἔτι ἀγωνιᾷ; ὅτι οὐκ ἀρκεῖται τῷ μελετῆσαι. τί οὖν θέλει; ἐπαινεθῆναι ὑπὸ τῶν παρόντων. Vgl. III 23, 19. 23ff. Der stoische Erzieher rührt hier ein sehr aktuelles praktisches Problem an: Die Schwachheit des antiken Menschen für Lob und Beifall, und anderseits seine Empfindsamkeit gegen den ψόγος, die λοιδορία, den Spott. Hegel spricht bei dem griechischen Menschen von “dem unendlichen Trieb der Individuen, sich zu zeigen, zu bekunden, was jeder aus sich machen kann und dann durch das, was er dadurch bei den andern gilt, sich zu genießen”. Dieser Trieb ist zwar gewiß allgemein menschlich, aber Hegel sagt wohl mit Recht, daß “die agonale Tätigkeit die Hauptbestimmung und das Hauptgeschäft der Griechen” ist (K. Leese, *Die Geschichtsphilosophie Hegels,* 1922, 195f.); und der philosophischen Formulierung entspricht ein augenfälliger Charakterzug der griechisch-römischen Kulturwelt überhaupt. In diesem Zusammenhang ahnt man etwas von der Bedeutung des ἔπαινος sowohl im gewöhnlichen Menschenleben als in der populär-philosophischen Predigt. Die letztere bemüht sich ernstlich darum, den Einzelnen vom Urteil der Menschen, ob Lob oder Tadel, freizumachen und verpönt aufs strengste jedes Haschen nach menschlichem Lob.

Aus vielen Beispielen nur einige wenige: *Diss.* II 1, 34ff. warnt Epiktet vor jeder Ostentation; du sollst dich nur bemühen, im Inneren Gott treu zu bleiben, τῷ κεκληκότι σε ἐπ’ αὐτά. Was die äußeren Dinge betrifft, μηδὲ φωνὴν τις ἀκούσῃ σου περὶ αὐτῶν ποτε μηδ’ ἂν ἐπαινέσῃ τις ἐπ’ αὐτοῖς, ἀνέχου, δόξον δὲ μηδεὶς εἶναι καὶ εἰδέναι μηδέν. vgl. III 23, 19; Marc. Ant. IV 19:2: και˙ οὐ λέγω, ὅτι οὐδὲν πρὸς τὸν τεθνηκότα (sc. ἡ ὑστεροφημία), ἀλλὰ πρὸς τὸν ζῶντα τί ὁ ἔπαινος; – IV 20: “Jegliches Schöne ist schön durch sich selbst und in sich vollendet, so daß für ein Lob kein Raum an ihm ist (οὐκ ἔχον μέρος ἑαυτοῦ τὸν ἔπαινον). Wird es doch durch Lob (ἐπαινούμενον) weder schlechter noch besser ... Was wahrhaft schön ist, bedarf des Lobes ebensowenig als das göttliche Gesetz, die Wahrheit, die Güte, die Scham, usw.”

So muß der wahre Philosoph darauf gefaßt sein, verkannt und verachtet zu werden (Epiktet *Ench.* c. 13); es genügt aber das eigene Bewußtsein, *Ench.* c. 23: ἀρκοῦ οὖν ἐν παντὶ τῷ εἶναι φιλόσοφος˙ εἰ δὲ καὶ δοκεῖ βούλει, σαυτῷ φαίνου καὶ ἱκανὸς ἔσῃ. *Gottes Lob,* dagegen, ist ihm eine Hauptsache: ἐξουσίαν ἔχει ἄνθρωπος μὴ ποιεῖν ἄλλο ἢ ὅπερ μέλλει ὁ θεὸς ἐπαινεῖν, καὶ δέχεσθαι πᾶν ὁ ἂν νέμῃ αὐτῷ ὁ θεός, Marc. Ant. XII 11. – Man wird schon aus den angeführten Beispielen sehen, daß ἔπαινος und ἐπαινεῖσθαι bald mehr ausgesprochen vom Beifall, der bewundernden Kundgebung steht, bald im allgemeineren Sinn von der Anerkennung der Eigenschaften und des Wertes eines Menschen von Seiten der Umwelt. Auch auf diese letztere meint der Stoiker verzichten zu sollen.

Nach alle dem dürfte es psychologisch erklärlich sein, wie Paulus, indem er den wahren Juden schildert, auch auf dessen ἔπαινος zu sprechen kommt. Wo das Innere gegen das äußere Gebahren hinausgespielt wird, muß auch Stellung genommen werden zu dem von allen so heiß erstrebten Gut: dem ἔπαινος der Menschen, ihrer positiven Anerkennung und Wertschätzung des betreffenden Individuums. Die Stoiker accentuierten dem gegenüber das Bewußtsein des Einzelnen von seiner inneren Qualität, seiner Harmonie mit der Natur (mit Gott); *Paulus* muß, seinen religiösen Voraussetzungen gemäß, dem ἔπαινος ἐξ ἀνθρώπων den ἔπ. ἐκ τοῦ θεοῦ entgegenstellen. Nur Gott sieht und schätzt das verborgene Wesen, den inneren Wert des wahren Juden.

Dieser Gedanke erhält 1 Cor. 4:5 eine eschatologische Wendung. Der Apostel warnt hier gegen ein πρὸ καιροῦ κρίνειν τι. Dessen soll man sich enthalten, bis der Herr kommt und alles aufhellt: καὶ τότε ὁ ἔπαινος γενήσεται ἑκάστῳ ἀπὸ τοῦ θεοῦ. Man wundert sich hier, daß als Erfolg des Gerichts bei der Parusie des Herrn ohne weiteres das göttliche *Lob* jedem in Aussicht gestellt wird.

H. Lietzmann: "Es ist nur von ἔπαινος die Rede, doch wohl weil an Paulus, Apollos, Kephas und ihresgleichen hier als an die zu richtenden gedacht ist". – J. Weiss ähnlich, denkt aber an einen "besonderen Lohn." – Ph. Bachmann: "Der Schlußsatz ... zeigt, daß der letzte Anlaß zu jener Auseinandersetzung in einem unzeitigen Loben gelegen war, das in Korinth laut wurde ... und vergaß, daß das letztlich allein gültige Lob von dem Herzenskündiger allein kommen kann und muß." Ein völlig schiefer Gedanke, der dem vorhergehenden κρίνειν nicht gerecht wird. – Ähnlich Robertson-Plummer: "He will have his praise, what rightly belongs to him, which may be little or none, and will be very different from the praise of the partizans here."

Die Schwierigkeit löst sich, wenn wir auf den oben nachgewiesenen Gebrauch von ἔπαινος achten: Die Erkenntnis und die Schätzung des im Inneren des Menschen verborgenen Wertes, seines wahren Ichs. Indem Paulus 1 Cor. 4:4f. von der Aufhellung des Verborgenen und der Offenbarung der Herzensgedanken spricht, fließt ihm von selbst das Wort ἔπαινος in die Feder; da soll ein jeder in seinem wahren, früher vielfach verkannten Charakter aufgezeigt werden. Nicht weil Paulus besonders an sich, Apollos und Kephas denkt, schreibt er ἐπ., auch nicht weil er gegen ein übertriebenes Loben von Seiten der Korinthier reagiert, sondern weil dieses Wort überhaupt den Gegensatz in sich birgt zwischen menschlicher Kurzsichtigkeit, die nur das Äußere sieht, und Gottes Kenntnis des Verborgenen.

Zum Stil des paulinischen Peristasenkatalogs 2 Cor. 11,23ff.

(1928)

In seiner Polemik gegen die judaistischen Agitatoren in Korinth macht Paulus einen geradezu schlagwortartigen Gebrauch von der Wortgruppe καύχησις, καύχημα, καυχᾶσθαι (10,7–12,10 über ein dutzend Mal). Ob er den Ausdruck aus dem Vokabular der Gegner aufgegriffen hat, oder ob das judaistische Gebahren einen Lieblingsbegriff bei Paulus auslöste, braucht nicht ausdrücklich entschieden zu werden; Hauptsache ist, der Apostel läßt sich mit glänzender geistiger Überlegenheit auf einen ἀγών mit den selbstbewußten Herren aus Jerusalem ein und spielt dabei mit dem Gedanken der καύχησις in vielfach überraschenden Wendungen. Die ganze Geschichte ist ihm widerlich (er spricht nicht κατὰ κύριον sondern ὡς ἐν ἀφροσύνῃ 11, 17), aber man verspürt doch seine geheime Freude am Spiel: er hat alle Trumpfe auf der Hand, will er sich rühmen κατὰ σάρκα, hat er alle aristokratischen Vorzüge des Volljuden (11,22), will er den christlichen Gesichtspunkt anlegen (als διάκονος Χριστοῦ, 11,23ff.), so hat er auch diesen Köcher voller Pfeile. – Also:

διάκονοι Χριστοῦ εἰσιν;
παραφρονῶν λαλῶ, ὑπὲρ ἐγώ˙
ἐν κόποις περισσοτέρως, ἐν φυλακαῖς περισσοτέρως, ἐν πληγαῖς ὑπερβαλλόντως,
1. ἐν θανάτοις πολλάκις˙
ὑπὸ Ἰουδαίων πεντάκις τεσσεράκοντα παρὰ μίαν ἔλαβον, τρὶς ἐῤῥαβδίσθην, ἅπαξ ἐλιθάσθην, τρὶς ἐναυάγησα, νυχθήμερον ἐν τῷ βυθῷ πεποίηκα.
2. ὁδοιπορίαις πολλάκις,
κινδύνοις ποταμῶν, κινδύνοις λῃστῶν,
κινδύνοις ἐκ γένους, κινδύνοις ἐξ ἐθνῶν,
κινδύνοις ἐν πόλει, κινδύνοις ἐν ἐρημίᾳ,
κινδύνοις ἐν θαλάσσῃ, κινδύνοις ἐν ψευδαδέλφοις,
3a. κόπῳ καὶ μόχθῳ, ἐν ἀγρυπνίαις πολλάκις,
3b. ἐν λιμῷ καὶ δίψει, ἐν νηστείαις πολλάκις,
3c. ἐν ψύχει καὶ γυμνότητι˙
χωρὶς τῶν παρεκτὸς, ἡ ἐπίστασίς μοι ἡ καθ' ἡμέραν,
ἡ μέριμνα πασῶν τῶν ἐκκλησιῶν˙
τίς ἀσθενεῖ, καὶ οὐκ ἀσθενῶ;
τίς σκανδαλίζεται καὶ οὐκ ἐγὼ πυροῦμαι;
εἰ καυχᾶσθαι δεῖ, τὰ τῆς ἀσθενείας μου καυχήσομαι, ὁ θεὸς καὶ πατὴρ τοῦ κυρίου Ἰησοῦ οἶδεν, ὁ ὢν εὐλογητὸς εἰς τοὺς αἰῶνας, ὅτι οὐ ψεύδομαι. ἐν Δαμασκῷ ὁ

ἐθνάρχης Ἀρέτα τοῦ βασιλέως ἐφρούρει τὴν πόλιν Δαμασκηνῶν πιάσαι με, καὶ διὰ θυρίδος ἐν σαργάνῃ ἐχαλάσθην διὰ τοῦ τείχους καὶ ἐξέφυγον τὰς χεῖρας αὐτοῦ.

1.

Das alles ist von Paulus unter dem Gesichtspunkt des καυχᾶσθαι zusammengestellt, und so erhebt sich die Frage von selbst, ob nicht der Stil des Peristasenkatalogs dem einer Ruhmesliste nachgebildet ist, m. a. W. ob nicht Paulus mit vollem Bedacht die Aufzählung seiner Leiden und Demütigungen streckenweise formell zu einem *cursus honorum* gestaltet hat. Eine solche Kühnheit, eine solche paradoxe Formgebung ist ihm ohne weiteres zuzutrauen.

Eine gewollte Gliederung der Gedanken ergibt sich ungezwungen aus der Perikope selbst, so wie aus dem oben abgedruckten Text leicht ersichtlich ist. Das allgemeine, tematische ὑπὲρ (ἐγώ) wird zunächst dreifach umschrieben, es handelt sich um κόποι, φυλακαί und πληγαί; das Mehr (ὑπέρ) wird in dem doppelten περισσοτέρως und dem abschließenden variierenden ὑπερβαλλόντως aufgenommen und eingehämmert. Neben κόποι, φυλακαί, πληγαί treten dann θάνατοι, ὁδοιπορίαι, ἀγρυπνίαι und νηστείαι, in drei Ansätzen, je durch ein πολλάκις markiert. Das Mehr (ὑπέρ) ergibt sich von selbst aus der erdrückenden Fülle von περιστάσεις; man kann auch sagen, daß das vergleichende Interesse einer mehr *epischen* Einstellung weicht[1]: wir bekommen eben hier einen höchst originellen *cursus honorum*.

Dabei kreuzen sich rhetorische Gliederung und sachliche Stoffverteilung: die κίνδυνοι, welche zu den ὁδοιπορίαι gehören, treffen vielfach mit den θάνατοι zusammen. In den ersten Gruppe (θάνατοι) verweilt der Gedanke bei den gefährlichen Situationen selbst; in den zweiten (ὁδοιπορίαι) sind sie als Momente im ruhelosen Reiseleben des Missionars aufgefaßt.

2.

Wenn man dem Aufbau und den Einzelzügen des Peristasenkatalogs einige Aufmerksamkeit widmet, muß sogleich eins auffallen: die Funktion des viermal wiederkehrenden πολλάκις. Die funktionelle Kraft dieses Wortes in diesem Zusammenhang zeigt sich darin, daß es sozusagen mit Gewalt hereinbricht in ein sachlich und stilistisch geschlossenes Komplex:

κόπῳ καὶ μόχθῳ, [ἐν ἀγρυπνίαις πολλάκις]
ἐν λιμῷ καὶ δίψει [ἐν νηστείαις πολλάκις]
ἐν ψύχει καὶ γυμνότητι.

[1] s. Windisch z. St.

Paulus empfindet offenbar einen gewissen Stilzwang, die einmal begonnene πολλάκις-Linie durchzuführen, und er sucht Begriffe, die sich an θάνατοι und ὁδοιπορίαι anreihen lassen. Da stellt sich ihm ἀγρυπνίαι ein als vorstellungsmäßig und im Sprachgebrauch nahe sowohl mit ὁδοιπορίαι als mit κόπος und μόχθος verwandt.

Es möge in diesem Zusammenhang auf einige Plutarchstellen hingewiesen werden: ἀγρυπνίαι καὶ πλάναι καὶ περιδρομαί, *praec. de tuenda san.* XXII (p. 135 E), vgl. ibid. XXV (p. 137); πόνοι, ὁδοιπορίαι, ἀγρυπνίαι, *Sertorius* XIII (p. 574 C); ἀγρυπνία καὶ πόνος, *Antonius* XLVII (p. 938 A), vgl. *Lucullus* XVI (p. 501 F); κόπος καὶ ἀγρυπνία, *praec. de tuenda san.* XIV (p. 129 D) vgl. ἀγρυπνίαι καὶ κόποι, *Sulla* XXVIII (p. 470 C), *Aratus* XXIII (p. 1037 D); ἔνδεια καὶ ἀγρυπνία, *Philopoemen* 111 (p. 357 D) [vgl. ἀγρυπνία καὶ ἱδρώς, 2 Macc. 2,26].

Νηστείαι wiederum ist die Zusammanfassung von λιμός und δίψος.

Man fragt sich, wie dies durchgehende πολλάκις zu erklären ist. Ich glaube, es ist der Stil der *Ruhmeschronik,* deren vornehmsten Vertreter wir in dem Monumentum Ancyranum besitzen. In diesen Chroniken ist die Knappheit der Inschrift mit einer gewissen epischen Breite verbunden, und so treten neben die genauen Angaben auch die ungefähren, mehr allgemein gehaltenen. So z.B. Mon. Anc. 5, 8ff.: ἐκ τούτων τῶν εὐχῶν πλειστάκις ἐγένοντο θέαι (im lateinischen Text *saepe*). Ferner 16,16f.: πρὸς ἐμὲ ἐξ Ἰνδίας βασιλέων πρεσβεῖαι πολλάκις ἀπεστάλησαν (lat. *saepe,* vgl. I 22–24). In der Inschrift des Antiochos I von Commagene (*Or. Graec. inscr.* sel. 383 Z. 65): μίμημα δίκαιον φυλάσσων ἀθανάτου φροντίδος, ἣ πολλάκις ἐμοὶ παραστάτις ἐπιφανὴς εἰς βοήθειαν ἀγώνων βασιλικῶν εὐμενὴς ἑωρᾶτο. Im Monumentum Adulitanum (*Or. Gr. inscr.* 199 Z. 25): ἄλλα δὲ πλεῖστα ἔθνη ἑκόντα ὑπετάγη μοι ἐπὶ φόροις.

Auf diesem Hintergrunde erklärt sich vielleicht die eigentümliche Verwendung von πολλάκις 2 Cor. 11; es bietet sich dem Apostel dar als willkommenes Stilmittel, wo er seine Leiden zusammenfassen und aufzählen will, dieses zur Chronikenterminologie gehörige, bequeme und dabei amplifizierende und anschauliche "oftmals".

3.

Freilich bekommen wir daneben auch die präzisen Angaben. Und hier ist die Stilform der Chronik offenbar. Das Mon. Anc. hebt sogleich an im Ich-Stil, das Verbum im Aoristus: ἡτοίμασα, ἠλευθέρωσα usw., und bald setzen die Zahlenangaben ein: δὶς ἐνίκησα παρατάξει (1,18); δὶς ἐπὶ κέλητος ἐθριάμβευσα, τρὶς ἐφ' ἅρματος (2,9); εἰκοσάκις καὶ ἅπαξ προσηγορεύθην αὐτοκράτωρ (2,10) usw., vgl. 2,15–20. 22–31; 4,10; 9,12ff.; 12,2–12; so in der Inschrift des nubischen Königs Silko (*Or. Gr. inscr.* 201) mehrfach. Wenn man bei Paulus liest:

ὑπὸ Ἰουδαίων πεντάκις τεσσεράκοντα παρὰ μίαν ἔλαβον,
τρὶς ἐῤῥαβδίσθην,
ἅπαξ ἐλιθάσθην,
τρὶς ἐναυάγησα ...

da ist der Gedanke nicht abzuweisen, daß eine Nachbildung des Stils der Ehrenchronik vorliegt.

Diese Formeln finden sich auch in der *Biographie,* wie bei Plutarchus *Gracchen* 1: der Vater der Gracchen wird bezeichnet als δὶς ὑπατεύσας καὶ θριάμβους δύο καταγαγών, vgl. *Marcellus* 1: πεντάκις ὑπατεύσας; *Camillus* 1: δικτάτωρ δὲ πεντάκις etc. In der *Diatribe* Epictet *Diss.* III 22. 27: ἐν ἀρχῇ οὐκ ἔστιν (sc. ἡ ἐλευθερία). εἰ δὲ μήγε, ἔδει τοὺς δὶς καὶ τρὶς ὑπάτους εὐδαίμονας εἶναι· οὐκ εἰσὶ δέ..

4.

Unter diesen Umständen fällt auch nicht die Aretas-Episode, die zum Schluß (11,32f.) kurz berichtet wird, so sehr auf, wie man es gewöhnlich empfindet: Es ist der epische Chronikstil, der hier wieder einsetzt, nachdem er eine Weile vom strophischen Schema verdrängt war.

Zu beachten ist schließlich, daß die περιστάσεις auch in der Ruhmeschronik ihren Platz haben, nämlich wo der Betreffende die von ihm überwundenen Schwierigkeiten und ausgehaltenen Strapazen schildert, wie z.B. im Monumentum Adulitanum (*Or. Gr. inscr.* 199):

καὶ Σεμῆνε ἔθνος πέραν τοῦ Νείλου ἐν δυσβάτοις καὶ χιονώδεσιν ὄρεσιν οἰκοῦντας, ἐν οἷς διὰ παντὸς νιφετοὶ καὶ κρύη καὶ χιόνες βαθεῖαι ὡς μέχρι γονάτων καταδύνειν ἄνδρα, τὸν ποταμὸν διαβὰς ὑπέταξα. Es liegt aber dem Paulus fern, wirklich mit seinen Drangsalen und Mühen renommieren zu wollen; er schaut zurück auf sie weder mit dem Stolz des triumphierenden Siegers noch mit der inneren Genugtuung des Stoikers; für ihn sind diese Widerfahrnisse samt und sonders Leiden, Demütigungen, ἀσθένειαι, ein Teil seines Martyriums. Und nur unter diesem Gesichtspunkt will er sich rühmen, nämlich insofern Gott ihn dieses Übermaßes von Leiden gewürdigt und ihm die Kraft sie zu tragen verliehen hat.

Wenn der Apostel trotz dieser christlichen Grundstimmung des Martyriums und der Schwäche sich dem Stil der Ruhmeschronik anschließt, zeugt das von einer gewissen Spannung in seinem Wesen zwischen menschlichem Selbstbewußtsein und christlicher Selbstentäußerung; einer Spannung, die in der paradoxalen Diskrepanz zwischen Form und Inhalt des Peristasenkatalogs hervorbricht.

Peristasenkatalog und *res gestae*

Nachtrag zu 2 Cor. 11, 23ff.

(1929)

Als ich vor kurzem diese Frage behandelte (Symb. Osl. VII [1928] p. 25–29) und dabei besonders gewisse Stileigentümlichkeiten des Paulus mit dem Stil der augusteischen Ruhmeschronik, des Monumentum Ancyranum, verglich, kannte ich noch nicht die Studie von E. Kornemann: *Mausoleum und Tatenbericht des Augustus* (Leipzig 1921). Die Lektüre dieser wichtigen und belangreichen Untersuchung veranlaßt mich, nochmals das Wort zum obigen Thema zu ergreifen. Die von Kornemann vorgetragenen Ansichten bestärken mich in der Überzeugung, daß meine These von einer Stilübernahme von seiten des Apostels richtig ist[1]. Ich skizziere im folgenden zunächst kurz die springenden Punkte der Kornemann'schen Ausführungen, um schließlich ihre Bedeutung für die von mir angeschnittene Frage anzudeuten.

1.

Kornemann führt den Nachweis, daß der Tatenbericht des Augustus nicht am Mausoleum selbst, sondern *vor* demselben an zwei freistehenden Inschriftenpfeilern angebracht war: "Augustus hat sich keine Grabinschrift, sondern eine Ehreninschrift setzen wollen, vor einem Monument, das den Ruhm seines Geschlechts für alle Zeiten verkünden sollte, und an einem Platze, der der großen Menge öffentlich zugänglich war. Mit anderen Worten, die *res gestae* sind ein historisch-politisches Dokument ersten Ranges, berechnet auf die Wirkung auf die römische Plebs, auf deren guter Stimmung der neue Kaiserthron ruhte, und geschrieben im Interesse des neuen Geschlechts und der aus ihm hervorgehenden neuen Dynastie" (p. 18).

Es fragt sich nun, wo das Vorbild dieser ganzen Anlage zu suchen ist. Was das Mausoleum betrifft, findet Kornemann Nachahmung teils des altitalischen

[1] Ich freue mich der Zustimmung von Gunnar Rudberg in seinem neu erschienenen Buch *Hellas och Nya Testamentet,* Stockholm 1929, p. 110ff. 117ff.

Grabhügels *(tumulus)*, teils der alexandrinischen Königsnekropole. Die Anbringung der Inschrift an vorgelagerten Pfeilern hat viele griechische Analogien. Es treffen sich also hier römische, griechische und orientalische Stilarten und gehen eine Verbindung ein.

2.

Uns kommt es aber hier auf die Inschrift selber an, ihren Zweck und literarischen Charakter.

Sie ist also *keine Grabschrift* – das ist auch für den Vergleich mit 2 Cor. 11 wichtig –, sondern eine Demonstration der eigenen Ruhmestaten, die zwar in diesem Falle mit dem Grabmal verbunden wurde, die aber auch mit anderen Monumenten zusammengestellt werden konnte[2].

Von der *Biographie* unterscheidet sich die Ruhmeschronik u.a. darin, daß nur die Taten, die im Dienst des Öffentlichen getan sind, Aufnahme finden[3].

Schließlich ist auch zu unterscheiden zwischen den *res gestae* und dem *cursus honorum*. Letzterer enthält nur die von dem Verstorbenen erlangten offiziellen Ehrenämter und Ehrungen.

Dabei hat natürlich die Ruhmeschronik Züge, die ihr und der *Biographie* bzw. dem *cursus honorum* gemeinsam sind; sie umspannt aber ein engeres Gebiet als die Biographie, ein weiteres als der *cursus honorum*.

Das entscheidende formale Merkmal der *res gestae* ist aber die *Ichform*. Man kann also den Inschriftentypus des Monumentum Ancyranum folgendermaßen definieren: *Eine Ehreninschrift, die einer sich selbst setzt, in welcher er seine Taten im Dienste des Vaterlandes und die dafür erhaltenen Ehrungen aufzählt, und zwar in der Ichform.*

3.

Wo liegt das Vorbild zu diesem Inschriftentypus? Schon Mommsen weist auf den Osten hin[4] 1. Auch diese Frage untersucht Kornemann, und zwar handelt es sich um zweierlei: die *Ichform* und die *Gruppierung des Stoffes*.

Was die letztere Frage betrifft, so verweist Kornemann auf das in hellenistischer Zeit unter orientalischem Einfluß ausgebildete *Herrscherenkomion* (βασιλικὸς λόγος), das charakterisiert ist durch *Verbindung von Taten und Tugenden* und durch die σύγκρισις oder ἀντιπαραβολή.

---

[2] Kornemann verweist p. 95 auf Plutarchus *Vit. X.* or., *Lykurg* p. 277 (die Stele mit der Inschrift wird errichtet vor der Palästra), und Diodor I, 27, Lactantius I 11, 33.

[3] Kornemann p. 86.

[4] *Ges. Schr.* IV p. 256, vgl. W. Otto in *Litt.-Zentralblatt* 1908 Nr. 40, Sp. 1287, Kornemann p. 81.

Das Reden in erster Person ist mit Mommsen zurückzuführen auf das Vorbild orientalischer Herrscher, die in ihren Ruhmeschroniken im Ichstil reden[5]. *Jedoch deutet Kornemann auch eine andere Möglichkeit an (Exkurs VIII): "Augustus hat in seinem großen Schlußrapport an das römische Volk die Form der amtlichen Berichte an Senat und Volk bis zum Reden in der ersten Person beibehalten"*[6].

Mir scheint, wenigstens vorläufig, die letztere Alternative etwas überflüssig. Es handelt sich ja um einen *Inschriften* typus, und da liegt doch die Analogie orientalischer Königsinschriften näher als die der amtlichen Berichte[7].

4.

Was ergibt sich nun aus alle dem für die stilistische Beurteilung des paulinischen Peristasenkatalogs?

Zunächst dürfen wir getrost annehmen, daß die literarische Gattung der *res gestae* dem Apostel wohlbekannt war. Die große Ruhmeschronik des Augustus wurde bald vorbildlich und wird zur Zeit des Apostels viele ähnliche Inschriften erzeugt haben.

Ferner fällt ein helles Licht auf die Tendenz der Aufzählung: Wesen des Tatenberichts ist ja die σύγκρισις[8]. Zwar ist diese im Monumentum Ancyranum eine indirekte, während Paulus sie offen ausspricht (ὑπὲρ ἐγώ, περισσοτέρως, ὑπερβαλλόντως). Aber das ist nur in den einleitenden Worten, und es wird gewissermaßen entschuldigt (παραφρονῶν λαλῶ). Das καυχᾶσθαι mag er nicht, er tut es nur gezwungen und hebt die καύχησις dadurch auf, daß er sich nur von seinen ἀσθένεια rühmen will[9].

Zum Schluß einige Bemerkungen zur Gruppierung der Taten, zum Stil und Rhytmus. Charakteristisch für die orientalischen Herrscherinschriften ist die

---

[5] Vgl. die Dareiosinschrift von Behistun und die Inschrift des Kommagenerkönigs Antiochos (Dittenberger *OGI* 388).

[6] Caesar dagegen hat die amtlichen Berichte an den Senat, die seinen Commentarien zu Grunde liegen, aus der ersten in die dritte Person umgesetzt.

[7] Eine Analyse und Charakteristik der *res gestae* der orientalischen Könige gibt S. Mowinckel: *Statholderen Nehemia,* Kristiania (Oslo) 1916, p.124–155, vgl. derselbe in Festschrift für Hermann Gunkel, Göttingen 1923, I, p. 278–322.

[8] Das ist schon im alten Orient der Fall, nicht erst im Hellenismus (Mowinckel in der Festschrift für Gunkel p. 304ff.).

[9] Zum Begriff der καύχησις bei Paulus s. R. Asting in *Norsk Teologisk Tidsskrift* 1925, p. 129–204, und Genths in *Neue Kirchliche Zeitschrift* p. 501–521. Zur Beleuchtung der eigentümlichen zwiespältigen Stellung des Apostels zum Rühmen mag hingewiesen werden auf die abgedämpfte Verwendung, die der Jude Nehemias von dem orientalischen Königsinschriftenstil macht, s. Mowinckel, *Statholderen Nehemia* p. 95ff. Nur mit Vorbehalt kann ein frommer Jude oder Christ dies Stilschema verwenden; das folgt aus seiner Stellung als δοῦλος θεοῦ, Χριστοῦ.

Aufzählung in kurzen, abgehackten, lapidaren Sätzen. Eine durchgedachte Disposition der Großtaten besteht nicht, vielmehr waltet der Zufall der Assoziation. Bisweilen macht sich indessen eine *epische* Tendenz geltend, die Aufzählung nähert sich der Erzählung oder der Schilderung, ohne jedoch in eine solche überzugehen. Und endlich stellt sich häufig der *Hymnenstil* von selbst ein.

Auch bei Paulus herrscht die *Aufzählung*. In derselben waltet aber der griechische Geist der Ordnung, der Disposition: θάνατοι, ὁδοιπορίαι, ἀγρυπνίαι-νηστεῖαι. Dabei verleugnet der griechisch schreibende Apostel den Orientalen nicht: die Disposition ist nicht straff durchgeführt; innerhalb der einzelnen Gruppen waltet die Assoziation, Kontrastprinzip, Komplementprinzip und kein Prinzip lösen sich ab. Die achtmalige Anapher hält das Ganze sachlich und klanglich zusammen.

Neben der griechischen Rhetorik bricht der orientalische Hymnenstil durch:

τίς ἀσθενεῖ, καὶ οὐκ ἀσθενῶ;
τίς σκανδαλίζεται, καὶ οὐκ ἐγὼ πυροῦμαι;

Schließlich mündet der Katalog in epische *Erzählung* aus: das schmähliche Abenteuer in Damaskus. Aber auch diese fällt nicht aus dem Stilschema hinaus; denn die Episode wird erzählt eben mit der lapidaren Knappheit und strengen Konzentration auf die konkreten Tatsachen, die den orientalischen Königsinschriften eigen ist.

So schließen sich die einzelnen Züge des Peristasenkatalogs zu einem einheitlichen Bild zusammen. Und das Ganze spiegelt die eigentümliche kulturelle Situation des Apostels in der hellenistischen Welt ab.

Exegetisches zu den Paulusbriefen

(1930)

1. Röm. 3,1

Τί οὖν τὸ περισσὸν τοῦ Ἰουδαίου, ἢ τίς ἡ ὠφέλεια τῆς περιτομῆς; πολὺ κατὰ πάντα τρόπον.

Sachlich bieten diese Sätze keinerlei Schwierigkeiten oder besondere Probleme, können aber vielleicht unter dem Gesichtspunkt der paulinischen Rhetorik ein gewisses Interesse beanspruchen. Daß der Apostel sich häufig der Frage bedient um seine Gedanken zu entwickeln, ist wohlbekannt, vgl. z.B. Gal 3,19: τί οὖν ὁ νόμος; τῶν παραβάσεων χάριν προσετέθη. Und zwar haben wir in diesen und ähnlichen Fällen nicht die rein "rhetorische" Frage vor uns, sondern vielmehr die lehrhafte.[1] Diese Redeform, die das Thema der folgenden Ausführung als einleitende Frage gestaltet, wurzelt wohl im mündlichen Unterricht, wo die Frage ihren natürlichen Ort hat, und ist von da aus als belebendes Stilmittel in den mündlichen Vortrag und schließlich auch in die geschriebene Darstellung hinübergegangen. Der Ursprung dürfte in der Schriftgelehrtenschule zu suchen sein; auf jeder Seite im Talmud sieht man ja, wie der Rabbi eine Frage als Ausgangspunkt seiner Belehrung nimmt.[2]

Etwas Überraschendes hat auch die Doppelung unserer Frage nicht. Sie entspricht der großen Vorliebe des Apostels für Parallelismen.[3] Es genügt zu erinnern an 1 Kor 15,50, wo ebenfalls das zweite, synonyme Glied das erste genauer umschreibt:

σὰρξ καὶ αἷμα βασιλείαν θεοῦ κληρονομῆσαι οὐ δύναται,
οὐδὲ ἡ φθορὰ τὴν ἀφθαρσίαν κληρονομεῖ.

---

[1] Mit Recht wird in den neueren Kommentaren die Frage abgelehnt, wer hier dem Apostel in die Rede fällt, der Heidenchrist oder der Judenchrist (vgl. B. Weiß z.St.)

[2] Auch die Gleichnisrede wird häufig mit einer Frage eingeleitet, vgl. Strack-Billerbeck zu Mark 4,30. Bultmann scheint unsere Stelle in die "dialogische Redeweise", die für die Diatribe kennzeichnend ist, einordnen zu wollen (*Der Stil der paul. Predigt* usw., S. 67); das kann ich nicht für unbedingt richtig halten.

[3] Siehe J. Weiß, *Beiträge z. paul. Rhetorik,* 1897, u. Bultmann a. a. O.

Jedoch wird man sich sagen müssen, daß die Formgebung Röm 3,1 recht singulär ist: Der Fragekomplex ist nicht aufgelöst (wie etwa 1 Kor 15,29ff.) sondern ist streng geschlossen, macht beinahe einen formelhaften Eindruck.

Sie erinnert gleich an die Einführungsformel der Gleichnisse Mark 4,30 (vgl. Luk 13,18; 7,31):

πῶς ὁμοιώσωμεν τὴν βασιλείαν τοῦ θεοῦ,
ἢ ἐν τίνι αὐτὴν παραβολῇ θῶμεν;

Diesen leicht variierten Pleonasmus möchte man ohne weiteres als typisch semitisch ansprechen (vgl. E. Klostermann zu Mark 4,30). Gleichwohl hat man den Eindruck, daß die Variation Röm 3,1 bewußter und bedeutsamer ist als der sachlich lose Pleonasmus im Evangelium.[4] Es ist da zu beachten, daß Ähnliches auch auf griechischem Boden zu finden ist, so daß eine Konvergenz verwandter Stilerscheinungen erwogen werden muß. Was besonders Röm 3,1 betrifft, so habe ich eine Stelle notiert, die hier angeführt werden mag: Dio Chrysostomus *Or.* II 24, 1 (Nr. 74 ed. de Budé II, pag. 347). Die Rede ist περὶ εὐδαιμονίας und führt u.a. aus, daß die meisten Menschen nicht nach Sinn und Kern des Lebens fragen, sondern nur gedankenlos ihren mannigfaltigen Interessen nachgehen, Reiten, Wettkämpfen, Musik, Landwirtschaft, Redekunst,

ἥντινα δὲ χρείαν αὐτοῖς ἔχει τούτων ἕκαστον,
ἢ τί τὸ ὄφελος αὐτῶν γίγνοιτ᾽ ἄν,
οὐκ ἴσασιν οὐδὲ ζητοῦσιν.

Vermag diese Stelle etwas Licht zu werfen auf die hier behandelte paulinische Formulierung? Bei der Lektüre hellenistischer Verfasser von dem Typ des Dion sieht man überall, wie der Hang zur "Fülle des Ausdrucks" sich breitmacht; und man fragt sich, ob nicht auch darin eine gewisse Regelmäßigkeit, eine Art Tradition sich ausgebildet hat in der Form einer relativ festen Synonymik, die den Rednern und Schriftstellern zur Verfügung stand, die aber leicht und mannigfach variiert werden konnte. Besonders der Prusäer kann kaum eine einzige Sache mit einem einzelnen Wort bezeichnen, er bedarf immer deren zwei oder mehrerer, und gewisse Kombinationen kehren bei ihm oftmals wieder (so z.B. ὠφέλιμος καὶ χρηστός).

Den konventionellen Charakter solcher Doppelungen ersieht man ja auch aus anderen Beispielen im N.T., wo nicht der ganze Satz, sondern nur ein Satzglied wiederholt ist, wie z.B. χρόνοι und καιροί 1 Thess 5,1, Act 1,7, vgl.

---

[4] Eine formell sehr ähnliche Stelle bei Dio Chrysostomus, *Or.* II 20,1 περὶ ἀναχωρήσεως (Nr. 70 ed. de Budé II, pag. 324):
Τί γάρ ποτε τὸ τῆς ἀναχωρήσεως ἐστι
καὶ τίνας χρὴ τιθέναι τοὺς ἀναχωροῦντας;
Die Frage stellt das Thema des folgenden Vortrags. Die Doppelung ist vorwiegend rhetorisch, zielt auf die klangliche Wirkung; aber die Variation ἀναχώρησις – ἀναχωροῦντες ist sachlich nicht ganz bedeutungslos.

Demosthenes *de Ol.* 3.16: τίνα γὰρ χρόνον ἢ τίνα καιρὸν τοῦ παρόντος βέλτιον ζητεῖτε; ἢ πότε ἃ δεῖ πράξετε, εἰ μὴ νῦν; Ferner ἡμέρα und ὥρα Mark 13,32, Matt 24,36.

Auch eine Stelle wie 1 Petr 1,11 glaube ich als rein pleonastische Stilvariation beurteilen zu sollen: ἐρευνῶντες εἰς τίνα ἢ ποῖον καιρὸν ἐδήλου τὸ ἐν αὐτοῖς πνεῦμα Χριστοῦ. So lesen wir bei Euripides, *Iph. Taur.* 256:

ἐκεῖσε δὴ' πάνηλθε, πῶς νιν εἵλετε
τρόπῳ θ' ὁποίῳ· τοῦτο γὰρ μαθεῖν θέλω.

Und bei Kallimachus im *Hymnus auf Delos,* V. 29:

τὴν ἱερήν, ὦ θύμε, τίνα χρόνον ἢ 'ς πότ [5] 'ἀείσεις Δῆλον ...;

Man wird also wohl an solchen Stellen mit Beeinflussung von literarisch-rhetorischer Tradition rechnen müssen und nicht mehr oder weniger weitreichende exegetische Schlüsse aus der Doppelung ziehen dürfen.[6]

2. Röm. 13,8

Μηδενὶ μηδὲν ὀφείλετε, εἰ μὴ τὸ ἀλλήλους ἀγαπᾶν.

Man kann hier sagen: Paradoxie oder Wortspiel? Will der Apostel den Begriff und die Vorstellung der "Schuld", die zunächst in ὀφείλειν liegt, auch im zweiten Glied (nach εἰ μή) festhalten, oder spielt er einfach mit der doppelten Bedeutung von ὀφείλειν: Schuld und Pflicht (Schuldigkeit)? Also entweder: Keine Schuld soll unerledigt bleiben außer der (unabtragbaren) Schuld der gegenseitigen Liebe; oder: Keine Schuld soll unerledigt bleiben; nur die Schuldigkeit (Pflicht) zur gegenseitigen Liebe (soll bleiben).

Überblickt man die Geschichte der Auslegung, sieht man gleich, daß die erstere Deutung vorwiegt, oder vielmehr, daß sie fast alleinherrschend ist. Origenes has sie später von allen zitierte und variierte Paragraphe geschaffen: *permanere tamen et nunquam cessare a nobis debitum caritatis; hoc enim et quotidie solvere et semper debere expedit nobis.* Ähnlich Chrysostomus: τοιοῦτος γάρ ἐστιν τὸ χρέος, ὡς καὶ διδόναι καὶ ὀφείλειν ἀεί. Augustinus: *(caritas) nec um redditur amittitur sed potius reddendo multiplicatur.* Thomas: *quia scilicet dilectionis debitum ita semel redditur, ut tamen semper maneat.* So auch fast alle Neueren.

[5] So wird wohl zu lesen sein, s. J. Vahlen, *Opuscula academica* I, 1907, S. 421 ff. Die Variation von ἤ und καί ist offenbar irrelevant.

[6] Wie z. B. B. Kühl zu 1 Petr 1,11. – Die Anwendung solcher halb poetischer Wendungen stimmt gut zu dem von Radermacher (*ZNW* 1926) nachgewiesenen literarischen Charakter vom 1. Petri.

Einige betonen jedoch, daß im zweiten Glied vom Bewußtsein der bleibenden Liebesschuld die Rede ist, also man konstatiert ein Hinübergleiten des Gedankens von der objektiven Feststellung hinüber zur subjektiven Empfindung. So schon Theodoret: ἡ γὰϱ ἀπόδοσις πολυπλασιάζει τὸ χϱέος. θεϱμοτέϱαν γὰϱ τὴν ἀγάπηv ποιεῖ. Erasmus in der Paraphrase: *Illis (exactoribus) si penderis quod exigunt, desinis debere: charitas etiam si satisfaciat aliis, sibi ipsa nunquam satisfacit, semper officia aemulans officiis.* Diese Tiefsinnigkeiten sind abgestreift, aber das Subjektive beibehalten bei Fritzsche: *ad Romanorum opinionem refertur: nisi ut mutuum amorem vos debere existimetis.* Ihm folgt u. a. Bernhard Weiss: "ὀφείλειν subjektiv, vom Bewußtsein der Unabtragbarkeit der Liebesschuld." – Dagegen sagt Kühl: "ὀφείλειν muß ... objektiv verstanden werden; also nicht: nur in bezug auf die Liebe zueinander sollt ihr euch dauernd schuldig fühlen, sondern: nur in bezug hierauf soll und darf ein dauerndes Schuldverhältnis bestehen ..."

Kühl hat natürlich Recht, wenn er behauptet, hier wird ein objektiver Tatbestand festgestellt, das liegt auf der Hand. Warum wollen denn einige feinfühlige Ausleger einen Übergang ins Subjektive annehmen? Statt der tatsächlichen Schuld soll nach εἰ μή das *Bewußtsein* von der (bleibenden) Schuld treten, – in Widerspruch zur exegetischen Tradition? Wahrscheinlich sind sie diesen Weg gegangen, weil sie die Empfindung hatten, wenn der objektive Schuldbegriff festgehalten werden soll, muß man zu viel aus dem konzentrierten Ausdruck herauslesen –, eben den Gedanken einer trotz ehrlichem Bemühen unabtragbaren Schuld: Der Bruderliebe stellen sich immer neue Anforderungen. Das klingt etwas zu sein und geistreich, und so möchte man den Gedanken umbiegen: Das stetige Bewußtsein von der Liebesschuld soll bleiben.

Dadurch wird die traditionelle Auslegung modifiziert, aber durchaus nicht in überzeugender Weise. Besser steht es nicht mit der Auslegung, die ὀφείλετε als Indikativ fast und nicht als Imperativ (de Dieu, Semler, Koppe, Flatt und vor allem Reiche): Alle eure Pflichten sind in der Pflicht der gegenseitigen Liebe einbeschlossen und werden somit durch die Erfüllung des Liebesgebotes erfüllt.[7] Das scheitert natürlich schon am μηδενί und μηδέν und paßt außerdem nicht in den Gedankenzusammenhang des Abschnittes hinein. Der Deutungsversuch ist aber symptomatisch, er verrät Bedenken an der herkömmlichen Interpretation.

Wie steht es nun? Darf man den an sich tiefen und wahren Gedanken von der unabtragbaren Schuld der gegenseitigen Liebe aus den Worten des Apostels in seinem Sinne herauslesen? Liegt eine beabsichtigte zugespitzte und überraschende Redewendung vor? *(argute dictum,* Erasmus; *acute, salse dictum,* Fritzsche; "nicht ohne Anflug von Scherz," Tholuck). Sanday – Headlam

[7] So auch Alex. Pallis, *To the Romans* (1920), S. 142. Er verweist auf Jannaris § 1818.

bemerken z.St.: "By this pregnant expression St. Paul suggests both the obligation of love and the impossibility of fulfiling it. This is more forcible than to suppose a change in the meaning of ὀφείλειν: Owe no man anything, only Ye ought to love one another." Es fragt sich aber, ob man diesen ästhetischen Gesichtspunkt anlegen darf. Das einfachste und nächstliegende ist jedenfalls ein Wortspiel anzunehmen mit der doppelten Bedeutung von ὀφείλειν: Schulden und verpflichtet sein. Dafür spricht vor allen Dingen der Umstand, daß Röm 15,27 mit derselben Doppelbedeutung von ὀφείλειν gespielt wird: Die Gläubigen in Makedonien und Achaia haben beschlossen eine Kollekte zu sammeln für die Jerusalemer, denn sie sind ihre Schuldiger (ὀφειλέται). Wenn nämlich die Heiden Anteil bekommen haben an den geistigen Schätzen der Jerusalemer, so sind sie verpflichtet (ὀφείλουσιν) ihnen auf dem irdischen Gebiete Dienste zu leisten. Wie leicht Schuld und Pflicht einander ablösen, sieht man hier klar.

Wenn Paulus Röm 13,8 die Vorstellung einer Schuld mit bewußter Paradoxie auch im zweiten Gliede festhalten wollte, würde er sich kaum so kurz und gedrängt geäußert haben. Für die feingeschliffene, bis zum äußersten zugespitzte Geistreichheit fehlte ihm der Sinn. Man vergleiche sein Verfahren in einem solchen Falle, wo er eine Vorstellung leugnet, um sie gleich nachher zu bejahen, 1 Kor 14,20:

μὴ παιδία γίνεσθε ταῖς φρεσίν,
ἀλλὰ τῇ κακίᾳ νηπιάζετε,
ταῖς δὲ φρεσὶν τέλειοι γίνεσθε.

Man sieht, wie breit er das ausführt ohne jeden Versuch, den Gedanken formell zuzuspitzen und so zu einer Paradoxie zu gestalten.[8]

Ich glaube also, man faßt am besten Röm 13,8 als ein leichtes und natürliches Wortspiel. Das hat freilich den Nachteil, daß der Satz im Deutschen unübersetzbar wird; die deutsche Sprache hat kein Zeitwort, das die beiden Bedeutungen von ὀφείλειν deckte.[9]

Es ist vielleicht in diesem Zusammenhang nicht ohne Interesse darauf zu verweisen, daß das jüdische *chajab* genau so wie ὀφείλειν beide Bedeutungen

[8] Eine ähnliche Negation und Position eines und desselben Begriffes begegnet bei Dio Chrysostomus in seiner dritten Rede περὶ βασιλείας 111 (Nr. 3 ed. de Budé I, pag. 66): ἐν μὲν οὖν τοῖς ἄλλοις οὐ πάντως ὑπερβάλλειν τοὺς ἰδιώτας ὁ τοιοῦτος βασιλεὺς βούλεται ... ἐν μόνῃ δὲ φιλίᾳ βούλεται πλεονεκτεῖν. Der den beiden Satzhälften gemeinsame Begriff "Vorrechte haben" ist sprachlich variiert (ὑπερβάλλειν, πλεονεκτεῖν, vgl. bei Paulus: παιδία γίνεσθαι – νηπιάζειν). Die Worte erinnern gewissermaßen an Röm 13,8, insofern als das, was auf anderen Gebieten nicht sein darf, auf dem Gebiete der Freundschaft (Liebe) sein soll.

[9] Anders auf Latein und in den romanischen Sprachen. *Nemini quidquam debeatis, nisi ut invicem diligatis. Non dobbiate nulla ad alcuno, se non di amar i gli uni gli altri.* Richtig auch Goodspeed *(The New Testament. An American Translation):* "Owe nobody anything – except the duty of mutual love ..."

in sich beschließt: Schulden und verpflichtet sein.[10] Das Wort ist sehr häufig in den Halacha-Texten (Mischna, Tosephta, Halachische Bestandteile der Talmude) und steht teils mit *l* ^{e} und einem Substantiv, teils mit *l* ^{e} und Infinitiv. Einige Beispiele: "Wir bezeugen von N.N., daß er seinem Nächsten 200 zuz schuldig ist" *(chajjab lachabero.* M. Makk. 1:2; vgl. M. Sanh. 3:6). "Man ist verpflichtet Gott zu preisen für das Böse sowohl als für das Gute" (*chajjab adam l* ^{e} *barek*. M. Ber. 9:5; vgl. M. Pes. 10:5). Delitzsch übersetzt Röm 13,8: *v* ^{e}*al tihju chajjabim l* ^{e}*isch dabar zulati ahabat isch äth-re* ^{e}*ehu.* Das entspricht genau dem griechischen Wortlaut und dessen Sinn.

3. 1 Kor. 3,9

θεοῦ γάρ ἐσμεν συνεργοί· θεοῦ γεώργιον, θεοῦ οἰκοδομή ἐστε.

Die anscheinend recht gewaltsame Verknüpfung[11] von zwei grundverschiedenen Bildern, dem des Ackerbaus und dem des Hausbaus, habe ich schon früher durch eine Platonstelle illustriert.[12] Die sachliche Voraussetzung der Verbindung der beiden Bilder suchte ich darin, daß "die beiden genannten Tätigkeiten charakteristisch sind für das Leben auf dem Lande einerseits, für das in der Stadt andererseits". Diese Ansicht wird bestätigt durch folgende Beobachtungen aus Dio Chrysostomus: *Or.* II 69,3ff. περὶ ἀρετῆς (Nr. 52 ed. de Budé II, pag. 220) klagt der Redner darüber, daß alle Menschen zwar die Tugend loben, aber ihre praktischen Bestrebungen auf allerlei andere Ziele richten: γεωργία, ἐμπορία, στρατεία, ἰατρική, οἰκοδομική, ναυπηγική usw. Aber keine von diesen Tätigkeiten ist unentbehrlich, man kann gut und rechtlich leben, ohne Musikanten, Schuster, Erzieher, Redner und Ärzte, οἶμαι δ' ἐγὼ καὶ δίχα γεωργῶν καὶ οἰκοδόμων. Für die letzte, als kühn empfundene Behauptung wird verwiesen auf die Skythen, die als Nomaden weder Häuser bauen, noch den Boden bepflanzen, noch besäen und dabei als gerechte und gesetzestreue Bürger leben. Gleich nachher werden wieder γεωργοὶ καὶ οἰκοδόμοι zweimal zusammen genannt (6–7). – *Or.* II 71,2.5 περὶ φιλοσοφίας (Nr. 54 ed. de Budé II, pag. 228f.): Der Philosoph hat seine besondere Fertigkeit geradeso, wie die Handwerker, die Häuser bauen, Schiffe zimmern, schmieden, weben und ackern (γεωργοῦντα); im folgenden spielen nun das Bauhandwerk und die Landwirtschaft die Hauptrolle, und schließlich wird zusammengefaßt: τοῦτο γὰρ οὐκ οἷόν τε, τοῦ τέκτονος τὸν ἰδιώτην ἄμεινον ποιῆσαί τι κατὰ τὴν τεκτονικὴν ἢ τοῦ γεωργοῦ τὸν οὐκ ὄντα γεωργίας ἔμπειρον ἐν τῷ ποιεῖν τι

[10] Dr. H. Odeberg hat mir freundlichst die folgenden Stellen ausgesucht und zusammengestellt.

[11] J. Weiß spricht von dem "schroffen Wechsel des Bildes" *(Beiträge z. paulin. Rhetorik,* S. 207).

[12] *Leg.* 643 B. Siehe *Theol. Stud. u. Krit.* 1922, S. 185f.

τῶν γεωργικῶν ἐμπειρότερον φανῆναι. – *Or.* II 44,6 fin. φιλοφρονητικὸς πρὸς τὴν πατρίδα (Nr. 27 ed. de Budé II, pag. 89): οὐδὲ οἰκίαν ἢ χωρίον ἐκτησάμην παρ' ἑτέροις, ὡς μηδὲν ᾖ μοι σημεῖον ἀλλαχοῦ πατρίδος (vgl. *Or.* II 39,5).

Wie eng die beiden Begriffe miteinander verbunden waren, sieht man auch bei Philo, zum Beispiel *Leg. all.* I,47f.: Daß Gott Adam in den Paradiesgarten setzte, will besagen, daß er τὸν νοῦν τίθησιν ἐν τῇ ἀρετῇ. ἵνα δηλονότι μηδὲν ἄλλο ἢ ταύτην καθάπερ ἀγαθὸς γεωργὸς τημελῇ καὶ περιέπῃ. Nun heißt es aber (Deut 16,21): οὐ φυτεύσεις σεαυτῷ ἄλσος κτλ. Was soll das heißen? ὅτι πρέπει τῷ θεῷ φυτεύειν καὶ οἰκοδομεῖν ἐν τῇ ψυχῇ τὰς ἀρετάς κτλ. – Hiermit ist zu vergleichen *de cherubim* 100ff.: Das rechte irdische Haus des unsichtbaren Gottes ist die unsichtbare Seele, und die θεμέλιοι dieses Hauses sind εὐφυΐα καὶ διδασκαλία, auf denen aufgebaut werden sollen (ἐποικοδομείσθωσαν) ἀρεταὶ μετὰ καλῶν πράξεων. Das Bild des Hauses wird nun in allen Einzelheiten ausgeführt, aber mitten drin taucht plötzlich die Vorstellung von einem Baum und dessen *Wurzeln* auf (102). – Zur Häufung der Bilder ist außerdem zu vergleichen *Quis rer. divin. her.* 116 und *Leg. all.* II,42. An der ersten Stelle wird gefragt: τέχναις δὲ καὶ ἐπιστήμαις οὐ πηγὴ καὶ ῥίζα καὶ θεμέλιοι καί, εἴ τι ἄλλο πρεσβυτέρας ὄνομα ἀρχῆς ὑπόκειται ἡ φύσις, ᾗ πάντ' ἐποικοδομεῖται τὰ καθ' ἑκάστην θεωρήματα; – an der anderen Stelle: πάντα γὰρ ὅσα πάσχει ἡ αἴσθησις, οὐκ ἄνευ νοῦ ὑπομένει, πηγὴ γὰρ οὗτός ἐστιν αὐτῇ καὶ θεμέλιος ᾧ ἐπερείδεται.[13]

Die angeführten Stellen aus Platon und Dion spiegeln die Spezialisierung der Arbeit, die sich im Altertum vollzogen hatte.[14] Es ist aber auch zu bedenken, daß unter primitiveren Verhältnissen Haus und Boden, Hausbau und Ackerbau sachlich aufs engste zusammengehören als die beiden konstitutiven Momente des Lebens überhaupt. Das ist der Hintergrund biblischer Aussagen wie Jer 1,10, Deut 20,5f., Luk 17,28 (vgl. Philo *de virtut.* 18, *de execrat.* 139). Wiederum von zwei Seiten fließen Traditionsströme zusammen und begegnen sich im Gedankengang und in der Terminologie des Apostels.

4. Phil. 3,1

Τὸ λοιπόν, ἀδελφοί μου, χαίρετε ἐν κυρίῳ· τὰ αὐτὰ γράφειν ὑμῖν ἐμοὶ μὲν οὐκ ὀκνηρόν, ὑμῖν δὲ ἀσφαλές.

Zu dieser vielgequälten Stelle bemerkt M. Dibelius (in Lietzmanns *Handbuch):* "In οὐκ ὀκνηρόν wird man es mit einer stilistischen Formel wie οὐκ ὀκνῶ und ähnliches zu tun haben ...; also ist bei der Übersetzung dem

[13] Vgl. Eph 3,17 und Lohmeyer zu Kol 2,7.

[14] J. Kaerst, *Geschichte des Hellenismus,* Bd. II. Kap. 3.

abgeblaßten Sinn solcher Wendungen Rechnung zu tragen." D. fasst τὰ αὐτὰ (γράφειν) als Bezug auf 2,18 und nicht als Einleitung zu 3,2: "Die dort folgende Warnung bedarf keiner besonderen Einführung, da der Stil der Paränese zusammenhängende Auseinanderreihung von Mahnungen mit sich bringt"; vgl. auch 4,4.[15] – Dieser Auffassung ist sicher beizustimmen. Zwei Äusserungen des Dio Chrysostomus scheinen ihr ein gewisses Relief zu verleihen. In seiner *Rhodiaca (Or.* I 31,36, Nr. 14 ed. de Budé I, pag. 292) sagt Dion: ὃ τοίνυν ἀρχόμενος εἶπον, οὐδ' ἂν νῦν ὀκνήσαιμι εἰπεῖν, ὅτι πανταχοῦ μὲν οἰκεῖον ἐστι φαίνεσθαι τοὺς ἀγαθοὺς ἄνδρας ὑγιεῖς καὶ μηδὲν παλίμβολον ἔχοντας μηδὲ δυσχερές κτλ. Dion führt seine Wiederholung mit einer oratorischen Phrase ein, – das entspricht dem sorgfältig ausgearbeiteten Charakter seiner Rede; Paulus dagegen läßt eine ähnliche Wendung einfließen, nachdem er schon die wiederholte Mahnung zur Freude diktiert hat.

Die Formel οὐκ ὀκνῶ (ὀκνήσαιμι), ἐμοὶ οὐκ ὀκνηρόν, nimmt der Wiederholung das Lästige dadurch, daß dieselbe als eine Aufopferung oder als ein Wagnis des Redners bezeichnet wird. Für Paulus ist es nun charakteristisch, daß er außerdem den Nutzen hervorhebt, den die Leser davon haben, und zwar hat er mit vollem Bedacht die konventionelle Redewendung in dieser Richtung ergänzt, vgl. die strenge Stilisierung des Ausdrucks: ἐμοὶ μὲν ... ὑμῖν δὲ ...

Auch über den Nutzen der Wiederholung vgl. ὑμῖν ἀσφαλές äußert sich Dion *Or.* II 17,2 περὶ πλεονεξίας (Nr. 67 ed. de Budé II, pag. 307): Die Aufgabe des Philosophen ist nicht so sehr den Zuhörern Neues beizubringen und so ihre ἄγνοια zu überwinden, als immer wieder an die bekannten Pflichten zu erinnern (συνεχῶς ἀναμιμνήσκειν) und Gehorsam ihnen gegenüber einzuschärfen; ὥσπερ γὰρ οἶμαι καὶ τοὺς ἰατροὺς καὶ τοὺς κυβερνήτας ὁρῶμεν πολλάκις τὰ αὐτὰ προσταττόντας, καίτοι τὸ πρῶτον ἀκηκοότων οἷς ἂν κελεύωσιν, ἀλλ' ἐπειδὰν ἀμελοῦντας αὐτοὺς καὶ μὴ προσέχοντας βλέπωσιν, οὕτως καὶ κατὰ τὸν βίον χρήσιμόν ἐστι γίγνεσθαι πολλάκις περὶ τῶν αὐτῶν τοὺς λόγους, ὅταν εἰδῶσιν μὲν οἱ πολλοὶ τὸ δέον, μὴ μέντοι πράττωσιν.[16] – Ähnliche allgemeine pädagogische Erwägungen werden auch die Worte des Apostels diktiert haben.

---

[15] Lohmeyer z.St. bezieht auch τὰ αὐτά auf 2,18, will aber 3,1 als Übergang zum Folgenden verstehen. Das beruht auf seiner besonderen Deutung des tragenden Gedanken dieses Abschnittes.

[16] Ähnliche Gedanken *Or.* I 34,16 (ed. de Budé I, pag. 408).

Paulus *abortivus*

Zu 1 Kor. 15, 8

(1932)

Im fünfzehnten Kapitel des ersten Korintherbriefes erwähnt Paulus die Offenbarungen des Auferstandenen Herrn, er zählt sie auf der Reihe nach mit Kephas anfangend, um dann schließich bei sich selbst anzulangen: ἔσχατον δὲ πάντων ὡσπερεὶ τῷ ἐκτρώματι ὤφθη κἀμοί. Die Wortfolge mit der vorangestellten Apposition zeigt, daß ἔσχατον nicht nur die Reihenfolge angibt sondern auch die Rangfolge andeutet: es ist das Gegenteil gemeint von *last but not least:*[1] Der Apostel will nicht betonen, daß nach ihm keine weiteren Offenbarungen vorkamen. Und er will nicht nur sagen, daß er zuletzt an die Reihe kam (ὕστερον[2]). Sondern er meint, daß er als der unwürdigste unter den Aposteln auch als der letzte berufen wurde. Das Abschätzige im ἔσχατον πάντων kommt im folgenden Satz zum Vorschein (V. 9): "Ich bin ja der geringste (ὁ ἐλάχιστος) unter den Aposteln, der ich nicht geeignet (würdig? ἱκανός[3]) bin Apostel genannt zu werden, weil ich die Kirche Gottes verfolgt habe". Ὁ ἐλάχιστος und οὐχ ἱκανός sprechen den Gefühlsgehalt im ἔσχατον πάντων aus; ja, in Anbetracht des folgenden Bildes vom ἔκτρωμα könnte man fast aus dem ἔσχατον ein allerschärftes Urteil heraushören wollen: Saulus war das allerschlimmste Scheusal unter allen Menschen.[4]

Wie soll man aber des näheren feststellen, was der Apostel mit dem Bilde

---

[1] πάντων ist natürlich Genitiv von πάντες und nicht von πάντα. – Das Überraschende, fast Unglaubliche in der Offenbarung an einen solchen Sünder wie dem Saulus schafft sich Ausdruck im καί (κἀμοί), das auf der Grenze des "sogar" liegt (vgl. κἀκεῖνοι, Röm. 11,23).

[2] Vgl. Mt. 22, 27 ὕστερον δὲ πάντων ἀπέθανεν [καί] ἡ γυνή (so auch Luk. 20, 32; Mk. 12, 22 ἔσχατον πάντων).

[3] ἱκανός kann (sachlich) "tauglich" oder (religiös und moralisch) "wert" heißen, im letzteren Falle gleich ἄξιος (Mk. 1,7; Mt. 8,8). Hier, wo sowohl Tauglichkeit als Würdigsein auf dem religiös-ethischen Verhalten beruht, machen die beiden Alternative keinen sachlichen Unterschied.

[4] Zur harten Selbstbeurteilung des Apostels vgl. Eph. 3, 8 (ἐμοὶ τῷ ἐλαχιστοτέρῳ πάντων ἁγίων ἐδόθη ἡ χάρις αὕτη). – Zu ἔσχατος im Sinne des äußersten Elends vgl. 1 Kor. 4,9; Alkiphr. 3, 7,5; Dio Cass. 4, 25; Diod. Sic. 8,13. Gegensätzliche Ausdrucksweise 1 Tim. 1, 16 ἁμαρτωλοί . . . ὧν πρῶτός εἰμι ἐγώ.

ὥσπερεὶ τῷ ἐκτρώματι sagen will? Und wie ist er auf dies sonderbare Bild gekommen?

Was zunächst die erstere Frage betrifft, ist zu betonen, daß das Bild vom ἔκτρωμα ein Urteil enthält über den Apostel in seiner vorchristlichen Verfolgerzeit, nicht aber eine Charakteristik seines Christwerdens oder Apostelseins. Als der Herr sich auch ihm offenbarte, war er so gut wie ein ἔκτρωμα, und wenn er sich selbst ὁ ἐλάχιστος τῶν ἀποστόλων nennt, meint er natürlich nicht, daß er *als Apostel* der geringste ist (gleich nachher sagt er ja das Gegenteil, V. 10), sondern daß er persönlich der untauglichste und unwürdigste zu diesem hohen Amte sei. Er spricht in diesem Bilde nicht von dem, was er durch Gottes Gnade ist, sondern von dem, was er einst war, und das ihn als den Begnadeten immer noch bedrückt und demütigt.[5] Also, den Verfolger Saulus nennt er ἔκτρωμα. In welchem Sinne? Es gilt das *tertium comparationis* zu finden, und da gehen nun, wie gleich zu zeigen ist, die Deutungen sehr auseinander. Hier soll ein Versuch gemacht werden, die Auslegung auf festeren Boden zu stellen.

Ein ἔκτρωμα ist ein Erzeugnis einer vorzeitigen Geburt, ein unreifes Embryo.[6] Die Eigenschaften, die ein solches auszeichnen, sind einerseits Leblosigkeit oder wenigstens geringe Lebenskraft, anderseits mangelhafte körperliche Entwicklung oder gar Deformität.[7] Es ist aber nicht wahrscheinlich, daß irgend ein besonderes von diesen Merkmalen dem Apostel vorschwebte und also der Deutung des Bildes in seinem Sinne zu Grunde zu legen ist, sondern es ist an den *unheimlichen Gesammteindruck* eines nicht vollgeborenen Embryos zu denken: Es ist etwas Dämonisches, Unmenschliches, ein Mensch ohne Menschlichkeit, ein Scheusal.[8] Ein solches war der Christenverfolger Saulus.

---

[5] In diesem Sinne, vom Andenken an seine Vergangenheit belastet, nennt sich Paulus den geringsten unter den Aposteln, genau so wie sich der Pseudo-Paulus im Epheserbrief den geringsten unter allen Christen und im 1 Tim. den ersten unter Sündern nennt.

[6] Hesychius: ἐκτρωθείς, φθαρείς˙ ἔκτρωμα, παιδίον νεκρόν, ἄωρον, ἐκβολὴ γυναικός˙ Ἄμβλωμα, ἔκτρωμα. – Aristoteles unterscheidet zwischen ἐκρύσεις und ἐκτρωσμοί (*de gen. an.* 4,5,4, p. 773 b. 18); Eusthat. in *Il.* τ p. 1239,29 φασὶ οἱ παλαιοὶ οὕτω˙ ἀμβλῶσαι τὸ φθεῖραι βρέφος ἐν γαστρί, καὶ ἀμβλωθρίδιον τὸ τοιοῦτον˙ ἐκτρῶσαι δὲ καὶ ἔκτρωμα τὸ μήπω τετυπωμένον. – Phrynichus warnt vor dem Wort (208f. Lob.): ἐκτρῶσαι καὶ ἔκτρωμα, ταῦτα φεῦγε˙ λέγε δὲ ἐξαμβλῶσαι καὶ ἄμβλωμα καὶ ἀμβλίσκει. – Philo verknüpft beides (*legg. all.* I, 76): οὐ πέφυκε γόνιμον οὐδὲ τελεσφορεῖν ἡ τοῦ φαύλου ψυχή˙ ἃ δ' ἂν δοκῇ προφέρειν, ἀμβλωθρίδια εὑρίσκεται καὶ ἐκτρώματα. Ob Philo dabei an mehr und weniger fortgeschrittene Entwicklungsstadien des Embryo denkt, oder nur das feinere Wort mit dem mehr volkstümlichen verbindet, mag dahingestellt sein.

[7] Vgl. einerseits Phryn.: παιδίον νεκρόν. Num. 12:12 (LXX) μὴ γένηται ὡσεὶ ἴσον θανάτῳ, ὡσεὶ ἔκτρωμα ἐκπορευόμενον ἐκ μήτρας μητρός. Hiob 3,16; Eccl. 6,3. – anderseits Eusthat.: τὸ μήπω τετυπωμένον. Irenäus *adv. Haer.* I 1,7 ἄμορφος καὶ ἀνείδεος ὥσπερ ἔκτρωμα; 3,25,6; 4,35,3 *(informis, infigurata, sine specie, quasi abortivum);* Tertull. *adv. Val.* 14 *(nec forma nec facies ulla).* Hippol. *Refut.* (Wendland) VI, 31, 1–2; VII, 27, 7.

[8] Vgl. Sueton. *Claud.* 3,2: *Mater Antonia portentum eum hominis dictitabat, nec absolutum a natura (=* ἀτελής oder ἀτελεσφόρητος), *sed tantum incohatum.* Monströse Geburten und Fehlgeburten wurden als etwas Teuflisches, Unheilbringendes angesehen: Frazer, *The Golden Bough,* III, S. 179, 152ff. 211–213; von Nagelein, *Traumchlüssel des Jagaddeva,* S. 17,

Wie ist aber Paulus auf diesen überraschenden Vergleich gekommen? Es ist sicher anzunehmen, daß er eine von den Gegnern geprägte und in Umlauf gesetzte Bezeichnung aufgegriffen hat.[9] So erklärt sich am besten der Artikel τῷ (ἐκτρώματι), der hier etwa unser Anführungszeichen vertritt.[10] Indem nun Paulus das Urteil der Gegner sich zu eigen macht, markiert er die übertragene Anwendung durch ein ὡσπερεί "sozusagen".[11]

Bei dieser Auffassung erhebt sich die Frage, in welchem Sinne denn die Gegner den Paulus ein ἔκτρωμα genannt haben. Etwa in dem Sinne wie er selbst: Ein widerwärtiges, menschenähnliches Scheusal? In dem Falle müßte man sich denken, daß ἔκτρωμα in Palästina oder Korinth ein geläufiges Schimpfwort war, und zwar ein so drastisches, ja rohes und profanes Schimpfwort, daß man sich schwerlich vorstellen kann, daß Christen es auf die Zunge nehmen wollten.[12] Die gegnerische Charakteristik des Paulus als ἔκτρωμα muß irgendwie einen *religiösen* Gehalt gehabt haben: Wenn die Gegner der paulinischen Mission den Apostel eine Fehlgeburt nannten, werden sie das getan haben im Hinblick auf die Wiedergeburt; diese sei mit ihm nicht gelungen, er sei eine Fehlgeburt der ἀναγέννησις ein unvollgeborener, mangelhafter, mißratener Christ und somit als Apostel unmöglich.

Dieses harte Urteil nimmt der Apostel auf und bezieht es auf sich, so wie er war in der Zeit, als er die Kirche Gottes verfolgte und der Herr sich ihm offenbarte. Damals war er sozusagen das ἔκτρωμα, als welches die Gegner ihn bezeichneten, ein unmenschliches Scheusal ohne wahres Leben. Als solches war er der letzte unter allen, erhielt deshalb als der letzte die Offenbarung des auferstandenen Herrn und empfindet sich immer noch als den geringsten, den unwürdigsten unter den Aposteln.

Die Deutung des Bildes vom ἔκτρωμα schwankt in der Geschichte der Auslegung bis auf den heutigen Tag und hat zuweilen seltsame Ansichten gezeitigt.[13]

66f., 172f. Die Fruchtabtreibung macht kultisch unrein, s. S. Wide im *Archiv für Religionswissenschaft,* 12 (1909), S. 224ff.

[9] So schon J.J. Wettstein *(Novum Testamentum Graecum* etc. 1751/52): *"Pseudapostoli videntur Paulo staturam exiguam obiecisse,* 2 Cor. 10,10" (!).

[10] So P.W. Schmiedel im *Hand-Commentar z. N. T.* II, 1, 1891.

[11] ὡσπερεί wird in der Schrift περὶ ὕψους (32) charakterisiert als μείλιγμα τῶν θρασέων μεταφόρων. Zur Anwendung vgl. Platon *Crat.* 442 A; Aristoph. Lys. 146, Eccl. 537; Plut. *de lib. ed.* 7 C ἀλλὰ ταῦτα μὲν ἐκ παραδρομῆς μαθεῖν ὡσπερεὶ γεύματος ἕνεκεν; 12 C δύο οὖν ταῦτα ὡσπερεὶ στοιχεῖα τῆς ἀρετῆς εἰσιν, ἐλπίς τε τιμῆς καὶ φόβος τιμωρίας.

[12] Auf eine Anwendung als Schimpfwort deutet vielleicht Rufin. *de bell. Jud.* 6,19: *servos se et convenas et degeneris gentis abortiones confessi sunt* (vgl. Juv. *Sat.* 2, 33). –Aber dieser Sinn bleibt unsicher und jedenfalls im Munde der Gegner des Apostels unwahrscheinlich. Dem Apostel selbst aber war kein Wort zu hart und kein Sinn zu schroff, wenn er seiner Verfolgerzeit gedachte. Auch sonst scheut er drastische Ausdrücke nicht (κύνες, κατατομή Phil. 3,2; ἀποκόπτεσθαι Gal. 5, 12).

[13] Sehr beliebt war lange statt τῷ (ἐκτρώματι) τῳ (= τινί) zu lesen, ohne zu beachten, daß dadurch die übertragene Anwendung des Wortes gefährdet wurde. Tatsächlich paraphrasiert auch van Hengel: Paulus sah nicht Jesus oculis corporis (Blindheit des Embryo!). Heydenreich

Absonderlich ist z. B. die alte Deutung des ἔκτρωμα als "Spätgeburt", im Alter nachgeborener, Spätling.[14] In der alten Kirche[15] bezog man das Bild teils (richtig) auf den Zustand des Apostels bei der Berufung, teils auf die Art der Berufung, im letzteren Falle ohne zu bedenken, daß ἔκτρωμα das Produkt, nicht der Akt ist. Diesen Fehler machen auch Neuere wie Grotius *(subita vi)*, Calvin, Heinrici, Robertson-Plummer, auch Lietzmann.[16] Aber mit Recht stellt Ed. Schwartz fest: Ἔκτρωμα heißt nicht "Frühgeburt" sondern "Fehlgeburt"; Paulus hatte ja zunächst geleugnet, daß Jesus der Messias sei.[17] Und Harnack äußert "In den Worten ἔσχατον δὲ πάντων etc. muß dem Worte ἔκτρωμα ein Sinn gegeben werden, der dem ἔσχατον und dem ὡσπερεί gerecht wird. Der Artikel beweist, daß den Korinthern diese Bezeichnung des Apostels

---

gibt gar ἔκτρωμα eine Beziehung zu ὁ ἐλάχιστος (τῶν ἀποστόλων): "velut abortivi solent esse minutuli exilesque statura". Man hat auch unsere Stelle aufhellen wollen mit Hilfe von Sueton, *Oct.* 33: *Erant semper mille* (senatores) *et quidem indignissimi; et post necem Caesaris per gratiam et praemium allecti, quos abortivos* (richtige Lesart: orcinos) *vulgus vocaret.* Paulus wäre also extra numerum vocatus (D.I. Rosenmüller, *Scholia in N. T.* 1806). An Textverbesserungen hat es auch nicht gefehlt, so hat man z.B. vorgeschlagen ὥσπερ τῷ ἐκτρώματι, oder man hat Fehllesung eines hebräischen Wortes vermutet ([א]יחט: "abortus et peccator", Bolten, also ὥσπερ ἐν ἁμαρτωλῷ).

[14] Theophylact (Migne *PG.* 124) τινὲς δὲ τὸ ὕστερον γέννημα (= filius postremo loco natus) ἔκτρωμα ἐνόησαν διότι καὶ αὐτὸς ἔσχατος τῶν ἀποστόλων. Daran schließt sich an J. Schulthess in Tzschirners *Analekten,* I, 4, S. 212f.

[15] Zur älteren Schriftauslegung vgl. J.C. Suicer, *Thesaurus Ecclesiasticus,* 2. Aufl. (1728), I, S. 1073 und J.C. Wolff, *Curae philologicae in IV priores Pauli Epistolas,* 2. Aufl. (Hamburg 1737). Zitiert zu werden verdient Theodoret (Migne *PG.* 82) ἀμβλωθριδίῳ ἑαυτὸν ἀπεικάζει ἐμβρύῳ, ὃ τῷ τῶν ἀνθρώπων οὐκ ἐγκατείλεκται καταλόγῳ. Vgl. J.M.A. Scholz, *Die heil. Schrift des N. T.,* III (1830): " – ebensowenig auf den Namen eines Apostels Anspruch habe, wie eine unzeitige Geburt Mensch genannt zu werden verdiene". Unrichtig ist hier nur die straffe Beziehung der Vorstellung zum Apostolat; denn Paulus vergleicht sich ja zunächst (V. 8) nicht nur mit den Aposteln, sondern mit *Allen,* die eine Offenbarung empfingen, erst mit V. 9, wird der Gesichtskreis auf die Apostel eingeengt.

[16] G. Heinrici, *Das erste Sendschreiben des Paulus an die Korinthier* (1880): "Waren die Zwölf den normal entwickelten Früchten vergleichbar, welche zur rechten Zeit, lebensfähig und ausgetragen, das Licht erblickten, als ihm der Geist die Herrlichkeit des Herrn offenbarte, so trug bei ihm die Bekehrung den Charakter des Gewaltsamen". A. Robertson & A. Plummer, *A Critical and Exegetical Commentary on the First Epistle of St. Paul to the Corinthians* (The International Critical Commentary) (1914): *"In calling himself the* ἔκτρωμα among the Apostles, he refers to the suddenness and violence of the transition (ἐκτιτρώσκειν), while he was still in a state of immaturity. – Theirs was a gradual and normal progress; his was a swift and abnormal change". – H. Lietzmann, *An die Korinther,* 3. Aufl. (1931): "Erst erscheint der Herr den Söhnen, dann zuletzt dem Schmerzenskind des Hauses (daher der Artikel τῷ ἐκτρ.) Das tertium comparationis mit dem ἔκτρωμα ist das Anormale der Geburt und die Unreife des Geborenen im Vergleich mit den übrigen Söhnen." Hier werden Verfolger, Bekehrung, Apostel durcheinander gemischt. Wie kann Paulus seine Bekehrung mit einem ἐκτιτρώσκειν vergleichen und sein neues Leben in apostolischer Vollmacht mit einem ἔκτρωμα? Daß er der geringste unter den Aposteln ist, will doch nur besagen, daß er auch als Apostel den Schmach seines früheren Lebens nicht vergessen kann.

[17] *Nachr. d. K. Gesellsch. d. Wiss. zu Göttingen, Phil.-Hist. Kl.*, 1907, S. 276.

nicht unbekannt gewesen ist, sei es, daß Paulus sich selbst (wie Ignatius[18], aber dieser wohl nicht unabhängig von Paulus) schon früher so genannt hat, sei es, daß ihn seine Gegner – und das ist wahrscheinlicher – so beschimpft haben. An ἔκτρωμα als Frühgeburt kann nicht gedacht werden, denn dazu paßt ἔσχατον wie die Faust aufs Auge. Vielmehr muß hier ἔκτρωμα lediglich als Ausdruck vollkommener Unwürdigkeit – der unzeitige Fötus, der sich nicht sehen lassen kann – aufgegriffen sein (V. 9): Der Unwürdige kommt zuletzt; diesen einfachen Gedanken koloriert Paulus, indem er das Schimpfwort aufnimmt."[19] Ähnlich Bengel, Olshausen, De Wette, Von Hofmann, Schmiedel, B. und J. Weiß.[20]

Bachmann[21] weist mit besonderer Energie die Deutung ab, die ἔκτρωμα auf die Plötzlichkeit und Unvermitteltheit der Bekehrung des nicht langsam zum Glauben ausreifenden Paulus bezieht. Der Artikel gibt dem Bilde eine Beziehung zu dem Vorangehenden und benennt somit Paulus als den, der im Verhältnis zu den vorher genannten *das* ἔκτρωμα ist. Und zwar ist das geistige Israel des Glaubens als die Mutter der Gläubigen gedacht: Das Normale für einen Israeliten war zu glauben; der Unglaube des Paulus kennzeichnet ihn als eine lebensunfähige Mißgeburt.

Dabei hat wohl Bachmann, bei richtigem Ausgangspunkt und gesunden Intentionen, das Bild über die Grenzen des Erlaubten gepreßt. Wenn man den Artikel so wie er erklärt: *die* Mißgeburt unter den Mitchristen, so entsteht die Frage, wie Paulus auf dieses bizarre Bild gekommen ist, und da wird man gezwungen, das Bild in Einzelkeiten durchzuführen, man muß fragen: wer ist die Mutter, die die Christgläubigen geboren hat und im Falle des Paulus eine Mißgeburt erlebte? – was offenbar methodisch bedenklich ist.[22] Denn zwar kennt Paulus die Vorstellung von der geistigen Mutter der Gläubigen (Gal. 4), aber einen solchen Realismus hat er wohl kaum diesem Begriff beigemessen, daß er von einer Fehlgeburt dieser Mutter sprechen würde.

Anders liegt die Sache, wenn man den Artikel vor ἔκτρωμα auf einen von den Gegnern geprägten Ausdruck bezieht; da ist nicht zu fragen, wieso Paulus *das* ἔκτρωμα (unter den Mitaposteln) sei, sondern in welchem Sinne zunächst die Gegner ihn, dann er sich selbst ein ἔκτρωμα genannt haben.

---

[18] Ign. *Rom.* 9,2; vgl. J.B. Lightfoot, *The Apostolic Fathers,* II (1889); W. Bauer, *Die apostol. Väter,* II (1920). (Ergänzungsbd. zu Lietzmanns *Handbuch z. N. T.).*

[19] *Sitz.-Ber. d. Preuß. Akad. d. Wiss. zu Berlin*, 1922, S. 70. Anm. 3.

[20] J. Weiß, *Der erste Korintherbrief* (1910) (Kritisch-exegetischer Kommentar über d. N. T. begr. von H. A. W. Meyer, 9. Aufl.).

[21] Ph. Bachmann, *Der erste Brief des Paulus an die Korinther,* 2. Aufl. (1910) (Komm. z. N. T. herausgeg. von Th. Zahn, Bd. VII).

[22] Wenn man den Artikel vor ἔκτρ. auf diese Weise deutet, muß man die Vorstellung einer *Familie* voraussetzen. Nach Bachmann ist diese Familie das geistige Israel des Glaubens mit dessen Kindern. Lietzmann denkt offenbar an die Apostel als eine Brüderschar im Hause Gottes ("das Schmerzenskind des Hauses"), ähnlich F. Godet, *Corinthiens* (1886): Fast in jeder Familie gibt es ein *"enfant mal venu"*.

Wenn die hier vorgelegte Ansicht richtig ist, daß die Gegner den Apostel Paulus ein ἔκτρωμα der ἀναγέννησις genannt haben, fällt von da aus ein gewisses Licht auf ein interessantes und dunkles Problem des Urchristentums: Wie dachte die Urkirche über Fälle, wo getaufte Christen durch ihr Benehmen sich als unchristliche Persönlichkeiten erwiesen? Bei dem kräftigen Realismus in der Auffassung des Taufsakraments, der damals herrschte, war diese Frage eine sehr heikle. Man mußte unter dem Druck der Tatsachen damit rechnen, daß die Taufe mißlang, daß die Wiedergeburt sich als eine Fehlgeburt entpuppen, zu einem dämonischen Resultat führen konnte. Heranziehen kann man da vielleicht das Wort des Paulus Gal. 4,19: τεκνία μου, οὓς πάλιν ὠδίνω μέχρις οὗ μορφωθῇ Χριστὸς ἐν ὑμῖν. Es ist nicht unmöglich, daß Paulus hier Sakramentales in Persönliches übersetzt, und daß wir somit daraus erschließen können, daß die Wiedergeburt in der Urkirche als ein Prozeß vorgestellt wurde, durch den Christus den Gläubigen durchdrang und ihn gestaltete.[23] Wo dieser Prozeß nicht gelang, kam, durch die mystische Kraft des Taufsakraments hervorgetrieben, ein teuflisches Gebilde zu stande.

---

[23] Eine verwandte Vorstellung, auf die auch Ed. Schwartz a. a. O. verweist, in dem Brief der gallischen Gemeinden bei Euseb *K.H.* 5,1,45 ἐγένετο πολλὴ χαρὰ τῇ παρθένῳ μητρί (der Kirche), οὓς ὡς νεκροὺς ἐξέτρωσε, τούτους ζῶντας (durch das Martyrium) ἀπολαμβανούσῃ. – Von "Fehlgeburten des Glaubens" (Apostasie? Häresie? Todsünden?) wird gesprochen *Inscriptiones christianae,* ed. G.B. De Roosi, II, 1 (Rom 1888), S. 274,4:

Gloria nostra dei crux est miranda, triumphans,
in qua certa salus firmissima permanet, atque
ni fidei aburtibus et per gesta sinistra
. . .
efferus hanc metuit rabie chelydrus venenata, etc.

Epikureisches im Neuen Testament?

(1933)

Phil. 2,6f. (Christus Jesus) ὃς ἐν μορφῇ θεοῦ ὑπάρχων οὐχ ἁρπαγμὸν ἡγήσατο τὸ εἶναι ἴσα θεῷ, ἀλλ' ἑαυτὸν ἐκένωσεν μορφὴν δούλου λαβών, ἐν ὁμοιώματι ἀνθρώπων γενόμενος κτλ. – Statt des viel umstrittenen ἁρπαγμόν schlug ich seiner Zeit vor, ἄπραγμον zu lesen. Diese Konjektur trug ich vor im Philologischen Verein zu Oslo im Frühjahr 1923 und veröffentlichte sie dann in der *Revue d'Histoire et de Philosophie religieuses* im selben Jahre[1]. Erst vor wenigen Wochen erfuhr ich[2], daß Salomon Reinach schon längst dieselbe Textänderung gemacht hatte, nämlich am 31. Juli 1914 in der *Academie des Inscriptions* [3], und sie dann veröffentlichte in der *Revue des Etudes grecques* [4], abgedruckt in *Cultes, Mythes et Religions* (t. V, 1923, S. 301–6) mit der Überschrift *"L'indolence des dieux"*. Er verweist auf die epikureische Götterlehre, zitiert Lucrez V 161ff., Vergil *Aen.* IV 379f. (ironische Anspielung an Epikur) und betont den scharfen Gegensatz zwischen griechischer und orientalischer Gottesvorstellung, der sich bei den Juden im Schimpfwort "Epikureer", d.h. ungläubiger Freigeist ausdrückte[5]. – Reinach hält das überlieferte ἁρπαγμόν für unbegreiflich und findet es sehr natürlich, wenn man bei Paulus einem epikuräischen Gemeinplatz begegnet.

Ich meinerseits bin einem etwas anderen Gedankenzuge gefolgt. Ich kann den Ausdruck οὐχ ἁρπαγμὸν ἡγήσατο nicht an sich unbegreiflich finden, nämlich wenn man den Gesichtspunkt anlegt, den W. Jäger geltend macht[6], daß hier eine *volkstümliche* Redewendung begegnet, in der ἁρπαγμός einem ἕρμαιον, εὕρημα o. dgl. entspricht[7]. Was mich aber stutzig macht, ist einerseits

[1] 1923, S. 441f.

[2] Durch eine Notiz im *Theol. Handwörterbuch* herausgeg. von G. Klttel (S. 472).

[3] *Comptes rendus,* S. 521.

[4] XXIX (1916), S. 238–44.

[5] Reiches Material jetzt in *Jüdisches Lexikon* herausgeg. v. Herlitz und Kirschner und *Encyclopaedia Judaica* herausgeg. v. Klatzkin, s. v. Epikuros. – A.H. Krappe in *Rev. d. Et. grecques* 39 (1926), S. 351–54 will im Buche Job eine Anspielung an epikuräische Denkart finden, nämlich 22, 12-15. Schon E.F.C. Rosenmüller (*Scholia in N. T.* 1806, V p. 542) zitiert zu dieser Stelle Vergil *Aen.* IV 379f. und Lucrez. – Einen anderen Hintergrund hat das Wort im Johannesevangelium: ὁ πατήρ μου ἕως ἄρτι ἐργάζεται κτλ. (5, 17).

[6] *Hermes* 1915, S. 537ff.

[7] Vgl. z. B. Heliodor *Aeth.* Vll 20: οὐχ ἅρπαγμα οὐδὲ ἕρμαιον ἡγεῖται τὸ πρᾶγμα.

das Vorkommen einer alltäglich-volkstümlichen Phrase in dieser feierlich erhabenen Aussage; noch unbegreiflicher wird das, wenn, wie z. B. Lohmeyer will[8], der Abschnitt ein urchristlicher Psalm ist. Anderseits ist natürlich die Form ἁρπαγμός statt ἅρπαγμα verdächtig. Man wird den Eindruck nicht los, daß hier etwas nicht in Ordnung ist.

Schon vor Reinach hat man zu bessern versucht[9]. S. A. Naber schreibt in *Mnemosyne* (1878, S. 102f.) vom überlieferten Text: "Absurde, uti vides. Quid dicet Apostolus? *Illud, opinor, cum in sinu dei esset, judicavisse Jesum sua non referre* τὸ εἶναι ἴσα θεῷ ... *Non contentus fuit divina sorte:* οὐχὶ πρᾶγμα ἡγήσατο τὸ εἶναι ἴσα θεῷ. Πρᾶγμα in ἅρπαγμα *abiit; deinde nescio quomodo* ἅρπαγμα *corruptum fuit ulterius, ut fieret* ἁρπαγμόν. *Sic* πραγμάτων *et* ἁρπαγμάτων *confusa reperies* Platon *Epist.* VII, p. 335 b".

Dieser Emendation Nabers stimmt H.P. Berlage bei[10], verwirft dagegen seine Deutung. Der Ausdruck οὐχὶ πρᾶγμα ἡγήσατο könne nicht bedeuten: "non contentus fuit (sua sorte)", sondern müsse übersetzt werden: "Er machte nichts daraus, es war ihm nichts daran gelegen." Dabei unterscheidet Berlage zwischen der Gottesebenbildlichkeit und der Gottgleichheit; die letztere, die messianische Herrlichkeit, besaß Jesus in seiner Präexistenz noch nicht, und es kam ihm auch nicht darauf an, sie zu erlangen (obgleich er die Möglichkeit dazu hatte). Im Gegenteil, er veräußerte sich des göttlichen Seins und bekam nun die Weltherrschaft als Lohn.

Offenbar ist in jeder Hinsicht, schriftbildlich und sachlich, ἄπραγμον eine bessere Emendation als πρᾶγμα. Jedoch ist der Versuch Nabers interessant und bezeichnend. Reinach hat alle Bedenken überwunden; auch F. Kattenbusch, dem ich vor 10 Jahren in einem Gespräch meine Vermutung (ohne sie als ernsthafte Konjektur zu bezeichnen) erwähnte, hat den Gedanken aufgenommen und energisch durchgeführt[11].

Kattenbusch bricht entschlossen mit der traditionellen Auslegung unserer Stelle, welche die Vorstellung der Menschwerdung eines himmlischen Gottwesens in ἑαυτὸν ἐκένωσεν findet[12]. Subjekt der Selbstentäußerung ist nach Kattenbusch nicht der präexistente Gottessohn, sondern Jesus in seinem irdischen Messiasdasein: Jesus als Mensch war, so denkt Paulus, Gottes Ebenbild (ἐν μορφῇ θεοῦ ὑπάρχων), aber diese Gottgleichheit (τὸ εἶναι ἴσα θεῷ) betrachtete er nicht als ein ἄπραγμον, ein otium, ein Befreitsein von jeglicher bindenden und zwingenden Pflicht. Im Gegenteil, er entäußerte sich.

Das Bild der ἀπραγμοσύνη sollte somit von der Terminologie menschlichen,

---

[8] *Kyrios Jesus* (Abhandl. d. Heidelb. Akad. 1928).

[9] E. Barnikol, *Philipper* 2. Kiel 1932, S. 124.

[10] *Theol. Tijdschrift* 1880, S. 80ff.

[11] *Theol. Studien und Kritiken* 104 (1932), S. 373–420.

[12] Vgl. F. Loofs, *Das altkirchliche Zeugnis gegen die herrschende Auffassung der Kenosisstelle. Theol. Stud. u. Krit.* 100 (1927–28), S. 1-102.

bürgerlichen Privatlebens herkommen. Es wäre die Lage dessen, der, ökonomischen Rücksichten überhoben und fern vom politischen Getriebe, das behagliche Leben des unabhängigen, nur seinen Interessen und Genüssen lebenden Menschen führt[13], das pflichtlose Individuum. Ein solches Dasein lehnte Jesus für sich ab.

Mir scheint, dieser Deutung gegenüber, daß Reinach einem richtigen Instinkt gefolgt ist, wenn er die ἀπραγμοσύνη als *Gottesprädikat* versteht und das ἄπραγμον der epikuräischen theologischen Terminologie entnimmt: Der Christus in seiner himmlischen Herrlichkeit und Seligkeit wollte kein *deus otiosus* sein, was ihm leicht möglich wäre, sondern nahm auf sich alle die πράγματα, die die menschliche Existenz *als solche* bedrücken.

Kattenbusch's Interpretation der Kenosisstelle steht und fällt ja keineswegs mit der hier besprochenen Textverbesserung; im Gegenteil finde ich, daß das von ihm vorgezogene ἄπραγμον eher von seinem Gedankenkreis abführt und in die alten Bahnen der präexistentiellen Auslegung zurücklenkt. Bei seiner Auffassung der Stelle würde ich die von Jäger befürwortete Deutung der Redewendung οὐχ ἁρπαγμὸν (= ἕρμαιον) ἡγεῖσθαί τι für ausreichend, ja natürlich halten; denn da befände sich Jesus im Gegensatz zu einem *irdisch-menschlichen* μακάριος ἀνήρ, der ein Götterleben auf Erden als einen wahren Glücksfund schätzen würde.

Die Verbesserung des ἁρπαγμόν zu ἄπραγμον stellt uns vor den Gegensatz zwischen Gott und Mensch, zwischen himmlischer und irdischer Existenzweise[14]. Wenn man diesen Gesichtspunkt anlegt, fällt ein scharfes Licht auf den Gegensatz ἐν μορφῇ θεοῦ ὑπάρχων und ἐν ὁμοιώματι ἀνθρώπου γενόμενος καὶ σχήματι εὑρεθεὶς ὡς ἄνθρωπος. Als äußerste Stufe dieses Gegensatzes kommt der Tod; er ist das schwerste der menschlichen πράγματα. – Wie erscheint nun in diesem Lichte das sachliche Verhältnis zwischen den beiden Bestimmungen ἐν μορφῇ θεοῦ ὑπάρχειν und εἶναι ἴσα θεῷ? Wenn es heißt οὐκ ἄπραγμον ἡγήσατο τὸ εἶναι ἴσα θεῷ, so ist damit ja schon gesagt, daß die Gott*gleichheit* auch mit πράγματα verbunden sein kann. Der Ausdruck kann sich also nicht auf die Existenzweise, sondern nur auf die göttliche *Rangstellung*[15]Jesu beziehen, die er von Ewigkeit bei Gott hatte, und die er auch in seiner Erniedrigung als festes Eigentum besaß. Die Gott*ähnlichkeit* aber beschließt notwendig in sich die ἀπραγμοσύνη und muß aufgegeben werden, wenn das himmlische Wesen Mensch wird. Die Ansicht von der sachlichen

---

[13] Vgl. ζῆν ἡδέως ἀπράγμονα, ἀπραγμόνως ζῆν ἡδύ (Apollod. Com. 1,1; Eurip. *fragm.* 193), ῥᾳδίως καὶ ἀπραγμόνως ζῆν (Dio Prus. *Or.* IV, 11).

[14] S. das Material, das ich zusammengestellt habe in der *Revue d. Hist. et de Philos. religieuses*, 1923, aus Cicero, *de nat. deor.* lib. I, Seneca, *de benef.* IV, *Epicurea* ed. Usener. Tertullian, *Apologet.* 47 sagt: *Epicurei (deum adseverant) otiosum et inexercitatum* (= ἀπράγμων καὶ σχολαῖος), vgl. Ael. Arist. *Or. in Sarap.* am Anfang: εὐδαίμων καὶ πραγμάτων ἀπηλλαγμένος.

[15] So auch Kattenbusch, S. 405–6.

Identität der beiden Bestimmungen muß aufgegeben werden; es ist zu unterscheiden zwischen wechselnde Existenzweise und dauernde innere Qualität[16].

Recht merkwürdig und m. E. bisher noch nicht einwandfrei erklärt ist das ἑαυτὸν ἐκένωσεν. Ob man hier mit den gewöhnlichen Übersetzungen, "entleerte, entblößte, entäußerte sich", auskommt, ist mir sehr zweifelhaft; der anderweitige Gebrauch von κενοῦν bei Paulus scheint nicht dafür zu sprechen[17]. Ich kann hier auf diese Frage nicht weiter eingehen, möchte nur die Vermutung äußern, daß der eigentümliche Ausdruck auf *Jesu Stellung im Geisterreich* Bezug nimmt: Er verzichtete auf seine Hoheitsstellung in der Geisterwelt, machte sich zu einem Nichts in den Augen der ἄρχοντες τοῦ κόσμου τούτου[18]; es wird ein mythisch-gnostischer Terminus sein. Wenn das richtig ist, versteht man besser die überschwängliche Schilderung seiner Erhöhung, das ὑπερύψωσεν, das ὄνομα τὸ ὑπὲρ πᾶν ὄνομα usw. (V. 9ff.).

---

[16] Kattenbusch sagt (S. 405): "Das τό gibt den weiteren Worten (εἶναι ἴσα θεῷ) den Charakter von Wiederaufnahme des zuvor von dem Messias als ὑπάρχων Gesagten". Er scheint nicht beachtet zu haben, daß der Artikel unentbehrlich ist vor dem Infinitiv (εἶναι), der als Objekt zu ἡγήσατο steht.

[17] I Kor. 9,15; Röm. 4,14; I Kor. 1,17 bedeutet κενοῦν ungefähr so viel als καταργεῖν. Man darf nicht von κενός im Sinne "leer" ausgehen, sondern es muß angeknüpft werden an die Bedeutung "kraftlos, wesenslos, nichtig" (= μάταιος, s. W. Bauer, *Lex.*).

[18] So tritt ἑαυτὸν ἐκένωσεν in Parallele zu ἐταπείνωσεν ἑαυτόν, V. 8.

Ἰσόψυχος = ebenbürtig, solidarisch

(1938)

Das Wort ἰσόψυχος kommt selten vor; nur drei Stellen sind bekannt: Aeschyl. *Agam.* 1470; Ps. 54,14 LXX und Ep. Pauli ad Philipp. 2, 20.[1] Die Auslegung der leztgenannten Stelle veranlaßte ein näheres Studium der Vokabel, weshalb mit dem Paulusworte Anfang und Schluß gemacht werden soll.

1.

Der gefangene Apostel schreibt an die Christen in Philippi 2, 19–22: (19) Ἐλπίζω δὲ ἐν κυρίῳ Ἰησοῦ Τιμόθεον ταχέως πέμψαι ὑμῖν, ἵνα κἀγὼ εὐψυχῶ γνοὺς τὰ περὶ ὑμῶν. (20) οὐδένα γὰρ ἔχω ἰσόψυχον, ὅστις γνησίως τὰ περὶ ὑμῶν μεριμνήσει· (21) οἱ πάντες γὰρ τὰ ἑαυτῶν ζητοῦσιν, οὐ τὰ Χριστοῦ Ἰησοῦ. (22) τὴν δὲ δοκιμὴν αὐτοῦ γινώσκετε κτλ. – In der Deutung von ἰσόψυχος gehen die Ausleger auseinander: soll man dazu ein ἐμοί oder αὐτῷ (τῷ Τιμοθέῳ) ergänzen? Seit den Vätern war das erstere Tradition. Chrysostomus sagt: ἰσόψυχος τουτέστι τῶν ὁμοίως μοι μεριμνώντων, – ἀντὶ τοῦ ὁμοίως ἐμοὶ κηδόμενον ὑμῶν καὶ φροντοζόμενον. Theodoret: τὴν οἰκείαν περὶ αὐτοὺς ἐνδεικνὺς διάθεσιν, ὅτι ὃν μόνον ἔχει ψυχαγωγοῦντα, τοῦτον διὰ τὴν αὐτῶν ἀπέστειλεν διάθεσιν. Theophylakt: ἠδυνάμην καὶ ἄλλον πέμψαι, ἀλλ' οὐδεὶς οὕτως ἰσόψυχός ἐμοι ὡς οὗτος. Ambrosiaster: Erat apostolo unanimis, quare et circa eos sollicitior signatur. Luther: der so gar meines Sinnes sei. Bengel: Paulus alter, Timotheus.

Calvin und Beza aber haben eine andere Ansicht begründet, indem sie übersetzen: "ihm (Timotheos) gleichgesinnt" *(pari animo affectum);* Beza: *Timotheum non secum sed cum aliis comparare.* So die meisten Neueren, z.B. Lightfoot, Lipsius, Holsten, B. Weiss, Haupt, Ewald, Loisy, Goodspeed, Dibelius, Lohmeyer, Michaelis.[2] Diese neuere Auslegung scheint mir vor der älteren den Vorzug zu verdienen. Denn ἰσόψυχος heist sicher nicht so ganz im

[1] ψυχή kommt auffallend oft vor eben im Philipperbrief: μιᾷ ψυχῇ 1, 27; σύμψυχος 2, 2; ἵνα εὐψυχῶ 2,19; ἰσόψυχος 2, 20; παραβολευσάμενος τῇ ψυχῇ 2, 30.

[2] Eine eigentümliche Deutung von σύμψυχος und ἰσόψυχος bei Clemens Alex. *Strom.* IV 13 (92, 4f.). Ἰσόψυχος sagt Paulus περὶ Τιμοθέου καὶ ἑαυτοῦ γράφων.

allgemeinen "gleichgesinnt", sondern hat qualifizierten Sinn. Die Qualifizierung liegt aber nicht im -ψυχος, das an sich neutral ist (vgl. μεγαλόψυχος, μικρόψυχος), sondern in ἴσος, das oft ein Moment der Auszeichnung in sich beschließt. Die Komposita mit ἴσος haben durchgängig etwas Vornehmes an sich. Im N. T. haben wir neben ἰσόψυχος noch ἰσότιμος (1 Petr. 1, 1) und ἰσάγγελος (Luc. 20, 36; Marc. 12, 25 und Matth. 22, 30 schreiben einfacher ὡς ἄγγελοι). In LXX kommen solche Komposita nur in den Maccabäerbüchern vor: ἰσαστήρ, ἰσοδύναμος, ἰσόθεος, ἰσόμοιρος, ἰσοπολίτης. Also, wer ἰσόψυχος ist, ist nicht nur gleicher, sondern *gleichwertiger* Denkweise.[3] Wenn somit ἰσόψυχος ein gewähltes, qualifiziertes Wort ist, etwa = "gleich edler Gesinnung", so ist es undenkbar, daß Paulus es auf sich selbst als Vergleichsobjekt bezogen hätte. Es bleibt bei dem Urteil von Beza: *Timotheum non secum sed cum aliis comparat Paulus.*

Vielleicht müssen wir aber jedoch auch diese Deutung etwas modifizieren, nachdem wir den Inhalt des Wortes näher bestimmt haben.

2.

In einem sehr interessanten Zusammenhang finden wir ἰσόψυχος Ps. 54, 14 LXX (also im dritten vorchr. Jahrhundert): Der Sänger klagt über falsche Freunde; nicht Feinde schmähen ihn,

σὺ δέ, ἄνθρωπε ἰσόψυχε, ἡγεμών μου καὶ γνωστέ μου,
ὃς ἐπὶ τὸ αὐτὸ ἐγλύκανας ἐδέσματα,
ἐν τῷ οἴκῳ τοῦ θεοῦ ἐπορεύθημεν ἐν ὁμονοίᾳ.

Der Angeklagte ist nicht eine individuell gleichgestimmte Persönlichkeit, sondern offenbar ein *Standesgenosse*. Hinter ἰσόψυχος liegt ein hebräisches Wort, אֱנוֹשׁ בְּעֶרְכִּי, d.h. einer, der zur selben Schätzungsklasse gehört, der sozial Gleichgestellte, der Tisch und Kultgenosse. Die Isopsychie wurzelt im gemeinsamen Klassenbewußtsein und ist keine rein individuelle Seelenhaltung, sondern eine *typische* Gesinnung oder Denkweise. Wir können also ἰσόψυχος etwa mit "Gesinnungsgenosse" wiedergeben, und dieser Begriff kann sich nach verschiedenen Richtungen hin nuancieren: "ebenbürtig", "verbunden", "solidarisch". So erklärt sich das sonst Unbegreifliche, daß der "Gleichgestimmte" den Sänger schmäht. Die Isopsychie ist eben keine subjektive Stimmung, sondern eine objektive Gegebenheit, die mit einer typischen Denkweise verbunden ist. Diese Denkweise fordert an sich, normal, Solidarität mit dem Standesgenossen, braucht aber keine individuelle Seelenverbundenheit mit ihm zu bedeuten. Deshalb kan man ἰσόψυχος dem anderen gegenüber sein und

---

[3] Vgl. W. Bauer, *Wörterbuch z. N. T.* 3. Aufl. 1937: "von gleicher Seelengröße, ebenso vortrefflich".

bleiben, auch wenn man ihn schmäht. Aber natürlich ein *schlechter, abnormer* ἰσόψυχος, ein unsolidarischer Genosse. Das schlechte Verhalten kann aber nicht den objektiven Tatbestand aufheben, auch wenn es mit der dazu gehörigen geistigen Haltung in Widerstreit steht. Nicht Stimmung, sondern Lage und Haltung drückt ἰσόψυχος aus: *Standesgenosse, Gesinnungsgenosse, ebenbürtig, solidarisch.*

Mit diesem Ergebnis treten wir an die einzige klassische Stelle heran, die zu unserer Verfügung steht: Aesch. *Agam.* 1470. Der Chor, an der Totenbahre des erschlagenen Agamemnon stehend:

δαῖμον, ὃς ἐμπίτνεις δώμασι καὶ διφυίοισι Τανταλίδαισιν
κράτος [τ'] ἰσόψυχον ἐκ γυναικῶν,
καρδιόδηκτον ἐμοί κρατύνεις ...

Wilamowitz (*Aischylos, Interpretationen,* 1914, S. 199) paraphrasiert: "Dämon, der du in den Häusern der beiden Atriden gleichmächtig in den Frauen lebst ..." vgl. Keck: "... und eine gleiche Macht in diesen beiden Weibern offenbarst". (κράτος) ἰσόψυχον sollte also poetisch für ἴσον stehen, was wenig überzeugend ist. Ansprechender ist die Deutung bei Mazon: "tu te sers de femmes aux âmes pareilles." Er löst den gedrungenen Ausdruck κράτος ἰσόψυχον ἐκ γυναικῶν auf in κράτος ἐκ γυναικῶν (ἀλλήλαις) ἰσοψύχων. Die Weiber sind Helena und Klytaimnestra; Helena, die "alleine so viel, ja so zahllos viel vor Troja der Seelen geopfert" (1419f.), und die Mörderin des Aigisthos. Durch diese beiden blutbefleckten Weiber übt der "finstere Geist, der schwer Tantalos' Haus heimsucht" (1469), seine furchtbare Herrschaft aus. Was besagt nun ἰσόψυχος in diesem Zusammenhang? Man kann vielleicht schwanken, ob man die Isopsychie auf den Dämon beziehen soll: κράτος ἐκ γυναικῶν (σοὶ) ἰσοψύχων, – das ergäbe einen etwas paradoxen Gedanken, er herrscht durch ihm (an Bosheit) Ebenbürtige; oder ob die Weiber als ἰσόψυχοι bezeichnet sein sollen: beide sind sich ebenbürtig sowohl an königlichem Rang als an bodenlosem Frevel. Wir werden uns wohl für die letztere Alternative entscheiden müssen. Den Doppelsinn, der da in ἰσόψυχοι liegt ("gleichen Schlages"), kann man auch leicht aus dem hier vorgeschlagenen Äquivalent heraushören: "Du übst deine teuflische Gewalt aus durch ebenbürtige Weiber!"[4]

[4] Man sollte vielleicht bei Aesch. auch an den Begriff der *Solidarität* denken können; Klytaimnestra hat eben Helena verteidigt (V. 1464 μηδ' εἰς Ἑλένην κότον ἐκτρέψῃς) gegen die Anklagen des Chors.–Wilamowitz übersetzt (*Griechische Tragödien* II 1919, S. 105): "–... der du dem Weibe gabest des Mannesmutes Stärke" (anders in den "Interpretationen"). Er legt wohl da zu viel in ἰσόψυχος hinein.

3.

Kehren wir nun zu Phil. 2,20 zurück! Es muß jetzt mindestens als fraglich hingestellt werden, ob wir die Worte οὐδένα γὰρ ἔχω ἰσόψυχον ohne weiteres übersetzen sollen: "ich habe niemand gleich trefflich gesinnt (wie er)". Wir würden ja nämlich in dem Falle einen rein *individuellen* Vergleich bekommen, wo Timotheos persönlich die Norm abgibt. Dagegen ἰσόψυχος ein *sozialer* Begriff ist und eine *typische* Denkweise mit einem dem entsprechenden Verhalten kennzeichnet. Ich schlage deshalb vor, zu ἰσόψυχον ein ὑμῖν zu ergänzen: *Ich habe*[5] (außer ihm[6]) *niemand, der zu euch solidarisch steht;* niemand, der sich mit euch verbunden fühlt, eine Verpflichtung euch gegenüber empfindet. Daran schließt sich ausgezeichnet der Relativsatz ὅστις γνησίως τὰ περὶ ὑμῶν μεριμνήσει: welcher (also) in "echter" Weise sich um eure Angelegenheiten kümmert. ὅστις etc. hat konsekutive Funktion und entfaltet den Inhalt von ἰσόψυχος.[7]

Da fällt auch Licht auf die Wahl von γνησίως: Eben innerhalb der Isopsychie, in der Sphäre der sozialen Solidarität, besteht und betätigt sich die Echtheit; man handelt γνησίως, d.h. man unterscheidet nicht zwischen dem eigenen Interesse und dem der Genossen. Von der großen Mehrzahl dagegen (οἱ πάντες[8]) sagt der Apostel: τὰ ἑαυτῶν ζητοῦσιν. Das ist die unsolidarische, "unechte" Haltung.

So bekommt alles einen guten Sinn und Zusammenhang: Paulus begründet die Sendung (γάρ) gerade von Timotheos, der ihm in seiner jetzigen Lage als unentbehrlich erscheinen könnte: Ich habe nämlich (außer ihm) keinen mit euch Verbundenen, der echte Sorge für eure Dinge hat.

4.

Das mehr persönlich-individuelle "gleichgesinnt" heißt ὁμόψυχος, vgl. 4 Macc. 14, 20 ἀλλ' οὐχὶ τὴν Ἀβραὰμ ὁμόψυχον τῶν νεανιῶν μητέρα μετεκίνησεν ἡ συμπάθεια τέκνων. Die Mutter der gefolterten Jünglinge legt dieselbe Gesinnung an den Tag wie Abraham beim Opfer des Isak. Das bezieht sich auf eine bestimmte Situation, nicht auf eine typische Haltung. Die Komposita mit ἰσο- und ὁμο- kongruieren zwar in einigen Fällen, zeigen aber meist charakteristische Unterschiede. Wir haben einerseits:

---

[5] ἔχω = ich habe hier, zu meiner Verfügung, vgl. Joh. 5, 7 und das anderwärts zitierte *Scholion* zu *Il.* 7, 295 πολλοὺς γὰρ εἶχεν ἰσοθύμους.

[6] οὐδένα ist natürlich nicht absolut, als ob Paulus überhaupt keinen ἰσόψυχον bei sich hätte und deshalb den Timotheos *faute de mieux* schicken müßte. Hinzuzudenken ist ein ἄλλον, Vgl. οἱ πάντες V. 21 = οἱ ἄλλοι πάντες.

[7] Blaß-Debrunner[5] § 379, *"qui ... solicitus sit"*.

[8] Vgl. Anm. 3, auf voriger Seite [= Note 6, above, (Ed.)].

ἰσῆλιξ	ὁμῆλιξ
ἰσοδυναμέω	ὁμοδυναμέω
ἰσόκληρος	ὁμόκληρος
ἰσόκτυπος	ὁμόκτυπος
ἰσοπληθής	ὁμοπληθής
ἰσοταχής	ὁμοταχής
ἰσοτελής	ὁμοτελής
ἰσότιμος	ὁμότιμος
ἰσότονος	ὁμότονος
[ἰσόχροος	ὁμόχροος]

In allen diesen Fällen ist das zweite Glied der Komposita ein qualifiziertes Wort, so daß es auf dasselbe hinauskommt, ob man eine Gleichwertigkeit (ἴσος) oder eine Gemeinsamkeit oder Ähnlichkeit (ὁμός, ὅμοιος) aussagt. Aber sonst waltet ein ausgesprochener Unterschied:

ἰσό-βιος lebenslang	-ὁμό = gemeinsam lebend
-γραφον kopie	= ὁμόγραμμος
-δαίμον gottgleich	denselben δαίμων habend
-δίαιτος auf demselben Fuß lebend	Lebensgenosse
-δοξος = ἰσοκλεής	gleicher Meinung
-δουλος sklavengleich	Mitsklave
-δρομέω gleichen Schritt halten	mitlaufen
-ζυγέω gleichgewichtig machen	zusammengekoppelt sein.
-κέλευθος vgl. ἰσόδρομος	
-λογία = ἰσηγορία	Bekenntnis. Geständnis etc.
-μήτωρ der Mutter gleich	= ὁμομέτριος [ὁμομήτριος Ed.]
-παις einem Kinde gleich	Zwilling
-πολίτης Gleichberechtigter	Mitbürger
-πτερος = ἰσότιμος	Kamerad
-στοιχος = ἀντίστοιχος	in derselben Reihe stehend
-τεχνος gleich tüchtig	Handwerksgenosse
-τοιχος gleichseitig	mit gemeinsamer Wand
[τράπεζος den Tisch ausfüllend	Tischgenosse]
[τριβής]	
-τυπος gleichgebildet	gleichlautend
-τύραννος Despot	Mit-Tyrann
ἰσουργός dasselbe tuend	Gefährte
-φθογγος gleichlautend	gemeinsam tönend
-φρων gerecht	einig
-φυής symmetrisch	von derselben Gestalt
-χρονέω gleichaltrig sein	gleichzeitig sein
-ψηφος mit derselben Stimmzahl	mitstimmend

Öfter decken sich die Komposita mit ἰσο- mit denen mit ὁμοιο- (-βαρής, -κατάληκτος, -μερής, -πλατής, -πτερος, -ταχής, -τιμος, -τονος, -τυπής, -χρονος). Dagegen weichen ὁμοιο-κλινής, -λογία, νομος, -ρροπος, -τεχνος (= ὁμότεχνος), -τύραννος von den Zusammensetzungen mit ἰσο- der Bedeutung ab. Neben ἰσόβιος und ὁμόβιος haben wir auch ὁμοιόβιος, dasselbe Leben führend, und neben ἰσο- und ὁμόγραφος auch ὁμοιόγραφος gleichgeschrieben. – Die Zusammensetzungen mit ὁμο- haben oft Entsprechungen in den Komposita mit συν- (ὅμασπις-συνασπιστής, ὁμο–, συν-αὐλία, -έστιος, -εὐνητής, -ήθεια, -ῆλιξ, -βιος, -βλαστέω, -βλαστάνω, -βουλέω, -βουλεύω, -βωμος, -γάλακτος, -γαμβρος, -γαμος, -γένεια, -γνώμων, -γονος, -γραφος, -δαις, -δαίτωρ, -δειπνος, -δίαιτος, -δοξέω, -δοξάζω, -δουλος, -δρομος, -εργός, -ζυγος, -ζυξ, -θρονος, -θυμέω, -κλινής, -μετρος, -πάθεια, -πλοος, -πολίτης).

Ein besonderes Interesse haben für uns die Komposita mit -ψυχος, -φρων, -νους, -θυμος:

ἰσόψυχος	ἰσόφρων		ἰσόθυμος
σύμψυχος	σύμφρων	σύννοος	συνθυμέω
ὁμόψυχος	ὁμόφρων	ὁμόνοος	ὁμόθυμος

Ἰσόφρων bedeutet gerecht, billig denkend, enthält also diese besondere Nuance von ἴσος. Dagegen ἰσόθυμος entspricht ἰσόψυχος im oben angegebenen Sinne; es findet sich *Schol. Hom. Il.* 7, 295, wo Hektor zu Aias spricht:

ὡς σύ, τ' εὐφρήνῃς πάντας παρὰ νηυσὶν Ἀχαιούς,
σούς τε μάλιστα ἔτας καὶ ἑταίρους, οἵ τε ἔασιν.

Dazu der Scholiast: ἔτας· πολλοὺς γὰρ εἶχεν ἰσοθύμους, d.h. die als Landsleute sich mit ihm solidarisch fühlten.

Σύμψυχος habe ich behandelt in der *Philol. Wochenschrift* 58 (1938) Sp. 910f.; σύν ist hier = ὅλος, wie in συννοέω, σύννοια, σύννοος, die Gedanken sammeln, konzentrieren: von ganzer Seele, völlig. Dagegen drücken σύμφρων und συνθυμέω die Übereinstimmung aus, gleich ὁμόψυχος, ὁμόφρων, ὁμόνοος und ὁμόθυμος (außerdem ὁμοθυμέω, ὁμονοέω, ὁμόνοια, ὁμοφρονέω, ὁμοφροσύνη).

Im folgenden mögen die wichtigsten Komposita mit -ψυχος zusammengestellt werden:

ἀντί- (= ἀντίλυτρον)
ἀ- (leblos; ἄνοος, ἄφρων, töricht; ἄθυμος niedergeschlagen, mutlos).
βαρύ- (nebst βαρύθυμος und βαρύφρων).
δί- (daneben δίφροντις, δίθυμος, LXX, ist zwieträchtig).
ἐμ- (belebt, lebhaft; daneben ἔνθυμος, ἔμφρων und ἔννους, verständig).
εὔ- (bei gutem Mut; ebenso εὔθυμος, doch auch: gut gesinnt, wie εὔφρων, εὔνοος, freundlich.
ἡμι- (semianimis).
κακό- (= κακόνοος, -φρων, κακόθυμος).
καλό- (καλόφρων = εὔψυχος, εὔφρων).
καρτερό- (καρτερόθυμος, -φρων).
μακρό- (daneben μακρόθυμος)

μεγαλό- (nebst μεγάθυμος, μεγαλόνοια, μεγαλόφρων)
μικρό- (μικρόθυμος, μικρόφρων).
πάμ- ("in Lebensfülle").
πονηρό-
φιλό- (das Leben liebend; φιλόφρων = freundlich).
ἀφιλό-
[πονοψυχία (Seelennot)].

Ἰσόψυχος ist also "gleich hinsichtlich der Denkweise"; ein anderes Verhältnis zwischen den beiden Bestandteilen des Kompositums besteht in der Anwendung des Wortes in den Scholien zu Eurip. *Androm.* 419. Andromache spricht:

πᾶσι δ' ἀνθρώποις ἄρ' ἦν
ψυχὴ τέκν'· ὅστις δ' αὖτ' ἄπειρος ὢν ψέγει,
ἧσσον μὲν ἀλγεῖ, δυστυχῶν δ' εὐδαιμονεῖ.

Dazu *Schol.*: ὅστις δὲ τὰ ὑπ' ἐμοῦ ῥηθέντα ὑπὲρ τέκνων ψέγει, λέγων ὡς ἰσόψυχα τοῖς ἀνθρώποις οὐκ εἰσὶν τὰ τέκνα, ὁ τοιοῦτος κτλ. Hier ist ἰσόψυχα offenbar = "der (eigenen) Seele gleichwertig" (in Anschluß an ἦν ψυχὴ τέκν' im Texte); vgl. ἰσόβιος und ἰσοτράπεζος.

Die Verwendung bei Eustathius zu *Il.* 17, 695ff. (ἰσοψυχεῖν = ἴσον θυμὸν ἔχοντες usw.) wirft für die klassische Zeit nichts ab.

Neutestamentliche Wortforschung

Themelios, 1. Kor. 3, 11

(1946)

Das Bild des Baues und des Bauens bei Paulus ist neuerdings behandelt worden von W. Straub (*Die Bildersprache des Apostels Paulus,* Tüb. 1937, S. 85 ff.) und Ph. Vielhauer (*Oikodome,* Diss. Heidelb. 1939, S. 78 ff.) vgl. auch K. L. Schmidt im *ThWBzNT* s. v. θεμέλιος. Vielleicht gibt es jedoch immer noch etliches dazu zu sagen, besonders gelegentlich der oben angegebenen Stelle: θεμέλιον γὰρ ἄλλον οὐδεὶς δύναται θεῖναι παρὰ τὸν κείμενον.

1.

Ich vermute, daß dieser Satz eine bautechnische Formulierung enthält, nämlich ὁ κείμενος (θεμέλιος). Diese Annahme stützt sich auf eine lesbische Bauinschrift (*IG* XII 2, 11) aus dem 3. vorchristl. Jahrh., die O. Viedebantt behandelt hat in Hermes 50 (1915), S. 34 ff. Es handelt sich um die Anlegung eines Verstärkungsfundaments an der östlichen Längsseite des Tempels; die Inschrift enthält die detaillierten Vorschriften für die Ausführung dieser Arbeit. Hier heißt es nun u. a. Z. 5, der Unternehmer soll eine Baugrube aufwerfen bis zu demselben Baugrund, auf dem *das schon daliegende Fundament* aufsitzt: ἐπὶ τὸ αὐτὸ ἔδαφος τῷ νῦν κειμένῳ θεμελίῳ. Denselben Ausdruck haben wir Z. 14. In Z. 15 steht: die obere Lagerungsfläche der neuen Mauer ist mit der Bleiwaage nach Maßgabe *des liegenden Fundaments* (πρὸς τοῦ κειμένου θεμελίου) waagrecht abzuebnen, vgl. denselben Ausdruck – auch diesmal ohne νῦν – in Z. 16. Offenbar ist ὁ κείμενος θεμέλιος ein terminus technicus, den Paulus aufgreift, indem er schreibt παρὰ τὸν κείμενον anstatt – was man nach V. 10 erwarten sollte – παρ' ὃν ἔθηκα. M.E ist die Wahl des unpersönlichen technischen Ausdruckes diktiert von einer Scheu vor dem nun offen ausgesprochenen Namen, Jesus Christus; der Apostel möchte nicht ausdrücklich den Herrn als Objekt seines Handelns darstellen (vgl. J. Boehmer, Die neutestamentliche Gottesscheu, Halle 1917).

2.

Der θεμέλιος ist nicht der ganze (felsige) Baugrund (ἔδαφος, Z. 5), sondern die denselben begrenzenden Grundmauern, auf denen der Tempel ruht. Die Inschrift kann auch von den θεμέλια sprechen (Z. 10), d. h. den 4 Mauerzügen, die zusammen das Fundament ausmachen; aber ebenso oft wird deren Gesamtheit ὁ θεμέλιος genannt, vgl. Eph. 2, 20, wo die Nennung des ἀκρογωνιαῖος bezeugt, daß die Vorstellung von einem Hausfundament aus 4 zusammenhängenden Mauerzügen bestehend vorschwebt. Vgl. auch Luk. 6, 48 ἔθηκεν θεμέλιον ἐπὶ τὴν πέτραν. Wer ὁ θεμέλιος sagt oder schreibt, kann also je nachdem auf das ganze Fundament oder auf einen Teil desselben Bezug nehmen. Bei seiner Verwendung des Bildes vom Bauen reflektiert Paulus nicht auf den Baugrund (τὸ ἔδαφος), auf dem der θεμέλιος aufliegt. Im Wort Jesu an Petrus (Matth. 16,18) herrscht dagegen die Vorstellung von der tragenden Funktion des Felsengrundes (πέτρα); wahrscheinlich macht sich hier semitisches tempelarchitektonisches Denken wahrnehmbar, das dem Felsen irgendeine kosmische Stellung beimißt, während Paulus sich in griechischen Kategorien bewegt. –

3.

Wie ist nun V.11 im Zusammenhang des Gedankenzuges V. 10–15 zu beurteilen? M. E. ist V. 11 nicht als eine Parenthese zu betrachten, die die Gedankenlinie von V. 10 unterbricht mit einer feierlichen Erklärung, die sich gegen gewisse Kritiker oder Neuerer richtet. Daß Paulus hier einen Stoß führen will gegen Leute, die tatsächlich "einen andern Grund" legen wollen (etwa Judaisten oder Gnostiker), halte ich für unglaublich; wenn eine solche Gefahr vorgelegen hätte, würde der Apostel einen viel schärferen Ton angeschlagen haben.[1] Ich glaube, man trifft das Richtige, wenn man auf die ganze Schreibweise des Apostels in 1.Kor. 1–4 achtet. Die Gemeinde ist in Gruppen zersplittert, deren Autoritäten gegen den Apostel ausgespielt werden. Die Ausführungen des Paulus in seinem Briefe bekämpfen das Parteiwesen teils dadurch, daß der Apostel überhaupt die Parteiungen verwirft, teils so, daß er den richtigen Gesichtspunkt angibt für die Beurteilung seines Verhältnisses zu den anderen Autoritäten der Gemeinde. Dabei betont er ihre prinzipielle Gleichgestelltheit als θεοῦ συνεργοί (3, 5–9); aber er vindiziert jedoch gleichzeitig für seine Person eine Sonderstellung als Gründer der Gemeinde (vgl. besonders ener-

[1] So z. B. A. Hilgenfeld, *Einleitung in das NT,* 1875, und noch J. Weiss z.St.: "er (Paulus) spricht damit nicht nur die völlig sichere Überzeugung aus, daß er in Kor. das Rechte gepredigt hat, sondern auch wohl eine Verwarnung gegen solche, die einen ἄλλος 'Ιησοῦς oder ein anderes Ev. predigen wollen." Ähnlich auch A. Schlatter, *Paulus der Bote Jesu,* S. 133.

gisch 4, 14ff.). In dieser Beziehung statuiert er einen unbedingten Unterschied: er hat den Grund gelegt, sie bauen weiter darauf (ἄλλος ἐποικοδομεῖ). An sie richtet er eine Warnung: ἕκαστος δὲ βλεπέτω πῶς ἐποικοδομεῖ. Absichtlich bewegt er sich in allgemeinen, unpersönlichen Redewendungen: ἄλλος, ἕκαστος. Bei dem ἕκαστος mußte wohl aber Paulus die kritische Frage vernommen haben: warum richtest du die Warnung nur an die ἐποικοδομοῦντες? Wie steht es mit deinem eigenen Werk? Die Antwort kommt V. 11, und das γάρ bezieht sich auf die unausgesprochene Zwischenfrage: Ich brauche diese Warnung nicht (eben hat er sich ja auch als σοφὸς ἀρχιτέκτων bezeichnet), denn ich habe das einzig mögliche, das einzig tragfähige Fundament gelegt, Jesus Christus. Οὐδεὶς δύναται bedeutet somit nicht: "kein anderer (etwa Judaist oder Gnostiker) kann ein anderes Fundament legen als das von mir gelegte", sondern: "keiner überhaupt (auch ich nicht)..." Das Wort θεμέλιος hat jedenfalls prägnanten Sinn (echtes, haltbares Fundament), ganz so wie εὐαγγέλιον Gal. 1, 6, wo ausdrücklich gesagt wird: ὃ οὐκ ἔστιν ἄλλο. Also Paulus schreibt: was mich betrifft, bin ich sicher; ich habe das einzig in Frage kommende Fundament gelegt.[2] Für die aber, die darauf bauen, ist die Lage eine andere, ihnen ist größte Vorsicht vonnöten.[3] Die Adresse der Warnung ist deutlich vernehmbar: es sind die Parteileute, die zu ernstem Nachdenken angehalten werden sollen.

---

[2] So z.B. H.Lietzmann z.St.: "Art und Zuverlässigkeit des von mir gelegten Grundes ist über jeden Zweifel erhaben."

[3] Wenn man, wie gewöhnlich, V. 12 als *Konditionalsatz* auffaßt, ist er eigentlich ein recht seltsames Gebilde: "Wenn jemand auf den Grund Gold, Silber usw. baut, so wird eines jeden Werk (im Gericht) offenbar werden ..." Man erwartet eigentlich: Wenn jemand baut, *so soll er bedenken,* daß eines jeden Werk offenbar werden wird. Indessen der Apostel will offenbar sagen: Wer auf den Grund (εἴ τις fast gleich ὅστις), dessen Werk wird im Gericht offenbar werden, da es sich zeigen wird, ob er Gold, Silber usw. gebaut hat. Wenn Paulus die Materialien – die doch erst im Gericht zutage treten – proleptisch in der Vordersatz hineinzieht als Objekt zu ἐποικοδομεῖ, so ist das eine starke Verschränkung, die aber dem Paulus wohl zuzutrauen ist. Es ist diese Verschränkung, die V. 12 so unlogisch gestaltet hat. – Man fragt sich aber, ob nicht der εἰ-Satz als vorangestellter abhängiger *Fragesatz* verstanden werden kann: "Ob einer (jetzt) auf den Grund Gold, Silber usw. aufbaut – eines jeden Werk soll offenbar werden." So wird der Satz logisch; dafür muß man eine leichte Verschiebung der Satzkonstruktion in den Kauf nehmen, aber das ist ja eine bei Paulus sehr häufige Erscheinung.

Neutestamentliche Wortforschung

"Nicht für Raub achten", Phil. 2, 6

(1946)

Im *Faust* I, V. 258f., sagt Mephistopheles:

> Leb mit dem Vieh, und *acht es nicht für Raub,*
> den Acker, den du erntest, selbst zu düngen.

Die hier durch Kursivdruck ausgezeichnete Redewendung hat *Goethe* auch in einem Briefe an Lavater vom 24. Nov. 1783: "Du erfahrener Arzt, der es *nicht für einen Raub hältst* [1], zu quacksalben..." Daß die Phrase irgendwie auf Phil. 2, 6 zurückgeht, kann nicht fraglich sein; dafür spricht schon die Tatsache, daß sie ausschließlich in negativer, nie aber in positiver Form vorkommt. Aber wann, wie und wo ist sie entstanden? Goethe hat sie natürlich nicht geschaffen, er greift eine allgemeine Redensart auf, die aber in der deutschen Literatur sehr spärlich vorkommt. In der Tat habe ich außer den beiden Goethe-Zitaten nur noch einen einzigen Fall feststellen können, nämlich bei Thomas Mann in dessen Roman *Joseph und seine Brüder I, Die Geschichten Jaakobs* (Berlin, Verlag S. Fischer, 1934) S. 378, wo die Begegnung zwischen Jaakob und seinem Schwiegervater Laban geschildert wird. Laban hat Jaakob verfolgt, um seine gestohlenen Hausgötter zurückzufordern, und beschuldigt ihn des Diebstahls. Jaakob sagt: "Jetzt hör mich an. Es ist gut, daß du da bist und *hast's nicht für Raub gehalten,* hinter mir drein zu ziehen so viele Tage um dieser Sache willen ..." – Anders liegt die Sache in Dänemark und Schweden, wo die Redewendung "etwas nicht für Raub achten" seit dem 19. Jahrhundert sehr verbreitet ist, und zwar sowohl in der lebendigen Rede als im literarischen Stil (reiches Material bei E.Låftman in *Nysvenska Studier,* 1944, S. 90ff.). In Norwegen scheint sie unbekannt zu sein. Sie dürfte wohl (über Dänemark?) von Deutschland nach Schweden gelangt sein. – In der Redensart "etwas nicht für Raub halten" hat ja das Wort "Raub" einen andern Sinn als im Zusammenhang der Bibelstelle. Es bedeutet nicht "kostbarer Besitz", "günstige Gelegenheit" u.

[1] Die alten deutschen Übersetzungen haben Phil. 2, 6 teils und meist "hielt er's nicht für Raub", teils "hat er's nicht für Raub geachtet". Die letztere Form ist feierlicher und mehr poetisch, wird deshalb im Faust verwendet.

dgl., sondern etwas Schlechtes, Niedriges. Bei Goethe sowohl als bei Mann ist die Meinung offensichtlich: "etwas für nicht unter seiner Würde halten", "sich nicht der Mühe entziehen". Wie kann aber "Raub" diesen Sinn angenommen haben? Die richtige Erklärung hat wohl das große Wörterbuch der schwedischen Akademie (*Svenska Akademiens Ordbok* I, Sp. 857), wenn es vermutet, man habe bei ungenauer Erinnerung an die Bibelstelle Phil. 2, 6 den Satz "er hat es nicht für Raub geachtet" (mit Ueberspringung der Worte "Gott gleich zu sein") mit dem Satz: (sondern) "entäußerte sich selbst und nahm Knechtsgestalt an" verbunden, und so wurde der Sinngehalt von Raub ein ganz anderer als der biblische. Diese Erklärung scheint mir recht plausibel.[2] Wenn man da überhaupt über den Sinn von "Raub" im Zusammenhang der Redensart nachgedacht hat, wird man wohl das Wort als "Beraubung" (seiner selbst) gedeutet haben. Im Schwedischen ist dann allerdings die Entwicklung weitergegangen, und "Raub" hat die Bedeutung von "Unrecht", "Schande", "Frechheit" angenommen. Beispiele (bei Låftman): "Herr W. hat es nicht für Raub gehalten, unverfroren als dessen Advokat aufzutreten" (geschrieben im Jahre 1842). "Der Leutnant hat es nicht für Raub gehalten, sich bei einem Offiziersball zu drücken" (im Jahre 1943). Ob diese Verwendung unserer Redensart im pejorativen Sinn auch auf deutschem Gebiet vorkommt, ist mir unbekannt. Belege fehlen bisher. Für die Aufhellung der ganzen Frage wären eventuelle Mitteilungen wünschenswert.

[2] Wenn der negative Satz: "er achtete nicht für Raub" von seinem positiven Komplementärsatz: "sondern entäußerte sich selbst" getrennt und verselbständigt wurde, mußte ἁρπαγμός in seiner eigentlichen Bedeutung (Beraubung, Räuberei) verstanden werden und der Sinn für seinen übertragenen Gebrauch verlorengehen. Die Frage, was ἁρπαγμὸν ἡγεῖσθαί τι bei Paulus besagen will, muß sich letztlich entscheiden am Gegensatz: ἀλλὰ ἑαυτὸν ἐκένωσεν – zwischen den beiden antitetisch koordinierten Begriffen muß eine innere Entsprechung bestehen, die den Deutungsmöglichkeiten bestimmte Grenzen zieht. Zu ἑαυτὸν ἐκένωσεν Wichtiges bei K. Petersen in *Symbolae Osloënses* XII (1933), S. 96f.

The Apostle and His Message

(1947)

When Paul in Romans introduces himself as a κλητὸς ἀπόστολος he characterizes himself as an eschatologic person. He is a man who has been appointed to a proper place and a peculiar task in the series of events to be accomplished in the final days of this world; those events whose central person is the Messiah, the Christ Jesus, crucified, risen, and returning to judgment and salvation. In order to understand the meaning of the title ἀπόστολος, as used by Paul, we must therefore grasp the eschatological way of thinking which dominated Jewish apocalyptic as well as Jesus and the Primitive Church.

Among the traits characteristic of this line of thought we emphasize the two following: firstly, the events of the final era follow each other according to a fixed plan leading up to a definitive goal: the destruction of the old world and the establishment of the new, eternal aeon. Secondly, this predetermined series of eschatologic events is bound up with certain elected persons who have a distinct and particular place in God's plan of salvation, and who have been given to play a strictly defined rôle in the great final drama, a rôle to which they, and they alone, are called–and for which they are specially equipped. Person and ministry are here inextricably one. These men are chosen and set apart. They are not ordinary people, but they are, so to speak, official personages of the kingdom of God on the same line as the chosen Old Testament instruments of God's dealings with Israel: Abraham, Moses, the prophets. It is significant that, speaking of himself, Paul says: "God who has appointed me when I was in my mother's womb" (Gal. 1,15), thereby applying to himself what Jahve said to the prophet Jeremiah, when He called him to his task (Jer. 1,5). It is also significant that, according to Rev. 21, 14, the names of the Twelve Apostles will be inscribed on the twelve foundation stones of the New Jerusalem. This fundamental eschatological conception which places the chosen apostle in a special position reserved to him, must be remembered as we attempt to understand the meaning of Paul's words when he declares himself an apostle of Jesus Christ.[1] Without that background one

[1] For recent literature on the notion of "apostle" in the Primitive Church cf. the article ἀπόστολος (by Rengstorf) in *Theologisches Wörterbuch zum N. T.* herausgeg. von Kittel (= *ThWB)*, I, 406–446. – Further E. Haupt, *Zum Verständnis des Apostolats in den synoptis-*

cannot grasp his apostolic selfconsciousness nor understand his arguments and actions.

This was the way of thinking also of Jesus and the Primitive Church as a whole. It is quite obvious that the Christian congregations in Jerusalem, Judea, and Galilee looked upon their situation from an eschatological point of view. They regarded themselves as living in the last days. The series of final events had begun to move, and had passed a decisive point: the death and resurrection of the Messiah. Jesus Christ had now taken His place on the right hand of God in heaven. What remained was his *parousia* and the coming of the Kingdom of Heaven in power and glory. To this situation Paul refers his apostolate. He regards his vocation and task, his person and total existence as main factors in that which has to happen before the Lord would return.[2] And here we are confronted with an important question: this idea that an *apostolate* is to stand in the centre of the eschatologic development between the resurrection and return of the Messiah, whence does it originate?

1.

It is obvious that the Primitive Church in Palestine expected the return of the Lord within a short time. We see also without difficulty that they expected persecutions and tribulations because of the name of Christ. But were they – *from the beginning* – convinced that, in the meantime of waiting, the church had to be active and that this activity was a part of what, according to God's plan and will, would have to happen and would happen in the last days?

This question belongs to the most difficult problems of the history of primitive Christianity. It is true that we read in the Gospels and in Acts that Jesus taught His disciples that the gospel would have to be preached in all the world before the Messiah appeared in His glory.[3] And Matthew and Luke as well as Acts relate that the risen Lord commanded the disciples to preach salvation to

chen Evangelien, 1895; S. Odland, *Apostolatets begreb og oprindelse,* Oslo 1897; H. Monnier, *La notion de l'Apostolat des origines à Irénée,* 1903; G. Sass, *Apostelamt und Kirche* (Forschungen zur Geschichte und Lehre des Protestantismus. Neue Reihe, Bd. II), München 1939; *The Beginnings of Christianity* Part I, vol. V, p. 37–58; H. Mosbech, "ΑΠΟΣΤΟΛΟΣ hos Paulus", in *Studier tilegnede Fr. Buhl,* Copenhagen 1925, p. 151–166; O. Cullmann, "Le caractère eschatologique du devoir missionnaire et de la conscience apostolique de Saint Paul", in *Revue d'Histoire et de Philosophie religieuses* XVI (1936), p. 210–245; H. Boddeke, *Jeruzalem-Antiochië*, Roermond-Maaseik 1938; H. Sasse, "Apostel, Propheten, Lehrer", in *Luthertum*, 1942; R. Liechtenhan, *Die urchristliche Mission*, Zürich 1946; Ed. Schweizer, *Das Leben des Herrn in der Gemeinde und ihren Diensten*, Zürich 1946; R. Liechtenhan, "Paulus als Judenmissionar", in *Judaica*, 1946.

[2] Compare Rom 11,13 with 11,25 ff.: Paul is ἐθνῶν ἀπόστολος ἄχρι οὗ τὸ πλήρωμα τῶν ἐθνῶν εἰσέλθῃ. Then comes the end. "*Now* is a day of Salvation!" 2 Cor. 6,2.

[3] Mc. 13,10; Acts 1,8.

all the nations, cf. also John 20, 21.[4] But we must put the critical question, whether these accounts are not fashioned *post eventum*, so that what actually happened later has been dated back to the beginning. This seems indeed to be the case. How then did the apostolate, in its Pauline, eschatological meaning, emerge in the Primitive Church?

When we try to form an opinion as to how this conception rose and prevailed, we come up against great difficulties. The account of the primitive congregation in Jerusalem, as we read it in Acts, does of course contain very valuable details; but, on a whole, it is strongly coloured by Luke's theology and historical view, and does not therefore give us a true idea of what actually happened. Luke concentrates everything to Jerusalem. But we know that many important things happened outside of Jerusalem, in Galilee and Syria.[5] There was a primitive church in Galilee as well as in Jerusalem. Luke draws an ideal picture of the church in Jerusalem under the leadership of the Twelve.[6] Into this ideal picture pieces of invaluable historical tradition are inserted, details which break through the ideal picture; thus, for instance, the schism between the Aramaic-speaking and the Hellenists. But these traditions, too, have been retouched by Luke in his account, so that we can no longer see clearly how everything actually happened. We are, for instance, not by a single word informed of how it came, that James, the brother of the Lord, rose to a leading position in Jerusalem, and of what the nature of his relations to the Twelve was. All of a sudden James emerges in ch. 15 as a first class authoritative personality in the church of Jerusalem.[7] In short, we should like to know the answers to a lot of questions in the history of the Primitive Church between 28 and 60 A. D., but sources are lacking. This is the case also concerning the question about the eschatological apostolate. Must we then leave this problem entirely unsolved? – Surely, we are here standing on precarious ground. All the same, we may dare to take a few cautious steps forward without falling into merely hypothetical speculations.

As to the situation of the church of Jerusalem in the thirties, we see that leading men there testified publicly about Jesus on certain occasions and argued with the Jews in the synagogues about his messiahship (St Steven). Individu-

[4] Mt. 28,18–20; Lk. 24,48: ὑμεῖς μάρτυρες τούτων, cf. Acts 1,8.

[5] E. Lohmeyer, *Galiläa und Jerusalem,* 1936; R.H. Lightfoot, *Locality and Doctrine in the Gospels,* 1938.

[6] Characteristic of Luke in Acts is his description of the outpouring of the Holy Ghost, Acts ch. 2, as a great manifestation of the Gospel to a great crowd representing all peoples in the world, immediately followed by the baptism of those who believed. That this is an entirely theological construction, is evident. Cf. Kirsopp Lake, *The Beginnings of Christianity* V, p. 120f.

[7] About 34 A. D. we find James in Jerusalem (Gal. 1,19). He was already at that time one of the "pillars" (Gal. 2,9); that we may conclude from the fact, that Paul at his first visit in Jerusalem entered into contact only with him besides Cephas.

ally, the Christians witnessed in their own circles. The same was surely the case in the Primitive Church of Galilee. So the Christian faith was rapidly spread in Judea, on the coastal plain, in Galilee, and Syria. Philip evangelized in Samaria and elsewhere. Perhaps Christianity was brought to Rome and Alexandria as early as in these years.[8] But was there any *apostolate* in the full sense of this term? Was there a mission which could, from an eschatological point of view, be regarded as official.

Of course, there were plenty of ἀπόστολοι. The Jewish world was in New Testament times full of *schelichin.* The princes, the Sanhedrin, the synagogal authorities, all employed messengers for different purposes, persons who had received a special commission for fulfilling a task on behalf of their commissioners. Private people frequently acted through *schelichin* entrusted with some business or other. Jesus sent out twelve chosen disciples to preach the gospel to Israel; and here we have a sort of eschatological apostolate, but only for a short time. When the Apostles returned to their Master after having accomplished their task, their apostolate expired; they were no longer the *schelichin* of the Messiah, but His *talmidin.* We may also conceive that the leading men of the Christian churches in Palestine frequently used ἀπόστολοι in order to keep contact with the believers and congregations spread throughout the country and in the neighbouring countries. But even those were temporary apostolates. How, then, did a permanent, fully eschatologic apostolate come into being? An apostolate in the real sense of the word as found in Paul?

I think Paul himself gives us precious help here. In Gal. 2, 7–8 referring to his transactions in Jerusalem, he writes: "... they saw that the gospel of the uncircumcision was committed unto me, as the gospel of the circumcision was unto Peter. For he that equipped Peter to the apostleship of the circumcision, the same equipped me unto the Gentiles." Here Paul expressly parallels his own apostolate with that of Peter. From this I think we may draw the conclusion that Peter had once, just as later Paul, been called and equipped to become the apostle of the circumcision. How this happened we do not exactly know. But Peter's apostolate was of course older than that of Paul, the historical and psychological background of which must have been Peter's apostolate to the circumcision (cf. Gal. 1, 17 οἱ πρὸ ἐμοῦ ἀπόστολοι). Obviously Paul pictures to himself the eschatologic situation of the world in this way: In this world, soon disappearing, the centre is Jerusalem with the primitive community and the Twelve, surrounded by the mission-field divided between two apostles: one sent by the Lord to the circumcised, the other to the Gentiles. Peter and Paul himself are the chosen bearers of the gospel, flanking the portal of the world to come. It is wholly in concordance with this view that the only relations in

[8] Cf. Léon Herrmann, *Du Golgotha au Palatin,* Bruxelles 1934. This book, fantastically fanciful as it is, deserves our attention as containing several remarks of importance.

Palestine mentioned by Paul are those to Peter, apostle to the circumcision, and James, leader of the Jerusalem church (Gal. 1,19; 2,11).[9]

As to Paul, we have in Acts some traditions about his conversion and vocation[10], and in the epistles some occasional remarks of his about this event. As to Peter, matters are different; we have no informations about his vocation to become an apostle to the circumcision. But the parallelism between the two, stressed by Paul, permits us to understand that Peter, too, had received his ministry and authority through a revelation. The vestiges of this revelation we have no doubt in John, ch. 21: "Feed my lambs, shepherd my sheep!"[11] In some way this tradition must be related with Peter's calling to be an apostle to Israel outside of Jerusalem. What was then the implication of his apostolate? First of all, of course, that he should preach the gospel to the Jews in the Jewish world. Paul hints at his journeys in 1 Cor. 9,5. But, apart from that, he must have had the supervision over the other missionaries, and have been the final court of appeal in all matters of contention and disciplinary cases. Peter was an apostle to the circumcision because of a special vocation, authorization and equipment. But this fact, of course, did not signify that he had a monopoly on the preaching to the Jews. He was, however, the shepherd of the flock of Messiah, of the people of the New Covenant, installed by Christ Himself.[12] *So the apostolate in*

[9] It is highly significant, that Paul, relating the revelations of the risen Lord, especially mentions those to Cephas and James (1 Cor. 15,5.7). These informations Paul had received from those two persons at his visit in Jerusalem.

[10] Acts ch. 9; 22; 26. E. Pfaff, *Die Bekehrung des H. Paulus in der Exegese des 20. Jahrhunderts.* Rome 1942; Fr. Smend in *Angelos* 1 (1925), 34ff.; E. Hirsch in *Zeitschr. für die neutestl. Wiss.* 28 (1929), 305ff.; H. Windisch in *Zeitschr. für die ntl. Wiss.* 31 (1932), 1ff.; W. Nestle in *Archiv für Religionswissenschaft,* 33 (1936), 264ff.

[11] It is probable that the narrative John 21 has been developed out of different old traditions about revelations of the risen Lord to his disciples. Two of these visions were localized to Galilee, one on the beach of the Lake, one at a meal. The revelation to Peter may have originally happened later and cannot be identified with the first revelation of the risen Christ to him (1 Cor. 15,5; Lk 24,34). These three visions have been combined so as to form a single coherent narrative, in which Jesus, on the pattern of 20,19–29, has intercourse with his disciples, still being in a state of a certain materialization, not yet having ascended to the Father (20,17). – The dialogue between Peter and the Lord, 21,15–17, with its threefold repetition betrays the original character of the scene: it was an audition (cf. 1 Sam. 3,1–8; G. Meloni, Saggi, Roma 1913, p. 288ff.). – The prediction of Peter's martyrdom, 21,18f., I hold to be an old prophecy emanating from some christian prophet in Peter's lifetime (cf. Agabus, Acts 21,10–14) and conserved in the tradition as a word of the Lord.

[12] The call to shepherd the flock of the Lord places Peter at the head of the Jewish church (τὰ πρόβατα ἐκ τῆς αὐλῆς ταύτης, John 10,16). The same position he receives through the words of Jesus Mt. 16,19: "I will give you the keys of the kingdom of heaven" etc., which I consider as another form of the same tradition (John 21, 15–17). – As shepherd and keeper of the keys to the kingdom of heaven Peter was not properly called to apostleship (ἀποστολὴ τῆς περιτομῆς), but rather to some sort of episcopacy (מְבַקֵּר). It was Paul who interpreted Peter's ministry as an "apostolate to the circumcision" which he could rightly do, as the vocation of Peter also included the preaching of the gospel. – The vocation lying behind John 21,15–17 and Mt. 16,19 marks a new stage in the eschatological function of Peter. At first he was the

its full and definite sense began with the calling of Peter. Thereby the church of Christ received its first great *apostolos,* Kephas, one of the Twelve, and the idea of an ἀποστολή comprising the entire existence and activity of a chosen instrument for the development of things in the last days.

Some few years later the apostleship to the Gentiles was created by the calling of Saul from Tarsus. He found himself in charge of a mission-field where the gospel was preached by many witnesses beside himself, his disciples and assistants. Paul fully respects their work, and makes it a rule not to encroach upon their sphere of work. But he regards himself as responsible for the whole. He does not attempt to claim any direct authority as a superior overseer, but it is

rock upon which the Lord built his ecclesia (Mt. 16, 18), which means that he was the central person in the Church of Jerusalem. Later on, probably after no long time, he was entrusted with the entire Jewish missionfield. Perhaps we may suppose a certain connection between this new vocation of Peter and the taking over of the ecclesiastical government in Jerusalem by James, the brother of the Lord? – It seems, then, that neither Peter nor the other ones of "the Twelve" ever were "apostles" in the proper sense of this term. Οἱ δώδεκα (1 Cor. 15,5; John 6,71) were no apostles (except during their short ministry in the lifetime of Jesus) but were the designated co-regents of the Messiah; they were to sit on twelve thrones judging the twelve tribes of Israel (Mt. 19, 28). About the authenticity of this logion we have no reason to doubt; and at any rate it expresses the idea of the Church of Jerusalem. Here we see that Jesus looked forwards to a millennial reign of the Messiah over Israel (Acts 1,6 κύριε, εἰ ἐν τῷ χρόνῳ τούτῳ ἀποκαθιστάνεις τὴν βασιλείαν τῷ Ἰσραήλ; for it is unthinkable that Jesus should have imagined the coming eternal world as an interminable reign of the Messiah surrounded by his twelve chosen representatives of the twelve tribes. The promise to the Twelve has in view their place in the intermediate space between the parousia and establishment of the new aeon (H. Bietenhard, *Das tausendjährige Reich,* Zürich 1944, p. 290). So the Twelve were in the Church of Jerusalem, as the designated co-regents of the Messiah, persons of the highest religious dignity. But they did not, all of them, play an active role in the life of the community. Only Peter and the two sons of Zebedee have left any trace in the tradition. The memory of the other members of the sacred college very soon faded away, and after the year 70 the Church did not even possess an accurate knowledge of their names. – But how did it come that in later time the Twelve became the twelve apostles of the Church? This much debated question we cannot discuss at length here. But I think they are right, who maintain that Paul has laid the foundation to this view. Paul applied the category of "apostle" to Peter and his submissionaries with their operation-base in Jerusalem. When he writes, Gal. 1,17.19 οἱ πρὸ ἐμοῦ ἀπόστολοι, ἕτερος τῶν ἀποστόλων, he does not mean οἱ δώδεκα . When enumerating the revelations of the risen Lord, 1 Cor. 15, 5. 7, he writes ὤφθη Κηφᾷ, εἶτα τοῖς δώδεκα, but Ἰακώβῳ, εἶτα τοῖς ἀποστόλοις πᾶσιν. [sic this sentence (Ed.)].These "apostles" must have been the messengers chosen by James to carry the message of the risen Christ out to the disciples of Jesus in all parts of Palestine. Before starting they had a collective revelation. – In fact, Paul never calls the Twelve "Apostles". But by stressing the parallel between his own apostolate and the commission of Peter he started the process which should lead to the result, that the Twelve became "the twelve apostles", beside whom Paul only with some difficulty could maintain his claim to the title. – In the later books of the N. T. the Twelve are "the apostles", so in Acts, in Ephesians and in Revelation. The synoptic gospels evidently mean that the Twelve were called by Jesus to a lifelong apostolate (Lk 6,13 δώδεκα, οὓς καὶ ἀποστόλους ὠνόμασεν). From Peter the title had passed over to the other eleven. A motive which supported and promoted this process I think we may find indicatcd in Eph. 2, 20, where "the holy apostles and prophets" together constitute the foundation of the Church: to the twelve prophets of the O.T. correspond the twelve apostles of the New Covenant. Cf. Lk. 11,49.

obvious that he has tried to assert his position and his doctrine also in the non-Pauline missionary churches of the Gentiles. Proof of this is provided by Ephesians, which, in my opinion, represents the type of letters Paul used to write to those churches which he had not himself founded. Proof is also Romans, where, in the introduction, Paul describes himself as an apostle of Jesus Christ to promote obedience of faith among *all* the Gentiles (ἐν πᾶσιν τοῖς ἔθνεσιν) for His name's sake.[13] I believe that the main motive of Romans is to assert, in a discreet way, the apostolic authority and teaching of Paul in the church of Rome. Paul has not aspired to apostolic dominion over the churches among the heathens, but as the "apostle to all the Gentiles" he endeavoured to wield his influence over the whole of the area. The Epistle to the Romans is probably one link of an extensive correspondence of Paul's with the non-Pauline churches in the Mediterranean – a correspondance which usually kept the trend of Ephesians, but in this special case assumed a particular character.

Characterizing the position of the Primitive Church in the fifties we see, therefore, that it is determined by three main factors: the church in Jerusalem under James, the brother of the Lord; Peter active as an apostle to the circumcision; and Paul active among the Gentiles. The actual conditions can, of course, not be grasped by this simple outline. Many apostles were busy, different currents of thought arose, and dissimilar standpoints emerged in the many practical problems which presented themselves to the young churches; crises and complications appeared in Jerusalem, Antioch, and outside. Here, we are not going to follow all these vicissitudes, but concentrate our attention on the preaching of the two principal persons, Peter and Paul.

2.

Both had been entrusted with the preaching of the gospel, Peter to the circumcised, and Paul to the Gentiles (Gal. 2,7). Constitutive of the ministry of an *apostolos* is that he has been given a message to proclaim; and the proclamation of this message is essential to his whole activity.[14] The apostolate also comprises other tasks, but they are of secondary importance compared with the preaching of the gospel: "Christ did not send me to baptize but to preach the gospel" (1 Cor. 1,17). We are now faced with the question whether Peter and Paul each had his own gospel, or, rather, his own form of the gospel.

[13] Cf. ἐν παντὶ τόπῳ, 2 Cor. 2,14; ἐν πάσῃ κτίσει τῇ ὑπὸ τὸν οὐρανόν, Col 1,23.

[14] See the article εὐαγγέλιον *ThWB* II, 705ff. – Analyzing Mt 10, we find the following elements constituting the pericope on the sending out of the 12 apostles: a) authorization; b) names; c) missionfield; d) message; e) instructions, prediction of persecutions and sufferings; warnings, promises. This combination of motives is typical. Here we are specially concerned with the definition of the missionfield and the message as being essential to the vocation of an apostle (cf. Gal. 1, 10–12. 16).

Recent scholarship has been inclined to deny this: there was only *one* gospel, and when, in Gal. 2,7, Paul distinguishes between "the gospel to the circumcised" and "the gospel to the uncircumcised", he is, according to a view generally held, only marking a difference between areas and not with regard to the message itself.[15] But if so, what does Paul mean by phrases like "my gospel", "the gospel which I preach", or "which was preached by me"?[16] – In my opinion, it is simply impossible not to interpret these statements so that Paul had been entrusted with the gospel in a distinct form which was revealed and handed over to him personally through a special call. He was not called to preach the gospel in general, but to proclaim quite a peculiar and characteristic message of his own, the deliverance of which was to be accomplished as an essential part in the eschatological programme. Hence the message cannot be separated from his own person; it stands or falls with him. Anyone wanting to attack his gospel is bound to dispute his apostolic *exousia*. – What, then, was this gospel like, with which Paul had been entrusted?

In 1 Cor. 15,1 ff. we find what it had in common with the Gospel of Peter.[17] It is the Christological *kerygma* concerning the Messiah who "died for our sins in accordance with the Scriptures", and "was raised on the third day according to the Scriptures". About these things Paul says: "Whether then it were I or they, so we preached and so you believed" (1 Cor. 15,11). The divergence between the Petrine Gospel and that of Paul makes its appearance only when we have to define the signification of the Messiah's (death and) resurrection.

What does Peter say about this? The sermons of Peter contained in the Acts give us sufficient information: "God has made him both Lord and Christ, this Jesus whom you crucified" (2,36). "The God of our fathers raised Jesus, whom you killed by hanging him on a tree. God exalted him at his right hand as Leader and Saviour, to give repentance to Israel and forgiveness of sins" (5,30f.). "Repent therefore, ... that times of refreshing may come from the presence of the Lord, and that he may send the Christ appointed for you, Jesus" (3,19f.). – In other words, Peter interprets the significance of the resurrection of Jesus from a Jewish point of view: "God, having raised up his servant, sent him to you first" (3,26). The resurrection of Jesus from the dead means that He is now, as the heavenly Messiah of Israel, ruling over the new-covenant people consisting of those Jews who believed in him. The way of salvation is open to all children of

[15] For instance E. Molland, *Das paulinische Evangelion*. Oslo 1934; G. Friedrich, *ThWB* II, 731.

[16] τὸ εὐαγγέλιον ἡμῶν, 2 Cor. 4,3; 1 Thess. 1,5; 2 Thess. 2,14; τὸ εὐαγγέλιόν μου, Rom. 2,16; 16,25; 2 Tim. 2,8; τὸ εὐαγγέλιον ὃ εὐηγγελισάμην ὑμῖν, 1 Cor 15,1; τὸ εὐαγγέλιον τὸ εὐαγγελισθὲν ὑπ' ἐμοῦ, Gal. 1,11; τὸ εὐαγγέλιον ὃ κηρύσσω ἐν τοῖς ἔθνεσιν, Gal. 2,2.

[17] γνωρίζω ὑμῖν τὸ εὐαγγέλιον ὃ εὐηγγελισάμην ὑμῖν ... τίνι λόγῳ εὐηγγελισάμην ὑμῖν "let me recall to your minds, brethren, the good news which I announced to you ... (stating) through which word I announced it to you." The kerygma is ὁ λόγος τοῦ εὐαγγελίου, the Pauline conclusion is ἡ ἀλήθεια τοῦ εὐαγγελίου (Gal. 2,5. 14).

Abraham; one has only to believe in Jesus as the crucified and exalted Messiah. This form of gospel is all through based upon the priority of Israel as the covenant-people of the world; they are the people of prophecy now experiencing its fulfilment. It is a typical "gospel of the circumcision."[18]

The gospel which Paul was given to proclaim to all Gentiles draws another conclusion from the fact of Christ's resurrection from the dead: through His resurrection Jesus has been exalted to the state of Lord of the universe (Phil. 2). All mankind, all cosmical powers, the whole universe, now belong to Him. As a result of this, all men now have access through faith to His kingdom and to salvation. The new and true Israel has been disengaged from any national basis. Baptism, not circumcision, constitutes the new covenant.

It is this conception that underlies Paul's summary of his gospel in Rom. 1,1f.:

"set apart for a gospel of God ...
concerning his Son,

a) who became one of the descendants of David according to the flesh
b) and was installed as Son of God in power, according to Spirit of holiness by resurrection from the dead."

Unto the main attribute "concerning his Son" there are joined two parallel statements, asyndetically co-ordinated, and, in my opinion, we cannot rightly understand Paul unless we notice a certain contrast between them. These two antithetical statements give a Pauline interpretation to the main attribute: "Son of God." This so-called "double kerygma" is not part of a creed common to the whole apostolic church, but is a specifically Pauline formula, as can be expected in the preamble to such a writing as Romans. We have here an antithetical *parallelismus membrorum:* over against the statement a): "descended from David according to the flesh" stands the other b): "(installed as) Son of God in power." In other words, through His resurrection from the dead, Jesus, formerly the Messiah of the Jews, has been enthroned as Lord and Saviour of the whole world. Thereby the old Jewish limitations have been done away with,

[18] The speeches of Peter in Acts do not lack an universal outlook, cf. ὑμῖν πρῶτον, 3,26; 2,39: πᾶσιν τοῖς εἰς μακράν, ὅσους ἂν προσκαλέσηται κύριος ὁ θεὸς ἡμῶν. These sentences may be due to the Lukan redaction. But there can be no doubt that Peter expected the calling of the elected amongst the heathens at the end of time. This did not, however imply the idea of a Christian mission in the pagan world in the meantime before the parousia. The conversion of the Gentiles should be God's own work and be a great salvation wonder. – I think we may consider the Petrine speeches in Acts as typical of the way of preaching the gospel to the Jews. Peter no doubt spoke like that when announcing the message of the crucified and risen Christ to Israel. – When I speak, in this paper, of "the Petrine gospel", I mean this type of preaching. My intention is by no means to try to revive the doctrine of the Tübinger School by opposing Peter to Paul. That Peter was no Judaizer is *quite* evident. See further on p. 13. – For literature to the speeches in Acts vid J. Cadbury in *Beginnings* vol. V, p. 402–426; O. Bauernfeind, *Die Apostelgeschichte* (Theol. Handkommentar zum N. T.), 1939, p. 62–71.

circumcision and the Law have been cancelled. The new and true Israel comprises those who believe in the Son and are baptized in His name.

The antithesis between "the descendant of David" and "the Son of God in power" is of course not an absolute, but a relative one, indicating two successive stages in the career of Jesus. Even as a descendant of David, in his capacity of a Jewish Messiah, Jesus was of course also the Son of God but in humiliation, not "in power".

The other antithesis, between the statements "according to the flesh" and "according to the Spirit of holiness", is also a relative one, and does not mean that Jesus received the holy Spirit only through His resurrection; He had the Spirit even in His humiliation, but it was concealed under His human appearance. Through the resurrection from the dead, however, the Spirit became the all-dominating factor in Jesus. His new creation or re-birth effectuated through the Spirit by the resurrection from the dead is set in a certain contrast to His natural birth in the lineage of David.[19]

Thus the situation of the Gentiles has been radically changed by the enthronement of Jesus as the Son of God in power. This fact constitutes the gospel for the uncircumcision, for the Gentiles, the gospel which Paul was called to proclaim in the interval between the resurrection of Jesus and his *parousia.* Whoever acknowledges the apostolic calling of Paul, also has to accept this message. And whoever rejects the message, is also bound to deny the apostolic authority of Paul.

Speaking of this gospel, Paul, in Gal. 1,11f., says that it is "not after man". "For neither did I receive it from man, nor was I taught it through man, but through a revelation of Jesus Christ." People have often been wondering how Paul can express himself so categorically whereas, later on, he explicitly states that he had himself received the gospel which he had passed on to the Corinthians (1 Cor. 15,1ff.). How then can Paul in Gal. frankly deny what he openly states in 1 Cor.?[20] – This difficulty disappears if we reckon with a special Pauline

---

[19] Concerning Rom. 1,1-4 I hold an opinion contrary to most interpreters f.i. Dodd, *The Ep. to the Romans,* p. 5, who says: "It is probable that Paul is citing, more or less exactly a common confession of faith which would be known and recognized at Rome. The statement is pretheological." I think this is to underrate the polemical strain in Romans.

[20] H. Schlier, in his commentary on *Galatians* (Kritisch-exegetischer Kommentar über das N. T. herausgeg. von H. A. W. Meyer, Göttingen 1939), tries to explain the (seeming) contradiction by distinguishing between the gospel itself and the λόγος of the gospel (p. 20): "Das Evangelium das von Paulus verkündet wird, ist also deshalb nicht ein 'menschliches', weil es in dem die eschatologische Enthüllung vorwegnehmenden Geschehen der direkten und totalen Enthüllung Jesu Christi selbst an den Apostel seinen Ursprung hat und diesem nicht in der Form einer durch Lehre angeeigneten Überlieferung zuteil wurde. ... Das Evangelium des Paulus ist ein Produkt des unmittelbaren und offenbaren Gegenwärtigwerdens des erhöhten Herrn und nicht seiner mittelbaren Vergegenwärtigung im Logos der Predigt. Das schließt nicht aus, daß der Apostel nicht *auch* Tradent einer Evangcliums-Überlieferung sein kann, wie 1 Kor. 11,23 und 15,1 ff. deutlich zeigen. Aber das betrifft einen fixierten λόγος (1 Kor. 15,2) des Evangeliums, das ihm seiner Substanz nach mit der Erschei-

message to the Gentiles on the basis of the common *paradosis*. The Pauline gospel contained an interpretation of Christ's death and resurrection which was essential to the Gentiles. And at the same time it is evident that Paul could very

---

nung des Erhöhten gegeben war, das aber schon als Überlieferung der anderen Apostel in der Kirche wirkte. Auf seinen Ursprung und damit auf seine 'Substanz' gesehen, ist auch das paulinische Evangelium als Kunde, die den Glauben bewirkt, διὰ ῥήματος Χριστοῦ, mittels des Tatwortes Christus'." – The distinction made by Schlier between the "substance" of the gospel and its λόγος is not convincing. I raise two objections a) The λόγος τοῦ εὐαγγελίου,1 Cor. 15,1, is not the gospel as developed in teaching and preaching but the kerygma, the very essence of the gospel and *thema* of the preaching and teaching (see note 17). b) If Paul distinguishes between the gospel as "Tatwort" (revelation by Christ Himself) and Christian tradition and teaching in the Church, why does he expressly deny that he has received his gospel through διδαχή and παράδοσις? One should rather expect him to deny that he had *heard* it (ἀκοή). As Paul expresses himself, I find it extremely difficult to interprete his words on the line of Schlier. The apostle's aim is, according to Schlier (and to Oepke) to maintain his *apostolic authority:* he is called by Christ Himself. Paul is not here concerned with the doctrine which he taught the Gentiles, but only with his apostolic legitimacy. This legitimacy he proves by declaring "The gospel announced by me is not κατὰ ἄνθρωπον." Can that really mean "Announcing to you the gospel (common to all the apostles), I do that, I assure you, only because I am called and committed by Jesus Christ Himself" –? "I am a real, authorized ἀπόστολος Ἰησοῦ Χριστοῦ" – ? I do not find this interpretation natural. Τὸ εὐαγγέλιον (τὸ εὐαγγελισθὲν ὑπ' ἐμοῦ) cannot be the "Tatwort". It goes without saying that such a word cannot be κατὰ ἄνθρωπον. To deny that one has received a "Tatwort" by διδαχή and παράδοσις would be a flagrant truism. Oepke (*Der Brief des Paulus an die Galater.* Theologischer Handkommentar, 1937) had already before Schlier made the distinction between gospel and tradition; he says (p. 22): "... nirgends sagt der Apostel, daß man das Evangelium *lernt* ... Am allerwenigsten aber macht das Lernen Apostel." Well, but if that is a general and essential truth, how then can Paul expressly deny his having "learnt" the gospel which he preaches? According to the interpretation of Oepke and Schlier, Paul's argumentation Gal. 1,11f. is merely abstract, operating with unreal alternatives. Τὸ εὐαγγέλιον τὸ εὐαγγελισθὲν ὑπ' ἐμοῦ cannot be exactly the same notion as the notion associated with the absolute τὸ εὐαγγέλιον: it must be something which can be taught and learnt, in other words it is the Pauline message to the Gentiles, cf. v. 9 εἴ τις ὑμᾶς εὐαγγελίζεται παρ' ὃ παρελάβετε (!). Of this message Paul states that it is not κατὰ ἄνθρωπον. One should perhaps expect that he would explain this rather vague statement by declaring (γάρ) that he had not devised his gospel *himself*. Now he declares that he has not "received" it from man. To him as a Jew it was natural to treat every doctrine as a παράδοσις, and so he contrasts human tradition with divine revelation. I do not now think it necessary to ask, from what man Paul was suspected to have received his gospel (cf A. Fridrichsen, "Die Apologie des Paulus Gal 1", Gießen 1931, in *Paulus und die Urgemeinde. Zwei Ahhandlungen* von L. Brun und A. Fridrichsen; J.H. Ropes, *The Singular Problem of the Epistle to the Galatians*. Harvard Theological Studies XIV, 1929). Ropes writes on 1,1 ("Paul, Apostle, not from man nor through a man but through Jesus Christ"). "We need not infer from his language that his apostleship had been expressly denied, but it seems clear that someone had affirmed that it came to him 'through a man' and that he therefore lacked independent divine authority for his teaching". And on 1,11ff.: "The charge which he repels seems to have been that he had been dependent for his gospel on one or more of the apostles". I now think this is an unneccessary conclusion from what Paul writes 1,1 and 1,11f. The contrast ἀπ' ἀνθρώπων, δι' ἀνθρώπου – διὰ Ἰησοῦ Χριστοῦ is typical of Paul and of his way of thinking: to him the apostolate and the gospel is not valid which is not received directly from Christ Himself. That does not mean that Paul rejects every apostle who has not been called by Christ Himself. But the situation of Paul as an apostle to the Gentiles endowed with a particular message is unique and demands divine authoriza-

well claim to be preaching the same gospel as Peter and the other apostles, since the basic substance of his gospel was this very same primitive *paradosis* concerning Christ's death and resurrection. He had no difficulty in accepting Peter's gospel about the risen Messiah, the King and Saviour of Israel, as long as this gospel was presented to Jews only. Within the Jewish sphere, circumcision was the token of the covenant and so the undisputed startingpoint. A different situation would arise if the Petrine gospel were to step over the Jewish boundary into the domain of the Gentiles, because there it could not but end with the demand that the Gentiles should become Jews if they wanted to partake in the New Covenant and enjoy its blessings. Thereby the Petrine gospel would become something quite different from what it had been within Jewish territory; it would, in spite of the common basic *paradosis,* mean a flat denial of the Pauline gospel. In a Pauline congregation the Petrine gospel would of necessity appear as "a different gospel", a false doctrine. The Judaizers were falsifying the gospel by not drawing the right conclusions from the resurrection of the Messiah. In its Judaizing form, the Petrine gospel is no more a gospel; it has lost its character of a gospel; if this gospel were right, Christ would have died in vain.[21]

tion. If we suppose with Ropes that he had been attacked by the Judaizers in Galatia as being instructed and commissioned by men – eventually by the leaders in Jerusalem – one cannot see how such dependence could be used against him. No, it is Paul himself who formulates the alternative "of man – through Christ". We could sooner imagine that the propagandists in the churches of Galatia attacked Paul on the ground that he was *not* instructed and authorized by the church-leaders in Jerusalem. Paul's emphatic denial of his being dependent of man is therefore entirely rhetorical and serves only to stress the positive statement through Christ. What Paul will say is simply this: I have received my message to the Gentiles directly from Christ personally, and so he who rejects my gospel rejects Christ's own word. The following short account of his conversion and relations to Jerusalem will in the first place demonstrate his complete independence of the Church there, – an independence which corresponds to his divine vocation. Even in giving this account I do not believe that Paul is defending himself against the calumnies of his adversaries. He is all the time showing that he is really ἀπόστολος ἐθνῶν διὰ Ἰησοῦ Χριστοῦ. If the agitators in Galatia had attacked Paul personally – what they naturally had – we cannot reconstruct their criticism on the basis of Gal. 1–2. I think their attacks followed the line we catch a glimpse of in 2 Cor. 4: Paul preaches himself, and his gospel is his own device When it suits him he can even preach circumcision (Gal. 5,11) – Paul can speak of "our (= my) gospel" without reference to his special message to the Gentiles (1 Thess. 1,5; 2 Thess. 2,14). But in Rom. 2,16 κατὰ τὸ εὐαγγέλιόν μου must allude to some point in the special pauline doctrine. Concerning 2 Cor. 4,3 see note 27.

[21] 2 Cor. 11,4 Paul speaks polemically about ὁ ἐρχόμενος, who preaches ἄλλον Ἰησοῦν bringing with him πνεῦμα ἕτερον or εὐαγγέλιον ἕτερον. "Another" Jesus must be a Jesus who remains within the bounds of judaism; who only is the Messiah of the Jews. A gospel announcing such a Saviour is a "different" gospel, no real gospel at all. And the Spirit which the believers in this gospel receive, is a "different" Spirit, a false Spirit. – We see, then, that what in the Jewish Church is a true gospel giving to the believers the Spirit of God, is in the Church of the Gentiles entirely false! It is extremely difficult to grasp the thought of Paul concerning Jewish Christianity and fully understand his attitude towards it. W.L. Knox in his book *St Paul and the Church at Jerusalem* (1925) does not, so far I can see, discuss this question. But see note 25.

Over against this attempt to falsify the gospel Paul summons all his strength in the effort to preserve "the truth of the gospel", the true significance of the death and resurrection of Christ, for his churches (Gal. 2,5.14).[22] And since this significance stands or falls with his own apostolic authority, his first concern in the controversy with the Judaizers in Galatia is to prove that he is called by the Lord Himself, and has received the gospel from Him alone (1,11ff.). It is because of this that he reminds them about his former fanaticism in persecuting the church of God, and tells them how it had pleased God to reveal His Son to him, in order that he might proclaim Him among the Gentiles (1,16).[23]

Paul then goes on to tell them about his relations to Jerusalem, laying special stress on his negotiations with those who were "esteemed" there (2,1ff.): "I laid before them the gospel which I proclaim among the Gentiles." He was successful in convincing them that he was entrusted with the gospel for the uncircumcision. He succeeded in obtaining recognition from the "pillars" by unfolding the contents of his gospel, i.e. by receiving their approval of his interpretation of the basic kerygma. Paul could prove the genuineness of his call to preach to the uncircumcision and was able to refer to the visible results of his missionary work: "they saw that I had been entrusted with the gospel to the uncircumcision." From the *calling* (ἐπιστεύθην) his thought passes to the *equipment* (ἐνήργησεν καὶ ἐμοὶ εἰς τὰ ἔθνη), the bestowal of capacity to fulfill the task; and finally passes over to the palpable *result:* "recognizing the grace given to me." On this threefold ground the "pillars" of the church of Jerusalem gave to Paul and Barnabas the right hand of fellowship "that we should go the Gentiles, and they to the circumcision".[24]

Through this agreement the missionfield was divided in a strictly geographi-

---

[22] The expression ἡ ἀλήθεια τοῦ εὐαγγελίου Gal. 2,5.14 is very important. It shows that τὸ εὐαγγέλιον as a general notion is concentrated in the kerygma, common to Peter and Paul. But this common substance of the Gospel could be interpreted falsely as to its consequences for the Gentiles. Paul defends the right interpretation (ἡ ἀλήθεια τοῦ εὐαγγελίου), given in "his gospel".

[23] ἐν ἐμοί, Gal. 1,16, is likely to be understood as equivalent to ἐμοί. A. Oepke in *ThWB* II, 534; Blass-Debrunner, *Neutestl. Grammatik,* 7. Aufl. 1943, § 220 (p. 101).

[24] When Paul writes: "I laid before them the gospel which I proclaim among the Gentiles", it should be quite clear that he speaks of the special form of the gospel with which he was entrusted. Why should he lay his gospel before the pillars in Jerusalem if it were the same as theirs? Schlier, though denying the existence of a special Pauline gospel, speaks here of Paul's "Heiden-Evangelium", and Oepke says: "... die von ihm unter den Heiden ohne gesetzliche Auflage, d.h. unter Nichtbeachtung der in Jerusalem durchweg anerkannten Grundsätze, verkündigte Heilsbotschaft." Does Oepke think that the Pauline gospel to the Gentiles was a purified, a reduced Jewish-Christian message? A gospel containing law should Paul never acknowledge as a "gospel", not even in the Church of the circumcision. Paul only knows *one* gospel. The gospel to the circumcision was essentially the same as the gospel to the uncircumcision. But as soon as the former raised its claim among Gentiles, it assumed an element of law, and *this* gospel Paul calls "a different kind of gospel (ἕτερον), though there does not exist another gospel (ἄλλο)", Gal. 1,6.

cal sense: Palestine on one side, on the other side the world outside the Holy Land. The geographical character of the division is proved by the fact that Paul regarded himself as sent not only to the Gentiles, but also to the Jews among them (Rom. 1,13f.; 1 Cor. 9,20, Acts *passim).* From this we may draw a couple of important inferences. Firstly, in the opinion of Paul the Jewish Church was bound to the Holy Land and had no existence *as a Church* outside of its boundaries. This explains, why he expects of Peter that he during his visit in Antioch enters into table communion with his brethren of the Gentiles. Secondly we may infer that Peter did not come to Antioch in order to carry out missionary work among the Jews there but for some other reason. For if he had come in order to preach to the Jews he should have thereby infringed upon the agreement recently concluded. Probably he came as a guest of the Church of Antioch and a friend of Paul. That his secret aim was to work against the fusion of Jewish and Gentile Christians in Antioch I hold to be impossible. I fully agree with E. Hirsch (*Zeitschrift für die neutestamentliche Wissenschaft* 29 (1930), p. 63–76) in that he maintains against Ed. Meyer (*Ursprung und Anfänge des Christentums,* III, 1923, 424ff.) and H. Lietzmann (*Sitzungsberichte der Berliner Akademie der Wissenschaften*, 1930) that Peter was no judaizer. He had wholeheartedly approved the apostolate and gospel of Paul. But he belonged to those Jews – and they were probably the majority – who were not able to draw the consequences of the admission of the Gentiles to the Church of Christ as regards the interrelations between Christians of the circumcision and such of the uncircumcision outside of Palestine. In this respect Peter was a man of compromise, one of those who stood behind the decree of the apostolic council in Jerusalem (Acts 15). And so he was not able to keep his position against those, who "came from James", but "drew back and separated himself, fearing those who were of the circumcision" (Gal. 2,12).[25]

We must, however, here leave aside the conflict between the two great apostles in Antioch and return to Paul and his gospel. There can be no doubting the fact that Paul had received his ministry as an apostle of the uncircumcision directly from the Lord. But it is hardly probable that this revelation of his

[25] It almost seems that the expression οἱ ἐκ τῆς περιτομῆς in Gal. 2,12 has the signification "members of the Church of Jerusalem", which is in accord with 2,9 αὐτοὶ εἰς τὴν περιτομήν: the missionfield belonging to Jerusalem. – I think it is essential in order to understand the attitude of Paul to the Jewish Christianity to be aware that to him Jerusalem and Palestine has a particular religious quality. His thoughts about this matter are intimately connected with the role Israel played in his theology (cf. N. Månsson, *Paul and the Jews [Paulus och judarna],* Stockholm 1947). I hope to return to this question one day trying to elucidate the different aspects of Paul's attitude to Jerusalem. Clear is that Paul did not approve of nor even tolerate the compromise of Jerusalem regulating the interrelations between Jew and Gentile in the churches outside of Palestine. Here he demanded of the Jewish believers a full and unreserved commission with their brethren of the Gentiles. I think Hirsch *(op. cit.)* is quite right when he assumes that Romans contains an indirect polemic against the compromising attitude of the Jewish Christians in the Church of Rome.

calling coincided with the vision which led to his conversion. He says himself, Gal. 1,16: "when God was pleased to reveal his Son to me, so that I might preach the gospel of him to the heathen." The words suggest that this revelation was the original and fundamental one. But it is probable that the calling to the apostleship for the uncircumcision took place on some later occasion.[26] On this occasion he arrived at his insight into the "truth of the gospel". That is what we may conclude from Eph. 3, where Paul speaks of himself and the gracious commission which God had given him to bring to the Gentiles. This refers to the mystery of Christ which has been disclosed to him: that "the Gentiles are fellow-heirs and fellow-members of the body, fellow-sharers of the promise in Christ Jesus through the gospel, of which I became a servant according to the grace of God, which was given me by his inworking power" (here again ἐνέϱγεια, cf. Gal. 2,8). – It is true that it is hardly the apostle himself who has written these words. When we read that the mystery has been revealed "to God's holy apostles and prophets by the Spirit", then we get a strong impression that we hear the views of a later period and listen to the terminology of the church at a time which regarded the apostles as forming a solid unity, a holy ecclesiastical body. But, on the other hand, we must be open to the possibility that genuine Pauline ideas are at the bottom of Ephesians, a letter which no doubt emanates from the apostle's school. For this reason we cannot altogether leave it aside as we attempt to grasp the thought of Paul.

Ephesians treats particularly the position of the Gentiles in the Church. And it is highly probable that the thoughts expressed about this theme in the epistle originate in the teaching of Paul and reflect his thought. Once the Gentiles were aliens from the commonwealth of Israel and strangers to the covenant of promise, without hope, and without God in the world. But now, in Christ Jesus, you who once were far have become near by the blood of Christ. Christ has by His death broken down the wall of partition between the Jews and the Gentiles, and reconciled the two in one body. – Obviously, we here have theological arguments, reflections about the significance of the death of the Messiah for the acceptance of the Gentiles into the church. But

[26] The development of Paul's religious thought we cannot follow. It is highly probable that in the first years after his conversion he was active as a missionary among the Jews in Arabia and Damascus. The fact that the Messiah had been killed by the Jewish authorities (1 Thess. 2,14f.) and the persecutions from the synagogue may – together with personal religious experience – have called forth and incited his reflexions on law, righteousness and the access of the Gentiles to Salvation. But he must also have received a direct and special vocation to become an apostle to the Gentiles. This revelation is perhaps reflected in the passage of his speech to the Jews, Acts 22,17–21, where he narrates the revelation he received in the Temple of Jerusalem. If that is right, it is very significant, that Paul was called to an apostolate to the Gentiles on the most sacred spot of Israel, in the very Sanctuary, to which nobody outside of Israel had access.

behind these reflections there is a fundamental insight inspired by revelation, by a definite and concrete declaration from the Lord: the Gentiles now belong to Him in the same way as the Jews, and they have in faith free access to His people and covenant. When Paul speaks of "the mystery which by revelation has been disclosed" to him, this should be understood in a verbal sense. Such a revelation must have set in motion Paul's theological thinking over Israel, the Law and the Gentiles. The revelation of the mystery concerning the Gentiles and the Kingdom of God gave him the impulse to interpret the Christological *kerygma* in a special direction. And this interpretation and the basic substance of the gospel merged in Paul's preaching into one absolute unity, *"my gospel"*.

This gospel Paul's adversaries characterized as "veiled", κεκαλυμμένον, 2 Cor. 4,3. What did they mean by this? Several different attempts have been made in order to throw some light on this word, and explain the underlying meaning. But against them all one common objection must be raised: they do not take into consideration the term "our, my gospel". This refers to the message which Paul preaches among the Gentiles and not to his teaching (διδαχή).[27] We have above repeatedly said that the message of Paul to the Gentiles, which he calls "my gospel", was based on the common Christian *kerygma,* but interpreted this kerygma in a special direction. Now, when Paul's adversaries call this gospel of Paul's "veiled" (κεκαλυμμένον), I think they did so with a view to the fact that Paul himself declared that this gospel has been "unveiled" to him, that he had received it by an unveiling (ἀποκάλυψις) of the mystery of God concerning the heathen. I do not doubt that, in designating the gospel of Paul as "veiled", the antagonists of Paul in Corinth alluded to the apostle's own terminology. But, of course, they also implied something real by applying the attribute κεκαλυμμένον to the message of Paul: One could not see that his interpretation of the basic kerygma was intrinsic in the very substance of the common apostolic creed. The conclusion which Paul drew from the facts of the death and resurrection of the Messiah was "veiled" to other people. In other

[27] Several different attempts have been made in order to throw some light on the expression "veiled gospel" and explain the underlying meaning. a) Paul's doctrine (teaching) is "veiled", i. e. incomprehensible, it goes against all tradition and reason; b) Paul's teaching is difficult to understand with its tortuous arguments and queer ideas (2 Pet. 3,16); c) In his preaching Paul hides parts of the truth, for instance the glory and blessing of the Mosaic Covenant; or the real doctrine of Jesus; such objections would come from the Judaizing campus; d) Paul conceals something which he does not dare to show: the real consequences of his doctrine of grace; or his personal interests and ambitions, which would be the real motive for his mission work. – With almost all interpreters I hold that Paul in his polemic 2 Cor. 4 aims at his judaizing adversaries in Corinth; they are the ἀπολλυμένοι, the ἄπιστοι, – in spite of their πίστις, because they reject the gospel of Paul and work against him. The construction of the sentence is somewhat strange: ἐν οἷς ὁ θεὸς τοῦ αἰῶνος τούτου ἐτύφλωσεν τὰ νοήματα τῶν ἀπίστων, but I think Lietzmann is right in assuming, that Paul's intention was to write τὰ νοήματα αὐτῶν but in the last moment he put in the harsher term ἀπίστων.

words, this conclusion was Paul's own invention serving his personal ambitions: to be the great authority among the Gentiles and enjoy the privileges and advantages connected with such a position.

Paul answers to this: "If our gospel is 'veiled', it is veiled to those who are going to ruin; in whom the god of this world has blinded the thinking of the unbelieving, so that the light of the gospel of the glory of Christ, who is the image of God, may not shine in." These harsh words give us an impression of the bitter earnestness which this question implied for the apostle. If they do not see the evidence of his gospel, it is because Satan himself has blinded their thinking. As he continues his reply to the charges of a "veiled" gospel, the apostle – as we clearly see – identifies himself with his message. He says: "For we are not proclaiming ourselves but Christ Jesus, our Lord." The charge that Paul is proclaiming himself and not Jesus Christ, must have a connection with his practice to speak of "my gospel". This term was expressing his conviction of having received a special calling to become an apostle to uncircumcision, and to preach a special gospel to the Gentiles – a gospel which had been revealed to him, and before that had been a mystery. This was misinterpreted by his enemies, who claimed that in speaking of "my gospel" he wished to place himself in the foreground and call attention to his special authority. Therefore Paul declares that he does not act by his own initiative: "it is the God who said: light shall shine out of darkness, who has shone in our hearts, bringing the light of the glorious knowledge of God in the face of Christ" (2 Cor. 4,6). The new knowledge which Paul possesses and spreads among the heathen is God's work, not the apostle's own device *in majorem sui gloriam.* And what a work it is! Paul puts it on a par with the creation of light in the beginning. He cannot find a stronger expression for his conviction that he has received a revelation of unique importance and of cosmic scope, a knowledge which is a main element in the development of the eschatological situation. It is very significant that Paul's thought here goes back to creation in the beginning. He himself is with his gospel active in the new creation at the end of time. Beginning and end correspond. What happened then, and now happens again, surpasses all human thought and conditions. It has an absolute and eternal significance.

So we return here to the eschatologic view to which we called attention in the beginning of this paper – this characteristic view with its absolute categories. Here the Pauline idea of the apostle has its place. In Paul this idea has taken on a more intense personal colour than in any other personality of the Primitive Church. Paul was called to become not only an apostle, but also more especially an apostle to the uncircumcision. And he had received not only the gospel, but a special gospel which was his own. A unique "revelation of the glory of God in the face of Christ" had been given to him, of a glory which embraces all mankind and the whole world, a glory which by far surpasses the δόξα of God in Israel, the *Shekinah.* This glory Paul had learnt to behold in the face of the risen

Christ. This vision made him an apostle to the Gentiles, endowing him with his gospel, τὸ εὐαγγέλιόν μου, ἡμῶν which he had to preach to promote obedience of faith among all the Gentiles, ἐν πᾶσιν τοῖς ἔθνεσιν.

Part Four

Varia

The New Testament and Hellas[1]

(1930)

The title of this paper already indicates that what follows is a response to Professor Gunnar Rudberg's book *Hellas och Nya Testamentet* ("Hellas and the New Testament") which was published last year.[2] In his work Rudberg examines the main points in the synthesis of Jewish religion and Hellenistic culture which we find in the books of the New Testament. It is quite natural that this synthesis occurred unconsciously and spontaneously. We cannot rule out that some Jesus-*logia* received a Greek wording already during the life time of Jesus in the strongly Hellenized Galilean environment. In addition, we can certainly take for granted that many stories about the great and popular preacher and miracle worker circulated among the Greek speaking population in Palestine. We do not, however, know anything for certain concerning this.

The Hellenizing of the Gospel tradition and the message of the resurrection gained strength in the Hellenistic part of the *early Church* in Jerusalem. We can still feel the gap and the tension between this group of Messianic believers and the strongly Jewish Orthodox majority in Acts, if only in a much weaker form. Evidently a breach developed, and the Hellenists established their own *ekklesia* led by a group of seven men along with the Aramaic community led by "the twelve."

Acts tell us that the Hellenistic group soon was split up and banished by fanatical Jews, thus giving rise to the first Christian mission among Gentiles with Antioch in Syria as its base in the East. Rome and Alexandria were also reached early on by the Gospel in ways that are unknown to us. In the mid 40's Paul of Tarsus began his large scale missionary activity that brought him to almost all the great cities of Asia Minor, Macedonia and Achaia.

This led to the synthesis, mentioned above, of the Aramaic Gospel and Greek culture – in many places and in many ways. Nonetheless, the result must show a certain unity, because the whole movement had a common starting point: the tradition about Jesus and the message concerning his resurrection.

---

[1] A lecture in the "Videnskaps-Akademiet" in Oslo on February 28, 1930.

[2] See *Norsk Teologisk Tidsskrift* 1929, pp. 271 ff.

We must also reckon with the influence of the Greek Bible (the Septuagint) on the Christian mission. It certainly coloured its language and the Christian world of concepts to a high degree. We also have to reckon with Paul's position as the most important Apostle who has deeply influenced the whole Gentile mission, as is clear from the fact that the whole epistolary corpus of the New Testament is heavily influenced by Paul.

It is also evident, however, that the basic unity that is so characteristic of the New Testament does not rule out a great variety: factual, formal, and linguistic. It is sufficient to mention the Synoptic Gospels and the Gospel of John as examples. As we continue to study the synthesis of a Jewish gospel and a Hellenic culture, which we find in the New Testament, we will build upon the foundation which Rudberg has made firmer and more clear, and on the presuppositions that he has specified. It then will be necessary to examine the variations within the New Testament and to subject the different parts within this unity to an individual and at the same time a comparative discussion. We must also consider this synthesis from the *Semitic* side; we must follow the whole process from the starting point through the receptive medium all the way to the end result. This must not be looked upon as two competing methods for the study of the New Testament against its Greek Hellenistic background (as Rudberg does) and against its Oriental Palestinian background, but rather they make up two sides of the same task. In this regard, the New Testament occupies approximately the same position as the rest of the Jewish Greek literature that is not simply translated. Only through a study of the New Testament from both of these perspectives will it be possible to understand the part the New Testament plays in spiritual history in a fully realistic and comprehensive way.

For the time being the task is not to search for a formula for this position. What is necessary, however, is to do sensitive and detailed studies based on correct and fruitful viewpoints. But we can now, of course, point to those basic topics which throw light on the whole question of the New Testament and show the direction in which we can search for a summarizing characterization. One such topic, and the most important one, is the *language*. The New Testament certainly is written in Greek, but most of it is not in a Greek of a literary type. Instead we find a popular koiné based upon a Semitic substratum. Even those authors who show some literary ambitions; authors like Paul, the authors of Hebrews, Luke and 1 Peter use a language that is permeated by biblicisms. We will discuss another element here that points in the same direction but has not yet received the interest it deserves.

As was mentioned in the introduction of this article, we must look upon the Hellenization of the Gospel as a spontaneous and unconscious process. It was not a purposeful reinterpretation, a laborious conversion. This process was started and carried on by men who lived in both spheres of language, the Aramaic and the Greek, and thus could reshape the tradition unconsciously.

Here we find, however, an important symptomatic question: Do we find in the New Testament, in spite of its spontaneity in relation to the Hellenistic culture, a consciousness to engage something special and peculiar? Do the New Testament authors reveal any awareness of the special and unusual world-historical combination of the Gospel and Hellas? Do words like *Hellas, Hellenic* and *Hellenes* sound peculiar in their ears? It is important to know this. For if there was such a feeling for what is Greek, this would testify to a real inner encounter with the spirit of Hellenism, and we would expect to meet a real and thorough *interpretatio graeca* in the New Testament. If, on the other hand, we do not find such a feeling, this will imply a naive unconsciousness in the relationship to Hellenism, i.e. the Hellenization does not influence the basic core. Of course, a *naively radical* Hellenization of the Gospel is another option, but hardly for those who are born as Jews. It is reasonable to suppose that these were and remained Jews, although of a Greek type.

Thus, does the New Testament mirror a special impression, a specific view of Hellas?

It is of course ruled out that old nationalistic connotations still cling to the concept of "Hellenes." During this time "Hellenes" had become a cultural concept instead of an ethnical one. Already in 388 B.C., Isocrates said that the name of "Hellenes" no longer referred to descent but to character, the patterns of thought (ἡ διάνοια), "a Hellene is not the one who is of our blood, but those who share our education" (*Panegyricus* 50). Does the New Testament show any feeling for this distinctive character of Hellenistic culture?

Of course, we cannot expect to find anything like this in the early layers of *Mark* and in *the Logia-source.* The Syrophoenician woman (Mark 7:26) is called Ἑλληνίς, in this connection clearly identical with "Gentile", non-Jewish (cf. Acts 17:12, in contrast to the Jews). Otherwise Mark talks only about the proclamation of the Gospel "throughout the world" (Mark 14:9), mission territory being an undifferentiated whole.

In *Matthew,* however, we can find a certain orientation towards the East. In his farewell speech and the mission command to his disciples (Matt. 28:19) the resurrected Lord instructs them to make "all people" his disciples. He thus moves within the traditional Jewish scheme which distinguishes between two groups of people, Jews on the one side and "the nations" (τὰ ἔθνη) on the other. It may be significant in this connection that chap. 2 talks about "the Magi from the *East"* who arrive to worship the newborn king – evidently representing the whole of non-Jewish humanity.

Scholars have long thought of *the Gospel of John* as the most typical and the most consistent example of the Hellenization of the Gospel. It starts by considering Jesus as the *logos,* after which it uses great spiritualizing concepts like life, light, truth and freedom. Philo and the Alexandrian philosophy, which combines Plato and the Stoa and which interprets the Jewish Bible according to this

Greek spirit, seems to be the self-evident contemporaneous phenomenon that gives us the key to the riddle of the Fourth Gospel. This idea has always been contradicted by strong, but relatively isolated, insights which state that the language and concepts in John rather point to a strictly Semitic origin, even to Palestinian soil. It is only against such a background that the Gospel can bear a fruit of this kind (Schlatter, Burney). Reitzenstein's studies in early Asiatic Iranian-Babylonian syncretism have furthered such a view, and H. Odeberg's important work about the Fourth Gospel[3] has certainly proven that it is Jewish Oriental mysticism that has provided the terminology as well as concepts and inner structure to the Christ witness of the Johannine Gospel.

This is supported by the fact that we do not find the world of non-Palestinian peoples reflected in John in any other way than we did in Matthew. The "world" is an undifferentiated religious concept within which the "people" (11:51–52) occupy a special historical-religious position: "Jesus would die for the Jewish nation, and not only for that nation but also for the scattered children of God, to bring them together and make them one." The text on Jesus' cross is in Hebrew, in Latin and in Greek (19:20), the languages of the country, the administration and the oikoumene. When Jesus says (10:16): "I have other sheep that are not of this sheep pen. I must bring them also. They too will listen to my voice, and there shall be one flock and one shepherd," – these other sheep generally refer to the Gentiles. John, however, seems to be more oriented towards the West than Matthew was: The Jews ask whether Jesus intends to go "where our people live scattered among the Greeks, and teach the Greeks" (7:35). The Hellenes here evidently represent diaspora Jews speaking Greek. The same is the case in 12:20, where we read that some Greeks who went up to pray during the festival asked to see Jesus. The speech given by Jesus on that occasion (on the seed that is put into the ground to die and bear much fruit) seems to indicate that this event must be understood as a prediction of the universal effects of Jesus' death. It is significant that it is (Hellenistic) *Jews* who represent humanity as a whole. Along with them, the *Samaritans* appear as bearers of a universal longing for salvation and religious receptivity (John 4) – the horizon thus is typically Palestinian-Jewish.

The *Lucan books,* the two books to Theophilus, require our special attention in this connection. We find an author with a certain literary training, and he treats his subject from the perspective of a historian. Both these points may be the result of a conscious relationship to Hellenistic culture. But even Luke is totally bound by the traditional views about Jews and the Gentiles.

In the *Gospel,* Luke is almost totally dependent upon his sources which quite

[3] *The Fourth Gospel interpreted in its Relation to Contemporaneous Religious Currents in Palestine and the Hellenistic-Oriental World,* Uppsala 1929.

naturally move within the perimeters of Palestine. But even when he is free to choose his own words, these words are permeated by a theocratic Jewish thinking, something that is clear especially in the prehistory in chaps. 1–2 with their strongly biblical character and language, cf. the promises to Zechariah 1:14–17, Mary 1:32ff.; the Magnificat 1:46ff., the Benedictus 1:68ff., and the message from the angels 2:10–14. It is only in the words spoken by old Simeon over the child that we find universalistic tones in addition to the biblical ones. We also find a biblical universalism when Jesus' genealogy is traced all the way back to Adam, or when the widow in Zarephath or the Syrian Naaman are emphasized at the expense of Israel (3:38, 4:26ff., cf. 13:28ff.). The mentioning of "the nations" (τὰ ἔθνη, e.g., 21:24), all the peoples of the earth (12:30, 24:47) is, however, authentically Jewish. The mission will have its starting point in Jerusalem (24:47).

In *Acts* the mission programme is worded as follows: "you will be my witnesses in Jerusalem, and in all Judea and Samaria, and to the ends of the earth" (1:8). The story follows this line – and it ends in Rome. The first twelve chapters are dependent upon Palestinian sources. Luke still does not leave Jewish Christian patterns of thought when he composes his narrative more independently. In the list of peoples (chap. 2), a list whose purpose evidently is to give a universal impression, "Hellenes" are not mentioned among the many peoples. The word Ἕλλην, when used in Acts, signifies a Gentile in contrast to a Jew (11:20, 16:1,3, 17:4, 21:28, cf. Ἑλληνίς 17:12; Jews and Hellenes 14:1, 18:4, 19:10,17, 20:21), but also someone who speaks Greek and thus is no barbarian (28:4). This last mentioned contrast is genuinely Greek and gives voice to a true Hellenistic self-consciousness. In Luke, however, it is a purely literary convention, and it does not indicate any distinctive view of culture. "Hellas" is the term used for the province of Achaia (20:2), thus in accordance with the popular use of language. When a Jew is called ἑλληνιστής it only indicates that he uses the Greek language (6:1, 9:29).

In *Acts 17* Luke brings his reader to Athens and makes him a witness to a classical scene: the Christian missionary preaches for an audience that includes Epicurean and Stoic philosophers among others. We hear Luke's judgement on Athens and the Athenians: The city is full of idols (κατείδωλος), and the Athenians are all busy relating or cross examining new things. Even the foreigners who live among them are infected by this all-absorbing curiosity. These are the two main characteristics of the cradle and centre of the Greek culture. The Athenian *deisidaimonia* was proverbial and known everywhere. The Jew and the Christian, however, looked at it with particular feelings: Ever since Antiochus Epiphanes tried to Hellenize the Jews and their piety, Hellenism stood for paganism, for Satan and for the demons. Athens certainly was the stronghold and the main seat of godlessness. If we combine this view with the contemptuous characteristic of the Athenians and with the foolish appearance of the philosophers against Paul, it does not seem reasonable that Luke would have found any deeper meaning in this meeting between the Gospel and Hellas on the most classical ground of antiquity, a meeting that for us may be perceived as a world historical event. It is true that it is difficult to ward off the impression that something specific must have been intended with this unique scene: Paul on the Acropolis, but this still is to insert our understanding of history into the motives of the early Christian missionary author.

It is of course of a certain importance for our problem as to how we consider this part of Acts literarily and historically. If we are of the opinion that Luke has created the story about Paul in Athens all by himself, he may very well be influenced by his conviction that the scene on Acropolis was quite important, even if he treats the representatives of the culture of antiquity disrespectfully. If however, he builds upon an actual tradition (Harnack, Ed. Meyer) or he follows a literary cliché (Ed. Norden), then we do not need to evaluate the inner importance of this event. Luke has probably known and used a tradition about how Paul preached the Gospel in Athens. We do not know for certain what importance, if any, the philosophers already had in this tradition. It may, however, be worthwhile to note that the speech – which certainly is a literary composition based upon typical motives – does not use a general philosophical thesis as its starting point, but rather a *cultic* formula that could be used anywhere. Probably the philosophers have been part of the tradition concerning Paul's discussing with Stoics and Epicureans in Athens. Luke, for whom a "philosopher" was more or less identical with a professional cheat (see Lucian), has described them as unsympathetic and superficial listeners to the Apostle's message.

Having arrived at this negative result, we come to the greatest cultural personality of the early Church, the Apostle *Paul.* Born in Tarsus in Cilicia, he spoke Greek from his childhood and ever since his early youth he was well acquainted with Greek general education. Later he received a strictly Jewish form of training as a Pharisee and a disciple of Rabbi Gamaliel II, and finally he devoted his life to Christian mission in the Eastern and Northern Mediterranean countries, thus on Greek soil in the strict sense of the word. This career moved Paul widely within the cultural world of his time and deep into both a Jewish-Aramaic and a Hellenistic environment, while also lifting him above both of these spheres. This must have given him the best possible qualifications to develop an understanding of Hellenism as a cultural phenomenon and a spiritual power.

We must never forget, however, that Paul was no cool and objective observer; neither was he an open and receptive wanderer between two worlds. He was a missionary. He was deeply engaged in his vocation, and he did not think of anything else other than the winning of as many people as possible. We must also remember that Paul's thoughts are totally Jewish, shaped by the Old

Testament and the Jewish self-consciousness *vis-à-vis* "the ...nations." He brings both of these elements with him into his Christian thinking, but elevated them to a higher plain. Thus we can hardly expect to find comments on Hellenism, but rather reflections of the experiences that the Apostle had while working on Greek soil. Have these experiences influenced his letters in any way?

As could be expected, Paul, like the other New Testament authors, writes about the "nations" (τὰ ἔθνη), the undifferentiated non-Jewish Gentile world (e.g., Rom. 1:5,13, 3:29, 9:24, 11:13, 15:16,18, Gal. 1:16, chap. 2). And the word "Hellene" is used as a synonym for "Gentile," thus in a fixed phrase that occurs frequently, "Jew and Hellene" (Rom. 2:9ff., 3:9, 10:12, 1 Cor. 10:32). It is significant that the combination "Jews and Hellenes" is replaced by the combination "Jews and Gentiles" in 1 Cor. 1:22ff. At some places "Jews and Hellenes" is used in the meaning of "Jewish Christians and Gentile Christians" (Rom. 1:16, 1 Cor. 1:24, 12:13, Gal. 3:28, Col. 3:11).

Paul emphasizes many times when he writes about Jews and Hellenes (contrary to Jews and Judaizers) that the two groups are *in the same situation* as far as religion is concerned: Jews and Hellenes are all under sin (Rom. 3:9), there is no difference between Jews and Hellenes (Rom. 10:12), Jews and Hellenes are all baptized into one single body (1 Cor. 12:13), they are all one in Jesus Christ (Gal. 3:28, Col. 3.11). But sometimes he indicates a certain *difference* with the word πρῶτον in spite of the basic similarity. Salvation and judgement is given to all on the same conditions but *to the Jew first,* then to the Hellenes (Rom. 1:16, 2:9,10). Many scholars want to make this πρῶτον refer both to the Jew and to the Hellenes in a way that brings these two groups together and distinguishes them in relation to the rest of humanity. If this is so, then this wording is an interesting witness that Paul grants the Greek (those who live within the Greek culture) a spiritual advantage that gives him a higher *religious* position, just as the Jew has. Thus it is not necessarily according to Paul's spirit to identify the "nations" with the "Hellenes." When Paul describes the "Hellene" as the second human category beside the Jew and summarizes the whole of humanity in these two groups, this is because these are in fact the two groups among whom he is working.

This interpretation, which is fully possible grammatically (see Acts 26:20 for the word πρῶτον placed in between: τοῖς ἐν Δαμασκῷ πρῶτόν τε καὶ Ἱεροσολύμοις ... ἀπήγγελλον), is supported by the fact that Paul now and then differentiates between Hellenes and *barbarians:* "I am bound both to Greeks and non-Greeks, both to the wise and to the foolish," (Rom. 1:14), cf. Col. 3:11: "Here there is no Greek or Jew, circumcised or uncircumcised, barbarian, Scythian, slave or free." But "Jew and Greek" and "Hellene and barbarian" are rather two independent schemata, both of which cover all humanity. In Colossians the combination "Jews and Hellenes" is used synonymously with the following "circumcised and uncircumcised", and the combination barbarian[4] and the Scythian is hardly more than pleonasms.

None the less, it is certainly not unimportant that Paul knows and uses the contrast "Hellenes and barbarians" and adds the circumlocution "wise and foolish". Thus we find that Paul not only is conscious of Hellenism as the dominating cultural factor – something which is self-evident – but also that he values it for what it is. It is important for us to grasp this assessment.

When Paul gives the Jew the first place among all humans without distinction and without exception ('Ιουδαίῳ πρῶτον), he does so because of Israel's unique position as the elected people (Rom. 3:1f., 9:4ff.). Paul has never questioned this position: what is new in his proclamation is not that the advantage of the Jews was an empty imagination, but that the Gentiles in their totality were included in the blessing of Abraham (Gal. 3:6–8), that they now have received their share in the privileges of Israel (cf. the metaphor of the root and the branches in Rom. 11:17ff.). Thus far there is a total equality, but the Jews are and will remain the first according to salvation history, even if their majority for the time being has rejected salvation.

Paul thus calls the non-Jewish humanity "the nations" as well as "Hellenes." These two words are certainly interchangeable, but they are not identical. The Apostle also distinguishes between Greeks and barbarians. Now when "Hellenes" can replace the wider concept of "the nations" (the Gentiles), is this only possible because the majority of the peoples were Hellenistic and the Hellenes in fact were those Gentiles whom Paul encountered? Or is it possible that Paul looks upon the Hellene as *the typical Gentile?*

As has been mentioned above, this was the traditional Jewish view since the time of the Maccabees, and this view gained in strength through the success of Hellenism in Palestine under the Herodians. The Greek city culture brought with it an abundance of temples, altars, idols, Gentile cultic rites and events, but also prostitution, theatre, circus – all of these things belonging together and being abominations for the Jew. We find the reaction against all of this in the first two chapters of Romans. Paul, however, does not restrict himself to a general Jewish judgement upon the Hellenes as the most significant representatives of idolatry and the moral degeneration that was dependent upon this idolatry. The Hellene dominates the Gentile world because he represents *human self-glorification,* he adores *"wisdom."*

In Rom. 1:14 Paul uses the words σοφοὶ καὶ ἀνόητοι for "Hellenes and barbarians".[5] He, of course, considers his readers to be "wise" (cf. οὕτως etc. in

[4] We seem to find a combination of the two schemata "Jew and Hellene" and "Hellene and barbarian" in Col. 3:10. The Scythian probably represents the climax of barbarism. It is hardly possible, as is stated by Th. Hermann supported by late authors (in *Theologische Blätter* 1930, nr. 5), that the barbarian represents the black and the Scythian the white race.

[5] Like Kühl and Lietzmann I understand "Hellenes and barbarians" and "wise and foolish"

1:15 = so [i.e. because of my universal obligation] I am eager to preach the Gospel also to you who are in Rome); it is consistent that he declares in 1:16 that he is not ashamed of the Gospel, not even in Rome with its beauty. We can trace an unmistakably critical view of "wisdom" in these courteous words. Paul relates critically to this wisdom. We will not be surprised when we consider what he writes on "wisdom" in 1 Cor.

The Apostle constantly feels and experiences opposition both to Jews and to Hellenes: His message is a stumbling block to Jews and folly to Gentiles (1 Cor. 1:23). These words characterize the two groups mentioned in v 22: Jews demand signs, and the Hellenes seek "wisdom" (σοφία). Paul, however, has much in common with the Jews; his proclamation of righteousness and judgement, maybe even of a suffering Messiah, does not necessarily sound like meaningless words in their ears. But it sounds offensive to them that it is this crucified Galilean who is the Messiah, and it must necessarily be proven through great signs, that are irrefutable. There must be some kind of *legitimation.*

The Hellene looks upon this message in a totally different way. For him the message of the cross is folly. He has – contrary to the Jew – no inner connection to the Gospel, his thoughts are altogether in the categories of "wisdom." This wisdom is his great curse, since it caused the world to not understand God (οὐκ ἔγνω ὁ κόσμος διὰ τῆς σοφίας τὸν θεόν, 1:21). As a consequence humanity fell victim to idolatry as well as spiritual and moral degradation (Rom. 1:22: φάσκοντες εἶναι σοφοὶ ἐμωράνθησαν).

Thus what is typical for Hellenism stands out for Paul as a "wisdom" that is folly in the eyes of God, as human thoughts without any background in reality, as an illusion altogether contrary to "God's power." There is a deep chasm between Paul and Hellenism – or rather between all genuine Judaism and the Greek culture. In addition, the whole New Testament is on Paul's side. This makes it most problematic to formulate a synthesis of the Gospel and Hellenism. In spite of its Hellenization the New Testament remains not only non-Greek but even anti-Greek.

It is not possible here to discuss in any detail how Paul comprehends Greek "wisdom." A few points must be made, however. The contrast between the Hellene wisdom and the *pneumatic* wisdom which Paul prefers to find among mature Christians (1 Cor. 2:6ff.) is enlightening. This latter wisdom reveals God's transcendent mystery of salvation. Greek wisdom, on the other hand, is

to be parallel expressions for the same thing. Most scholars are of another opinion. The first expression is said to distinguish between languages, the second between education och spirituality. They together include the whole of humanity without distinction; thus it is wrong to ask where to place the Romans. Thus, e.g., Jülicher, Zahn, Lagrange, R.A. Lipsius, Sanday-Headlam, O. Holtzmann. But this interpretation fails on the words that follow: "I am not ashamed ..." Paul here stands face to face with "wisdom", with the "Hellenistic culture". We will discuss later on what is meant when the barbarians are characterized as ἀνόητοι.

totally worldly, tied to this age and its rulers, destined as they are for destruction. The Greek world-view and life style looks like that for the Apostle – correctly so from his presuppositions. As Paul rejects this worldly culture he also instinctively rejects Greek rhetoric and dialectic (οὐκ ἐν σοφίᾳ λόγου 1:17; οὐκ ἐν πειθοῖ[ς] σοφίας [λόγοις] 2:4), the *artistry of words* that is the legitimate child of this culture.

It seems strange against this background that Paul in Rom. 1:14 writes about the "wise" Hellene in contrast to the barbarian who is said to be ἀνόητος. The word ἀνόητος is often translated "uneducated" – hardly its correct meaning – thus presupposing that Paul places the barbarian lower than the Greek. But if there is some kind of polemical irony in the word σοφοί, then we may also understand ἀνόητοι *cum grano salis:* It is the Greek, in his self-conscious cultural pride, who characterizes the barbarian in this way – he is stupid. Paul himself would probably prefer the naiveté of the barbarian to the intelligent and flexible thinking of the Greek (see Juvenal's third satire).

Thus we have found that Paul distances himself from Hellenism as he has encountered and experienced it and considers it as totally unrelated to the Gospel, that is where he expresses himself concerning it. We may speak of a *negative* result in the full meaning of this word. This result is interesting and unusual in a person who owes Hellas so much as the Apostle did. Did he really have no feeling for his debt to Hellenism? Did he lack all understanding of the invaluable preparation for the mission to the world that the Greeks had made in so many ways?

His immediate and spontaneous relation to Hellenism shows, however, that this is the case. Language and concepts, views and forms of style were his spiritual inheritance from his early childhood and on. The synthesis of his spiritual heritage – Judaism, and later on the Gospel – and Greek philosophical categories was made unconsciously and by itself. For this reason Paul is able to criticize so devastatingly the culture which was the air which he breathed so to speak.

Thus this criticism is not ingratitude, but rather the necessary result of his religious might. It is the reaction of this powerful religiosity against his rich experiences of Hellenism. This is typical for Paul. He always takes a strong position on any question; he judges and decides without any compromises. And we must admit that he takes a negative position with full right; the contradiction between Hellas and the New Testament in its totality is well expressed by Paul. In his strong religious personality the latent tension becomes an open and implacable contradiction. When we consider the problem of Hellenism in Paul, we must study the larger historical problem of the early Church, a problem that is hidden in the fact that a Semitic spiritual inheritance conquered a Greek milieu only to become absorbed into it. This led to a Hellenization, which, however, never became thorough. Early Christianity, even in its Hellenized form, remained a religion based upon Judaism, upon the Old Testament and upon the history of Palestine, i. e. it remained non-Greek in its basis.

By pointing this out and emphasizing it, I want to add something to Rudberg's valuable treatment of "Hellas and the New Testament." All of the specific observations that have been gathered and systematized are united on a higher level by Rudberg's conception of a cultural synthesis, its essence, laws and expressions. There is also another basis however: Rudberg poses the question about the enduring distinctive character of the New Testament, even when the Gospel was rephrased and absorbed into its new environment. He finds the answer in Jesus Christ, the creative personality (pp. 252ff.), who organized and developed the synthesis.

We have reached the central and decisive point. Rudberg, however, goes on to emphasize that "Hellas and Christianity also means opposition up to this very day ..." (p. 251). He expounds his views, in the main, from the idea that history is created through cooperation and antagonism between opposing, but at the same time convergent powers. Thus the relationship between Christianity and Greek culture and religion was not a mortal but a fruitful opposition. I want to stress and throw light upon this important idea by emphasizing that the Greek New Testament itself knows Hellas as a mortal enemy, but at the same time uses the riches of this enemy. This is most clear in Paul, who has left his personal stamp on the synthesis of the Gospel and Hellenism and has given voice to what was unconscious for the others.

This strange fact throws light upon all the detailed work within the field of the relation between Christianity and Hellenism. Here we can find the reason why the analysis of New Testament words and concepts (like "righteousness", "truth", "flesh", "knowledge", "perfection" etc.) is so problematic. It also throws light, however, on burning questions in the world of Christian culture today, a Christianity that is conscious of its spiritual inheritance and experiences the contradictions in it as a real problem. Here history may be our teacher and show us the way to go by revealing the very laws of history.

“Sich selbst verleugnen”

(1936)

Mc 8,34 lesen wir:

εἴ τις θέλει ὀπίσω μου ἐλθεῖν,
(1) ἀπαρνησάσθω ἑαυτὸν καὶ
(2) ἀράτω τὸν σταυρὸν αὐτοῦ,
καὶ ἀκολουθείτω (= ἵνα ἀκολουθῇ) μοι.

Die Paralleltexte bei Mt (16,24) und Lc (9,23) zeigen nur unbedeutende Varianten: Lc hat (1) ἀρνησάσθω und (2) καθ' ἡμέραν.

In der Logiendublette (Mt 10, 38f.; Lc 14, 27) fehlt die Selbstverleugnung, und das bestätigt den unmittelbaren Eindruck, den man schon von der Marcusrecension bekommt, daß bei Mc eine pleonastische Erweiterung vorliegt, es werden synonyme Leidensworte gehäuft. Kreuztragen und Selbstverleugnung sind sachlich eng verwandte urchristliche Leidenstermini. Ihr allgemeiner Sinn ist einigermaßen klar, kann aber vielleicht etwas schärfer gefaßt werden, als es gewöhnlich geschieht. Besonders gilt das dem eigentümlichen ἀπαρνεῖσθαι ἑαυτὸν, das als sprachliche Erscheinung einzig dasteht und nicht ganz eindeutig ist. Hier soll ein Versuch gcmacht werden, die Deutungsmöglichkeiten näher zu umreißen.

Ein durchgängiger Fehler bei der Auslegung dieses Wortes ist der, daß man nicht aufmerksam genug auf die nahe Beziehung zu dem folgenden Worte *“sein Kreuz aufnehmen”* achtet. Gewöhnlich bewegt man sich auch in ziemlich losen sprachlichen Assoziationen. – Fast durch die ganze Geschichte der Auslegung geht die Ansicht, daß die Selbstverleugnung eine rein *geistige Haltung* ist. “Sich selbst verleugnen” heißt, sein altes, natürlich-menschliches Wesen aufgeben oder es unterdrücken, bekämpfen. Bald faßt man das mehr radikal-religiös, bald mehr psychologisch-ethisch auf. Zur ersteren Kategorie gehören z.B. Origenes (der sogar an Gal. 2,20 denkt!), Chrysostomus,[1] Schoettgen, Gould, Schlatter, Schniewind (“sich selbst nicht kennen, ein völlig neues Ich!”). Zur späteren (alle seine menschlichen Wünsche verneinen, den eigenen Willen opfern, alle persönlichen Neigungen bekämpfen): Greg. Nyss., H. und

[1] ἡ παντελὴς τῶν παρελθόντων λήθη, καὶ ἡ τῶν θελημάτων αὐτοῦ ἀναχώρησις.

O. Holtzmann, Wohlenberg, Dausch, Hauck ("harter Selbstverzicht"), W. Bauer ("vollkommen selbstlos handeln, seine Persönlichkeit aufgeben"), wohl auch E. Klostermann ("seine ganze Person aufgeben")[2].

Das Verb ἀπαρνεῖσθαι wird dabei als "nicht kennen wollen", jede Beziehung ablehnen, gedeutet, so z. B. B. Weiss ("sein eigenes Wesen als fremdes behandeln"), Lagrange, Zorell, Schlatter ("dem Ich die Gemeinschaft aufsagen"), Schniewind (s. o.)[3].

Gegen diese an sich ansprechende Auslegung – "sich selbst verleugnen" d. h. sein altes Ich nicht mehr kennen wollen, wäre ein höchst expressiver Ausdruck für die Wiedergeburt oder Bekehrung[4] –, machen sich nun Bedenken geltend. Vor allen Dingen wegen der engen Nachbarschaft zum Begriff der Kreuzaufnahme. Zwar ist auch dieses Wort nicht eindeutig[5]. Aber soviel ist jedenfalls klar, daß das Kreuztragen mit *äußeren* Umständen verknüpft ist. Die Selbstverleugnung als synonymer Begriff wird also kaum auf die Wiedergeburt des Ichs zu beziehen sein; etwas rein praktisches ist von Anfang sicher damit gemeint.

Dieses praktische ist aber in der kirchlichen Auslegung spiritualisert worden, bis in die neueste Behandlung von Schlier hinein (*Theol. Wörterbuch* I 471), der ἀπαρνεῖσθαι ἑαυτόν im Gegensatz zu ὁμολογεῖν ἑαυτόν faßt: "Ich soll mich nicht zu mir, zu meinem Wesen bekennen und mich an mir festhalten, sondern mich in radikalem Verzicht auf mich selbst (nicht nur auf meine Sünden) preisgeben." Wie das zu verstehen ist, geht aus den folgenden Worten hervor: "Ich soll nicht mehr von mir aus mein Leben sicherstellen, sondern im Gegenteil in Entschlossenheit den eigenen Tod ergreifend von Christus mich sicherstellen lassen in der Nachfolge."

Die Selbstverleugnung ist also der Gegensatz zur Selbstbehauptung. Das mag als allgemeine Definition gelten. Aber was für Selbstbehauptung soll hier verneint und vernichtet werden? Sicher nicht die allgemeine Selbstbehauptung der menschlichen Persönlichkeit, des Ichs. Sondern ganz einfach der *Selbsterhaltungstrieb* (das θέλειν σῶσαι τὴν ψυχὴν αὐτοῦ Mc 8, 35). Es handelt sich um "die Sicherstellung des Lebens" in ganz konkretem Sinne; diese soll "preisgegeben" werden.

Im Gegensatz zur traditionellen Auslegung wird man behaupten müssen, daß "sich selbst verleugnen" an sich ein *ebenso profaner Ausdruck ist, wie "sein Kreuz aufnehmen" es von Haus aus war.*[6] Das spezifisch Religiöse liegt im Begriff ἀκολουθεῖν, der die beiden Worte umrahmt.

---

[2] Theophylakt sogar rein asketisch: τὸ ἡμετέρου σώματος ἀφειδεῖν.

[3] Vgl. Chrysostomus μηδὲν ἐχέτω κοινὸν πρὸς ἑαυτόν.

[4] Als religiöse Begriffsbildung würde er in ein jüdisches Milieu sehr gut hineinpassen!

[5] Ich werde nächstens auch dieses Wort behandeln, anschließend an meine Ausführungen in der (norwegischen) Festschrift für Lyder Brun, Oslo 1922.

[6] Mit Recht sagt von Campenhausen (*Die Idée des Martyriums in der alten Kirche,* 1936, S. 59, 3): "Es ist fraglich, wieweit hier überhaupt an den Kreuzweg Jesu gedacht ist und nicht eine ältere volkstümliche Redewendung zugrunde liegt".

Sprachlich wird es sicher unrichtig sein, ἀπαρνεῖσθαι ἑαυτόν aus der Bedeutung "nicht kennen wollen", die Bekanntschaft leugnen, herzuleiten. Vielmehr hat ἀπαρν. ἑαυτόν in diesem sprachlichen Zusammenhang einen *abgeschliffenen* Sinn, in dem freilich der Ursinn (sich irgendwie negativ zu etwas verhalten) klar hervorleuchtet. Persönlich bin ich der Überzeugung, daß ἀπαρν. ἑαυτόν die griechische Entsprechung zu dem offenbaren Aramaismus μισεῖν τὴν ψυχὴν ἑαυτοῦ ist[7]. Ob dabei ἀπαρνεῖσθαι ἑαυτόν eine *echt* griechische Bildung ist oder eine gräzisierende Nachbildung nach dem Aramäischen, ist bei der extremen Knappheit des Materials kaum zu entscheiden. Wie aber dem auch sei, klar ist, daß das (ἀπ)αρνεῖσθαι in dieser Beziehung (sich preisgeben, sein Leben aufs Spiel setzen, jede Vorsicht aufgeben) eine Bedeutungsentwicklung *innerhalb dem Griechischen* voraussetzt, die zur Bedeutung "preisgeben" geführt hat.

So weit ich sehe, sind Belege für die oben angenommene profane Bedeutung von ἀπαρνεῖσθαι mit persönlichem Objekt in der Gräzität selten. Wir haben solche Beispiele hauptsächlich in religiösen Zusammenhängen. Aber auch aus diesen läßt sich etwas erschließen. Eine Gottheit verleugnen heißt von ihr abfallen, ihren Kult aufgeben – das ist eine wohlbekannte sprachliche Erscheinung. Neben dem oft zitierten Jes. 31, 7 LXX τῇ ἡμέρᾳ ἐκείνῃ ἀπαρνήσονται[8] οἱ ἄνθρωποι τὰ χειροποίητα αὐτῶν kommt in Betracht Lucian, *De morte Peregrini* 337 ἐπειδὰν ἅπαξ παραβάντες θεοὺς μὲν τοὺς Ἑλληνικοὺς ἀπαρνήσωνται, τὸν δὲ ἀνεσκολοπισμένον ἐκεῖνον σοφιστὴν αὐτῶν προσκυνῶσι. – Wie man sieht, handelt es sich um ein äußeres, rein praktisches Verhalten: Man kehrt der betreffenden Gottheit den Rücken und geht zu einer anderen über (παραβάντες, s.o.). Von einer mündlichen oder gar inneren Absage ist keine Rede. Der Gegensatz zu ἀπαρνεῖσθαι ist nicht ὁμολογεῖν sondern προσκυνεῖν (s. die Lucianstelle).

Das wird natürlich anders in den christlichen Evangelien, wo eine *Verfolgungssituation* vorausgesetzt wird. Der Gläubige muß der Obrigkeit wegen seines Glaubens an Christus Rede stehen. Da bekommt ἀπαρνεῖσθαι seine Antithese in ὁμολογεῖν (die beiden Wörter bilden in der Sprache ein Gegensatzpaar, Joh. 1, 20, und bekommen jetzt einen vertieften Inhalt). In diesen Zusammenhängen erhält ἀπαρνεῖσθαι einen mündlichen, deklarativen, Charakter.[9]

Ganz besonders wird das natürlich der Fall in der Leidensgeschichte bei der *Verleugnung des Petrus*. Hier spitzt sich das ἀπαρνεῖσθαι auf eine Formel zu:

---

[7] Das haben mehrere Exegeten des großen humanistischen Zeitalters der Auslegung (z.B. Rosenmüller und Kuinoel) gesehen. Sie umschreiben ἀπ. ἑ. mit *"vitam suam contemnere"*, *"desertor sui"*, *"sui prodigus"*, und verweisen auf Lc 14, 26; Jes. 31, 7 LXX. – Bengel zieht Lc 14, 33 heran: ἀποτάξασθαι πᾶσιν τοῖς ἑαυτοῦ ὑπάρχουσιν (so schon Palladius, *Hist. Laus.* 64). Das ist zu eng.

[8] יִמְאָסוּן.

[9] Cf. Joh. 1, 21 Mt 10, 33; Lc 12, 9.

Ich kenne ihn nicht![10] Das ist aber durch den epischen Zusammenhang bedingt. Es wäre verfehlt, von hier aus die anderen Worte, die von Verleugnung Christi sprechen, inhaltlich und sprachlich zu bestimmen. Auch wo ἀπαρνεῖσθαι seine Antithese in ὁμολογεῖν hat, braucht es sich nicht immer oder vorwiegend um mündliches Bekennen und Verleugnen zu handeln, sondern es kann das praktische Verhalten, das Verhehlen seines Glaubens wenigstens miteinbegriffen sein[11].

Werfen wir nun einen Blick auf die übrigen Aussagen mit ἀπαρνεῖσθαι im NT.

1 Tim. 5, 8 Wer nicht seine nächsten Familienpflichten erfüllt, ἤρνηται τὴν πίστιν und ist schlimmer als ein Ungläubiger. Das bedeutet wohl weder daß er (subjektiv) dem Glauben Gehorsam verweigert, noch (objektiv) daß er sich in offenbaren Widerspruch zum Wesen des Glaubens gesetzt hat, sondern einfach: Er ist vom Christentum abgefallen, und so ist er schlimmer als einer, der nie Christ war. Umgekehrt Tit. 3, 12 ἀρνησάμενοι τὴν ἀσέβειαν καὶ τὰς κοσμικὰς ἐπιθυμίας: dem Heidentum den Rücken kehren und ein neues Leben führen (ἵνα ... σωφρόνως καὶ δικαίως καὶ εὐσεβῶς ζήσωμεν). An den Eindruck auf die Umgebung ist bei ἀρνησάμενοι nicht ausdrücklich gedacht[12].

2 Tim. 3, 5, am Schluß eines Lasterkataloges ἔχοντες μόρφωσιν εὐσεβείας, τὴν δὲ δύναμιν αὐτῆς ἠρνημένοι. Auch hier wieder wird es sich nicht um den äußeren Eindruck handeln: Äußerlich dem Christentum gehörig, zeigen sie durch ihr Verhalten, daß sie die lebendige und lebensgestaltende Kraft des Christentums nicht besitzen (so *Wohlenberg:* "Schreiender Widerspruch" zwischen Lehre und Leben). Sondern man muß μόρφωσις und δύναμις als *Gegensatzpaar* verstehen, nicht tote Form und lebendige Kraft, sondern äußere Form und innerer Lebenskern (ἡ δύναμις = ἡ ἀλήθεια). Mit dem Perfektum ἠρνημένοι muß Ernst gemacht werden: Diese Leute haben definitiv mit dem wahren, echten Christentum gebrochen, sind davon abgefallen. Bei *Wohlenbergs* Deutung sollte man wenigstens ἀρνούμενοι erwarten[13].

Die übrigen Stellen haben für unsere Frage weniger Belang, weil nämlich da (ἀπ)αρνεῖσθαι nicht im abgeschliffenen Sinne als gewißermaßen technisches

---

[10] Mc 14, 68.

[11] Beachtenswert in diesem Zusammenhang ist die Variante des Verleugnungswortes bei Mc (8, 38): ὃς ἐὰν ἐπαισχυνθῇ με, das natürlich nicht nur auf die Stimmung, sondern auch, und vorwiegend, auf die Rückhaltung des Jüngers Bezug nimmt, er will nicht als Christ hervortreten.

[12] Ähnlich 4 Mac 8, 7 ἀρνηθέντες τὸν πάτριον ἡμῶν τῆς πολιτείας θεσμὸν καὶ μεταλαβόντες ἑλληνικοῦ βίου, vgl. 10, 15 οὐκ ἀρνήσομαι τὴν εὐγενῆ ἀδελφότητα: "ich werde (durch meinen Abfall) mich nicht von meinen Brüdern scheiden." Vgl. auch Joseph. *c. Ap.* 1, 191 μὴ ἀρνούμεθα τὰ πάτρια.

[13] B. Weiss übersetzt "nicht anerkennen", Schlatter: sie leugnen die Möglichkeit einer neuen Lebensgestaltung. Die Verleugnung geschieht aber durch die gesammte Lebenshaltung, nicht durch einen bewußten Denk- oder Willensakt.

Wort auftritt, sondern der *Inhalt* der Verneinung ist irgendwie angegeben oder geht aus dem Zusammenhang hervor.

Tit. 1, 16 θεὸν ὁμολογοῦσιν εἰδέναι, τοῖς δὲ ἔργοις ἀρνοῦνται sc. εἰδέναι αὐτόν: durch ihr praktisches Verhalten strafen sie ihre theoretische Bekenntnis Lüge, es liegt ein offenbarer Widerspruch vor zwischen Lehre und Leben bezüglich des εἰδέναι τὸν θεόν. – Ferner Mc. 14, 68. 70 m. Par.; Lc 8, 45; 22, 34; Joh. 18, 20; 18, 25. 27; AG. 4,16 (eine Tatsache leugnen); Heb. 11, 25 (sich weigern); 1 Joh. 2,22. Zu bemerken ist, daß der Inhalt der Verneinung, statt in einem Satze oder Infinitiv (Partizipium) entwickelt zu werden, in ein nominales Objekt konzentriert werden kann; so wird 1 Joh. 2, 22 dieser Inhalt mit einem ὅτι-Satz angegeben, im folgenden Verse steht gleichbedeutend ὁ ἀρνούμενος τὸν υἱόν, offenbar eine gekürzte Ausdrucksweise. Ähnlich Lc 22,34 ἕως τρίς με ἀπαρνήσῃ εἰδέναι und σήμερον ἀπαρνήσῃ με τρίς.[14] – Ferner fallen die Stellen weg, wo der Zusammenhang die Verneinung bestimmt: AG. 3, 13f., wo ἠρνήσασθε (den ihnen von Pilatus *anerbotenen* Jesus *ablehnen)* durch das folgende ᾐτήσασθε (sich ausbitten) bestimmt. – Ferner AG. 7,35: "Die Verleugnung von Mose besteht in der Frage: Wer hat dich zum Führer und Richter über uns eingesetzt?" – es handelt sich um die Ablehnung des Führer*anspruches* des Mose. Zu übersetzten ist etwa "Sie lehnten sich gegen Mose auf" ("den sie fortgestoßen hatten", *Beyer,* ist nicht ganz gelungen). – Ebenso Jud. 5 = 2 Petr 2, 1 dem δεσπότης den ihm zukommenden Gehorsam verweigern. Das man einem Gott seine Herrscherrechte vorenthält, wird auch außerhalb des NT mit ἀρνεῖσθαι ausgedrückt: Babrius (ed. Crusius) 152: Ein Rabe gelobte in der Not dem Apollo ein Opfer und wurde gerettet, hielt aber sein Gelübde nicht. Wieder in Not geraten ἀφεὶς τὸν Ἀπόλλωνα τῷ Ἑρμῇ ὑπέσχεν θῦσαι. ὁ δὲ πρὸς αὐτὸν ἔφη· ὦ κάκιστε, πῶς σοι πιστεύσω, ὃς τὸν πρότερόν σου δεσπότην ἠρνήσω καὶ ἠδίκησας[15];

Mit 2 Tim. 2,12 kehren wir zu ἀπαρν. ἑαυτόν zurück.

> εἰ ἀρνησάμεθα, κἀκεῖνος ἀρνήσεται ἡμᾶς.
> εἰ ἀπιστοῦμεν, ἐκεῖνος πιστὸς μένει,
> ἀπαρνήσασθαι γὰρ ἑαυτὸν οὐ δύναται.

---

[14] Vgl. *Die Briefe des Sokrates und der Sokratiker,* herausgeg. von Liselotte Köhler, p. 15, 25 ἀπαρνῆται ποιητικήν, gleich nachher φησὶν μηδὲν εἶναι ποίημα αὐτοῦ. *Anthol. Graec.* ed. Stadtmüller VII 473 (von zwei Selbstmördern): ζωὰν (= τὸ ζῆν) ἀπηρνήσαντο.

[15] Man kann hier fragen, ob die Verleugnung darin besteht, daß der Rabe den alten Herrn im Stich ließ (ἀφείς), oder darin, daß er ihm das gelobte Opfer nicht brachte. Ich halte das spätere für richtig. Nach griechischem Empfinden war der Übergang zu einer anderen Gottheit etwas durchaus normales. Also: "Wie soll ich dir Glauben schenken, wenn du deinem vorigen Herrn dein Gelübde nicht hieltst und ihm (so) schädigtest" (zu ἀδικεῖν = ökonomisch schädigen vgl. 2 Petr. 2,13).

"Wenn wir ihn preisgeben,
wird auch er uns preisgeben.
Wenn wir untreu sind,
bleibt er treu (seinem Worte, seiner Verheißung),
Denn er kann sich selbst nicht aufgeben."

In dem hier zitierten λόγος braucht nicht an die Verleugnung vor dem Richterstuhl gedacht zu sein[16], eine mündliche Absage, sondern ἀρνεῖσθαι ist, wie so oft, abfallen, preisgeben[17]. Dieselbe Bedeutung ist natürlich im abschließenden Satz zu finden: Christus kann sich selbst, seine Existenz, nicht aufgeben. Das würde er tun, wenn er seinem Heilswort und Heilswerk untreu werden wollte, das wäre seine Selbstaufgabe, das würde seine durch Tod und Auferstehung erkämpfte Stellung vernichten. Von einer Verleugnung des eigenen "Wesens", einem In-Widerspruch-Sein mit seinem eigenen Ich, ist nicht die Rede. Ein solcher Gedanke würde außerdem einen *praesentischen* Infinitiv, nicht Aorist, erfordern[18].

Wir sind am Ende. Was Christus als göttliches Wesen nicht kann und darf, das muß sein menschlicher Jünger auf der Erde tun, wenn er am göttlichen Leben seines Herrn Anteil bekommen will: Sich selbst preisgeben, seine ganze Existenz aufs Spiel setzen, ἀπαρνεῖσθαι ἑαυτόν[19].

---

[16] Die Anspielung auf das Logion Mt 10, 33 ist klar, aber auch in diesem Wort ist nicht nur an mündliche Verleugnung gedacht. – Das gilt auch von Apoc. 2, 13; 3,8.

[17] Die Gemeinschaft brechen, nicht: sie leugnen.

[18] Es sollte klar sein, daß V. 13 den Gedanken des vorausgehenden λόγος umbiegt ("Paradox", Dibelius) und nicht ihn fortsetzt (so auch jetzt Joach. Jeremias). Jedoch wird dieser Gedanke auch nicht verneint und aufgehoben, denn ἀπιστεῖν ist weniger als der Abfall; es ist die Schwäche des Gläubigen, die sich an der unveränderlich festen Treue des Heilandes immer aufs Neue aufrichten muß.

[19] Ich freue mich der Übereinstimmung mit Rengstorf, dessen Lucas-Kommentar ich eben bei Abschluß dieses Aufsatzes zu Gesicht bekam (Neues Göttinger Bibelverk 3, 1937, S. 107): "... völliger Bruch mit dem Verfahren, daß man zuerst an sich denkt und *darauf bedacht ist, daß die Menschen einem Wohlgesinnt sind*" (von mir kursiviert). Das ist ein Bruch mit der traditionellen Auslegung, den ich lebhaft begrüße. Eine sprachliche Begründung fehlt leider. Als formale und sachliche Parallele zu Mt. 10,33; 2 Tim. 2,12 vgl. Hos. 4,6 LXX:

ὅτι σὺ ἐπίγνωσιν ἀπώσω,
κἀγὼ ἀπώσομαί σε ...
καὶ ἐπελάθου νόμον θεοῦ σου,
κἀγὼ ἐπιλήσομαι τέκνων σου.

und 1 Reg. 2,30 LXX:

τοὺς δοξάζοντάς με δοξάσω,
καὶ ὁ ἐξουθενῶν με ἀτιμωθήσεται.

Acts 26, 28

(1938)

King Agrippas' famous reply to Paul: ἐν ὀλίγῳ με πείθεις χριστιανὸν ποιῆσαι, has been the object of many reflections and comments, although, in reality, its composition is grammatically perfectly clear and the sense quite perspicuous. It is rather strange that interpreters should have approached Agrippas' words so enquiringly and perplexedly. A closer study of Greek grammar would have saved them quite a lot of superfluous reflections, and other people from several impracticable ideas and suggestions.[1]

We may at once disregard the Byzantine version χριστιανὸν γενέσθαι instead of χριστ. ποιῆσαι. Zahn prefers χριστ. γενέσθαι on the assumption that ποιῆσαι is *"sinnlos"*. Even Clark speaks of this version as being "absurd" (*The Acts of the Apostles,* Oxford 1933, p. 383), although he rejects γενέσθαι as a conjecture (p. LII).

The majority of interpreters have, however, attempted other ways out of the difficulty. The easiest way is, with A, to read πείθῃ (Clark, Naylor, *Class. Review* 1914, p. 227 ss.) or with Westcott-Hort to conjecture a πέποιθας: "In a short time thou takest it upon thyself to make me a Christian!" A peculiar suggestion is put forward by Whitaker (*Journal of Theol. Studies,* 1914, p. 82 s.): ἐν ὀλίγῳ με πείθειν χριστιανὸν ποιῆσαι "Don't trouble thyself to make me a Christian!" Usually, however the interpreters accept the most certified and apparently most difficult text:

ἐν ὀλίγῳ με πείθεις χριστιανὸν ποιῆσαι.

It is then the difficulties – unnecessarily – arise. Temporarily putting aside ἐν ὀλίγῳ we can register the following translations: "Thou persuadest me to make a Christian" i.e. to become a missionary, or: "to play the Christian" *(christianum agere,* cp. Schmiedel, *Encycl. Bibl.* I 754, Nairne, *Journ. of Theol. Stud.* 1920, p. 171). This is rejected with all justification by Clark (op. cit. LXII). – In his commentary on Acts, Wendt finds in this passage a contamination of two different constructions, a) Thou intendest to make me a Christian, and b) Thou persuadest me to become a Christian, – an unacceptable explanation! It is

[1] I have treated the question previously in *Symbolae Osloenses* IX, 1935; here I add some new points of view.

easier to think of a contraction of με πείθεις (ὥστε) χριστ. ποιῆσαί (με), "Thou tryest to win me over (so as) to make (me) a Christian".

One would have been spared all these artifices if the interpreters had considered what the Greek grammar has to say about the Accusative with the Infinitive: Where the Infinitive has the same Subject as the Principal Verb the Subject may be omitted. *The same thing applies to the Object* (cp. Kühner-Gerth 3rd ed. § 476, 2). Just at πείθω we find a very short abbreviation, cp. Xenophon *Mem.* I, 2, 49 ἀλλὰ Σωκράτης γ' ἔφη ὁ κατήγορος, τοὺς πατέρας προπηλακίζειν ἐδίδασκε, πείθων μὲν τοὺς συνόντας αὐτῷ σοφωτέρους ποιεῖν τῶν πατέρων. The complete sentence should be: πείθων τοὺς συνόντας αὐτῷ (ἑαυτὸν) σοφωτέρους ποιεῖν (αὐτοὺς) τῶν πατέρων. Now Acts 26, 28 is completely analogous: ἐν ὀλίγῳ με πείθεις (σεαυτὸν) χριστιανὸν ποιῆσαι (με). Syntactically the much discussed sentence is clear as crystal water. But in what relation does the positive content stand with the given grammatical interpretation?

It gives an excellent meaning! Paul has, in the speech for his defence, dealt with the resurrection of the dead and appealed to the King's belief in the Scriptures: πιστεύεις, βασιλεῦ 'Αγρίππα; οἶδα ὅτι πιστεύεις. Thus it is not a case of getting Agrippa to *become* a Christian, but Paul *presumes* that Agrippa believes in the Scriptures, he is a *"Believer"* (πιστεύων, the first Christians called themselves οἱ πιστεύοντες). This is too much for Agrippa, and irritated he exclaims: "You will make me believe that you, in the turn of a hand (ἐν ὀλίγῳ is to be connected with ποιῆσαι) have made me a Christian", i. e. *you treat me as if I were a Christian already!* There is much more irritation than irony in this word. Paul has pressed him too hard.

'Εν ὀλίγῳ can only mean "in a short time", not "with little effort" or "almost" (παρ' ὀλίγον, ὀλίγου δεῖ, ὀλίγου), cp. Blass ad. loc. To ἐν ὀλίγῳ = "in no time" cp. Polyb. XI, 16 τοῦτο δ' ἐστὶν ἐν ὀλίγῳ: "this goes in a hurry".

Paul's reply to the King is connected to the latter's formulation; the Apostle plays with words. It is in the nature of the play on words that it inflects the meaning of the expression which it makes its point of departure.[2] Therefore it is quite in order that Paul continues with καὶ ἐν ὀλίγῳ καὶ ἐν μεγάλῳ instead of, as we should expect, ἐν πολλῷ. But what does Paul mean by this surprising inflection of the King's phrase? Does he wish to say "howsoever", "in all circumstances", cp. 1 Macc. 3, 18 ἐν πολλοῖς ἢ ἐν ὀλίγοις, and 2 Chron. 14, 11 LXX οὐκ ἀδυνατεῖ παρὰ σοὶ σώζειν ἐν πολλοῖς καὶ ἐν ὀλίγοις). The line of demarcation between ὀλίγος and μικρός, πολύς and μέγας was not so pronounced in later Greek (cp. Hesseling, *Neophilologus* 1935, p. 129 ss.). I believe, however, that the sentence may be understood otherwise. The word order denotes that ἐν ὀλίγῳ καὶ ἐν μεγάλῳ is to be connected with εὐξαίμην ἄν,

---

[2] This is rightly argued by Lake and Cadbury in *Beginn. of Christianity* IV 1933, p. 322 ss.

not with the following γενέσθαι, and certainly we may suppose that these prepositional expressions with ἐν are equivalents to a dativus commodi: "I would to God, *concerning both small and great,* that all were as I". In ἐν μεγάλῳ lies assuredly an allusion to the King: Be it a person of low rank or the great and mighty of the world (οἱ μεγάλοι), Paul maintains his message indifferently. To the construction with ἐν equal to dativus commodi cp. 1 Cor. 14, 11; Gal. 1, 16 (H. Ljungvik, *Studien zu Sprache der apokryphen Apostelgeschichten,* 1926, p. 33).

Thus we must translate as follows: Agrippa: "You will make me believe that you, in small time, have made me a Christian". Paul: "I would to God, concerning both small and great, that not only You but also all that hear me today, were such as I am, except these bonds".

The Unity of the New Testament

(1941)

The subject of the unity of the New Testament is concerned with a question which is of central significance both for theology and for the Church: Is there in the New Testament a fundamental and pervading inner unity? Or do these very old, classical documents of Christianity deviate from one another, and represent different, incompatible types of religion, among which we must choose the one and reject the other? The question of the historical nucleus of Christianity is a *religio-historical* problem of the first magnitude. At the same time it is also a major *theological* problem, for here we stand at the foundations of the doctrine of faith. It is no less an ecclesiastical concern both for the servant of the Word and for the ordinary Bible reader: how is the strongly diversified witness of the New Testament to be understood? Does the same faith and one invariable ideal of life exist everywhere in the NT?

It is quite natural and necessary, following the discovery of the inner diversity of the New Testament, that scholarship should occupy itself primarily and most eagerly with this diversity. When it was found that the New Testament had a history, a new discovery with vast consequences had been made, – not merely a history of the Canon, but also an *inner* history. It became clear that the basic fact of history, Jesus, in his continued effects in interplay with historical circumstances, produced a great variety of expressions of faith, preaching, church life and theology, all of which were committed to writing in a literature, of which we still have a substantial part in the New Testament. The question is: Has this inner history, which cannot be denied, perhaps ruptured the original unity, missed its connection with the starting-point, produced new variations of religion, which the Church has held together and preserved in the mistaken belief that all these different matters were one and the same thing?

It was Ferdinand Chr. Baur, the great Tübingen theologian, who exactly one hundred years ago was the first one to see and formulate clearly the religio-historical problem of early Christianity, and thereby that of the New Testament. This problem ever since has incessantly occupied theological research, in which, as it is well-known, very different and conflicting standpoints have been put forth. The battle has often been intense and the waves run high in the ecclesiastical storms, which blew up along the paths of the theological debate.

In a field such as early Christianity, where so much is obscure, the debate can never stop or come to rest. Scholarship is constantly confronted with new finds and observations, and old views must be taken up for renewed examination, demanded by the questions of each generation. But it is obvious that the question of the *unity* of the New Testament has lately come to the foreground in connection with the study of the outlook and characteristics of the various groups of the New Testament writings. One does not wish to see only the differences but also the fundamental connection. Behind this attempt lies *inter alia* a deeper insight into and perception of the Jesus tradition and the person of Jesus, an understanding that has been facilitated by many different factors, which cannot be analysed here. However, *one* factor will be mentioned here briefly. This is the insight into the *eschatological* character of the New Testament.

Wherever one may turn within the province of the New Testament, one meets the fundamental conviction that with Jesus Christ a new epoch has been initiated in the life and situation of the world. This new epoch, however, is not a historical phase which has succeeded an older one in order that it may itself be succeeded by another one. The new era is the final one (τὸ ἔσχατον). In the expression "the final time" there lies primarily not something chronological, an order in the sequence of events, but something qualitative. The new epoch is characterized by a break-through which has transpired from above, from God's eternal world, which has now entered time and fills it with its transcendental life. But therewith the framework of time is exploded and time is condemned. The old, sinful world draws to its end. Even in this respect the new time is "the final one": it is on its way to the eternal goal of the history of creation, to the consummation of the work of creation through a transformation, which is simultaneously destruction and renewal.

This eschatological outlook, which was Jesus' own and was laid by him as the Church's foundation, binds together the various parts of the New Testament into a solid inner unity in spite of all the diversities. This basic outlook is set forth in varying terms: "the kingdom of God", "regeneration", "righteousness", "life", "Spirit", "the day of the Lord" etc. In all the authors of the New Testament we find the same conviction: We live in the final days! Judgment and salvation are now set before us. The situation is decisive and demands decision.

This situation, however, filled by τὸ ἔσχατον, is concentrated in a single person, in *Jesus*. This is the next element in the unity of the New Testament. No matter how different and varying the christological terms and ideas of the New Testament may be, they all cover the same content: Jesus comes with the new time. With him eternal life breaks into this world. With him begins the *"krisis"*, which will lead to the new world of eternal life. Whether Jesus himself is speaking of "the Son of Man" or John of "the Logos" or Paul of "The Lord", it is always Jesus as the personal bearer and bringer of "the eschaton" who comes to mind. Jesus considered himself as such, and for this reason it is impossible to detach him from the great New Testament context, and set him in opposition to Paul and John.

The unity of the New Testament is thus presupposed in its eschatological, fundamental outlook, concentrated on Jesus's person. We can, however, go further in determining this unity more closely. It concentrates itself around certain main elements, certain eschatological realities, which are presupposed with and through Jesus: *reconciliation, church, love.* With the help of these three concepts we can describe summarily the situation brought about by Jesus. Together they constitute the insignia of the final time.

1. Reconciliation

Judaism, which awaited the great change in time, expected it to come under the leadership of a triumphant victorious figure, filled with Yahweh's power and glory. This figure was to be a great miracle worker whether he was called Messiah or Son of Man *(bar nash)*. Jesus's path took him through the utmost humiliation. An outcast from his people and delivered by his own to the heathen world-power's representative in Jerusalem, he received the terrible fate of a great criminal, death on a cross. This death he anticipated and bore, conscious of its being an essential presupposition for the arrival of the new time: "The Son of Man has come to give his life as a ransom for many", i.e. for humanity. The New Covenant could only be established "in his blood", through his sacrificial death. This gives to the final time its innermost quality: the blood, the death; the atoning, the condemning and freeing death, the love that sacrifices everything and thereby triumphs. Here we stand at the heart of the New Testament, from where all lines of thought radiate and where they run together.

The thoughts of the New Testament about Jesus' death are inexhaustible. In the New Testament there is no theory, no dogma about reconciliation, because its thought world is wholly dominated and pervaded by Jesus' death. This, in its insoluble unity with the resurrection, is the principle of life and thought in the New Testament. The terms vary: reconciliation (καταλλαγή), atonement (ἱλασμός), redemption (λύτρον, ἀπολύτρωσις) etc. The thought-connections link on to every kind of sacral, sacramental and personal point of departure: the idea of sacrifice, revelation, substitution, the motive of battle, the mystical kinship-experience etc. New Testament thought at this point knows no logical or objectively demarcated categories. It simply interprets the reality of life in Jesus's death in every direction and from every point of view.

All of them, however, maintain that this is a death "for the many" (ἀντὶ πολλῶν), i.e. for the entirety of humanity. In the New Testament humanity is regarded as a unity: "God so loved the world ..." The Bible knows of no individualism, no private religion, but only of personal religion within the framework of the whole. Yahweh chose for himself Israel in order to win and save humanity through this people. Jesus proclaimed the Gospel, performed miracles, and and went to death, not in order to awake a larger or smaller number of people to a religious life, but in order to gather Israel as the holy firstfruits in God's *kingdom*. And when his own people rejected him, he organized and sanctified a new Israel through his word and his death, the people of the Son of Man, the eschatological community. At the threshold of death he gave it the table fellowship of the holy communion as substitute for his visible, bodily presence in its midst. Jesus founded his ἐκκλησία in the circle of Disciples upon the New Covenant in his blood and gave to it at his departure its cultic organization. Here we have the other element, which is connected directly with reconciliation.

2. The Church

In the New Testament the Church is the correlate of Christ, just as in the Old Testament Israel belongs together with and is one with its king, the Lord's anointed, the Messiah. Paul expresses this correlation, this unity, by saying that the Church is the body of Christ while John uses the image of the vine and the branches, of the shepherd and the sheepfold. The most complete expression of this relation is given in Ephesians where, with regards to Christ's work, it teaches that through his atoning death he broke down the wall of partition between Israel and the heathen world, and created a new, holy collective, a body, whose head is Christ. The eschatological reality which emerged from Jesus' death, is a New Covenant people, the Israel of the new covenant, the Church of Christ. With this, with its ordinances, spirit and activity, are connected life, salvation and blessedness. It is the unanimous view and teaching of the New Testament: "You are Peter, and on this rock I will build my *ecclesia*, ... and I will give you the keys of the kingdom of heaven; whatever you bind on earth will be bound in heaven, and whatever you loose on earth will be loosed in heaven". "Remain in me and I will remain in you. No branch can bear fruit by itself; it must remain in the vine. Neither can you bear fruit unless you remain in me". "For we were all baptized by one Spirit into one body – whether Jews or Greeks, slave or free – and we were all given the one Spirit to drink".

The New Testament concept of the church has two essential hallmarks: it is rooted in the *objective*, i.e. in the eschatological situation created and filled by Jesus, and it is *universal*. The Church is independent of all subjective decisions or human measures, and it is therefore in principle something quite different from an association, a union or an organization, which has come into being by pious initiative or on account of religious needs. The concept of the church in the New Testament, so eminently practical and so full of life as it is, is in itself strictly theological, dominated ideologically and bound to the Scriptures. The theocratic-sacral aspect taken over from the Old Testament in the light of the New Covenant's fact of Christ characterizes the thought and self-consciousness of the early Church. Any departure from the objective and universal is thus a departure from the New Testament idea of the Church, a disintegration of the very foundation of the Church. Where Christ is a living reality for man, there at the same time – if it is the whole biblical Christ – his Church must become the holy sphere of life, which gives life its content and form.

The spark of life in this sphere is love, ἀγάπη, the answer to and the consequence of divine love and sacrifice of its life.

3. Love

The central cultic act of the Church stands under the sign ὑπὲρ ὑμῶν, "for you". This, in conjunction with Christ's command and the whole early Christian tradition, places love at the center of the Christian life, at the center of Church life. Love, together with reconciliation and the Church, form an organic unity. Like the Church it is objectively motivated and universal, although it is exceedingly personal. Its objective presupposition and universality are both given simultaneously in the saying: "God so loved the world ..."*God's* relationship, his relationship to the *world,* i.e. to his creation, is the presupposition and the norm of all Christian ἀγάπη. When this universal love of God becomes the personal acquisition of the individual, he can love his neighbour without restriction, even his enemy and the one who injures him, even the one who comes quite accidentally in his way. Jesus expresses the same thing in the great double commandment: "Love the Lord your God ... and your neighbour as yourself". God and the neighbour are not co-ordinate concepts; the καί is not simply copulative, it marks an inner coherence. The commandment presupposes that man is conscious of belonging to God, of owing everything to him, of being indebted to him for everything.

Love is universal, it is concerned with one's neighbour, without exception. It receives all its meaning, however, all its power and richness, when the neighbour is a brother who exhibits signs of Christian life. There love becomes reciprocal: ἀγαπᾶτε ἀλλήλους, a union of soul with mutual understanding. In the Synoptic tradition there are several features which show how Jesus sought to train his Disciples to the reciprocity of such a love. He strongly opposes their natural ambitions and desire to assert themselves, to go their own way, and exhorts them to find their greatness in serving, which in itself also includes understanding, to understand in order to serve[1]. This exhortation goes like a scarlet thread through Paul's letters to the churches. In Jesus's farewell discourse and the Johannine letters this is a main theme.

In the New Testament the correspondence among reconciliation, the Church, and love is obvious. It is all the fruit of God's love for the world through the Son. This love creates the new people of God, whose law of life is love. Love receives its strength and riches in the mutuality of church fellowship. Love is, of course, not limited to the Church, but it is motivated and given form by the Church. Paul expresses this in the Song of Love, 1 Cor 13, in his own monumental way. With solemn words he explains that every great gift and achievement is worthless without ἀγάπη. It means that Christian religion and ethics, which are not incorporated in the holy fellowship, lack a foundation in God and that ultimately they serve only man's selfish interests. The same thought permeates the Johannine literature: "As the Father has loved me, so have I loved you. Now remain in my love", i. e. in the κοινωνία which Christ has created, and in which he is the driving and shaping force.

At every decisive point in the New Testament we stand before a solid and strong unity. Theology and the Church must discover, experience and hold fast this unity in order to have a correct and fruitful relationship to the diversity of Scriptures in research, proclamation and reflection. Then it will be fruitful to enter deeply into the diversity of the New Testament, to listen to the various voices and their strange sounds, to be engrossed with the characteristics of individuals, to follow the various trains of thought. The basic reality, which stands behind it all, receives in this way a much richer life, a much more brighter hue. Then we will understand that the right way of going about it is not to harmonize the New Testament, to take parts out of the Synoptics, Paul and John and to put them together in order to form a new, motley entity. Everyone of these areas forms a rounded, complete whole, a total view. And as *wholes* they illuminate and complete one another. That is why it is so important that the exegetical study of details be completed by a biblico-theological study, that seeks to present the overall pictures in their inner, organic coherence: Jesus' Synoptic proclamation, the Johannine witness, the mighty Pauline world of thought.

There remain here plenty of religio-historical and historical problems, with which scholarship may wrestle and over which the thinking preacher cannot either fail to ponder now and then. Let us, for example, take the *Johannine problem,* which is not at all the same question as who has written the Fourth Gospel. This is a fairly secondary question. The real question is how all this Jesus tradition has arisen and been formed, how this picture of Jesus has

[1] The Swedish of this last clause makes no sense, probably one or more words are missing. [Transl.]

received its shape. At this point theology stands before one of its greatest question-marks, before a gate, at which unceasingly, without break or rest, it pulls and pushes in order to get at least a crack to peer through, but up to now without any significant success. We see the contours of something here and there through the keyhole, but only the contours.

These closed doors and open problems do not, however, need to worry us in our experience of the basic unity of the New Testament, which has its ground in the unity found in the foundational fact of Christ. I have already pointed out that this unity appears in the consistently eschatological character of the New Testament. We can now vary this thought and say the same thing in a different way, by a well known saying: the entire New Testament is saturated and characterized by the thought of *fulfilment.* That which happens through Christ and his Apostles are, to be sure, historical events, but at the same time they are revelations of a supra-historical course of events. In this course of events that which was prepared earlier is now being fulfilled, – it is fulfilled and goes on to its consummation. The eternal light falls from the fulfilment over the history of the entire race, it reveals the hidden meaning of this history, and at the same time annuls history. As in the case of "the final events", τὸ ἔσχατον, we have in the New Testament concept of "fulfilment" a strange interplay of the temporal and the qualitative. It is a history through time, which arrives at its end and at the same time at its goal: the history of Israel in its intertwining with world history. And fulfilment is itself an historical process through historical persons. But in this process of fulfilment the supra-historical content of history is disclosed, i.e. the salvific will of God; and not only is it disclosed, it is realized. It was also at work in the preceding history, in which the situation became ripe for the fulfilment. Thus, when the fulfilment came it was the goal of previous history, but also its end. At the same time as a new world was opened, – God's kingdom, *regnum gratiae,* – the old world was condemned to destruction. The preparatory stage became a course of events belonging to the past. To desire to keep it in the new order of things becomes therefore a revolt against God, no matter how holy and venerable the traditions are, which one wishes to keep and preserve.

Fulfilment, judgment, and renewal find expression on every page of the New Testament, whether it speaks of God, Christ, or man, of faith or life. This strange situation, which is designated as "fulfilment" makes itself felt in everything. Therein lies the possibility and the risk for man, who lives in this strange time, the final time, the time of fulfilment.

From another perspective, therefore, we can determine the unity of the New Testament in so far as the New Testament in all its parts places man before one and the same decision. Wherever we turn in the Scriptures, we stand before *a* life-possibility and *a* death-risk. Not many possibilities to choose from, not different ways for a well-disposed choice, but just *one* possibility, *one* way. If more than one way is spoken of, then it is at the most two, and one of them leads to perdition. There is only *one* way that leads to life: *the narrow way*. It goes through the entire New Testament.

Our mention of the narrow way leads us to another aspect of the unity of the New Testament. "Enter through the narrow gate. For wide is the gate and broad is the road that leads to destruction and many enter through it; But small is the gate and narrow the road that leads to life, and only a few find it". What is it that makes the narrow road so little trafficked? It does not say that it is steep or stony or in some other way dangerous or difficult. It says only that it is *narrow*. This means that it is difficult to keep to. Only a few *find* it. As an almost invisible track it winds its way through the terrain. No large, grand gate, splendid and attractive, opens at its end; it ends up in a little, small door-opening in the wall. Only by engaging one's whole being seriously in the search can one discover the path that leads to life. This is the way in which the New Testament, too, in all its parts discloses its inner unity of life only to those who apply themselves to the study of Scriptures with all seriousness and energy. In truth, this study is no child's play. Just as the New Testament is one in its gift to those who find it, so it is also one in its demand to those who seek. The task is already large and heavy when one reads the wretched elements that are demanded for getting the first courses in the B.D. degree. How many have not felt and do feel discouraged before such a task! How many have not sighed and do sigh on the steep and stony road, which leads to the examination, which is related more with the Hesiodic image than with the biblical one about the way to ἀρετή: μακρὸς καὶ ὄρθιος οἶμος εἰς αὐτὴν καὶ τρηχὺς τὸ πρῶτον. No one can be spared the hours of discouragement in the scientific study of the Bible. But might not one thing help greatly in overcoming the tiredness and the discouragement: To take on oneself the still harder task of proceeding, in connection with the study of the Bible, to the narrow road that leads to life? For it is on that road that one discovers the secret of the New Testament, and a glimpse of this can give new courage to the discouraged one and new strength to the tired one. For courage and strength in scientific study ultimately come from courage and strength in *life*. Science is no isolated domain, even though it has its own character and makes its own altogether special demands and assigns its tasks. Science wants to serve life. But then it must remain in living contact with life in order to be able to fulfil its task rightly.

Study, with its variety of areas and problems, is nevertheless ultimately in itself still a unity of life. Basically everything belongs together organically and forms a whole. Often and during long periods one may forget this and lose oneself in details and special issues. But with maturing experience and a broad overview one rediscovers that unity and rejoices in the discovery. Now the details appear in new and richer light within the framework of the whole. This has been the case also with Scriptural theology during its long and changing trajectory through time. It (theology) has quite often forgotten the whole on account of the details, and fascinated by the diversity of the New Testament, it has lost sight of the unity. It has rediscovered this unity, however, and rejoiced in it. This joy of discovery also throws its reconciling light over erroneous and circuitous paths.

Scholarship is certainly not going to be spared such experiences in the future. For truth must always be tested and discovered anew. The wise Goethe said: "What you possess, you must acquire in order that you may posses it again". Thus, too, theology must go on towards new problems and continue wrestling with the old ones. It has, however, an increased experience. And to this experience belongs also this: theology must not forget *the Church*. For the ever current proof for the unity of the New Testament is the Christian Church. It lives and it can only live by the New Testament witness to Christ in the totality of all its variations and musical keys.

To be sure the Church does not receive its insights into the New Testament freely. The diversity of the New Testament also causes in the Church a continual anxiety and tension. Sometimes the unity of the Church has been ruptured on account of this diversity. But it is obvious that only by embracing the whole New Testament can the Church remain the Church, and avoid a distorted and one-sided development, which can only lead to the formation of sects and to isolation. The life of the Church is based on the unity and totality of the New Testament. It is the presupposition for all its limitlessly variegated and ramified activity, its innumerable individual differences, which must be held together in a living unity, in the totality of the spiritual wealth of the New Testament. This totality is the early Church's inalienable legacy. Goethe's words, however, apply also to this legacy : "What you have inherited from your fathers, acquire it, in order that you may possess it again!" In this endeavour perhaps the Church could receive some help from theology in repayment for all it has given to it.

Unity between Church and theology is, like the unity of the New Testament, sometimes difficult to see, but necessary to seek and to hold fast. The unity of Church and theology is not either obtained without cost. It is not found on the broad road, but on the narrow road. May both the men of theology and the men of the Church be willing to choose that road!

Sprachliches und Stilistisches zum Neuen Testament

(1943)

1. λοιπόν

Durch seine in Eranos veröffentlichte treffliche Studie über (τὸ) λοιπόν[1] hat A. Cavallin auch den Neutestamentler zum Dank verpflichtet. Die zerstreuten Beobachtungen zu diesem Wort, die schon seit langem in der exegetischen Literatur vorkommen, haben durch die umsichtigen und reich belegten Ausführungen Cavallins eine breite und tragfähige Grundlage erhalten. Da Cav. nur eine Auswahl des neutestamentlichen Stoffes behandelt, soll hier die Betrachtung auf sämtliche Stellen im N.T. ausgedehnt und so die Ergebnisse seiner Arbeit für den ganzen Bereich der neutestamentlichen Beispiele fruchtbar gemacht werden.

Das von Cav. beigebrachte Material zeigt sehr eindrucksvoll, daß die verschiedenen Bedeutungsnuancen von λοιπόν nicht einander ablösen, sondern in voller Lebenskraft unmittelbar neben einander bestehen. Man muß also jedesmal alle die verschiedenen Möglichkeiten ins Auge fassen. Jede Schematisierung ist unerlaubt. Daraus folgt, daß es bisweilen recht schwer sein kann, sich für die eine oder andere Alternative zu entscheiden. Zwei oder sogar mehrere Möglichkeiten müssen in solchen Fällen offen bleiben.

Besonders unsicher bleibt die Deutung von *Mc. 14,41 (*= Mt. 26,45). In Gethsemane findet Jesus zum drittenmal die Jünger in tiefen Schlaf versenkt und sagt zu ihnen: καθεύδετε [τὸ] λοιπὸν καὶ ἀναπαύεσθε· ἀπέχει! Die neue schwedische Bibelübersetzung lautet: "Ja, ihr schlafet noch immer ..." Die alte, klassische Übersetzung: "Ja, schlafet nun ..." faßt den Satz imperativisch auf. Er könnte auch als Fragesatz verstanden werden. Dafür könnte sprechen, daß Lc. (22,46) an der entsprechenden Stelle schreibt: τί καθεύδετε; Wenn der Satz als Frage zu verstehen ist, liegt es nahe, λοιπόν mit "also" zu übersetzen; "Ihr schlafet also ...?" In dem Falle würden wir hier ein Beispiel der "interjektionellen" Verwendung von λοιπόν haben (Cav. S. 136ff.). Daß der Satz affektbetont ist, zeigt in der Tat das bei Mc. folgende ἀπέχει, "sufficit".[2] Wenn

[1] Eranos XXXIX (1941). S. 121–144.

[2] Es scheint mir wahrscheinlich, daß dieses ἀπέχει in dem ἱκανόν ἐστι Lc. 22,38 weiterwirkt.

man das temporale Moment in diesem λοιπόν herausschälen will, wird man es etwa mit "in dieser Lage" paraphrasieren müssen, analog mit νῦν oder ἤδη. Ich möchte es also mit der alten schwedischen Übersetzung halten gegen die neue, und Mc. 14,41 als eine affektvolle Frage, beinahe als einen indignierten Ausruf verstehen: "Ihr schlafet also nun und ruhet euch aus! Genug (des Schlafens)!"

Zu *Apg. 27,20:* λοιπὸν περιῃρεῖτο ἐλπὶς πᾶσα τοῦ σῴζεσθαι ἡμᾶς, hat Cav. das nötige gesagt (S. 124). Viel Material zu diesem Sprachgebrauch schon bei G. Raphelius, *Annotationes philol. in N.T. ex Arriano et Polybio* (Hamburg 1715).

1. Cor. 1.16: λοιπὸν οὐκ οἶδα εἴ τινα [ἄλλον] ἐβάπτισα. Vgl. Cav. S. 133. ἄλλον ist hier etwas unsicher (es fehlt bei D it). Wenn es gestrichen worden ist, muß es als überflüßig neben λοιπόν empfunden worden sein. Umgekehrt, wenn es hinzugefügt wurde, hat man λοιπόν so zu sagen gedoppelt. Jedenfalls muß λοιπόν hier "darüber hinaus", "sonst" heißen und bezieht sich also auf die vorausgehende Aufzählung der von Paulus getauften Jünger.

1. Cor. 4,2: ὧδε λοιπὸν ζητεῖται ἐν τοῖς οἰκονόμοις ἵνα πιστός τις εὑρεθῇ. Cav. hat diese Stelle nicht besprochen. Er hat aber reichliche Belege für Kombination von λοιπόν mit ἤδη gegeben. Dadurch fällt auch ein Licht auf unsere Stelle. ὧδε λοιπόν ist ebenso zu beurteilen wie ἤδη λοιπόν und bedeutet "somit nun" (Menge: "bei dieser Sachlage"). Als Parallele verweist man gewöhnlich auf Epikt. *Diss.* II 12,24: ὧδε λοιπὸν ὁ κίνδυνος, μὴ πρῶτον μὲν εἴπῃ ... "dabei besteht nun die Gefahr ..." Lokales und Temporales fließen hier ineinander. ὧδε, hier, ist: "unter diesen Umständen"; was einem "folglich" oder "somit" nahe kommt. Bei λοιπόν ist die Bedeutung "also", gleich betontem οὖν, sehr gewöhnlich. – Zur Doppelung könnte man auch erinnern an Epikt. *Diss.* II 15,8: Man soll die Grundlagen seiner Entscheidungen kritisch prüfen, καὶ οὕτως λοιπὸν ἐποικοδομεῖν αὐτῷ τὴν εὐτονίαν, "und *dann erst* ..." – 1. Cor. 4,2 hat eine starke Texttradition: ζητεῖτε (imper.) statt ζητεῖται, das aber vielleicht auch imperativisch zu fassen ist.[3]

1. Cor 7,29: ὁ καιρὸς συνεσταλμένος ἐστίν· τὸ λοιπὸν ἵνα καὶ οἱ ἔχοντες γυναῖκας ὡς οἱ μὴ ἔχοντες ὦσιν ... Die meisten übersetzen hier λοιπόν mit "hinfort" oder "fürderhin". Ob das ganz richtig ist, scheint mir etwas zweifelhaft. Wir leben, sagt der Apostel, in den äußersten Tagen der Welt, nur eine kurze Frist noch, und das Ende kommt (ὁ καιρὸς συνεσταλμένος ἐστίν). In dieser Endzeit sollen die Gläubigen innerlich frei der vergehenden Welt und ihren Einrichtungen gegenüberstehen. Das ist natürlich eine allgemeine Regel, die Paulus dabei ausspricht. Sie galt schon früher und gilt immer in der Letztzeit. Was soll da ein "fürderhin" oder "hinfort"? Etwa nach dem Empfang des Apostelbriefes? Dieser Brief leitet doch keine neue Epoche innerhalb der Endzeit ein; Paulus schärft nur ein, was prinzipiell sein soll. Ich halte deshalb

---

[3] Vgl. *Coniectanea Neotestamentica* VII (1942), S. 5.

λοιπόν hier nicht für temporal, sondern für logisch: *also, mithin*. Der Imperativsatz mit ἵνα[4] formuliert die logisch-sachliche Konsequenz der voraufgehenden Feststellung: die Frist ist nur noch kurz. λοιπόν markiert ausdrücklich diese Konsequenz und steht gewissermaßen auf der Grenze zwischen der "logischen" und der "interjektionellen" Bedeutung. – Will man trotzdem an der temporalen Bedeutung des λοιπόν an unserer Stelle festhalten, sollte es am ehesten mit einem betonten jetzt, *nunmehr* übersetzt werden: In dieser Zeit, in der wir leben, soll man sich auf die rechte Weise einrichten. Die logische Bedeutung wird jedoch vorzuziehen sein. Ich vergleiche den Brief in *Aegypt. Urkunden aus dem Kgl. Mus. zu Berlin* III 864: λοιπὸν πέμψον εἴς με, παρακαλῶ ("like an emphatic οὖν", Moulton-Milligan).

2. Cor. 13, 11: λοιπόν, ἀδελφοί, χαίρετε ...
Phil.3,1: τὸ λοιπόν, ἀδελφοί μου, χαίρετε ἐν κυρίῳ.
Phil. 4,8: τὸ λοιπόν, ἀδελφοί, ὅσα ἐστὶν ἀληθῆ ... ταῦτα λογίζεσθε.
1 Thess. 4,1: λοιπὸν οὖν, ἀδελφοί, ἐρωτῶμεν ὑμᾶς ... ἵνα...
2. Thess. 3,1: τὸ λοιπὸν προσεύχεσθε, ἀδελφοί, περὶ ἡμῶν.

An allen diesen Stellen steht λοιπόν, um den *Übergang* zu einem neuen Gedanken oder den *Abschluß* einer Vermahnungsreihe zu markieren. Es ist also zu übersetzen: *also, nun* (unbetont), oder *schließlich* (so 2. Cor. 13,11; auch 2. Thess. 3,1, wo dann allerdings eine neue Vermahnung folgt). In 1. Thess. 4,1 eröffnet λοιπόν die Vermahnungsreihe und ist (in den meisten Handschriften) mit οὖν kombiniert. Etwas schwieriger zu beurteilen sind Phil. 3,1; 4,8. An der letzteren Stelle ist "schließlich" wohl am Platze. Im ersteren Falle muß man unsicher sein, ob der Apostel ursprünglich den Brief hier abschließen wollte, dann aber weiter schrieb, oder ob er schon mit diesem λοιπόν die folgenden polemischen Äußerungen gegen die Juden beabsichtigte. Wenn das letztere zutrift, ist λοιπόν lediglich Übergangspartikel (ähnlich wie so oft διό, καὶ νῦν usw.).[5]

2. Tim. 4,8: ... τὴν πίστιν τετήρηκα˙ λοιπὸν ἀπόκειταί μοι ὁ τῆς δικαιοσύνης στέφανος. Schon Raphelius sagt hierzu:"possis hoc etiam vertere itaque." Er zitiert mehrere Polyb-Stellen, die ein ähnliches λοιπόν enthalten. Menge übersetzt *nunmehr,* also temporal, und ebenso die neue schwedische Übersetzung. Man wird aber auch in diesem Falle gut tun, das logische und das temporale Moment nicht allzu streng zu unterscheiden. Man könnte etwa paraphrasieren: "so liegt denn nun für mich der Kranz bereit". Vgl. Cav. S. 134.

Hebr. 10.13: εἰς τὸ διηνεκὲς ἐκάθισεν ἐν δεξιᾷ τοῦ θεοῦ, τὸ λοιπὸν ἐκδεχό-

[4] Vgl. T. Kalén, *Selbständige Finalsätze* I (Skrifter utg. av K. Hum. Vet.- Samf. i Uppsala 34: 2), 1941, S. 55.

[5] Vgl. Cavallin, S. 137 ff. – Zu διό vgl. E. Molland in *Serta Rudbergiana,* 1931, S. 43–52. – Zu καὶ νῦν vgl. Joach. Jeremias in *ZNW* 38 (1939), S. 119 ff.

μενος ἕως τεθῶσιν οἱ ἐχθροὶ αὐτοῦ ὑποπόδιον τῶν ποδῶν αὐτοῦ. Menge übersetzt: "hinfort wartet er...", vgl. Cav. S. 124: "Hier bezieht sich τὸ λοιπόν auf die Zukunft." Meines Erachtens liegt es jedoch näher, hier τὸ λοιπόν in Beziehung zum *Vorhergehenden* zu setzen. Jesus hat ein einziges Opfer für die Sünden dargebracht; *nunmehr* (tut er nichts derartiges mehr, dagegen) wartet er... Dieser Gebrauch von λοιπόν als Schlußpunkt eines Geschehens (und damit als Anfangspunkt eines neuen Zustandes) ist bei Cav. sehr reichlich belegt. Ich möchte also Heb. 10,13 eher mit einem betonten *nun* (wie die alte und neue schwedische Übersetzung) als mit "fürderhin" übersetzen.

Eine Papyrusstelle sei noch kurz erwähnt, die, soweit ich sehe, bei Cav. nicht berücksichtigt ist. Es handelt sich um den Brief eines reuigen jungen Menschen (Deissmann, *Licht vom Osten,* 4. Aufl., S. 154). Der Briefschreiber bittet dringend: "Versöhne dich mit mir! λοιπὸν οἶδα τί ποτ' ἐμαυτῷ παρέσχημαι· πεπαίδευμαι. Deissmann übersetzt: "im übrigen weiß ich ..." Ich glaube, wir werden eher zu übersetzen haben: "*jetzt* (endlich) verstehe ich, was ich mir zugezogen habe, ich bin gezüchtigt", λοιπόν also gleich einem betonten νῦν. – Es ist übrigens bezeichnend, daß in einem kleinen Brief eines ungebildeten Jungen λοιπόν zweimal auftritt[6], und zwar in verschiedenen Nuancen. Dies ist ein Zeugnis unter vielen anderen von der großen Beliebtheit des Wortes und von seiner vielseitigen Anwendung in der alltäglichen Sprache.

2. Zu AG 12, 17

καὶ ἐξελθὼν ἐπορεύθη εἰς ἕτερον τόπον. Dies wird erzählt vom Apostel Petrus, der durch ein Wunder aus dem Gefängnis befreit worden war. Die Kommentatoren finden den Ausdruck εἰς ἕτερον τόπον recht auffallend. Er ist in diesem Zusammenhang, wo man einen Ortsnamen erwartet, so eigentümlich unbestimmt, daß man sich fragen muß, ob hinter den Worten etwas anderes als der schlichte Wortsinn zu suchen sei. In dem großen englischen Kommentar zu AG *The Beginnings of Christianity* I, IV S. 138 schreibt Kirsopp Lake zur Stelle: "τόπος may mean another house or another town. I think that it means town." Wellhausen glaubt, daß in der Quelle Antiochia stand (*Abh. d. Kgl. Wiss. Ges. zu Göttingen,* 1914). Bei der Einarbeitung der Quelle in die AG wurde die Ortsangabe verwischt mit Rücksicht auf 15, 1-34, wo Petrus wieder in Jerusalem weilt. Harnack findet in der unbestimmten Angabe den Rest einer alten Überlieferung von dem Weggang der Zwölf von Jerusalem zwölf Jahre nach dem Tode Jesu.[7] Also, was bei Wellhausen Redaktion ist, ist bei Harnack Urquelle! Lake scheint unseren Vers einer älteren Vorlage der AG zuzuschrei-

[6] Im oben zu 1. Cor. 7,29 erwähnten Papyrusbrief.

[7] *Chronol.* I, S. 243 f.

ben, in welcher 9,32ff. die Fortsetzung von 12,17 bildete. In 9,32ff. finden wir ja den Apostel auf einer durch mehrere Stationen verlaufenden Reise, die ihn schließlich nach Lydda führt. Lake will also 12,17 im Zusammenhang der AG verständlich machen.

Das ist natürlich die richtige Methode. Nur glaube ich, man muß da einen anderen Weg einschlagen als Lake, der ja übrigens das rein Hypothetische seiner Kombination von 12,17 und 9,32ff. kräftig betont. Das zunächst Überraschende im Ausdruck εἰς ἕτερον τόπον verschwindet, wenn man darauf achtgibt, daß τόπος hier ganz unbetont und farblos ist, und daß der Ton ganz und gar auf ἕτερον ruht: Petrus verließ Jerusalem (wo sein Leben bedroht war) und ging anderswo hin (wo er in Sicherheit sein konnte). ἕτερον ist gewissermaßen qualifizierend.

Eine gute Parallele zu dieser Ausdrucksweise gibt Dio Chrysostomus *Or.* XX, περὶ ἀναχωρήσεως (ed. Budé II, S. 325). Es geht hier um den rechten Begriff des ἀναχωρεῖν. Dio nennt einige Fälle, die nicht als ἀναχωρήσεις gelten können: Wenn ein Athener nach Megara oder Aigina geht, um sich dem Kriegsdienst zu entziehen; wenn ein reicher Mann die Stadt verläßt, um den Kosten der Liturgien zu entgehen; wenn ein Arzt an einen anderen Ort übersiedelt wegen einer lästigen Klientel von Freunden und Verwandten usw. All das ist keine ἀναχώρησις, sondern eine φυγή und ἀπόδρασις. Die Ausdrücke des Umziehens sind folgende: εἴ τις ἀπέλθοι ἐκ τῆς πόλεως – εἴ τις ἀποδημήσειεν εἰς ἕτερον τόπον – εἴ τις ἑτέρωσε ἀποχωροῖ ποι. Wir beobachten hier, daß ἀποδημῆσαι durch ἕτερον τόπον ergänzt wird; der Mann wandert aus, und zwar anderswohin (εἰς ἕτερον τόπον = ἑτέρωσε), wo er unbehelligt leben kann.[8]

Ähnlich Xenoph. *Inst. Cyr.* I, 2.3, wo von der sogenannten ἐλευθέρα ἀγορά der Perser die Rede ist. Der gemeine Pöbel ist hier ausgeschlossen: ἀπελήλανται εἰς ἄλλον τόπον, d.h. anderswohin, wo er aus dem Wege ist.

Kehren wir nun zu AG 12,7 zurück! Petrus verläßt das gefährliche Jerusalem und begibt sich an einen anderen Ort, wo er sicher ist. ἐπορεύθη εἰς ἕτερον τόπον besagt also mehr, als wenn es nur hieße ἐπορεύθη ἐντεῦθεν (vgl. Lc. 13,31). Wir vernehmen, daß der Apostel einen besseren Aufenthaltsort aufsuchte. Man sieht: es kann keine Rede davon sein, daß hier ursprünglich ein Ortsname gestanden hätte. Der Satz ist ganz und gar literarisch-lukanisch. Es kann auch keine Rede davon sein, daß hier eine Urquelle an den Tag träte.

Die Frage, ob Lukas wußte, wohin Petrus bei dieser Gelegenheit umzog, kann nicht auf Grund von AG 12,17 ohne weiteres verneint werden. Er *kann* so schreiben und sehr wohl das gewußt haben; aber der betreffende Ort hatte für ihn kein Interesse. Er will ja nicht die Biographie des Petrus schreiben. Ausge-

[8] Vgl. auch Plut. *Cons. ad Apoll.* 3 (*Mor.* 108 D): ὥστε εἰ καὶ προσέοικε μετάγειν εἰς ἕτερον τόπον ὁ θάνατος, οὐκ ἔστι κακόν. Der Tod versetzt anderswohin, wo die Verhältnisse ganz andersartig sind.

schlossen aber wären jedenfalls Antiochia und Rom. Denn eine Übersiedlung des Petrus dahin wäre ein kirchengeschichtliches Ereignis, das kaum unerwähnt bleiben könnte, wenn Lukas es in seiner Darstellung überhaupt berührt hätte.[9]

3. Zum Stil des Peristasenkatalogs

In einer polemischen Auseinandersetzung mit seinen judaistischen Gegnern in Korinth, die sich ihrer Vorzüge rühmen (καυχᾶσθαι), formt Paulus eine Periode, die von kräftigem Pathos und rhetorischem Stil geprägt ist, 2. Cor. 11,23ff. Er will sich nun seinerseits rühmen, und das tut er, indem er alle die Leiden und Widerwärtigkeiten aufzählt, die er hat durchmachen müssen. Diese Aufzählung hat mehrere Züge, die an die *res gestae* des Augustus erinnern. Diese Ähnlichkeiten habe ich behandelt in den *Symbolae Osloënses* VII (1928), S. 25ff. und VIII (1929), S. 78ff. Dort wies ich auch auf das literarische Vorbild der *res gestae* hin: die Ruhmeschroniken der orientalischen Herrscher im Ichstil. Es würde ausgezeichnet zu der ganzen Art des Apostels passen, daß er, wenn er nun *seine* Ruhmeschronik verfaßt, lauter πάθη, Leiden und Demütigungen (περιστάσεις) aufzählt. Allerdings hat auch dies einen gewissen Anhalt in den gewöhnlichen Ruhmeschroniken, insofern diese auch bisweilen die ausgestandenen und überwundenen Mühen und Strapazen des betreffenden Herrschers berichten.

Ich glaube nach wie vor, daß eine Beziehung zum Stil der *res gestae* bei dem paulinischen Peristasenkatalog anzunehmen ist. Daneben möchte ich aber auch auf eine andere Stilparallele aufmerksam machen, die auf einem ganz anderen Gebiete zu suchen ist, nämlich im griechischen *Roman.* Bekanntlich spielen in dieser Literatur die πάθη der Helden eine zentrale Rolle. Das Leben dieser Menschen ist ein großes Martyrium, eine Kette von ununterbrochenen schweren Prüfungen, die sie immer wieder bis an den Rand des Todes führen. Sowie die Lage sich etwas erhellt, trifft sofort ein neuer Schicksalsschlag die

[9] Ich glaube allerdings nicht, daß Lukas eine konkrete Kunde über den neuen Aufenthaltsort des Petrus besaß. Das kann man aber nicht aus seiner Ausdrucksweise schließen. Diese besagt nur: Petrus setzte sich in Sicherheit – Gelegentlich dieser Besprechung von τόπος möchte ich eine kurze Bemerkung zu Apoc. 18,17 machen: πᾶς κυβερνήτης καὶ πᾶς ὁ ἐπὶ τόπον πλέων καὶ ναῦται καὶ ὅσοι τὴν θάλασσαν ἐργάζονται ἀπὸ μακρόθεν ἔστησαν ... Ὁ ἐπὶ τόπον πλέων ist schwerbegreiflich. Man hat ἐπὶ πόντον lesen wollen; Heikel (*Stud. u. Krit.* 106 [1935–36], S. 317) schlägt vor: ὁ ἐπὶ [τὸν] τόπον (= Rom) πλέων. Mir scheint das nicht zu den anderen Kategorien zu passen: Steuerleute, Seeleute usw. Man erwartet eine Erwähnung der *Passagiere,* und vielleicht könnte diese Erwartung erfüllt werden, wenn wir ὁ ἐπίτοπον πλέων, "wer mit Gelegenheit segelt", lesen. Die antiken Schiffspassagiere fuhren ja fast immer mit irgendeiner "Schiffsgelegenheit" (vgl. AG. 27,6 κἀκεῖ εὑρὼν πλοῖον Ἀλεξανδρῖνον). Ἐπίτοπος ist zwar nicht literarisch belegt; aber ἐπιτόπως kommt vor (bei *Liddell-Scott:* "suitably").

armen, schon so vielgequälten Hauptpersonen. In diesem Zusammenhang begegnet uns auch der Peristasenkatalog im Munde des geplagten Helden. Es kommt vor, daß er das Bedürfnis empfindet, seine Leiden laut zu beklagen, und da nimmt er einen zusammenfassenden Überblick über alle die Nöte, die ihn befallen haben. Wir finden diese romantischen Peristasenkataloge bei Charito und Achilles Tatius:

Char. III, 8.9 τέθνηκα ἀνέζησα,
λελήστευμαι πέφευγα,
πέπραμαι δεδούλευκα ...
IV, 3.10 ἐπράθην διὰ σέ
καὶ ἔσκαψα
καὶ σταυρὸν ἐβάστασα
καὶ δημίου χερσὶν παρεδόθην ...
IV, 4.10 ἐπράθην ἐδούλευσα ἐδέθην
V,5.2 τέθνηκα καὶ κεκήδευμαι,
τετυμβωρύχημαι πέπραμαι δεδούλευκα,
ἰδοῦ τύχη, καὶ κρίνομαι.
VI, 4.6 πόσοις με παρέδωκας;
λησταῖς θαλάττη[10]
τάφῳ δουλείᾳ κρίσει
Achill.Tat. V, 18.4 διὰ σέ ἱερεῖον γέγονα καὶ καθαρμός[11]
καὶ τέθνηκα ἤδη δεύτερον,
διὰ σὲ πέπραμαι
καὶ ἐδέθην σιδήρῳ
καὶ δίκελλαν ἐβάστασα
καὶ ἔσκαψα γῆν
καὶ ἐμαστιγώθην.
Vgl. 2.Cor. 11,24: ὑπὸ Ἰουδαίων πεντάκις τεσσεράκοντα
παρὰ μίαν ἔλαβον
τρὶς ἐρραβδίσθην,
ἅπαξ ἐλιθάσθην,
τρὶς ἐναυάγησα ...

Die Romanparallele hat natürlich nur stilistisch-psychologischen Wert. Von einem sachlichen Zusammenhang kann keine Rede sein. Die aufgezählten πάθη sind bei Charito und Achilles Tatius ganz stereotyp; bei Paulus tragen sie die frische Farbe des Erlebten. Aber die Parallele ist unter stilistischem Gesichtspunkt interessant. Besonders die Asyndese, die dem Pathos entspricht. Diese Ausdrucksweise ist die natürliche Form einer leidenschaftlich erregten Auseinandersetzung mit der Wirklichkeit. Wir müssen vor allem einen psychologischen Gesichtspunkt anlegen. Kerényi (*Die griechisch-orientalische Romanliteratur in religionsgeschichtlicher Beleuchtung,* 1927, S. 103ff.) erinnert an den Stil der Mysteriensymbola:

[10] Vgl. 2. Cor. 11,26 κινδύνοις λῃστῶν ... κινδύνοις ἐν θαλάσσῃ.
[11] Vgl. 1. Cor. 4,13 ὡς περικαθάρματα τοῦ κόσμου ἐγενήθημεν.

ἐνήστευσα, ἔπιον τὸν κυκεῶνα
ἔλαβον ἐκ κύστης κτλ.
ἐκ τυμπάνου ἔφαγον, ἐκ κυμβάλου ἔπιον
ἐκερνοφόρησα, ὑπὸ τὸν παστὸν ὑπέδυον.

Vgl. 1 Tim. 3,16: ὃς ἐφανερώθη ἐν σαρκί,
ἐδικαιώθη ἐν πνεύματι,
ὤφθη ἀγγέλοις
ἐκηρύχθη ἐν ἔθνεσιν,
ἐπιστεύθη ἐν κόσμῳ,
ἀνελήμφθη ἐν δόξῃ.

Der Stil ist ausgesprochen hieratisch. Er stellt sich ein, wo die heiligen Erlebnisse oder Tatsachen zusammengefasst werden sollen; so entsteht die Formel. Der Stil stellt sich auch ein, wo der göttliche König seine Taten in ewige Worte fasst. Und wo der schicksalsgeplagte Märtyrer der Liebe sich mit seinem Schicksal auseinandersetzt. Der Apostel steht unter demselben psychologischen Stilgesetz. Es färbt seinen Stil. Aber nur zeitweilig und vorübergehend. Der paulinische Peristasenkatalog enthält eine reiche Variation von Stilelementen, die von der Selbständigkeit und der Originalität des Apostels zeugen. Er geht nie restlos im Schema auf. Und jedes Schema erfüllt er mit persönlichem Inhalt.

4. Leib und Reich

Zum paulinischen Begriff σῶμα Χριστοῦ ist viel antiker Parallelstoff gesammelt worden. Er ist übersichtlich zusammengestellt bei A. Wikenhauser, *Die Kirche als der mystische Leib Christi* (Münster i. W. 1937). Ich vermisse dort eine Stelle, die zwar isoliert dasteht, die aber vielleicht doch auf einige Aufmerksamkeit Anspruch haben könnte. Es handelt sich um Heliodorus, *Aethiopica* X, 4. Schauplatz ist die aethiopische Stadt Meroë, wo vom König Hydaspes und seiner Gemahlin Persina ein grosses Siegesfest gefeiert werden soll. Unter den bei dieser Gelegenheit zu opfernden Gefangenen befindet sich auch das Heldenpaar des Romans, Theagenes und Charikleia – die letztere ist in Wirklichkeit die verschwundene Tochter des Königspaares. Durch das übernatürliche Wissen des Vorstehers der äthiopischen Gymnosophisten, Sisimithres, wird das Mädchen im letzten Augenblick vor dem Opfertod gerettet und ihre Identität aufgeklärt. Als die Königin vor dem Fest die Gymnosophisten zur Teilnahme an der bevorstehenden Opferfeier einlud, gab Sisimithres nach Befragung der Gottheit seine Zusage, fügte aber hinzu: θόρυβον δέ τινα καὶ ταραχὴν προμηνύει τὸ δαιμόνιον ἐσομένην μὲν παρὰ τὰς θυσίας, εἰς ἀγαθὸν δὲ καὶ ἡδὺ τὸ τέλος καταστρέψουσαν, ὡς μέλους μὲν ὑμῶν τοῦ σώματος ἢ μέρους τῆς βασιλείας ἀπολωλότος τοῦ πεπρωμένου δὲ εἰς τότε τὸ ζητούμενον ἀναφαίνοντος.

Das Orakelwort weissagt natürlich die Entdeckung der verlorenen Tochter. Aber der Weise hat an diesem Zeitpunkt nur einen noch ganz allgemeinen Begriff erhalten von dem, was sich ereignen soll, und drückt sich entsprechend aus: Er spricht in dunklen Worten von einem "Glied an eurem Leibe", was dasselbe ist wie "ein Teil des Reiches". Diese Zusammenstellung von σῶμα und βασιλεία ist interessant. Das Reich scheint als der Leib des Herrschers vorgestellt zu sein; er, der König, ist eins mit seinem Herrschaftsbereich. Kerényi (S. 51) macht auf das Wortspiel μέρος – μέλος aufmerksam (Paulus hat μέλη ἐκ μέρους, 1. Cor. 11,27) und findet hier eine ägyptische Vorstellung, die in der Κόρη κόσμου zum Ausdruck kommt (Stob. *Ecl.* I, p. 411 Wachsmuth): die Erde liegt wie ein Mensch auf dem Rükken und schaut zum Himmel hinauf, Ägypten ist das Herz, Äthiopien der Kopf, μεμερισμένη δὲ καθ' ὅσα μέρη ὁ ἄνθρωπος μελίζεται. Der Zusammenhang dieser Vorstellung mit der Heliodor-Stelle will mir doch nicht recht einleuchten. Eher wird wohl daran zu erinnern sein, dass das Weltall vielfach als der Leib der Gottheit angesehen wird. Besonders gilt das für den Gott Aion, aber auch für Zeus und andere Götter (Wikenhauser S. 232f.). Wie die Welt der Leib der Gottheit ist, so ist das Reich der Leib des göttlichen Herrschers. Wahrscheinlich ist diese letztere Anschauung das erste und die kosmische Vorstellung vom Weltall als dem Leib der Gottheit davon abgeleitet.

Leider ist die Gleichung σῶμα – βασιλεία zu knapp bezeugt, als dass man davon irgendwie weitgehendere Schlüsse ziehen könnte. Es wäre sehr bestechend, diese Idee auf Christus und seine βασιλεία, die Kirche (Gemeinde) zu übertragen: als der göttliche βασιλεύς der Kirche hat Christus in ihr sein σῶμα.

Die Konstellation von σῶμα und βασιλεία führt den Gedanken auf die Frage des Paulus, 1. Cor. 1,13: μεμέρισται ὁ Χριστός; Der Apostel richtet die Frage an die korinthische Gemeinde, die von σχίσματα gespalten ist. Sie zerfällt in verschiedene Parteigruppen, und Paulus fragt entrüstet: "Ist denn der Christus zerteilt?" Das muss eine *Frage* sein; denn als Aussage oder Ausruf ist der Satz sinnlos. Aber was will er mit dieser rhetorischen Frage sagen? Offensichtlich etwas Unmögliches. Ein μεμερίσθαι des Christus kann nicht in Frage kommen, wäre aber gewissermassen die notwendige Entsprechung zu den Parteibildungen in Korinth, wenn diese legitim sein sollten. Christus ist aber eine ungeteilte Einheit, so muss auch die Gemeinde eine solche sein, da sie sein Leib ist. Nur wenn im Christus verschiedene μέρη bestünden, wäre eine in Gruppen geteilte Gemeinde, eine ἐκκλησία μεμερισμένη, berechtigt.

Ich glaube nicht, dass man μεμέρισται mit "zerstückt" (Lietzmann) oder "zerrissen" (J. Weiss) übersetzen darf.[12] μεμέρισται könnte "innerlich zerspalten" heissen, vgl 1. Cor 7,34, und diese Bedeutung wäre an unserer Stelle denkbar: "ist wohl der Christus (so wie seine korinthische Gemeinde) mit sich

---

[12] Da hätten wir eher ein μεμέλισται zu erwarten, als μεμέρισται.

selbst entzweit, in sich gespalten?" Da würden wir uns aber auf *psychologischem* Gebiet befinden, was nicht sehr wahrscheinlich der Denkweise des Apostels entsprechen würde. Er denkt nicht psychologisch, sondern objektiv, wo er vom Christus spricht. μεμέρισται ὁ Χριστός; muss m. E. heissen: Ist der Christus in μέρη zerlegt? Gibt es im Christus (so wie nun in seiner gespaltenen Gemeinde) verschiedene μέρη? Eine solche Redeweise würde man am leichtesten verstehen, wenn man in Korinth von "Gemeindeteilen" sprach. Die Gruppen betrachteten sich als μέρη τῆς βασιλείας, in Widerspruch zu der Anschauung, dass die einzelnen Gläubigen μέλη τοῦ σώματος sind. Paulus dagegen macht vollen Ernst mit der Gleichung σῶμα – βασιλεία. Da sind keine μέρη, nur μέλη. Und wenn die Gemeinde in "Teile" zu zerfallen droht, fragt er mit Schärfe: "Gibt es 'Teile' im Christus" Nein ! Er ist eine geschlossene, unzerteilbare Einheit, und seine Gemeinde ist als sein Leib ebenso unteilbar. Der σῶμα-Begriff wird dem Begriff der βασιλεία (zu dem auch die Vorstellung von μέρη gehört) unbedingt übergeordnet. Bei Paulus können μέλος und μέρος nicht dasselbe sein.

Bibliographical Notes

Anton Fridrichsen as Academic Teacher in the Service of the Church
by Erik Beijer

Translated by Chrys C. Caragounis from Swedish "A. Fridrichsen som akademisk lärare till kyrkans tjänst", by Erik Beijer, *Svensk Exegetisk Årsbok* 53 (1988), pp. 88–109.

Realistic Interpretation of the Bible: A Scientific Demand and a Practical Desideratum

Translated by Chrys C. Caragounis from Swedish "Realistisk bibelutläggning. Ett vetenskapligt krav och ett praktiskt önskemål", *Svensk Exegetisk Årsbok* 1 (1936), pp. 20–30.

The Logion concerning 'to carry one's cross: A Critical-exegetical Study

Translated by Tord Fornberg from Norwegian "Ordet om 'å bœre sit kors'. En kritisk-exegetisk studie", *Gamle spor og nye veier. Tydninger og Tegninger*, FS Lyder Brun, Kristiania 1922, pp. 17–34.

The Tripartite Formula in Matt. 28:19 and Baptism in the Three Names

Translated by Tord Fornberg from Norwegian "Den treleddede formel Mt 28.19 og dåpen til de tre navn", *Norsk Teologisk Tidsskrift* 23 (1922), pp. 65–81.

The Parables in Recent Research

Translated by Tord Fornberg from Norwegian "Den nyere tids parabelforskning", *Svensk Teologisk Kvartalskrift* 5 (1929), pp. 34–48.

The Conflict of Jesus with the Unclean Spirits

Theology 22 (1931), pp. 122–135, translated by Hugo Odeberg from Norwegian "Jesu kamp mot de urene ånder" *Svensk Teologisk Kvartalskrift* 5 (1929), pp. 299–314.

Who Did Jesus Claim to Be? The Historical Foundation of Faith in Christ According to Present Biblical Research

Translated by Chrys C. Caragounis from Swedish *Vem ville Jesus vara?* Kristustrons historiska grundval enligt nutida bibelforskning, Stochkolm 1931.

Excepta fornicationis causa

Translated by Chrys C. Caragounis from Swedish "Excepta fornicationis causa", *Svensk Exegetisk Årsbok* 9 (1944), pp. 54–58.

Neutestamentliche Wortforschung. Zu Matth. 11.11–15
Theologische Zeitschrift 2 (1946), pp. 470-471.

Jesus' Farewell Discourse in the Fourth Gospel: An Introduction to the Johannine Question
Translated by Chrys C. Caragounis from Swedish "Jesu avskedstal i fjärde evangeliet. En introduktion till den johanneiska frågan", *Svensk Exegetisk Årsbok* 3 (1938), pp. 1–16.

Bemerkungen zur Fußwaschung Joh 13
Zeitschrift für die Neutestamentliche Wissenschaft 38 (1939), pp. 94–96.

The Shepherd Chapter: Jn 10
Translated by Chrys C. Caragounis from Swedish "Herdekapitlet Joh 10", *Svensk Exegetisk Årsbok* 8 (1943), pp. 30–48.

Zur Auslegung von Röm 1.19f.
Zeitschrift für die Neutestamentliche Wissenschaft 17 (1916), pp. 159–168.

Die Apologie des Paulus Gal 1
Norsk Teologisk Tidsskrift Beih. 21 (1920), pp. 33–76.

Der wahre Jude und sein Lob. Röm 2,28f.
Symbolae Arctoae (= Symbolae Osloenses) 1 (1922), pp. 39–49.

Zum Stil des paulinischen Peristasenkatalogs 2 Cor 11,23ff.
Symbolae Osloenses 7 (1928), pp. 25–29.

Peristasenkatalog und *res gestae*. Nachtrag zu 2 Cor 11,23ff.
Symbolae Osloenses 8 (1929), pp. 78–82.

Exegetisches zu den Paulusbriefen
Theologische Studien und Kritiken 102:3 (1930), pp.291–301.

Paulus *abortivus*. Zu 1 Kor 15,8
Symbolae Philologicae O. A. Danielsson octogenario dedicatae, ed. A. Nelson, Uppsala 1932, pp.78–85.

Epikureisches im Neuen Testament?
Symbolae Osloenses 12 (1933), pp. 52–56.

'Ισόψυχος = ebenbürtig, solidarisch
Symbolae Osloenses 18 (1938), pp. 42–49.

Neutestamentliche Wortforschung. *Themelios,* 1 Kor. 3,11
Theologische Zeitschrift 2 (1946), pp. 316–317.

Neutestamentliche Wortforschung. 'Nicht für Raub achten, Phil 2,6 *Theologische Zeitschrift* 2 (1946), pp. 395–396.

The Apostle and His Message
Uppsala Universitets Årsskrift 1947:3, pp.3–23.

The New Testament and Hellas
A lecture in the "Videnskaps-Akademiet" in Oslo on February 28, 1930. First published under the title "Den nye testamente og Hellas", *Norsk Teologisk Tidsskrift* 31 (1930), pp. 201–215. Translated by Tord Fornberg from Norwegian.

Sich selbst verleugnen
Coniectanea Neotestamentica II, pp. 1–8 (Arbeiten und Mitteilungen aus den Neutestamentlichen Seminar zu Uppsala 4; Leipzig und Uppsala 1936.

Acts 26,28
Coniectanea Neotestamentica III (1938), pp. 13–16.

The Unity of the New Testament
Translated by Chrys C. Caragounis from Swedish "Nya Testamentets enhet", *Svensk Exegetisk Årsbok* 6 (1941), pp. 43–54.

Sprachliches und Stilistisches zum Neuen Testament
Kungliga Humanistiska Vetenskaps-Samfundet i Uppsala, Årsbok 1943, pp. 24–36.

Index of Passages

1. Biblical Passages

New Testament

Matthew

Mark

2 Corinthians

Galatians

2. Apocrypha

3. Pseudepigrapha

4. Christian Authors

5. Rabbinica

6. Ancient Authors

7. Inscriptions and Papyri

Index of Modern Authors

Wissenschaftliche Untersuchungen zum Neuen Testament

Alphabetical Index of the first and second series

– see *Hengel.*
Heiligenthal, Roman: Werke als Zeichen. 1983. *Volume II/9.*
Hemer, Colin J.: The Book of Acts in the Setting of Hellenistic History. 1989. *Volume 49.*
Hengel, Martin: Judentum und Hellenismus. 1969, ³1988. *Volume 10.*
– Die johanneische Frage. 1993. *Volume 67.*
Hengel, Martin and *Ulrich Heckel* (Ed.): Paulus und das antike Judentum. 1991. *Volume 58.*
Hengel, Martin and *Hermut Löhr* (Ed.): Schriftauslegung. 1994. *Volume 73.*
Hengel, Martin and *Anna Maria Schwemer* (Ed.): Königsherrschaft Gottes und himmlischer Kult. 1991. *Volume 55.*
– Die Septuaginta. 1994. *Volume 72.*
Herrenbrück, Fritz: Jesus und die Zöllner. 1990. *Volume II/41.*
Hofius, Otfried: Katapausis. 1970. *Volume 11.*
– Der Vorhang vor dem Thron Gottes. 1972. *Volume 14.*
– Der Christushymnus Philipper 2,6–11. 1976, ²1991. *Volume 17.*
– Paulusstudien. 1989, ²1994. *Volume 51.*
Holtz, Traugott: Geschichte und Theologie des Urchristentums. Ed. by Eckart Reinmuth and Christian Wolff. 1991. *Volume 57.*
Hommel, Hildebrecht: Sebasmata. Volume 1. 1983. *Volume 31.* – Volume 2. 1984. *Volume 32.*
Kamlah, Ehrhard: Die Form der katalogischen Paränese im Neuen Testament. 1964. *Volume 7.*
Kim, Seyoon: The Origin of Paul's Gospel. 1981, ²1984. *Volume II/4.*
– »The ›Son of Man‹« as the Son of God. 1983. *Volume 30.*
Kleinknecht, Karl Th.: Der leidende Gerechtfertigte. 1984, ²1988. *Volume II/13.*
Klinghardt, Matthias: Gesetz und Volk Gottes. 1988. *Volume II/32.*
Köhler, Wolf-Dietrich: Rezeption des Matthäusevangeliums in der Zeit vor Irenäus. 1987. *Volume II/24.*
Korn, Manfred: Die Geschichte Jesu in veränderter Zeit. 1993. *Volume II/51.*
Koskenniemi, Erkki: Apollonios von Tyana in der neutestamentlichen Exegese. 1994. *Volume II/61.*
Kuhn, Karl G.: Achtzehngebet und Vaterunser und der Reim. 1950. *Volume 1.*
Lampe, Peter: Die stadtrömischen Christen in den ersten beiden Jahrhunderten. 1987, ²1989. *Volume II/18.*
Lieu, Samuel N. C.: Manichaeism in the Later Roman Empire and Medieval China. 1992. *Volume 63.*
Löhr, Hermut: see *Hengel.*
Maier, Gerhard: Mensch und freier Wille. 1971. *Volume 12.*
– Die Johannesoffenbarung und die Kirche. 1981. *Volume 25.*
Markschies, Christoph: Valentinus Gnosticus? 1992. *Volume 65.*
Marshall, Peter: Enmity in Corinth: Social Conventions in Paul's Relations with the Corinthians. 1987. *Volume II/23.*
Meade, David G.: Pseudonymity and Canon. 1986. *Volume 39.*
Mell, Ulrich: Die »anderen« Winzer. 1994. *Volume 77.*
Mengel, Berthold: Studien zum Philipperbrief. 1982. *Volume II/8.*
Merkel, Helmut: Die Widersprüche zwischen den Evangelien. 1971. *Volume 13.*
Merklein, Helmut: Studien zu Jesus und Paulus. 1987. *Volume 43.*
Metzler, Karin: Der griechische Begriff des Verzeihens. 1991. *Volume II/44.*
Niebuhr, Karl-Wilhelm: Gesetz und Paränese. 1987. *Volume II/28.*
– Heidenapostel aus Israel. 1992. *Volume 63.*
Nissen, Andreas: Gott und der Nächste im antiken Judentum. 1974. *Volume 15.*
Noormann, Rolf: Irenäus als Paulusinterpret. 1994. *Volume II/66.*
Okure, Teresa: The Johannine Approach to Mission. 1988. *Volume II/31.*
Philonenko, Marc (Ed.): Le Trône de Dieu. 1993. *Volume 69.*
Pilhofer, Peter: Presbyteron Kreitton. 1990. *Volume II/39.*
Pöhlmann, Wolfgang: Der Verlorene Sohn und das Haus. 1993. *Volume 68.*
Probst, Hermann: Paulus und der Brief. 1991. *Volume II/45.*
Räisänen, Heikki: Paul and the Law. 1983, ²1987. *Volume 29.*
Rehkopf, Friedrich: Die lukanische Sonderquelle. 1959. *Volume 5.*
Reinmuth, Eckart: Pseudo-Philo und Lukas. 1994. *Volume 74.*
– see *Holtz.*

For a complete catalogue please write to the publisher
J. C. B. Mohr (Paul Siebeck), P. O. Box 2040, D-72010 Tübingen.